D1237529

From Performance to Print in Shakespeare's England

Redefining British Theatre History

General Editor: **Professor Peter Holland**

Redefining British Theatre History is a five-volume series under the general editorship of Professor Peter Holland. The series brings together major practitioners in theatre history in order to establish ways in which previous assumptions need fundamental questioning and to initiate new directions for the field. The series aims to establish a new future for theatre history, not least by making theatre historians aware of their own history, current practice and future.

Titles include:

Peter Holland and Stephen Orgel (*editors*)
FROM SCRIPT TO STAGE IN EARLY MODERN ENGLAND
FROM PERFORMANCE TO PRINT IN SHAKESPEARE'S ENGLAND

W. B. Worthen and Peter Holland (*editors*)
THEORIZING PRACTICE
Redefining Theatre History

Redefining British Theatre History
Series Standing Order ISBN 0–333–98219–3 (Hardback) 0–333–98220–7 (Paperback)
(*outside North America only*)

You can receive future titles in this series as they are published by placing a standing order. Please contact your bookseller or, in case of difficulty, write to us at the address below with your name and address, the title of the series and the ISBN quoted above.

Customer Services Department, Macmillan Distribution Ltd, Houndmills, Basingstoke, Hampshire RG21 6XS, England

From Performance to Print in Shakespeare's England

Edited by

Peter Holland

and

Stephen Orgel

Redefining British Theatre History Series
General Editor: Peter Holland
In Association with the Huntington Library

Introduction, selection and editorial matter
© Peter Holland and Stephen Orgel 2006
All chapters © Individual Contributors, 2006

All rights reserved. No reproduction, copy or transmission of this
publication may be made without written permission.

No paragraph of this publication may be reproduced, copied or transmitted
save with written permission or in accordance with the provisions of the
Copyright, Designs and Patents Act 1988, or under the terms of any licence
permitting limited copying issued by the Copyright Licensing Agency,
90 Tottenham Court Road, London W1T 4LP.

Any person who does any unauthorised act in relation to this publication
may be liable to criminal prosecution and civil claims for damages.

The authors have asserted their rights to be identified
as the authors of this work in accordance with the Copyright,
Designs and Patents Act 1988.

First published 2006 by
PALGRAVE MACMILLAN
Houndmills, Basingstoke, Hampshire RG21 6XS and
175 Fifth Avenue, New York, N.Y. 10010
Companies and representatives throughout the world

PALGRAVE MACMILLAN is the global academic imprint of the Palgrave
Macmillan division of St. Martin's Press, LLC and of Palgrave Macmillan Ltd.
Macmillan® is a registered trademark in the United States, United Kingdom
and other countries. Palgrave is a registered trademark in the European
Union and other countries.

ISBN-13: 978–1–4039–9228–4 hardback
ISBN-10: 1–4039–9228–2 hardback

This book is printed on paper suitable for recycling and made from fully
managed and sustained forest sources.

A catalogue record for this book is available from the British Library.

Library of Congress Cataloging-in-Publication Data
From performance to print in Shakespeare's England / edited by
    Peter Holland and Stephen Orgel.
      p.   cm. — (Redefining British theatre history series)
"In association with the Huntington Library."
Includes bibliographical references and index.
ISBN 1–4039–9228–2
1. Shakespeare, William, 1564–1616—Stage history—To 1625.
2. Shakespeare, William, 1564–1616—Stage history—England.
3. Shakespeare, William, 1564–1616—Dramatic production.
4. Shakespeare, William, 1564–1616—Criticism, Textual.   5. Theater—
England—History—16th century.   6. Theater—England—History—17th
century.   I. Holland, Peter, 1951–   II. Orgel, Stephen.   III. Redefining British
theatre history.
PR3095.F76 2006
792.9'50942—dc22   2005053787

10   9   8   7   6   5   4   3   2   1
15   14   13   12   11   10   09   08   07   06

Printed and bound in Great Britain by
Antony Rowe Ltd, Chippenham and Eastbourne

PR 3095
.F76
2006

061704828

Contents

List of Illustrations

Notes on Contributors

Anston Bosman is Assistant Professor of English at Amherst College. He has published essays and reviews on Renaissance culture and history in such journals as *Shakespeare Quarterly, ELH* and *MLQ*, and is at present completing a study of English traveling players in early modern Europe.

A. R. Braunmuller is co-general editor (with Stephen Orgel) of the New Pelican Shakespeare and is currently editing *Measure for Measure* for the Arden 3 series. He recently wrote an essay on the history of the design of editions of Shakespeare and gave a lecture at the conference to mark the 400th anniversary of the Treaty of London (King's College, London). He is professor of English and comparative literature at the University of California, Los Angeles.

Margreta de Grazia is the Joseph B. Glossberg Term Professor in the Humanities at the University of Pennsylvania. She is the author of *Shakespeare Verbatim* (Oxford, 1991) and co-editor (with Maureen Quilligan and Peter Stallybrass) of *Subject and Object in Renaissance Culture* (Cambridge, 1996), and (with Stanley Wells) *The Cambridge Companion to Shakespeare* (Cambridge, 2001). *'Hamlet' without Hamlet* is forthcoming (from Oxford University Press).

Gabriel Egan is Senior Lecturer in English at Loughborough University. His book *Shakespeare and Marx* was published by Oxford University Press in 2004 and his *Green Shakespeare: From Ecopolitics to Ecocriticism* will appear from Routledge in 2005. From 2000 to 2004 he was a Visiting Research Fellow in the English Department of King's College, London and the Globe Education Lecturer at Shakespeare's Globe London, in which capacities he ran the Globe side of the joint King's/Globe MA in 'Shakespearean Studies: Text and Playhouse'.

Lynn Enterline is Professor of English at Vanderbilt University and author of *The Tears of Narcissus: Melancholia and Masculinity in Early Modern Writing* (Stanford University Press, 1995) and *The Rhetoric of the Body from Ovid to Shakespeare* (Cambridge University Press, 2000). Her work moves between Greek, Latin, Italian, and English literary traditions in relation to contemporary literary, feminist, and psychoanalytic theories. The essay in this volume is part of her current project on 'Shakespeare's Schoolroom: Rhetoric, Discipline, Emotion'.

Peter Holland is the McMeel Family Professor in Shakespeare Studies in the Department of Film, Television and Theatre at the University of Notre Dame. Among his books are *The Ornament of Action* (Cambridge, 1979) and *English Shakespeares: Shakespeare on the English Stage in the 1990s* (Cambridge, 1997). He is currently editing *Coriolanus* for the Arden 3 series. He is editor of *Shakespeare Survey* and general editor (with Stanley Wells) of *Oxford Shakespeare Topics* for Oxford University Press.

John Jowett is Reader in Shakespeare Studies at the Shakespeare Institute, University of Birmingham. He is a member of the editorial boards of Arden Early Modern Drama, the Malone Society, and the Oxford *Collected Works* of Thomas Middleton, and is an editor of the Oxford Shakespeare *Complete Works*. He has edited *Richard III* and *Timon of Athens* for the Oxford Shakespeare series, and is currently editing *Sir Thomas More* for the Arden Shakespeare.

Gordon McMullan is Reader in English at King's College London. His publications include *The Politics of Unease in the Plays of John Fletcher* (1994) and three edited or co-edited collections of essays. His Arden edition of *Henry VIII* was published in 2000, and his Norton Critical Edition of *1 Henry IV* in 2004. He is currently writing 'Shakespeare and the Invention of Late Writing' and co-editing a collection of essays on early modern re-readings of medieval texts. He is a general editor of Arden Early Modern Drama.

Jeffrey Masten is Associate Professor of English at Northwestern University, specializing in early modern literature and culture, the history of sexuality and gender, queer theory, textual editing, and the history and theory of authorship. He has written *Textual Intercourse: Collaboration, Authorship, and Sexualities in Renaissance Drama* (Cambridge, 1997), and, with Peter Stallybrass and Nancy J. Vickers, has co-edited *Language Machines: Technologies of Literary and Cultural Production* (Routledge, 1997). He is currently writing 'Spelling Shakespeare, and Other Essays in Queer Philology'. He is also the co-editor (with Wendy Wall) of the journal *Renaissance Drama*.

Stephen Orgel is the Jackson Eli Reynolds Professor in the Humanities at Stanford. His most recent books are *Imagining Shakespeare* (Palgrave Macmillan, 2003), *The Authentic Shakespeare* (Routledge, 2002) and *Impersonations: The Performance of Gender in Shakespeare's England* (Cambridge, 1966). His many editions include *The Tempest* and *The Winter's Tale* in the Oxford Shakespeare, and *Macbeth, King Lear, Pericles, The Taming of the Shrew,* and *The Sonnets* in the New Pelican Shakespeare, of which he and A. R. Braunmuller are general editors.

Richard Preiss is Assistant Professor of English at the University of Utah and a Ph.D. candidate in English at Stanford University. Shortly to be completed, his dissertation examines the interdependence of stage clowning and authorial practices in early modern English theater, from the age of Tarlton to the Restoration. He has articles forthcoming in *Renaissance Drama* and in *Shakespeare Yearbook*.

Gary Taylor, Director of the Hudson Strode Program in Renaissance Studies at the University of Alabama, has worked as General Editor of the *Complete Works* of Shakespeare (Oxford, 1986; rev. 2005) and Thomas Middleton (Oxford, forthcoming). His many books include *Reinventing Shakespeare* (1991), and his most recent contributions to theater history include 'Hamlet in Africa, 1607' (in *Travel Knowledge*, ed. Ivo Kamps and Jyotsna G. Singh) and the forthcoming

Revels Plays edition of John Fletcher's *The Tamer Tamed* (co-edited with Celia R. Daileader).

Wendy Wall is Professor of English at Northwestern University, with a specialization in early modern literature and culture. She is author of *The Imprint of Gender: Authorship and Publication in the English Renaissance* (Cornell University Press, 1993) and *Staging Domesticity: Household Work and English Identity in Early Modern Drama* (Cambridge University Press, 2002), as well as co-editor for *Renaissance Drama*. She is currently at work on 'Reading Food: A Culinary History from Shakespeare to Martha Stewart'.

Series Introduction: Redefining British Theatre History

Peter Holland

On the surface, it doesn't look like much of a problem: conjoining the two words 'theatre' and 'history' to define a particular practice of scholarship has a long and illustrious history. Nor does it appear to over-complicate matters to add the word 'British', for all that the word is so furiously questioned at different moments of history (and especially at the moment). Yet what kind of history theatre history is and what kind of theatre theatre history investigates, let alone what the Britishness is of its theatre history, is endlessly problematic. For all the availability of shelves full of the outcomes of its practices, theatre history is in need of a substantial reassessment. This series is an attempt to place some markers in that vital project.

It is hardly as if theatre history is a new area of scholarly enquiry and academic publication. Within a general, varyingly academic mode of publication, one could point, in the UK, to the longevity of *Theatre Notebook*, a journal founded in 1945 by the Society for Theatre Research; its subtitle *A Journal of the History and Technique of the British Theatre* neatly sets out its scope and the assumed scope of theatre history. A number of US journals have had similar concerns, including *Theatre Survey* (from the American Society for Theatre Research) and more narrowly defined examples like *Restoration and Eighteenth-Century Theatre Research* or *Nineteenth-Century Theatre Research*. Lying behind such work is the complex institutional history of the formation of university drama and theatre departments on both sides of the Atlantic and their vexed and often still unformulated connection both to theatre training (the university as feed to a profession) and to departments of English Literature.

For the early modern period theatre historians might chart the subject's early twentieth-century history as being encapsulated by the work of E.K. Chambers (especially *The Elizabethan Stage*, 4 vols [Oxford: Clarendon Press, 1923]) or G.E. Bentley in his continuation (*The Jacobean and Caroline Stage*, 7 vols [Oxford: Clarendon Press, 1941–68]), phenomenal individual achievements of documenting theatrical events, theatre performers and theatrical contexts. Their work might be matched for a later period by, say, E.L. Avery et al., eds, *The London Stage 1660–1800*, 11 vols (Carbondale, Ill: Southern Illinois University Press, 1960–8) or Philip Highfill, Kalman Burnim and Edward Langhans, eds, *A Biographical Dictionary of Actors, Actresses, Musicians, Dancers, Managers and Other Stage Personnel in London, 1660–1800*, 16 vols (Carbondale, Ill: Southern Illinois University Press, 1973–93). Further back still comes the fundamental work of such people as Boaden (*Memoirs of Mrs Siddons*, 2 vols [London, 1827]) and Genest (*Some Account of the English Stage from the Restoration in 1660 to 1830*, 10 vols [Bath, 1832]), who saw themselves neither as scholars nor as academics and yet whose work implicitly defined the accumulative function of data collection as a primary purpose of theatre history.

Behind them comes the achievement of the greatest of eighteenth-century editors of Shakespeare, Edmond Malone.

Yet, seeing that there is a practice of theatre history is not the same as understanding or theorizing such a project. While many academics are engaged in the practice of something they would unhesitatingly term 'Theatre History' and while they would differentiate it carefully from a variety of other contiguous fields (e.g. performance theory or history of drama), there has been remarkably little investigation of the methodological bases on which the shelves of accumulated scholarship have been based or the theoretical bases on which Theatre History has been or might be constructed. Even within organizations as aware of the need for theoretical sophistication as IFTR/FIRT (Fédération Internationale pour la recherche théâtrale) the emphasis has been placed more squarely on performance theory than on the historiographical problems of theatre. In part that can undoubtedly be traced to the disciplines or institutional structures out of which the work has evolved: one would need to examine its early and still troubled connection to literary studies, to the analysis of drama and, most visibly, to the study of the history of Shakespeare in performance or, on another tack, to consider the ways in which theatre departments have structured their courses in the US and UK.

By comparison with the traditionally positivist accumulation of data that marks, say, *Theatre Notebook*, one could, however, see signs of the emergence of a new concern with the processes of historiography as it affects the specific study of a massive cultural institution like theatre in, to take just one significant example, the collection of essays edited by Thomas Postlewait and Bruce McConachie, *Interpreting the Theatrical Past: Essays in the Historiography of Performance* (Iowa City: University of Iowa Press, 1989). But, while individual theatre historians are demonstrating an expanding awareness of the specific areas of historiography relevant to their work (e.g. economic history) and while theorizing of performance including its historical traces has grown immensely over the past 15 years, there is little enough to set out on a large scale the parameters of something that might hope by now to see itself as a discipline. The shelves of libraries and bookshops and the reading lists of courses do not show major resources for understanding what theatre history is, while an unending stream of books offering to help students understand the history of theatre pours from presses. In part this may be connected to the absence of departments of theatre history and the further substantial absence, within theatre departments, of courses concerned to do more than teach theatre history as an assumed and shared methodology based on an acceptance of what constitutes evidence and of how that evidence generates the potential for meaning.

Redefining British Theatre History sets out, extremely ambitiously, to make a major statement by bringing together, in the course of its series of five volumes, some fifty major practitioners in theatre history in order to establish ways in which previous assumptions need fundamental questioning and in which a future for the field can be enunciated in modes as yet undervalued. It aims to be a significant review of where we are and what we think we are doing.

The project began from an unusual collaboration between research library and publisher. My gratitude goes first and foremost to Dr Roy Ritchie of the Huntington

Library and Josie Dixon of Palgrave Macmillan for contacting me to see whether I would develop a proposal that would create a series of conferences and subsequent volumes based on a single theme. Their support, not least financial, has been crucial in bringing the project to a reality both in the pleasures of the conference and the creation of this book. If we succeed, *Redefining British Theatre History* should chart the beginnings of a new future for theatre history, not least by making theatre historians newly and self-consciously aware of their own history, their practice and their future.

Introduction: Printing Performance

Peter Holland

On 13 December 1881 Henrik Ibsen published his new play *Ghosts*. There is nothing remarkable about the fact except that the play had not yet been performed and would not reach its stage premiere until May the following year. For *Ghosts*, as for all the plays he published from then until the end of his career, more or less at the steady rate of one every two years, publication preceded performance and Ibsen was far more interested in the profits from the sales of the printed text in the Christmas book-buying spree than with the income accruing from performance. Even though, for all the subsequent plays, the production process was well under way (usually for a first night in the middle of January), Ibsen's primary concern was to release the play into a print-culture for a reading-public, not to see the play appear first on stage.

From most perspectives, but perhaps especially for scholars working on early modern English theatre, there seems something almost perverse about the sequence. So much of the evidence for performance of individual plays seems locked into the printed text that the interrogation of print to understand performance seems at times the only activity scholars can undertake, however tentative, vulnerable, and hypothetical much of the work to find the right keys to unlock these texts may be. The early lists of plays, like the 'Exact and perfect Catalogue of all the Plaies that were ever printed' that was affixed to the first printing of *The Old Law* by Massinger and others in 1656 (with such marketing ploys as the assignment of *The Arraignment of Paris* and *Hoffman* to Shakespeare), tantalize us as much as the titles in Henslowe's 'diary' with their hints of plays unknown and now unknowable. Already, 14 years after the closure of the theatres, print-culture was the only way to know early modern drama.

While the normative movement of the early modern play is seen as being from writing to performance to print – though many plays never made the first step to production and many others were performed but not printed (and how many were in each category is another fertile field for guesswork) – there are other routes that the consideration of the twin poles, so often taken to be almost the binary opposites, of performance and print seem to pose. The essays in this collection take a fresh look at the materials, ask new questions, restate old enquiries, and offer varieties of answers.

At the heart of Stephen Orgel's enquiry is the question he poses at the outset:

> if the play is not its text (I won't say 'simply' or 'merely' its text, because there seems to me nothing simple or mere about the issue), what does the text of a play – the printed text, as it almost invariably is – represent?

For the printed text of any play negotiates with performance in a series of ways, a series defined by a hypothesized chronology. From the act of writing through rehearsal and performance to the transmission to the printing-house, each stage along the way points to and leaves traces of the processes of its own change and its signals of connection with that (at least normative) sequence. A word may hint at the actor's delivery and audience's understanding as well as the author's handwriting and the compositor's reading. A phrase that is part of a marketing ploy may define the play-text's link both to future performances and to past ones. An image may direct us back to performances and, complexly, define the early modern European cultural geographies within which the occasion, publication, and reception of plays vary so greatly.

But printed books are vulnerable documents: they can be written over and the writing may document or signal another transmission for the text: from print back into script. Its cuts witness historical change: that which can be spoken at one moment may not be at another. But it is in some senses then no longer a book at all:

> The playbook as promptbook is scarcely a book any more. It is a set of notations for production, and, as such, an archeological site of evidence about the play's physical, auditory, visual, spatial requirements and possibilities at a particular moment in theater history.

While the promptbook is a record of the actors' and other theatre workers' reading, how do we read a play as literature? Again, Orgel finds in the traces of reading (and of its absence) signs of readers' differing negotiations with performances and signs of the ownership and possession which the book makes as material object.

Where Orgel's approach argues from a wide range of examples, Gary Taylor's concern is with the publishing and marketing of one remarkably famous book, *Mr William Shakespeare's Comedies, Histories, and Tragedies*, the First Folio of 1623. Taylor first examines a connection between performance and print that has been ignored: the performative setting of the bookshop. For Taylor, as he shows with a host of examples, '[b]ookshops were performance spaces, where individuals acted out socially scripted interactive rituals of self-fashioning' with a standard cast of characters: the customer, the bookseller, and the bookseller's boy. The selling of books is another homosocial space like the theatre, indeed, one that is even more exclusively male, a space of smoking and gossip, reading and marketing, astute observation (the bookseller of the customer's likely interests) and economic exchange. Taylor sees it also as a space which negotiated with the concept of the author in contradictory ways, exemplified here by Thomas Walkeley's preface from stationer to reader prefixed to the 1622 quarto of *Othello*.

If Walkeley was unsure about how well Shakespeare's name would sell anything, he was strikingly unlike his contemporary, Edward Blount, who, at exactly the same time, was making a massive and, in business terms, quite probably completely disastrous commitment to Shakespeare's name. Although Taylor notes that the two events are not necessarily related, the change in Blount's fortunes before and after the publication of the First Folio is quite extraordinary:

> Between 1603 and the publication of the Shakespeare collection late in 1623, Edward Blount had published at least 72 titles, an average of 3.4 books per year. But from November 1623 until summer 1628 – that is, in the four and a half years immediately following publication of the Shakespeare folio – Blount did not publish a single book; in 1627 he lost his bookshop, which had been the foundation of his business for two decades.

Although our sense of the aesthetic value and cultural importance might make us wish it were otherwise, the plain fact is that F1 did not sell well. Taylor compares Blount's book with the bestsellers of the year and the comparison is not exactly flattering to Shakespeare.

Books, especially large folio productions, are complex material objects with their central raft of text surrounded by other texts: title-pages and portraits, letters to readers and commendatory poems. As Taylor examines the details of F1's elements (why these dedicatees and not the King? what are the prefatory poems saying?), the paratexts of theatre also come back into view: the prologues and epilogues, the acting company and their patrons, the props and costumes, and the large physical object that is the material fact of the theatre. The printed book proves to be a performance space too, just as much as the theatricalized shops in which it was sold. The printed book mimics theatre, theatre imitates the structures of print. Both perform and, in the complexities of their negotiations, as traced by all the contributors to this collection, the ways in which they witness histories of theatre and performance are substantially redefined.

Without F1, half of Shakespeare's plays might never have been printed at all. John Jowett's method is to work outwards from a specific passage in one of them, *Timon of Athens*, to ask what the evidence of the only early printed version of the play can tell us about the possibilities of early modern performance, a performance that, in this case, may never have preceded printing at all and may never have occurred. In his attempt to move from print to performance, reversing the conventional flow, as it were, Jowett is interested in the reader's envisioning of a theatre of the mind, a space in which performance is imagined. But he is also concerned with the full complexity of hearing and vision in the creation of a sensory world for the drama, what he defines as 'sense-scape', a space in which sounds and sights and even smells configure in the creation of the full splendour of performative event.

His choice of segment to examine is a sequence in the second scene of the play, a complex spectacle of the masque put on by Timon for his guests. But is it a masque of Amazons or of 'the fiue best Sences' who 'acknowledge [Timon] their Patron' or somehow both? The passage has posed difficulties for *Timon*'s editors, that particular species of reader, for it is not simply – indeed, never simply – a matter of assuming a hypothesized perfect state of the text. Each choice excludes others and alters the textual representation both of the print-text and of the performance-text. An apparently comparatively simple question – do the female masquers carry lutes? – proves a sign of cultural meaning: of the status of the women, of the link between this masque and other courtly performances, of female education and of female sexuality.

To consider the performance of a scene such as this is also to enter fully into the play's arguments and meanings, its interpretative possibilities and dramatic forms. The editor's deliberations about how the stage directions appear on the page is as much a question of moderation and excess as anything that Timon himself exemplifies throughout the whole play. To imagine performance is to engage with and even to become part of the meaning of *Timon of Athens*.

The economics of play-publication was, as Taylor shows, a distinctly rocky adventure, for plays in print hardly ever recouped the publishers' investment. Gabriel Egan's concern is with some of the strategies for marketing plays in print and, in particular, with the precise connections with performance that title-pages manifest, especially since the title-page was used to advertise and sell the book. While sixteenth-century printings often used the word 'play' to describe a play, Egan is struck by the way that the word vanishes from title-pages between 1581 and 1609, the date of the first publication of *Pericles*, announced as 'THE LATE, and much admired Play, Called Pericles, Prince of Tyre', both a description of its form (it is a play) and a reference back to its success on stage ('much admired').

Something seems to be happening at this juncture at the opening of the century: a new and growing tendency to see the play as continuing to be performed (now described as being 'As it is played' or with a signal of the company's 'playing usually') and a sequence of books that are plays (and yet not fully plays, for they are narratives of performances rather than scripts) leading up to *Pericles*, a 'play' that is a play. In addition, Egan links together a series of printed playtexts that share a typographical characteristic, a particular woodblock for the word 'the' or rather, since it is large and emphatic, 'THE'. The thread that connects these events proves to be the King's Men but Egan's enquiry is necessarily hesitant about the significance of the linkage.

If printed play-texts refer primarily to London performance, they were unquestionably used for production – as well as reading – elsewhere. Egan is concerned both with the general issue that intrigues Orgel: the printed play-text now used as script. But he is also, like Orgel, fascinated by the Simpson or Cholmley company, a group of recusant players who performed – or were said to have performed – both *King Lear* and *Pericles* when playing on their circuit in Yorkshire in 1609. When Richard Simpson claimed that 'That booke by which he and the other persons did act the said play...was a prynted book, And they onlie acted the same according to the contents...and not otherwise', he may have been committing perjury but he was also relying on the assumption that the printed book was an allowed version of the play and that their faithfulness to the print version would protect them. He was wrong but his claim was an intriguing one: as Egan puts it, the players 'excused themselves with the assertion that the books, not the players, were the authors of their performances'.

Jeffrey Masten begins with a consideration of one particular kind of problem in performance: what exactly is a boy and what does that mean for our understanding of Shakespeare's Viola? It might seem an obvious question but Masten argues that our concern with what it meant that boys played women on the early modern stage has stopped us asking what it meant that boys played boys. Exploring the state of between, of becoming, that is the early modern construction of youth leads Masten towards the erotics of desire for 'the categorical unfixity of "the boy"' and its implications for the breadth of forms of desire with which pederasty overlaps.

In *Philaster* the problems of desire are exacerbated by the difficulties in print of representing the ambiguities of the boy/woman that is Bellario. *Philaster* is a rich field for exploration, not least because of the sheer number of editions but also because they try to resolve the printed definition of the double gender in intriguingly different ways, from Q1's description of Bellario as both 'a Page' and 'Leons daughter' (with the speech-prefix 'Bel' replacing 'Boy' only when his/her gender is revealed) to the 'hybrid or dissonant presentation of the character' in Q3 and beyond.

But books were full of boys, for the ornament stock of early modern printing shops included numerous signs of boys, decorations that visualize boys, that make the readers see boys, especially boys reading, mimicking the activity of the reader who looks at them. In the margins of the text to which ornaments have been traditionally consigned, boys can be seen performing in print.

The modern Shakespeare editor has to negotiate boys' performances – and indeed all kinds of performances – in very different ways. Readers expect – or at least series editors and publishers tell us they expect – that editions of the plays talk about performance, are performance-aware, demonstrate the history of possibilities of the text that performance has charted. A single mark of punctuation can be the problem: when is a question mark a mark of exclamation and how can an edition show both the ambiguities and inflections a point is heir to when Lady Macbeth is printed as saying to her husband (in F1) 'We faile?'?

Braunmuller, reflecting on the fact that the anxiety may give the editor nearly as much sleeplessness as murder gives Macbeth, is well aware that the text, let alone its commentary, has to know how to start to recall, prefigure or represent an onstage event and, just as significantly, has to know when to stop. From marks of direct speech to italics of emphasis, from malapropisms to the ever-acute problem of stage directions (to add or not to add – and if the former then where do they go?), every corner of a Shakespeare play gives the editor pause – or should do. At a point at which the unformulated and often ill-conceived assumptions about what the reader wants are placed as demands before the editor, the sensitivity to what kind of performance is being printed is a large demand to make of scholars. For Braunmuller, editors' interventions (emendations, adjustments, formalizations, whatever we may call them) are often unnecessary and excessive. They are also representations of conflicting and frequently conflicted desires, an attempt to please all that may end by pleasing nobody.

At present, editions are seen as competing with each other, existing in a simultaneous present-tense of the marketplace. Wendy Wall is concerned to trace a history and lineage that underpins, often in complex ideological ways, the filiation of editions. Editions belong in family-trees, the stemmas that later editors construct (grow?) as means of representing in print the history of print. *Romeo and Juliet*, a play especially sensitive to the details of kinship ties and the social structures of family within a community, is also a play whose printed history has been subject to an editorial history of defining other kinds of kinship, structural relationships, and familial pressures. Yet the explanations can never be more than flawed:

> The model of vertical biological generations that tends to underpin editorial practice, however, tends to naturalize knowledge and fails to reflect the doubt at its core. The family model, that is, forces the texts into a reductive paradigm that can't allow for the interconnections between the texts that editors freely admit.

Recent textual theory has created a demand to keep early texts separate, to worry less about their kinship than their differences so that the precise performance work that each does can be more clearly seen, the stories they each tell more adequately narrated, and the actions they document more adequately read. Each early text not only witnesses different performances or possibilities of stage event but also performs itself differently. To use a different play as example, a playgoer who in 1603 wanted the text of *Hamlet* that she had seen at the Globe would have found the only edition she could buy disturbingly unlike the play she had watched. Like the extreme story of woe and the golden statue that stand beyond the end of *Romeo and Juliet*, solidifying its events, the text always threatens its own degeneration or transmutation into another form.

We are used now to the notion that our conceptualization of the performative cannot be restricted to the theatre. We are also used to the notion that plays were often performed in schools, that, indeed, performance was a function of the rhetorical training that all Elizabethan schoolboys underwent. But Lynn Enterline's is a revisionary concern with the ways in which the processes of literary production and the exercise (in many senses) of discipline (both the structure of behaviour and the punishment for failing to obey that structure) become sources for dramatic production (specifically Shakespeare's activity of writing in dramatic and non-dramatic forms) and become manifestations of what she sees as 'the theatricality of everyday life'.

Enterline's pedagogically primal scene is the 'daily performance of Latinity'. But Enterline opposes the traditional narrative of the educational system which created and maintained an assumed separation of oration from performance. As she puts it,

Because of our own anachronistic distinction between rhetoric and drama, moreover, we have not attended as carefully as we might to the school's habitual association between declamation and acting: schoolmasters thought *both* were good training in eloquence and gentlemanly behavior.

This association is present at the level of the word: '[s]everal school ordinances use the verbs "declame" and "play" as virtual synonyms.' Even more significantly, the activity of education was public, the boys' performing for their master and for the other pupils. The result is an ever-increasing theatricality of educational process:

> [It] is not simply that humanist schools made language training an increasingly public activity. Rather, the form this increasingly public education took became, thanks to the concentration on rhetoric, a matter of staging: performances and spectacles of imitation and punishment turned the school into a kind of *daily theater for Latin learning.*

Enterline goes further, seeing in the mode of this training a precisely thespian set of concerns, the kinds of distinction between 'seeming and being, *persona* and person, address and self-representation' that amount to a labile and dislocating movement, internally and in performance, from writer to actor to audience. It is not just that Elizabethan education trained boys to speak in public. Enterline shows, in effect, that it trained them to be good playgoers, teaching them how to watch and listen and how to understand the processes of performance. Her article opens up new fields for early modern theatre history in its exploration of the creation of a theatre-literate society.

This social history of the cultural training that creates audiences intersects with Anston Bosman's definition of theatre that develops in the cultural interstices between nations, between particular forms of language, genre and performance. Bosman starts from the design for a curtain for a Leipzig theatre in 1766 which depicts Shakespeare as a shadowy figure who, as Goethe put it, 'without predecessors or followers, unconcerned as to models, pursued his own way ... to immortality'. But his major concern is with a form of theatre, widely known but hardly read by Anglophone scholars, the work of the 'English Comedians' in Germany from the 1580s onwards, troupes who were soon not made up of English actors at all. The volume of their plays, printed in 1620, is, for Bosman, 'printed evidence, a textual capture, of an episode in the history of performance'. But the book poses as many questions as it answers. As Bosman reads its title-page, with its reference to the character 'Pickle-herring', the plays come to occupy a point where 'languages and cultures "meet"', the space of linguistic intersplicing that has 'the logic of the contact zone'. The plays' language is now defined as 'interlanguage' and Bosman uses recent work in cultural theory and sociolinguistics in order to see how the theory of 'intersystems' can enable a revision of the work of these troupes who existed, in complex ways, in the spaces between cultures, an 'intertheatre', both international and between cultures.

But while the companies worked in a complex cultural space between cultures, between nations, the history of analysis of their work has been culture-specific: German and British analysis of this theatrical intersystem has been nationally driven in surprising ways. Bosman's argument moves towards a moment at which scholarship and the dramas of this intertheatre become visible in performance: William Poel's production in 1924 of *Der bestrafte Brudermord*, a play with complex and as yet unresolved links to *Hamlet*, which Poel staged as *Fratricide Punished*. *Hamlet*, displaced into the version of the English Comedians, is displaced again into its originating theatrical tradition when performed by Poel's company in the context of his search for a reconstruction of Elizabethan theatre conditions. Performances and printings weave together in the travellings to and fro across Europe.

Bosman is interested in the recovery of the culture that generated a book. Richard Preiss's article concentrates on the recovery of a great performer from the surviving traces in print. Robert Armin became the clown of the King's Men in 1599, succeeding Kemp and usually described as the cause of the transition from clown to fool. Clowns, who have been conventionally seen as in many senses the radical opposition to the authority of the playwright, give way to the actor, 'a comedian who is now wholly the author's creature'. Preiss shows that this traditional narrative is deeply flawed, for Armin is a much more complex presence than this would suggest: Armin's project is

> an attempt to suspend two performance codes under one performer – keeping his Kemp-like profile intact while incrementally modulating it toward the mimetic possibilities his talents began to present. In so doing, ... Shakespeare followed Armin's lead, not vice versa, and that lead derived not from what he did in the play but from what he was doing after it.

Armin's playing of a role was also intimately a product of the forms of self that print created for him, both in his own writing (the pamphlets *Foole upon Foole* and *Quips upon Questions*, both appearing in 1600) and in *Tarltons Jests*, published the same year, in which Armin became the anointed descendant, the adopted son of the great clown Tarlton.

The persona of Armin is constructed (and reconstructed by Preiss) less from what he did during the play than through impromptu performance, signaled in its fragments in print, events that surround and extrapolate from the play-event itself. The performance becomes available to be read through print, the transitions from print to performance to print again marking modes of evidentiary presence through which Armin took on his cultural role, playing his parts on stage and off it, in print and in an oral culture. The final transition of the tension between clown/fool and author comes when Armin becomes visibly identified as playwright himself, the clown writing himself into his plays, the author as fool.

Preiss's work sees the presence of the performer stretching far beyond the stage. As the gap of time widens between a play and its first performances, even a play with a continuous performing tradition like *Hamlet* has to negotiate afresh, both in print and in performance, with its new cultural configurations. Margreta de Grazia focuses on the moment when Hamlet does not kill Claudius, when he might do it pat but does not, the moment when he unquestionably delays and postpones the event which will finally and necessarily complete the action of the plot, the act of killing Claudius that he here refuses to accomplish. In the eighteenth century, both in performance and in print, the scene was understood to pose a moral problem of immense import, for a Hamlet who will not kill Claudius unless he can damn his soul to hell was to be detested and himself damned. As Dr Johnson put it in 1765, 'This speech, in which *Hamlet*, represented as a virtuous character, is not content with taking blood for blood, but contrives damnation for the man that he would punish, is too horrible to be read or to be uttered'. The speech indeed was not uttered and was cut for centuries.

The editing for performance was one thing; the printed texts of Shakespeare, the plays in their repeated new guises put on them by successive editors, could not simply eliminate the problem by discarding the passage. De Grazia finds, though, as a crucial step in the cultural encoding of the play in print and performance, that the end of the eighteenth century can solve the problem, not through new editing and certainly not through new performance, but through the application of new theories of psychology. Hamlet is now able to be seen as deceptive in a wholly new mode, a victim or perpetrator, willing or without control, of self-deceit. As de Grazia summarizes the writings of Thomas Robertson and William Richardson, the two Scots critics who separately investigated the problem in the 1780s,

> It is to himself that he conceals his revulsion at the deed, thereby exhibiting 'a most exquisite picture of amiable self-deceit.' '[H]e endeavours to hide it from himself'; he 'shelters himself under the subterfuge' of a monstrous intention. Lines formerly regarded as indefensible...are now justified as a cover-up, devised by Hamlet to convince Hamlet that he is capable of vengeance *in extremis* when in fact – that is, deep down inside – he shrinks from the prospect.

How to perform this new psychological reading is quite another issue, how, that is, to translate the writing about the play into the performance of it. But de Grazia is also concerned with the ways this approach transforms the previous diabolic element in play and character so that psychology replaces the morality of damnation and interiority substitutes for 'diabolic virtuosity'.

Such fundamental rethinkings of individual plays are a recurrent feature of the print/performance history of Shakespeare. Gordon McMullan's concern is with the ways in which the entwined histories have produced a specific kind of narrative of Shakespeare's work, the assumption that there is a quality of lateness, a phenomenon that characterizes work by poets, dramatists, composers and others. Late Beethoven is supposedly like late Shakespeare. As with de Grazia's investigation of the historical construction of the psychology of Hamlet, McMullan is concerned with the effect of 'the disjunction between early modern and post-romantic understandings of Shakespearean authorship' and its links to 'the gulf between later critical and performance accretions of the plays we call the "late plays" and their origins'.

Central to McMullan's account of the history of the concept of 'lateness' in Shakespeare come two figures, scholar-critic and practitioner-critic, Edward Dowden and Harley Granville Barker. Dowden epitomizes the biographical reading of the plays: the qualities of late Shakespeare plays are a direct consequence of Shakespeare's mood at the time, the assumed retirement to Stratford and the mental state which Dowden called 'On the Heights'. It is Granville Barker's 1912 production at the Savoy Theatre of *The Winter's Tale* that moves the history of lateness into a new phase. The revolutionary production, which McMullan aligns visually with the work of the Ballets Russes and the performances of, say, Stravinsky's *Rite of Spring* at the same time, defines lateness not as an aspect of Shakespeare's retirement nor (in the scholarly rethinking of Dowden) as a consequence of the King's Men's move to the Blackfriars but instead as an aspect of an artistic avant-gardism that brings lateness in Shakespeare away from Lytton Strachey and towards Adorno.

From the printed texts of early modern English theatre to Stravinsky may appear a long journey. But it links together two moments of revolutionary performance, the possibilities of theatre newly redefined. And it leaves that permanent regret that there will never be as much known about early modern production as the rich records that trace the Ballets Russes, a regret balanced by an awareness of the ways that the new questions these essays have posed drive new modes of enquiry, new ways of moving back to that complex interaction of performance and text, the performance in print that bears the imprint of performance.

Part I
Performing the Book

1
The Book of the Play

Stephen Orgel

In an essay called 'Acting Scripts, Performing Texts' I raised some large questions about the relation of text to performance in early modern drama, and some very specific ones about what kind of evidence printed texts provide, since these are for the most part all that survive of the plays of Shakespeare's era. We have used the evidence of texts to attempt both to reconstruct the playwright's original manuscript, and to trace the archeology of performance and reconceive what the Elizabethan spectator saw in the theater. These, however, are two very different things, and we must be clear about the differences if we are to understand, for example, what 'the two hours' traffic of our stage' can mean in relation to texts that can rarely be performed in less than three hours or more, or discern the implications of Jonson's complaint that the actors misrepresented his plays. So the largest question is really the most basic one: what is the play? Is it what the actors do, or what the author writes? And if the play is not its text (I won't say 'simply' or 'merely' its text, because there seems to me nothing simple or mere about the issue), what does the text of a play – the printed text, as it almost invariably is – represent?

If there is any answer, there is a multitude. I shall conduct this investigation largely through specific examples. I start with a famous case of editorial intervention. When Lewis Theobald decided in 1733 that Falstaff's death had nothing to do with 'a table of green fields,' but rather that in dying, ' 'a babbled of green fields,' the emendation, indisputably a stroke of editorial genius, seemed to have restored what Shakespeare must actually have written. Bibliography here communicated with Shakespeare himself – or at least with Shakespeare's manuscript before it reached the printer. The revision, or restoration, which was almost universally accepted thereafter, also thereby rewrote the stage history of *Henry V*.

But let us pause over that history. If we agree that Theobald was correct, and that a compositor setting the type in the printing house was misreading Shakespeare's handwriting, what happened before the play got to the compositor? 'Table' is the 1623 folio's reading; so the folio's printer is the culprit. But the only other substantive text, the 1600 quarto, at this point reads not 'babbled' but 'talk,' and it is apparent that the folio text was not set up from the very garbled quarto, but from Shakespeare's manuscript. So neither of our two primary sources reads 'babbled': 'babbled,' even if it is impeccably correct, is all Theobald. Q seems to be a reported text provided by two actors, but if F's 'table' is a misreading resulting from a visual error in deciphering Shakespeare's handwriting, so would Q's 'talk' seem to be. In a reported text, however, the error ought to be an auditory one. If Q is really a reported text, then, the counter-argument here would have to be the one that Gary Taylor makes, that the reporters heard 'babbled' but remembered it as the simpler concept 'talk' (or 'talkd,' as it is usually emended).[1] This argument would be more persuasive if 'talkd' looked less like 'table.' Moreover, even if we agree that 'babbled' was what Shakespeare wrote, it might also be the case that Shakespeare's handwriting was hard to read for everyone, and was misread not only by the folio compositor but by the scribe who prepared the promptbook, who also would have been working from Shakespeare's manuscript – and the promptbook, after all, would have been the source of the actors' scripts too, and thereby of what the reporters heard, or misremembered. Maybe the actors were (incorrectly) saying 'table' or 'talkd' all along. For Theobald's purposes, however, what the actors said, what the reporters recalled, what all the audiences from 1599 to 1733 heard, was irrelevant; his communication was with Shakespeare's mind – or at least, with Shakespeare's putative bad handwriting.

The history of any text is also a history of its interpretation, and to elucidate a crux is not merely to solve a riddle. Riddles have solutions; but cruxes also have histories of debate and disagreement, and even if the cruxes ultimately seem to be resolved, their solutions do not cancel their histories. Admittedly not much is at stake in this example. The stage history of *Henry V* is, in fact, very short: the play was not a popular one, and does not seem to have been revived after the early years of the seventeenth century – there was a performance before the king in 1605, but the next recorded production was not until 1738, five years after Theobald's edition, and it included his revision.[2] Theobald's intuition could effectively abolish the performing tradition because what little stage life the play had was more than a century in the past.

Perhaps the oddest thing about this sort of puzzle is to decide where the playwright fits into it. In 1599, Shakespeare was on the spot to see that the promptbook and the actors got it right – how could 'table' (or 'talkd') be wrong? But in fact this is not a very persuasive argument: there are numerous perfectly obvious muddles in the Shakespeare texts. When Cassio is first mentioned in *Othello*, he is described as 'a fellow almost damned in a fair wife', but the wife is never mentioned again, and for the remainder of the play Cassio is clearly unmarried. The stage directions for the opening of Acts I and II of *Much Ado About Nothing* include an entry for Leonato's wife Innogen, but she has no lines and is never mentioned. Early in *The Tempest*, Ferdinand alludes to a son of Antonio's among those lost in the wreck, but thereafter Antonio has no son. In *The Comedy of Errors*, Adriana's servant Luce appears in 3.1, and in the next scene she is named Nell. These examples are evidence, no doubt, that Shakespeare sometimes changed his mind during the process of composition, the only puzzling aspect of which is why they remained a permanent feature of the texts. Didn't the actors playing Cassio, Leonato and Antonio wonder about their missing families? Didn't the boy cast as Luce or Nell demand to know, as soon as he got his part, what his name was? (Didn't Shakespeare thunder ' "babbled," not "table," idiots'; and why didn't the embarrassed prompter then immediately correct the error?) How did the confusion survive the first rehearsal? What, in short, is the relation between these texts and what Shakespeare wrote, on the one hand, and what went on on Shakespeare's stage, on the other?

And of course, play-texts, especially printed ones, are not only performing scripts. Even in those cases where they seem specifically to address actors, a larger, and different, audience is also being courted. For three decades in the mid-sixteenth century, published plays characteristically solicited performance by announcing, either on the title page or in the cast list, how many actors were required and how the parts were to be multiplied. 'Four may play it easily,' says the printed text of *The Longer Thou Livest the More Fool Thou Art*, published around 1569, and even supplies a chart dividing the 15 roles among four exceptionally adaptable players: Discipline, for example, is to double Incontinency, Impiety, and Confusion; Piety doubles Idleness and Ignorance; and (perhaps less of a stretch in the mid-sixteenth century) God's Judgment doubles Wrath and Cruelty. The assumption behind such advertising would seem to be that there is nothing to do with a play but perform it. However, a thoughtful audience, whether of spectators or readers, is also solicited by the title-page (Figure 1), which declares the play both 'a very merry and pithy comedy' and 'a mirror very necessary for youth, and specially for such as are like to come to dignity and promotion, as it may well appear in the matter following' – this is not simply an admonition to the actors to choose the right audiences. The merry comedy is 'matter,' a mirror for incipient magistrates, and its profit is not only in the moment of performance; it solicits a readership of 'such as are like to come to dignity.' The moral seriousness of the enterprise is emphasized, perhaps adventitiously, by the printer's use on the title-page of an emblem from Alciato signifying intelligence denied advancement by poverty, also interpretable as Icarus falling from the sky, and in either case serving as an appropriate admonition 'for such as are like to come to dignity and promotion.'[3] The same premonitory woodcut was to adorn the title-page of the first quarto of Marlowe's *Doctor Faustus* in 1604.

The typography too is worth pausing over: the smallest type on this page is used for the play's title and the name of the author. The printer's interests are seemingly quite different from the author's. The printer is concerned with the design of his page, a series of diminishing triangles. He would doubtless have replied to any complaints about the logic of his notion of typographic subordination that if the author had wanted the title, or his name, in large type, he ought to have put them at the top. The author, in fact, probably had little to do with the matter; but it is clear that for publishers, the title-pages of plays – the first thing readers saw, and the principal typographic inducement to buy – required no different style of presentation from the title pages of treatises or sermons. The reason for this was not some primitive insensitivity to the special nature of plays, but a very clear sense of the nature of reading in the age: readers did not skim, they started at the beginning and proceeded quite systematically. As they did so, serious readers made marginal notations of the subject, the progress of the argument, and whatever

Figure 1 *The Longer Thou Livest the More Fool Thou Art*, c. 1569, title-page. Reproduced by permission of The British Library

interesting matters they might wish to return to. For such readers, the hook would not be in the title, but in the characterization offered by the first line: '*A very merry and...*' – irresistible, no? Far more enticing than *The longer thou livest, the more fool thou art*, even if that could be got onto one or two lines of large type.

Thus Lewis Gager's *Life and Repentance of Mary Magdalene* in 1566 declares itself '*very delectable for those which shall heare or reade the same.*' What, then, about the purchasers and readers of plays? The title page of *Cambises* (1570) (Figure 2) promises a play in the mode of *Pyramus and Thisby*, 'a lamentable tragedy mixed full of pleasant mirth,' and pretty much delivers on the promise; but the format suggests more a textbook of Ramist logic than what Sidney called a 'mungrel tragicomedy.' Academic plays like *Gammer Gurton's Needle* and *Ralph Roister Doister* are overtly literary, domesticating the Roman comedy taught in schools. Nicholas Udall, the playwright of *Roister Doister*, had even published an *en face* translation of three Terence plays as a Latin conversation book, *The Flowers of Latin Speaking*; so for this playwright the boundary between reading and performance was almost nonexistent. *Gorboduc*, on the other hand, makes the fact of publication itself part of a miniature tragicomedy:

> This tragedy was... never intended by the authors thereof to be published; yet one W. G. getting a copy thereof at some young man's hand that lacked a little money and much discretion in the last great plague, anno 1565, about five years past (while the authors were away)... put it forth exceedingly corrupted: even as if by means of a broker for hire, he should have enticed into his house a fair maid and done her villainy, and after all to-bescratched her face, torn her apparel, bewrayed and disfigured her, and then thrust her out of doors dishonored. In such plight after long wandering she came at length home to the sight of her friends, who scant knew her but by a few tokens and marks remaining. They, the authors I mean, though they were very much displeased that she so ran abroad without leave, whereby she caught her shame, as many wantons do, yet seeing the case as it is remediless, have for common benefit and shame-fastness new apparelled, trimmed and attired her in such form as she was before. In which better form since she hath come to me, I have harbored her for her friends' sake and her own, and I do not doubt her parents the authors will not now be discontent that she go abroad among you good readers, so it be in honest company.

This is the preface to the second edition of the work, published by John Day in 1570. It is clearly addressed to a reading audience, but the appearance of the play as a book is assumed to require justification, and Day's allegory deals with the issues of authority and transmission by putting them into a patriarchal fable and gendering them. The manuscript of the play is not simply a material possession, it is female – initially a chaste maid, but once revealed through unauthorized publication a fallen woman, seduced and betrayed by venal men. The betrayal involves a double misrepresentation: the fact that the play was printed at all, and the incorrect text, 'exceedingly corrupted' – it is the maid who is dishonored by

A lamentable tragedy

mixed ful of pleasant mirth, conteyning the life of
CAMBISES king of *PERCIA*, from the beginning
of his kingdome vnto his death, his one good deed of ex-
ecution, after that many wicked deeds
and tirannous murders, committed by and
through him, and last of all, his odious
death by Gods Justice appoin-
ted. Doon in such order as
foloweth. By
Thomas Preston.

The diuision of the partes.

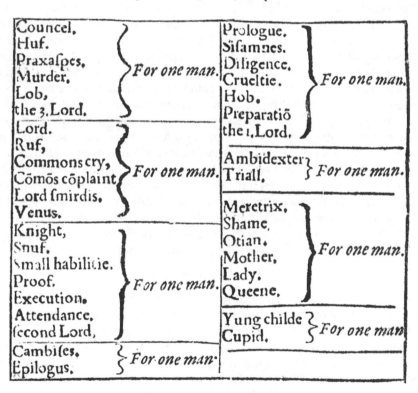

Councel. Huf. Praxaspes. Murder. Lob, the 3. Lord.	For one man.	Prologue. Sisamnes. Diligence. Crueltie. Hob. Preparatiõ the 1. Lord.	For one man.
Lord. Ruf, Commons cry, Cõmõs cõplaint Lord smirdis. Venus.	For one man.	Ambidexter, Triall.	For one man.
Knight, Snuf. Small habilitie. Proof. Execution. Attendance. second Lord,	For one man.	Meretrix. Shame. Otian. Mother, Lady. Queene.	For one man.
		Yung childe Cupid.	For one man
Cambises. Epilogus.	For one man.		

Figure 2 Thomas Preston, *Cambises*, 1570, title-page. Reproduced by permission of The British Library

these actions, not the mercenary purveyor or the unscrupulous publisher (the mysterious W. G.), and least of all the careless and absent authors, who are construed as the maiden-play's parents. Everyone involved in this melodrama, including the two parents, is male, with the sole exception of the play itself. Or rather, with the sole exception of the *script*. It is especially striking, in an age in which most published plays were anonymous, that the corruptibility of the text in the absence of the authors is conceived to be all but inevitable.

The corruption, however, is not simply a function of W. G.'s unauthorized publication. By the time it first appeared in print in 1565, the play had been published already, in the sense that it was circulating in manuscript. Manuscript duplication was in fact the most widely practiced form of publication for court and academic drama, as well as for poetry, until well into the seventeenth century. It is the translation of *Gorboduc* into print that is claimed to be the corrupting factor – despite the fact that the source of the printed copy, the manuscript acquired by W. G., would presumably have been similarly defective. But the easy multiplication of copies that printing enabled, and even more, their indiscriminate dissemination to any reader with the price of an octavo, are the crucially contaminating elements. Texts are construed within a social hierarchy: the world of manuscripts is limited, gentlemanly, and familiar; the print world into which the play has been seduced is limitless, classless, and anonymous.

This would seem to be the ideal world for publishers, a world in which anyone may buy. But literary audiences do not define themselves. Readerships must be solicited, and before they can be solicited they must be imagined. The problems printers faced in imagining who might want to read their products are visible like stigmata throughout the texts of early modern drama – as they are in the two initial printed incarnations of *Gorboduc*. John Day's preface of 1570 claims that his new edition corrects the unauthorized version of 1565 (Figure 3). The first of his changes is the title itself: the play is now not *The Tragedy of Gorboduc*, but *The Tragedy of Ferrex and Porrex*. Purchasers of the earlier edition might reasonably be expected to want to replace, or augment, their copies with a more correct or more complete version; but is the change of title really the correction of an error, or merely publishing politics? *Gorboduc* was already registered with the Stationers' Company, and changing the name would give the impression that the new edition was a different literary property – in fact, if Day had not changed the title, he could have been accused of piracy. Was this the point? Or was the new title not obfuscation but an advertising strategy: did a play about murderous sibling rivalry seem more likely to attract new purchasers than a play about a superannuated royal autocrat? If this was the point, it must be relevant that the next edition, in 1590, returned to the title of the supposedly corrupt, inauthentic text, and that the play has been known as *Gorboduc* ever since.[4] As for the unprincipled W. G., although Day pretends not to know his identity (the manuscript, he says, was acquired by 'one W. G.'), he was William Griffith, a perfectly reputable printer and bookseller, and Day certainly knew his name, since it is on the title page of his edition. If the initials are designed to keep clear of the libel laws, they hardly serve to conceal the printer's identity. Why the coyness about the name? It does,

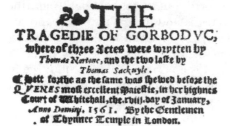

TRAGEDIE OF GORBODVC;
whereof thzee Actes were wzytten by
Thomas Nortone, and the two laste by
Thomas Sackvyle.
Ct hett forthe as the same was shewed befoze the
QVENES most ercellent Maiestie, in her highnes
Court of Whitehall, the.rviij.day of Januarp,
Anno Domini. 1561. By the Gentlemen
. of Chynner Temple in London.

IMPRYNTED AT LONDON
in Fleteltrete, at the Signe of the
Faucon by *William Griffith*: And are
to be fold at his Shop in Saincte
Dunstones Churchyarde in
the West of *London*.
Anno, 1565. *Septemb*.22.

¶The Tragidie of Ferrex
and Porrex,
fet forth without addition or alte -
ration but altogether as the fame was fhewed
on ftage before the Queenes Maieftie,
about nine yeares paft, *vz*. the
xviij. day of Ianuarie. 1561.
by the gentlemen of the
Inner Temple.

Seen and allowed. &c.

Imprinted at London by
Iohn Daye, dwelling ouer
Alderfgate.

Figure 3   The title pages of *Gorboduc* and *Ferrex and Porrex*, 1565 and 1570 (the latter appearing as part 6 of *All such treatises as haue been lately published by Thomas Norton*). Reproduced by permission of The Huntington Library, San Marino, California

ironically, imbricate the play even more firmly within the culture of publication, identifying Griffith by his logo, his initials – the printer reduced to his profession, the publisher as the letter P.

Whatever Day intended, however, most of his claims appear to be false. There is nothing corrupt about Griffith's 1565 text; as Greg says, 'the obvious errors are few, and the textual differences between the two editions neither frequent nor important, the only notable change in [Day's edition] being the omission, possibly on political grounds, of eight lines in V.i.'[5] That is, Day's edition is *less* complete and accurate than Griffith's, not more. Day's version was, moreover, clearly set up not from a new manuscript, but from a copy of the 1565 volume, lightly marked up – the basis for Day's text was the allegedly incorrect one. Finally, although there is a Stationers' Register entry for Griffith's book, there is none for Day's. Considering the number of unregistered books in the period this was certainly a minor infraction, though Day is an odd person to be breaking the rules: he was a charter member of the Company (so was Griffith), and subsequently became its Master; and he registered several other books for publication in the same year. Was the failure to register, like the change of title, another attempt to conceal both the infringement of a fellow Stationer's property and the true source of the text? In any case, if either edition is at all surreptitious, it is the later one.

We have here, then, a specially clear case of a publisher inventing a narrative designed to create a market and an audience. The two title-pages employ competing strategies as well. Griffith gives a great deal of information, and constitutes our only source for the division of authorial labor:

> The Tragedy of Gorboduc, whereof three acts were written by Thomas Norton and the two last by Thomas Sackville. Set forth as the same was showed before the Queen's most excellent majesty, in her higness' court of Whitehall, the 18 day of January, Anno Domini 1561. By the Gentlemen of the Inner Temple in London.

Day reveals much less:

> The Tragedy of Ferrex and Porrex, set forth without addition or alteration, but altogether as the same was showed on stage before the Queen's majesty, about nine years past, viz. The 18 day of January, 1561, by the gentlemen of the Inner Temple.

Sackville and Norton are discreetly mentioned only in the justificatory preface, and the details of composition are suppressed. The focus is on the production, the venue, the patrons, the audience, the performers; Whitehall, the presence of the queen, the Inner Temple, the gentlemen actors. Curiously, moreover, though the text has in fact been slightly improved (the changes involve not only the deletion of the politically incorrect passage, but also some amendment of metrics and occasional clarifications of sense), this is not conceived to be a selling point: the play claims, on the contrary, to be 'set forth without addition or alteration' – the most desirable text is assumed to be the one closest to the original performance. Day's title page claims to offer the reader direct access to that theatrical event in the past, not to the true or final intentions (or even the names) of the authors. The fact that the claim is entirely false indicates where the priorities lie.

This sort of claim remained a selling point for drama until well into the seventeenth century:

> A most excellent Comedie of Alexander, Campaspe, and Diogenes, Played beefore the Queenes Maiestie on twelfe day at night, by her Maiesties children, and the children of Poules.

> Gallathea. As it was playde before the Queenes Maiestie at Greene-wiche, on Newyeeres day at Night. By the Chyldren of Paules.

Thus Lyly's publishers, in 1584 and 1592. For certain kinds of theatrical texts this was always the essential marketing strategy:

> The Characters of two royal masques, the one of Blackness, the other of Beauty, personated by the most magnificent of queens Anne, Queen of Great

Britain, etc., with her honorable ladies, 1605 and 1608, at Whitehall, and invented by Ben Jonson.

Lovers Made Men, a masque presented in the house of the right honorable the Lord Hay, by divers of noble quality, his friends, for the entertainment of Monsieur le Baron de Tour, extraordinary ambassador for the French king, on Saturday the 22 of February, 1617.

For court masques especially, the occasion was essential, since there was no question of the text serving as a script for subsequent performances.

Published plays, however, sometimes pointedly indicate that the text is in fact much more than the performance. Consider the first two quartos of *Hamlet*:

The tragical history of Hamlet Prince of Denmark, by William Shakespeare. As it hath been diverse times acted by his highness' servants in the city of London, as also in the two universities of Cambridge and Oxford, and elsewhere.

Thus the 1603 quarto: this was apparently a performing text for a company on tour, and is, indeed, almost unique among Shakespeare texts in being the right length for the canonical two hours' traffic of his stage. The 1605 quarto, however, reads:

The tragical history of Hamlet Prince of Denmark, by William Shakespeare. Newly imprinted and enlarged to almost as much again as it was, according to the true and perfect copy.

Clearly the true and perfect copy includes a great deal more than you could see at the theater. Similarly, Humphrey Mosely announces that his Beaumont and Fletcher texts in the 1647 folio include 'both All that was *Acted*, and all that was not; even the perfect full Originalls without the least mutilation'[6] – performance mutilates the true and perfect copy, and if you want the whole play, the *real* play, you must buy the book.

One way of retaining the performative aspects of the playbook is to illustrate it. Humanist printers began doing this with classical drama very early, though curiously, only in editions of Terence, not Plautus or Seneca. This probably reflects the fact that Terence alone of the three was actually performed in schools, but the illustrations are in general more bookish than theatrical.[7] The title-page to the 1496 Strasbourg edition in Figure 4 has more to do with the Nuremberg Chronicle than with the performance of plays, and the illustration in the same edition in Figure 5 combines characters from two plays, *Adelphi* and *Heautontimoroumenos*, obviously not on stage – it is even provided with schematic guidelines to indicate what characters belong together. The title-page of a 1497 Venetian edition (Figure 6), however, does give a real sense of theater in action, and focuses, interestingly, on the academic audience rather than the performers. Many Terences include miniature scenes, for the most part in contemporary dress, but again give little sense of an

Figure 4 Title-page of Terence's *Comedies*, Strasbourg, 1496

actual performance.[8] The fact that such incunabular scenes were still being imitated in a Paris edition of 1552 (Figure 7) indicates how much more this sort of illustration has to do with the history of the book than with the history of theater. There are a few notable variations: the 1567 Paris edition in Figure 8 puts

Figure 5 A conspectus of characters from Terence's *Adelphi* and *Heautontimoroumenos*, from the 1496 Strasbourg edition

the plays on a Renaissance perspective stage, and even includes an audience. But in a sense this is archeology – the point of the perspective settings is that they are classical, based on Vitruvius as explicated by Serlio, not that they represent contemporary theatrical practice. As for modern plays, they were most commonly

COLISEVS SI VE THEATRVM

Figure 6 Frontispiece of Terence's *Comedies*, Venice, 1497, showing the Prologue addressing an academic audience

ACTVS IIII. SCENA V.

ARG. ADR. BARL.

IN hac fcena Chremes puerum ex Glycerio natum
audit, & illam ciuem effe Atticam, vt fic à nuptiis de_

Figure 7 A scene from the *Andria*, from Terence's *Comedies*, Paris, 1552

tur, pro deind
dent quæ peta
pugnafcere . [
Sic Virg. Heu
multam fruftr.
videtur non ef
tricis fatisfact
[Non eam, ne
gunt, qui fecur
Conftituam : v
meretricum co
lacrymæ côfié
[Exclufit, reuc
exclufit, potiu
quod erat mo
go fuperiore:
ret; inferiore
Bene de ea qu
tat, nec roget,
maiorem par
λογισμὸς quafi
medonteæ fer
Deeft, eft : vt,
do ad landem.

Trimetri .

PHAEDRIA adolefcens, PARMENO feruus .

VID igitur faciam? non eã?
ne nunc quidem,
Cum accerfor vltro? an potius ita me comparem,

Figure 8 A scene from the *Eunuchus*, from Terence's *Comedies*, Venice, 1567

illustrated not as if taking place on a stage, but with a conspectus of scenes and characters, as narrative poems were illustrated in the period. A characteristic plate in the 1602 edition of Guarini's *Pastor Fido* (Figure 9) shows not a scene, but a summary of a whole act. Virgil, Ovid, Ariosto, Tasso were imagined in the same way: the pictures represented not scenes but epitomes.

Figure 9   Battista Guarini, *Il Pastor Fido*, Venice, 1602. A conspectus of the action of Act 2

On the other hand, when it was the occasion, not the drama, that was important, the illustrations gave a very detailed and specific sense of performance: masques, balets de cour, royal entries, were often issued with splendid plates that provide a vivid particularity. The best known of these is the 1581 *Balet Comique de la Royne*. The view of the masquing hall (Figure 10) shows not only the scene in progress, in a great hall with dispersed settings, but the disposition of the audience, with the royal party on the floor of the hall and the rest of the spectators in a gallery. Other illustrations in the volume show costumes and pageants, and the text also includes music. In Figure 11, from a 1618 ballet de cour in which Louis XIII danced, a key is provided to identify the costumed dancers, so that the reader could not only reconstruct the action but penetrate the disguises. The book also shows the settings, and includes not only the music, but lute tablature as well, so that musically literate readers could reproduce it for themselves. Festival books, records of courtly spectacles, were among the most elaborately produced publications in the period; and clearly in these, although scenery and costumes were often lavishly depicted, the principal attraction for the original readers was not the performance but the royal patrons or the aristocratic venue.

Now let us cross the Channel. I believe that the only English masque published with illustrations was Campion's *Lord Hay's Masque*, 1607, which includes a single engraved costume design (Figure 12).[9] The uniqueness of this example indicates something about the market for printed masques in England – that it was not dependent on the elegance of the book. For plays, English publishers from the 1590s on occasionally provided, as a frontispiece or on the title-page, a scene from the play, generally as if in performance; R. A. Foakes has identified and described 28 of these.[10] As Foakes observes, the images rarely accord with the text: for example, the frontispiece to *The Spanish Tragedy*, in Figure 13, is not a scene from the play. It is rather a summary of the central action, conflating two separate moments. In the drama, Hieronymo is alone when he discovers his son's body; the murder of Horatio, his lover Bel-Imperia's cries for help, and her sequestration by the villains Lorenzo and Balthazar, have all taken place before he enters. Moreover, the dialogue that comes in ribbons from the characters' mouths exists nowhere in the text; it has been invented for the picture. Despite the fact that this illustrates a printed version of the play, the action here departs radically from its script – the scene depicted has been improvised by the artist, as if the play were not a text but a scenario. The sources of this kind of representation are images that, however dramatic, have no connection with plays or theater – early Annunciation scenes, for example, in which 'Ave gratia plena' emanates from the angelic messenger's mouth. And nothing here suggests a theater.[11]

For comparison, here is how Italian publishers were illustrating plays in the same period. A Florentine tragedy called *Il Solimano*, published in 1620, included double-page etchings of the stage sets and characters by Jacques Callot. These are scenically detailed, lavish and realistic – the settings did not change throughout, but the developing action is minutely rendered, with the final scene ending spectacularly in a conflagration (Figures 14 and 15). In 1637 another Florentine

Figure de la Salle.

Figure 10 Baltasar de Beaujoyeulx, *Balet Comique de la Royne*, Paris, 1582. The masquing hall with the opening scene

BALLET

Figure 11   Estienne Durand, *Discours au vray du ballet dans par le roy...*, Paris, 1617. Dancers in the first entry

publisher issued an edition of a comedy called *Le Nozze degli Dei*, with engravings by Stefano della Bella, after Alfonso Parigi, who had designed the settings (Figure 16). Both these sets of illustrations have become classics in the history of scenography. The publishers in such examples were certainly interested in producing a lavishly illustrated book, but the close alliance of book with performance was of the essence.

   The English had very little interest in this sort of thing, though Inigo Jones was creating stage sets as elaborate as those of Alfonso Parigi. The only English

Figure 12   Thomas Campion, *The Description of a Maske...*, London, 1607 (*Lord Hay's Masque*). Frontispiece. Reproduced by permission of the Folger Shakespeare Library

theatrical text issued in this format before the eighteenth century was Elkanah Settle's heroic tragedy *The Empress of Morocco*, 1673.[12] The volume was a real attempt to locate Settle's text in the theater: it had as a frontispiece the façade of the Dorset Garden (or Duke's) Theater, where the play was performed, and included five engravings of stage settings and action. These look, however, much more like book illustrations than theatrical performances; even at their most imaginative their decorative frames overwhelm them, and the sensationally gory conclusion especially, in Figure 17, is much too neatly contained – the stage, for this artist, is clearly constrained by the page. Dryden, who called the play 'a rhapsody

Figure 13 Thomas Kyd, *The Spanish Tragedy*, London, 1615. Title-page illustration. Reproduced by permission of the Folger Shakespeare Library

Figure 14 Prospero Bonarelli della Rovere, *Il Solimano Tragedia*, Florence, 1620. Frontispiece to Act 2

Figure 15   Il Solimano. Frontispiece to Act 5

of nonsense,' was especially contemptuous of its publication with illustrations, and attacked it in a pamphlet called *Notes and observations on The empress of Morocco, or, Some few errata's to be printed instead of the sculptures with the second edition of that play* (1674)[13] – the second edition, 13 years later, was indeed published without illustrations, as was the third in 1698. The play was a success, but London publishers clearly felt that play-texts would do well enough on their own. When publishers did issue elegant and expensive books of plays, collected (and usually memorial) volumes, they embellished them not with dramatic scenes, but with portraits of the author – Shakespeare, Jonson, Fletcher (no portrait of Beaumont was available), Cartwright, Killigrew, Sir Robert Howard. So plays become literature, visualizing the author rather than the stage.

How different performing texts were from published texts is strikingly illustrated by those cases where printed plays have actually served as the bases for performance – have been, in effect, turned back into scripts. A copy of the first folio in the library of the University of Padua preserves a very early example, the texts of *Measure for Measure* and *Macbeth* marked up, no later than the 1630s, for performance. I have written in detail about these; here I shall show only a single characteristic example (Figure 18). This is a page of *Measure for Measure*. The cutting has been relentless; and in fact, throughout this most dialectical of dramas the argumentation

Figure 16   Giovanni Carlo Coppola, *Le Nozze degli Dei*, Florence, 1637. Hell scene, Act 5

has been largely eviscerated. Long speeches are shortened, debates radically simplified, and – especially – poetic complexity has been removed. A certain quality of continuous explanation and self-justification (a quality that most modern readers would call essential) has disappeared too: gone are the Duke's opening speech about the properties of government, the first 15 lines of his charge to Angelo, including the reasons for making Angelo his deputy, and most of his subsequent explanation of why he left his throne. More strikingly, Claudio's exculpatory account of his failure to formalize his marriage to Juliet, because of dowry problems – that is, Angelo's plea of innocence – is cut. Even the revelation of Juliet's pregnancy – the smoking gun, so to speak – was originally deleted, though it was subsequently restored with a marginal 'stet.' In Isabella's interviews with Angelo, the arguments on both sides are effectively disemboweled; and indeed, the omission from this script of what were to become the most famous passages in the play would appear to be systematic, as if the reviser was gifted with a kind of reverse prophecy. The only major scene that is left even relatively intact is Isabella's interview with her brother in prison, which was presumably considered the only dramatically indispensable debate.

A similar pattern is evident in the cutting of *Macbeth*. The reviser speeds up the dialogue, often at the expense of logic and always at the expense of poetic complexity, and shortens nearly every scene – we can almost hear him muttering, 'More action, and less talk!' This sort of cutting is quite normal in Shakespeare productions on the modern stage – Peter Brook, for example, obviously believes

Figure 17   Elkanah Settle, *The Empress of Morocco*, London, 1673. Frontispiece to Act 5

that if you delete enough you will eventually get to the essential play; and Tom Stoppard's *Dogg's Hamlet* may well have proved him right – but the same assumptions are already at work in the early seventeenth century, almost within Shakespeare's lifetime.

36

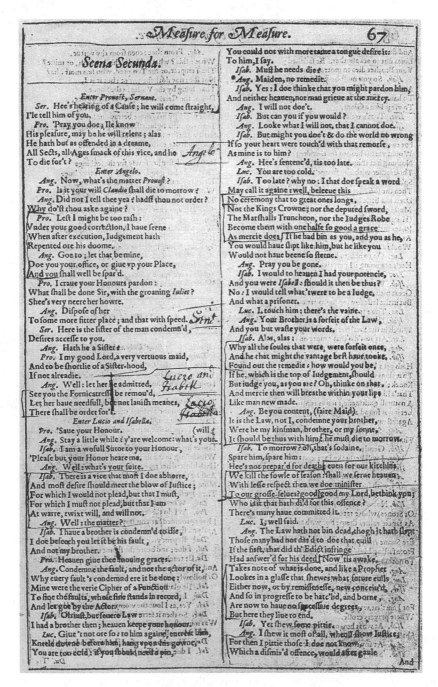

Scena Secunda.

Enter Prouost, Seruans.

Ser. Hee's hearing of a Cause; he will come straight,
I'le tell him of you,
Pro. 'Pray you doe; Ile know
His pleasure, may be he will relent; alas
He hath but as offended in a dreame,
All Sects, all Ages smack of this vice, and he   *Ang:lo*
To die for't?

Enter Angelo.

Ang. Now, what's the matter *Prouost?*
Pro. Is it your will *Claudio* shall die to morrow?
Ang. Did not I tell thee yea? hadst thou not order?
Why do'st thou aske againe?
Pro. Lest I might be too rash:
Vnder your good correction, I haue seene
When after execution, Iudgement hath
Repented ore his doome,
Ang. Goe to; let that be mine,
Doe you your office, or giue vp your Place,
And you shall well be spar'd.
Pro. I craue your Honours pardon:
What shall be done Sir, with the groaning *Iuliet?*
Shee's very neere her howre.
Ang. Dispose of her
To some more fitter place; and that with speed.   *Sene*
Ser. Here is the sister of the man condemn'd,
Desires accesse to you.
Ang. Hath he a Sister?
Pro. I my good Lord, a very vertuous maid,
And to be shortlie of a Sister-hood,
If not alreadie.
Ang. Well: let her be admitted,   *Lucio and Izabell*
See you the Fornicatresse be remou'd,
Let her haue needfull, but not lauish meanes,   *Lucio Izabella*
There shall be order for't.

Enter Lucio and Isabella.

Pro. 'Saue your Honour.   (will?
Ang. Stay a little while; y'are welcome: what's your
Isab. I am a wofull Sutor to your Honour,
'Please but your Honor heare me.
Ang. Well: what's your suite.
Isab. There is a vice that most I doe abhorre,
And most desire should meet the blow of Iustice;
For which I would not plead, but that I must,
For which I must not plead, but that I am
At warre, twixt will, and will not.
Ang. Well: the matter?
Isab. I haue a brother is condemn'd to die,
I doe beseech you let it be his fault,
And not my brother.
Pro. Heauen giue thee mouing graces.
Ang. Condemne the fault, and not the actor of it,
Why euery fault's condemn'd ere it be done:
Mine were the verie Cipher of a Function
To fine the faults, whose fine stands in record,
And let goe by the Actor.
Isab. O iust, but seuere Law:
I had a brother then; heauen keepe your honour.
Luc. Giue't not ore so: to him againe, entreat him,
Kneele downe before him, hang vpon his gowne,
You are too cold: if you should neede a pin,

You could not with more tame a tongue desire it:
To him, I say.
Isab. Must he needs die?
Ang. Maiden, no remedie.
Isab. Yes: I doe thinke that you might pardon him,
And neither heauen, nor man grieue at the mercy.
Ang. I will not doe't.
Isab. But can you if you would?
Ang. Looke what I will not, that I cannot doe.
Isab. But might you doe't & do the world no wrong
If so your heart were touch'd with that remorse,
As mine is to him?
Ang. Hee's sentenc'd, tis too late.
Luc. You are too cold.
Isab. Too late? why no: I that doe speake a word
May call it againe: well, beleeue this
No ceremony that to great ones longs,
Not the Kings Crowne; nor the deputed sword,
The Marshalls Truncheon, nor the Iudges Robe
Become them with one halfe so good a grace
As mercie does. If he had bin as you, and you as he,
You would haue slipt like him, but he like you
Would not haue beene so sterne.
Ang. Pray you be gone.
Isab. I would to heauen I had your potencie,
And you were *Isabell*: should it then be thus?
No: I would tell what 'twere to be a Iudge,
And what a prisoner.
Luc. I, touch him: there's the vaine.
Ang. Your Brother is a forfeit of the Law,
And you but waste your words.
Isab. Alas, alas:
Why all the soules that were, were forfeit once,
And he that might the vantage best haue tooke,
Found out the remedie: how would you be,
If he, which is the top of Iudgement, should
But iudge you, as you are? Oh, thinke on that,
And mercie then will breathe within your lips
Like man new made.
Ang. Be you content, (faire Maid)
It is the Law, not I, condemne your brother,
Were he my kinsman, brother, or my sonne,
It should be thus with him: he must die to morrow.
Isab. To morrow? oh, that's sodaine,
Spare him, spare him:
Hee's not prepar'd for death; euen for our kitchins
We kill the fowle of season: shall we serue heauen
With lesse respect then we doe minister
To our grosse selues? good, good my Lord, bethink you;
Who is it that hath di'd for this offence?
There's many haue committed it.
Luc. I, well said.
Ang. The Law hath not bin dead, thogh it hath slept
Those many had not dar'd to doe that euill
If the first, that did th' Edict infringe
Had answer'd for his deed. Now 'tis awake,
Takes note of what is done, and like a Prophet
Lookes in a glasse that shewes what future euils
Either now, or by remissenesse, new conceiu'd,
And so in progresse to be hatch'd, and borne,
Are now to haue no successiue degrees,
But here they liue to end.
Isab. Yet shew some pittie.
Ang. I shew it most of all, when I show Iustice;
For then I pittie those I doe not know,
Which a dismis'd offence, would after gaule,

And

Here is an example deriving even more directly from the playhouse; although a little later than the period we have been considering, its evidence relates to perennial issues of performance. The volume started out as the promptbook of a Colley Cibber production of Otway's Restoration tragedy *Venice Preserv'd*. The cast list, including Cibber, Elrington, and Thomas Sheridan, would date the production from the 1740s; but the promptbook, which was repeatedly altered, must also have served for a number of subsequent productions.[14] The text is the first edition of the play, published in 1682 – the book was already more than 60 years old. The dates emphasize both the durability and the malleability of play-texts. Figure 19 shows an entirely characteristic page. As in the Padua Shakespeare folio, most cuts are initially indicated simply by outlining the passages – sometimes a marginal 'Out' is present in addition, but the omissions are not inked out because they need to remain legible in a text which will serve for more than one production and must therefore accommodate numerous changes of mind. And as this page from Act 4 indicates, very few cuts remained deleted, and many of the restored bits were subsequently deleted in their turn. This page seems to represent at least five separate versions of the dialogue; by the end, the main problem was obviously no longer the legibility of the text, but how to indicate what lines were actually to be included. There is only one point in the promptbook where the cutting is irreversible, because it is literal – a page containing an inconclusive, mildly bawdy scene between the elderly lecher Antonio and the scornful courtesan Aquilina, has been excised. The scene was superfluous because Antonio's role had been cut; but what is striking is that this is the only instance of a permanent excision, one binding on future performances. The radical surgery doubtless records real discomfort: Antonio's scenes with Aquilina are, to modern readers, certainly silly and even embarrassing; they are also probably the closest Restoration drama, so notorious for its libertinism, actually comes to anything like kinky sex – which is to say, not very close (Rochester's *Sodom* is, in comparison, robustly healthy, in the sense that it is full of characters who really are interested in both sex and each other). But in the era of *Fanny Hill*, it is sexual failure that is unstageable, so 'obscene' (literally) that the promptbook must be mutilated to ensure that audiences will never be confronted with the elderly, unsatisfied lecher.

Figure 20 shows the stage manager's instructions for a single moment near the end of the performance, the beginning of Act 5: 'Longfield ready at bell.' No actor named Longfield is recorded in the theatrical dictionaries; he is rather the stagehand who rings the 'dismal bell' that will punctuate the final tragic interview between Belvidera and Jaffeir in about five minutes, and he is being told not to be ready at the *sound* of the bell, but to stand by to ring it.

'O. P.': Belvidera and Jaffeir exit at the side of the stage *opposite the prompter* (rather than 'P. S.', the *prompter's side*) – this was the standard shorthand way of dealing with the question, unresolved to this day, of whether 'stage left' and 'stage right' mean the actors' left and right (as in the UK) or the audience's (as in the US); the prompter throughout these various productions would always have sat on the same side. 'Carpet on' and 'stage cloth off' indicate a change in décor – the carpet is peculiar, since the scene is moving from inside the Doge's Palace to

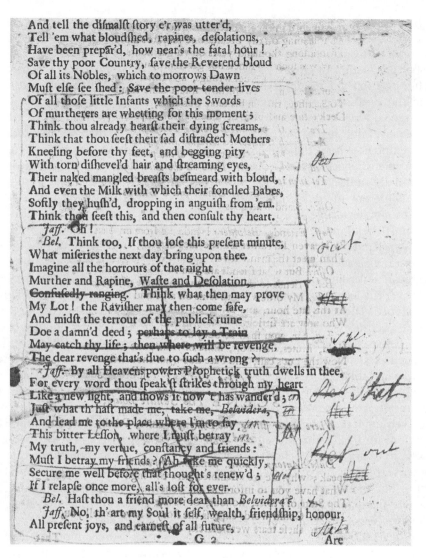

And tell the difmalft ftory e'r was utter'd,
Tell 'em what bloudfhed, rapines, defolations,
Have been prepar'd, how near's the fatal hour !
Save thy poor Country, fave the Reverend bloud
Of all its Nobles, which to morrows Dawn
Muft elfe fee fhed: Save the poor tender lives
Of all thofe little Infants which the Swords
Of murtherers are whetting for this moment ;
Think thou already hearft their dying fcreams,
Think that thou feeft their fad diftracted Mothers
Kneeling before thy feet, and begging pity
With torn difhevel'd hair and ftreaming eyes,
Their naked mangled breafts befmeard with bloud,
And even the Milk with which their fondled Babes,
Softly they hufh'd, dropping in anguifh from 'em.
Think thou feeft this, and then confult thy heart.
    Jaff. Oh !
    Bel. Think too, If thou lofe this prefent minute,
What miferies the next day bring upon thee.
Imagine all the horrours of that night
Murther and Rapine, Wafte and Defolation,
Confufedly ranging. Think what then may prove
My Lot ! the Ravifher may then come fafe,
And midft the terrour of the publick ruine
Doe a damn'd deed ; perhaps to lay a Train
May catch thy life ; then where will be revenge,
The dear revenge that's due to fuch a wrong ?
    Jaff. By all Heavens powers Prophetick truth dwells in thee,
For every word thou fpeak'ft ftrikes through my heart
Like a new light, and fhows it how 't has wander'd ;
Juft what th' haft made me, take me, *Belvidera*,
And lead me to the place where I'm to fay
This bitter Leffon, where I muft betray
My truth, my vertue, conftancy and friends :
Muft I betray my friends ? Ah take me quickly,
Secure me well before that thought's renew'd ;
If I relapfe once more, all's loft for ever.
    Bel. Haft thou a friend more dear than *Belvidera* ?
    Jaff. No, th' art my Soul it felf, wealth, friendfhip, honour,
All prefent joys, and earneft of all future,
                    G 2   Are

Figure 19   Thomas Otway, *Venice Preserv'd*, London, 1682. A page from the promptbook for a series of mid-eighteenth-century productions

outside it, but the removal of the 'stage cloth,' presumably with a painted interior setting, would have made the point. The prompter is also in charge of the commerce of theater; he calls for 'one ready to give out the play' – probably to announce the details of the next performance.

Act 5 takes place 'outside Pallace.' Priuli enters from 'P. S.', the prompter's side, opposite the one where Belvidera and Jaffeir have just made their exit. Priuli is 'Dressing' – hence, perhaps, the carpet, to mitigate the outdoor look of the scene. 'One ready below with Blood': below the trapdoor, atop which a scaffold is to be

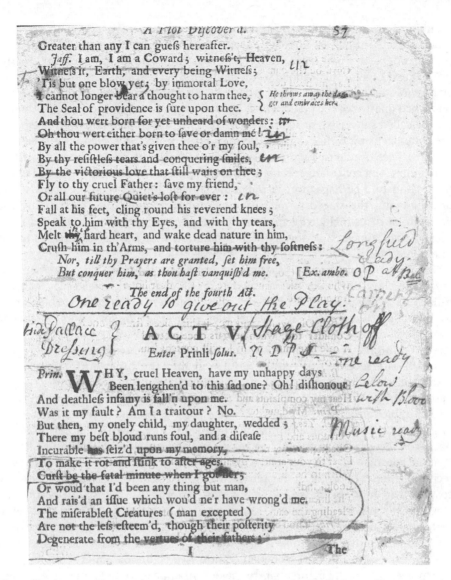

A Plot Discover'd.   57

Greater than any I can guess hereafter.

Jaff. I am, I am a Coward; witness't, Heaven,
Witness it, Earth, and every being Witness;
'Tis but one blow yet; by immortal Love,
I cannot longer bear a thought to harm thee,   { *He throws away the dagger and embraces her.*
The Seal of providence is sure upon thee.   {
And thou wert born for yet unheard of wonders:
Oh thou wert either born to save or damn me!
By all the power that's given thee o'r my soul,
By thy resistless tears and conquering smiles,
By the victorious love that still waits on thee;
Fly to thy cruel Father: save my friend,
Or all our future Quiet's lost for ever :
Fall at his feet, cling round his reverend knees;
Speak to him with thy Eyes, and with thy tears,
Melt his hard heart, and wake dead nature in him,
Crush him in th'Arms, and torture him with thy softness:
   Nor, *till thy Prayers are granted, set him free,*
   But *conquer him, as thou hast vanquish'd me.*   [*Ex. ambo.*

The end of the fourth Act.

ACT V.

Enter *Prinli solus.*

Prin. WHY, cruel Heaven, have my unhappy days
            Been lengthen'd to this sad one? Oh! dishonour
And deathless infamy is fall'n upon me.
Was it my fault? Am I a traitour? No.
But then, my onely child, my daughter, wedded;
There my best bloud runs foul, and a disease
Incurable has seiz'd upon my memory,
To make it rot and stink to after-ages.
Curst be the fatal minute when I got her;
Or woud that I'd been any thing but man,
And rais'd an issue which wou'd ne'r have wrong'd me.
The miserablest Creatures (man excepted)
Are not the less esteem'd, though their posterity
Degenerate from the vertues of their fathers;

I   The

Figure 20   A page of instructions for the stage manager in the *Venice Preserv'd* promptbook

revealed, on which Jaffeir will soon stab Pierre and then himself, whereupon they will both be covered with spurts of blood from 'below.' And 'Music ready', to accompany Belvidera's final entrance, 'distracted'.

The playbook as promptbook is scarcely a book any more. It is set of notations for production, and, as such, an archeological site of evidence about the play's physical, auditory, visual, spatial requirements and possibilities at a particular moment in theater history. All these are elicited from the text, to be sure, but the text is endlessly mutable – as the volume testifies, it changed from production to production.

Publication, in short, does nothing to fix the text of a play. When, therefore, a group of recusant players in Yorkshire were indicted in 1610 for performing Papist propaganda – the particular charge was that they had made additions to the printed text of a lost play about St Christopher; they had also performed *King Lear* and *Pericles* – they defended themselves by asserting that their scripts were the published quartos of the plays, which had been duly licensed and could not therefore be called subversive or seditious. This defense was inadequate in two respects: first, the licensing of books is a different matter from the licensing of theatrical performances. Audiences are large and unpredictable; their responses constitute much more of a civic danger than do the responses of the readers of printed plays. But second, and perhaps more to the point, the relation between the licensed text of a play and the staged script is quite simply imponderable. This is why the licensing of plays included a specific injunction that no more was allowed to be spoken than appeared in the script, a stipulation that was as essential as it was unenforceable.

Our promptbook shows us actors and producers reading. But what happens when the play really does become literature? How do readers read plays? In the earliest examples we have considered, the publishers assumed that the readers were in effect audiences; that, whether they were actors or spectators, what they wanted was to reconstruct a performance they either had seen or wished they had seen. And this has certainly always constituted a motive for reading plays. Moreover, from the late seventeenth century until well into the nineteenth, Shakespeare texts regularly indicated what sections were omitted from the performing versions – Restoration readers wanted Betterton's *Hamlet*, but they also wanted to know in what way Betterton's *Hamlet* was not Shakespeare's. I know of no early evidence of a reader actually using a printed text to reconstruct a particular performance; but some readers did imagine their texts on a stage. A sixteenth-century Italian student adorned his copy of a 1541 Aldine Terence with two nicely executed scenes: Figures 21 and 22 show a masked prologue and the first scene. These are costumed in modern dress, as Terence was performed in Humanist academies. However (to my disappointment, I must confess), these have nothing to do with performance and everything to do with books: the scenes are copied from two of the Terences we have just looked at. The prologue scene takes three figures from the frontispiece of the 1497 Venetian edition (see Figure 6: a later schoolboy has drawn eyes on on the actor's hat, to make him appear to be facing forward and masked, but his feet show that we are seeing his back); and the first scene, with its musical combo, is copied from the 1567 Venetian edition with the perspective settings (see Figure 8) – the schoolboy has not learned perspective yet.

As for readers using printed plays to reconstruct performances, I have no early example, but here is a Victorian one. Starting in the 1870s Henry Irving published his arrangements of Shakespeare plays to accompany his productions, as a kind of libretto. An anonymous reader annotated his copy of Irving's *Macbeth*, presented at the Lyceum in 1888–89. The pencilled glosses record stage business and interpretive detail, and occasionally even indicate the verbal accentuation, the most ephemeral element of the production. The notes seem to have been made during

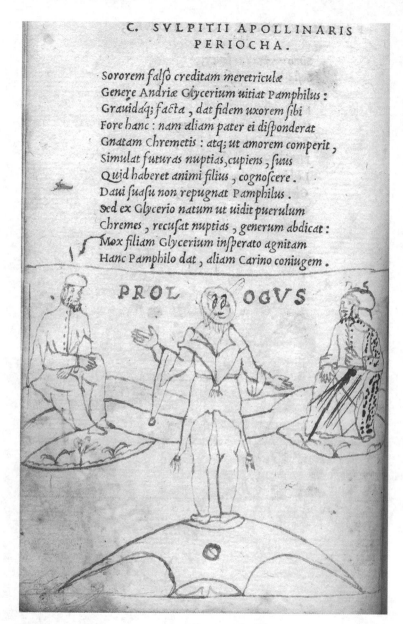

Figure 21   A contemporary drawing of the Prologue to the *Andria*, in *Terentii Comœdiæ*, Aldus, Venice, 1541

a performance (which would not have been easy, since Irving, almost alone of theatrical producers in the period, extinguished the house lights when the curtain was up; and this particular production was notorious for the murkiness of its stage lighting). Figure 23 shows the end of 1.7.

ANDRIA

Contaminari non decere fabulas.
Faciunt næ intellegendo, ut nihil intellegant.
Quj cum hunc adcusant, Nævium, Plautum, Ennium
Adcusant : quos hic noster auctores habet :
Quorum æmulari exoptat neglegentiam
Potius, quàm istorum obscuram diligentiam.
Dehinc ut quiescant, porrò moneo, & desinant
Maledicere, malefacta ne noscant sua.
Fauete, adeste æquo animo, & rem cognoscite,
Vt pernoscatis, ecquid spei sit reliquum,
Posthac quas faciet de integro comœdias,
Spectandæ, an exigendæ sint uobis prius.

INTERLOCVTORES.

Figure 22 A contemporary drawing of the first scene of the *Andria* in the Aldine Terence, 1541

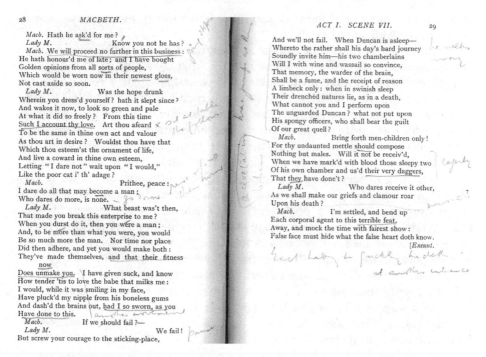

Figure 23   Macbeth, as arranged for the stage by Henry Irving, London, 1889. Two pages of 1.7 annotated by a member of the audience

Stresses and emphases are indicated. During Lady Macbeth's harangue Macbeth 'sit[s] at table / she follows.' At his assertion that 'I dare do all that may become a man,' 'Mac rise up / then turn' and then 'go down' – presumably downstage. Pauses are indicated. At the top of the next page, Macbeth 'walks away' as Lady Macbeth describes her plan for the murder, but also 'jumps at' it; his reply is spoken 'eagerly.' (As for the marginal 'music,' the production had incidental music by Arthur Sullivan, which would have been playing to accompany the banquet in the next room: I offer a prize for the best theory about why it is indicated only here and marked with a parenthetical query.) A clear indication that these are eyewitness notes, not based on access to the promptbook, is the awkward gloss at the scene's end: 'Exit Lady M quickly Macbeth at another entrance' – the promptbook would have said something much more efficient, like 'Exit Lady Macbeth left, Macbeth right.'

Nevertheless, our spectator did also have access to the promptbook at some point. He is careful to note throughout when more or less is spoken on stage than is in the text in his lap. At the beginning of the Porter's scene (2.3), he notes that the Porter's speech as edited by Irving has been cut by about half – what is omitted is eight lines, from 'Faith, here's an equivocator' to 'Here you may roast your goose.' The annotator's gloss reads, 'This speech partly cut / here is cut down to 'goose' and then marked stet.' Only in Irving's promptbook, which would have started with a full text of the play, could the annotator have found the missing lines restored with a marginal 'stet.'

These notes are obviously the work of an attentive, devoted, and literate spectator. The marginalia are therefore as interesting for what they omit as for what they include. For example, the *Daily Chronicle*'s reviewer admired Ellen Terry's 'steadfast gaze upon the portrait of her absent spouse carried in her bosom, after she has read the letter narrating his interview with the witches,'[15] but our annotator preserves for himself no record of this striking bit of stage business (there are no notes at all on Lady Macbeth reading the letter). Irving's *Macbeth* was both praised and ridiculed for its attempt to set the play in a historically accurate eleventh-century Scotland – scenery and costumes were very elaborate, and constituted a large element in the production's commercial success. Terry in her scenes as queen wore an astonishing opalescent dress made out of real beetles' wings – Oscar Wilde said of it that, though Lady Macbeth seemed to have patronized local cottage industries for her husband's clothes and the servants' livery, she did her own shopping in Byzantium.[16] None of this, however, is remarked in our spectator's marginalia. Audiences recall, and readers take note of, what interests them.

I turn now to those readers for whom the text is not a surrogate performance but a book – and who probably have always constituted most of the market for published plays. What does it mean for a play to be a book? The Padua Shakespeare folio, with two of its texts marked up for performance, is famous precisely because of its uniqueness. A folio in the Meisei University Library in Tokyo, annotated in a contemporary secretary hand, offers a less exciting but more normative example. I give only a transcription here, since the marginalia are largely illegible in reproduction. These are an early seventeenth-century reader's notes on the 'To be or not to be' soliloquy in *Hamlet*. The first two notes relate to the dialogue immediately preceding – Polonius gives Ophelia a prayerbook and tells her to pretend to have been reading it, remarking that shows of piety 'will sugar o'er/The devil himself,' and Claudius feels a sudden pang of guilt:

> our hipocrisie makes ws surpasse the
> devill in Wickednesse
> sting of conscience

Then Hamlet's soliloquy:

> question whether we ought to overcome our
> selves and our passions by extreame patience
> or die seeking desperat
> revenge

And above the second column,

> doubt what befalles after death
> Miseries and disgraces wherto we are subject
> Conscience makes ws cowards

The last two notes relate to Hamlet's ensuing dialogue with Ophelia:

> Rich gifts waxe poore when givers prove unkind
> Confession of many
> Vices[17]

The annotator provides subject headings and brief summaries, and elicits bits of wisdom or commonplaces – 'Conscience makes us cowards,' 'Rich gifts wax poor when givers prove unkind.' He also makes an interesting mistake in his reading of the soliloquy: Hamlet does not consider whether we should 'die seeking desperate revenge,' but whether we should commit suicide to escape an intolerable life – revenge is not an issue in the soliloquy. Possibly our reader misunderstands the metaphor, which compares attempting to fight back against life's miseries and injustices with the futility of taking arms against the sea (the idea that seventeenth-century poetry was difficult for seventeenth-century readers is one that we don't give much consideration). The misreading is, however, in its way a very shrewd one, because surely the question for Hamlet is *not* 'to be or not to be,' the question is, precisely, revenge, and the speech is, above all, an evasion of the question. This seventeenth-century reader marginally conceives an alternative hero who confronts what Hamlet is avoiding.

This is hardly what we would call a critical reading, but it is in its way an adversarial or corrective one, and it does give a good sense of how Renaissance readers read, and what they read for. Marginal guides, the extraction of wisdom, and on occasion the elucidation or amendment of the text are the stuff of early modern annotation; this is how students were taught to read – pen in hand, systematically epitomizing. Reading was also writing; you made yourself part of your book.[18] I now move to another reader of *Hamlet*, at the beginning of the next century.

My example is a copy of the last quarto, 1703, the fourth reprint of the quarto of 1676. This text, much shortened and slightly touched up by Davenant, was the version used by Betterton in his most famous role, although the omitted sections are also included in the volume, indicated by inverted commas. So a purchaser of any of the last five quartos had Davenant's and Betterton's *Hamlet* interlarded with passages from the original text, which in this case was that of the second quarto, not the folio. For one contemporary reader, this *Hamlet* was unsatisfactory, and he set about to rectify his copy.

To begin with he makes small changes, not especially systematic. Some correct misprints or lacunae, some restore Shakespearean readings in place of Davenant's revisions. Figure 24 is a characteristic bit from the first scene. The marginal 'Tush, tush,' 'illume' and 'harrows' transform Davenant back into Shakespeare; but 'let's sit down' is the annotator's own: the original text, in both Q2 and the folio, says 'sit we down.' In Hamlet's dialogue with Rosencrantz and Guildenstern about the arrival of the Players (2.2.333ff.), both Q2 and Davenant omit the section about the children's companies; the annotator copies it all into the margin, using as his text the fourth folio (Figure 25). He also throughout the book supplies stage directions, which are generally more readerly than performative – to the flourish indicated

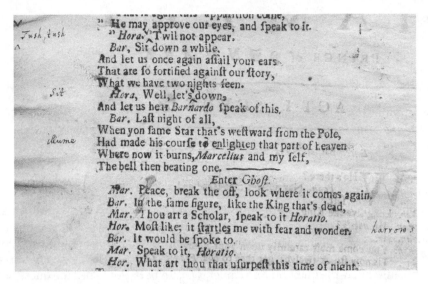

Figure 24   A section of 1.1 (*Hamlet*) with contemporary annotations

before the play within the play, he adds 'for the players'; Laertes does not merely weep for his sister, but 'wipes his eyes'. This is clearly not a text being prepared for either an editorial or theatrical purpose; it is the work of a reader revising to make the text both more Shakespearean and more his own.

These two *Hamlets* are firmly ensconced in the study. The earlier reader prepares a thematic guide, and elicits general and philosophical precepts from the play; the later reader corrects and augments the play from both textual sources and his own imagination. Neither has any interest in returning the play to the theater, or, indeed, treats it as in any significant way theatrical.

I conclude with two final examples of the play in the study, and then – much more precariously – in the library. Another way of asking what readers want out of plays is to consider what context their marginalia place the work in – rarely, as we have seen, the playhouse. The owners of a first edition of Heywood's *Iron Age*, Part Two, 1632, were sparing in their annotations. There are a few discreet corrections, and favorite passages marked. One of these gives a clue to the taste and character of the annotator. Figure 26 is a bit of the scene in which the idea for the Trojan Horse occurs to Synon:

> *Synon.* A horse, a horse.
> *Pyrrhus.* Ten Kingdomes for a horse to enter *Troy*.

Our reader simply marks Heywood's Shakespearean joke with an X – there is no showing off with a marginal reference to *Richard III*; the book is private and personal, and he knows why he has made the mark. Has this reader retreated from the theater to his playbooks? This is surely more than our small clue will reveal;

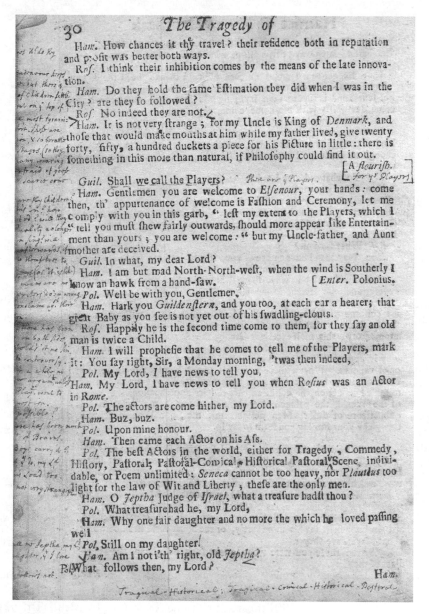

Figure 25 *Hamlet*, London, 1703, with marginal additions from the fourth folio

but it does suggest how far the world of books, even of playbooks, has moved from the world of the stage.

Figure 27 is the titlepage of a first edition of Thomas D'Urfey's revision of Chapman's *Bussy D'Ambois*, 1691. The scribbles are, I believe, the work of the original owner, a person obviously both messy and malicious. The epithet 'Poet

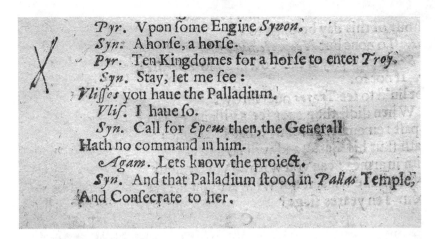

Pyr. Vpon fome Engine *Synon.*
Syn. A horfe, a horfe.
Pyr. Ten Kingdomes for a horfe to enter *Troy.*
Syn. Stay, let me fee :
Vliffes you haue the Palladium.
Vlif. I haue fo.
Syn. Call for *Epeus* then, the Generall
Hath no command in him.
Agam. Lets know the proiect.
Syn. And that Palladium ftood in *Pallas* Temple,
And Confecrate to her.

Figure 26 Thomas Heywood, *The Second Part of the Iron Age*, London, 1632. A minimal annotation

Stutter' alludes to a very malicious pamphlet by the satirist Tom Brown, published in the same year, called *Wit for money, or, Poet Stutter*, in which D'Urfey's verbal affliction is the least of his vices (writing for money is the worst). The remaining scrawls practice penmanship on D'Urfey's name and the Latin 'Hoc est' – there is some more rudimentary Latin on the final verso – and compose the beginning of a poem, 'So I live/So I dye,' otherwise unknown, but recalling the notorious temporarily Shakespearean 'Shall I die/Shall I fly?' Clearly there is little respect for plays, persons or books here; the title page is, after all, just paper. Internally, however, the text is quite clean (did the scribbler read beyond the title-page?), with the exception of a single marginalium to the prologue (Figure 28), beside the observation, in defence of satire, that

> ... no worthy man would break the glass
> That showed him handsomely his homely face.

The Greek says 'But what harm have I done you? None, unless a mirror harms an ugly man when it shows what he looks like.' It is a quotation from Epictetus as recorded by Arrian[19] – in short, a phenomenally learned parallel to an unremarkable commonplace, which Chapman might conceivably have run across, but which has nothing to do with theater, or drama, or, certainly, with D'Urfey, the most demotic of poets. I doubt that this is the same hand as that of the scribbler of the title page – though who knows? Had the malicious youth of 1691, who read scurrilous pamphlets and whose Latin didn't extend beyond 'Hoc est,' matured into an expert hellenist for whom the book he once treated so casually had become comparable to a classical text?

What do readers want out of plays? Many and various things, clearly, most of which have nothing to do with theater, and some of which, though they have

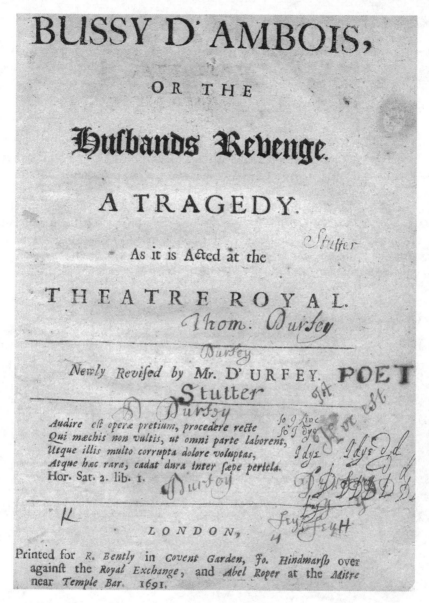

Figure 27   George Chapman, revised by Thomas D'Urfey, *Bussy D'Ambois*, London, 1691.
Title-page

everything to do with books, have little to do with reading. For example, the
nineteenth-century owner of the sad copy of William Cartwright's plays in
Figure 29 allowed the binder to cut it down so severely that not only some of
the title page but whole lines of text disappeared. The binder, however, also
covered the boards in handsome marbled paper and speckled the edges, and

> *I told him well writ Satyr wholfome was ;*
> *And that no worthy Man would break the Glafs,*
> *That shew'd him handfomely his homely Face.*
> *He anfwer'd, 'twas the Vice of all Mankind*
> *To be to their own Imperfections blind.*

Figure 28   Bussy D'Ambois, marginalium to the Prologue

thereby produced a very pretty little book – or rather something that looked like a book, a bibelot, best left unopened. This is all about possession, about books as objects, not as texts; Cartwright's plays have become the most mute and inert of performances.

I conclude with an institutional example. The Inns of Court were, throughout the sixteenth and seventeenth centuries, among the most avid patrons of theater; they regularly brought the London theater companies to perform for them, and commissioned, produced, and performed plays of their own. Lawyers wrote, read and collected play texts, and the libraries of the Inns have been, over the past two

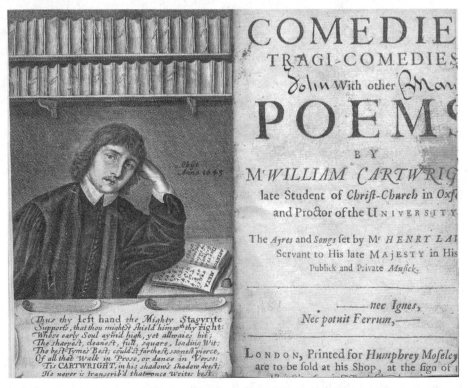

Figure 29   William Cartwright, *Comedies, Tragi-comedies, with other Poems*, London, 1651. Remnants of the frontispiece and title-page

centuries, a rich storehouse for English theater historians. And then about 30 years ago something happened, partly doubtless to do with budgets, but more profoundly to do with an institutional realization that London lawyers have not been reading plays (or for that matter, any old and valuable books) for a very long time, and that there was no reason to continue to bother with them. So the Inner Temple Library, in a series of purges, sold off a large percentage of its antiquarian holdings, including even law books from the library of Sir Edward Coke, which had been in its possession since his death in 1634.

The case in point is a copy of the first English translation of a play of Sophocles, *Electra*, by Charles Wase, published in The Hague in 1649, shortly after the execution of Charles I. It is dedicated to Charles's daughter Princess Elizabeth, and has prologues and epilogues drawing the obvious, explosive, political parallel. It is a beautiful little octavo; its contemporary binding has a royal stamp on both covers, C R crowned (this does not imply that it was in the royal library, but it does identify its owner as a royalist). Sometime in the eighteenth century this rare, valuable, and historically interesting book came to the Inner Temple Library, which added its own showy but elegant gold stamp to the binding, and inserted its very grand bookplate. These tasteful marks of ownership embellished the already handsome book, tokens of institutional pride. The Inner Temple's eighteenth-century librarians, however, also proceeded to beautify the book with red ink stamps: at various times two different ones were applied to the title page (Figure 30), and a third was impressed on the verso of the engraved frontispiece. These obviously had less to do with pride than with possessiveness; but even now the library had not sufficiently declared its ownership. The next page, the dedication, has another red Inner Temple stamp. So does the first page of the text, and the verso of its frontispiece. Nineteen pages later, in the midst of a wonderfully zany illustrated footnote explaining how to make an ancient Greek battle axe ('Take a plate of iron infinite, and describe in it a circle...'), the largest of the red Inner Temple stamps has been set (Figure 31); another small one appears on page 31, another at the beginning of the epilogue; and finally yet another, on the last page, smack in the middle of text. That is 12 separate library stamps in a book of about 75 pages, some imposed on pages that had already been stamped. Was this all done merely to discourage lawyers from stealing the book? I doubt that *Electra* was in any danger: I am quite sure that I am the only person to have read this copy in about three hundred years – it shows no signs of wear, and the only indication that any member of the Inner Temple ever opened it is the library stamps. The number of stamps seems far more pathological than practical, asserting, over and over, that the book is not reading matter but both property and paper, and manifesting the owners' wish literally to impress themselves upon it.[20]

Playbooks are not plays. They may be used as records of performances, or as surrogate performances, or even as scripts; but the evidence of that usage becomes part of the book too, a vestige of a particular reader's special kind of manipulation or attention. We might say, then, that nothing happens when

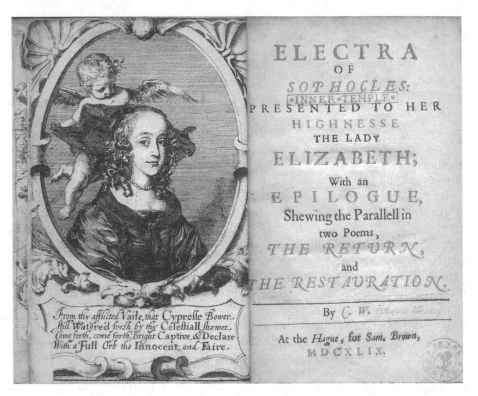

Figure 30   Charles Wase, *Electra of Sophocles*, 'The Hague' (i.e., London), 1649. Title-page with Inner Temple Library stamps. (The stamps and much of the printing is in red.)

plays become books – in this sense, plays do not, cannot, become books. The freefloating element in performance, the essential element unrepresented in the text and barely contained even by the script, the element that makes every performance unique, disappears with publication. But the playbook itself is amenable to performances of other kinds: as literary and scholarly touchstones, they enable imaginative re-creations, or inspire critical and editorial fantasias; as remnants of another era, they are archeological and bibliographical sites, historical and cultural archives; even reduced to their basic element, paper, they record culturally significant material practices as disparate as note taking, doodling, and ink stamping; conceived as objects, whether in 'Fine Bindings' and 'Fine Press' editions in a collector's library, or as bibelots on a drawing-room table, even unopened and unread, they declare that the making of books is a performative art; and finally, as simply a metonym for property itself, they are the containers, if not for the art of the stage and the work of the playwright, at least for whatever ways owners and connoisseurs have of enacting possession.

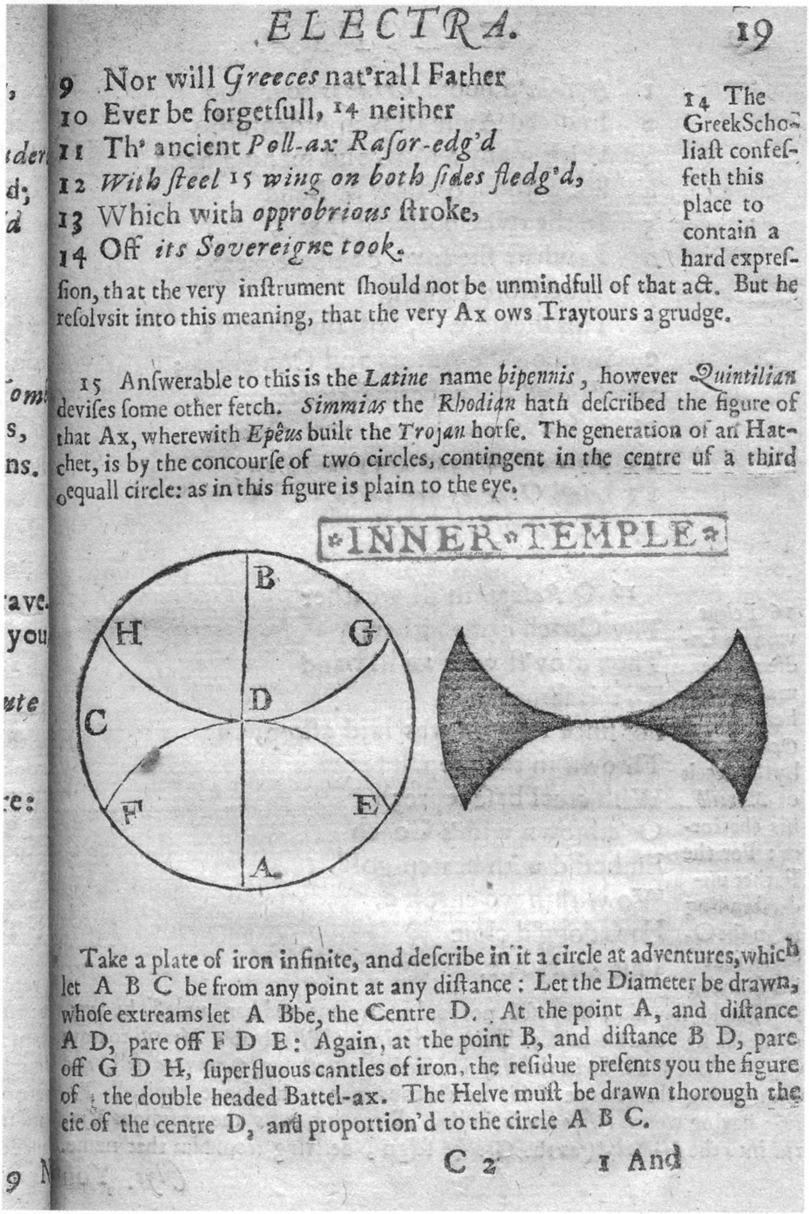

9 Nor will *Greeces* nat'rall Father
10 Ever be forgetfull, 14 neither
11 Th' ancient *Poll-ax Rasor-edg'd*
12 *With steel* 15 *wing on both sides fledg'd,*
13 Which with *opprobrious* stroke,
14 Off *its Sovereigne took.*

14 The GreekScho-liast confef-feth this place to contain a hard expref-

fion, that the very instrument should not be unmindfull of that act. But he resolvsit into this meaning, that the very Ax ows Traytours a grudge.

15 Answerable to this is the *Latine* name *bipennis*, however *Quintilian* devises some other fetch. *Simmias* the *Rhodian* hath described the figure of that Ax, wherewith *Epêus* built the *Trojan* horse. The generation of an Hat-chet, is by the concourse of two circles, contingent in the centre of a third equall circle: as in this figure is plain to the eye.

⁎INNER⁎TEMPLE⁎

Take a plate of iron infinite, and describe in it a circle at adventures, which let A B C be from any point at any distance : Let the Diameter be drawn, whose extreams let A B be, the Centre D. At the point A, and distance A D, pare off F D E : Again, at the point B, and distance B D, pare off G D H, superfluous cantles of iron, the residue presents you the figure of the double headed Battel-ax. The Helve must be drawn thorough the eie of the centre D, and proportion'd to the circle A B C.

C 2   1 And

Figure 31   The Inner Temple lays claim to a battle axe

Notes

1. Shakespeare, *Henry V*, ed. Gary Taylor (Oxford: Oxford University Press, 1982), 294.
2. Aaron Hill's 1723 adaptation of the play has no version of the scene.
3. See Andrea Alciato, *Emblemata* (Antwerp, 1608), no 120; and for Icarus, no 103.
4. With the mysterious exception of Greg, who lists the play as *Ferrex and Porrex (Gorboduc)* (see note 3).
5. W. W. Greg, *Bibliography of English Printed Drama* (London, 1939), 1.39–40
6. Francis Beaumont and John Fletcher, *Comedies and Tragedies* (1647), 'The Stationer to the Readers,' sig. A4r.
7. I am indebted to Gordon Hollis for information on early illustrated Terences.
8. The 1496 Strasbourg edition has individual scenes as well as its full-page conspectus plates.
9. Middleton and Rowley's *Courtly Masque: . . . the World Tost at Tennis* (1620), a public theater piece adapted from a masque, has what seems to be a stage illustration on the title-page.
10. *Illustrations of the English Stage, 1580–1642* (London: Scolar Press, 1985).
11. There is a similarly improvisatory quality about the famous Henry Peacham *Titus Andronicus* drawing, which shows a group of characters performing a scene that is not in the play, and accompanies it with dialogue that conflates quite different sections of the text.
12. Edward Ecclestone's opera on the Flood, *The Cataclysm*, was published in 1685 with illustrations that resemble stage sets, but the work was never performed.
13. The citation is from the Preface, a2r.
14. There are two separate casts listed. Neither coincides with any production recorded in *The London Stage 1660–1800*. Cibber and Elrington were performing the play together in Dublin in 1710–11, but Sheridan was not born until 1720. The three were acting together in London in the 1740s; there were, of course, many productions throughout the period for which no cast lists are preserved.
15. Quoted in Charles Hiatt, *Ellen Terry* (London: George Bell & Sons, 1898), 207.
16. The dress survives, and is on display in the Ellen Terry Museum in Smallhythe, Kent, though it has lost much of its sheen, along with many of its beetles' wings. Wilde's remark is quoted in W. Graham Robertson, *Time Was* (London, 1931), 151.
17. *The First Folio of Shakespeare*, ed. Akihiro Yamada (Tokyo: Yushodo Press, 1998), 237–9.
18. There is a wonderful miniature history of the subject in William H. Sherman's *John Dee* (Amherst: University of Massachusetts Press, 1995), especially 60–78. Erasmus, characteristically, wanted the practice systematized: 'you will, as you read the authors, methodically observe occurrences of striking words, archaic or novel diction, cleverly contrived or well adapted arguments, brilliant flashes of style, adages, example, and pithy remarks worth memorizing. Such passages should be marked by an appropriate little sign. For not only shouldn't a variety of signs be used, but they should be employed systematically so that it is clear to what sort of thing they refer. Erasmus, 'De Ratione Studii,' *Opera Omnia* 1,2 (1971), quoted in Ann Moss, *Printed Commonplace-books and the Structuring of Renaissance Thought* (Oxford: Clarendon Press, 1996), 98.
19. Dissertations, Book 2.14.21. I am indebted to David Sullivan for translating and identifying the quotation.
20. The three other Inner Temple books currently advertised for sale on the web have all been similarly treated: a great sixteenth-century English chronicle, a first edition of Salmasius's defense of Charles I bound with a first edition of Milton's reply, *Defensio pro Populo Anglicano*, and a magnificent 1678 Willoughby *Ornithology* with its 78 plates, every one stamped (to be sure, on the back) but intact.

2
Making Meaning Marketing Shakespeare 1623

Gary Taylor

Imagine that you are the sort of person who buys books. A bit of a stretch, I know, for most readers of this essay; but imagine that you live in a world without book auctions at Sotheby's, without Amazon.com, without mass-mailed sale catalogues: a world in which, if you want to buy books, you have to get off your ass and go to a bookshop. Imagine, in particular, that you are the sort of person who haunted bookshops in London in 1622. Imagine that, as you are standing in one of those very particular physical spaces where books were displayed and sold, you notice a new book – you can tell it's new because '1622' is printed on the title-page, but also and more reliably because the book has that aroma, as recognizable and exciting to every bookshop-haunter as the morning smell of coffee to another sort of addict, that aroma of new ink and new paper, not yet dissipated into the indifferent air, not yet smothered by the relentless accretions of dust – and in the bookshops of London in 1622, as in bookshops at all times and places, the new books tend to be congregated together, intensifying that chemical fog that tugs at the customer's unconscious. Anyway, as you peruse the books published since you last indulged yourself in this vice, you pick up a particular new book, entitled *The Tragedy of Othello, The Moore of Venice*; you open it, and the first thing you encounter, on signature A2, the first recto page after the title page, is a brief paragraph, headed 'The Stationer to the Reader.'

> *To set forth a booke without an Epistle, were like to the old English proverbe,* A blew coat without a badge, & *the Author being dead, I thought good to take that piece of worke upon mee: To commend it, I will not, for that which is good, I hope every man will commend, without intreaty: and I am the bolder, because the Authors name is sufficient to vent his worke. Thus leaving every one to the liberty of judgement: I have ventered to print this Play, and leave it to the general censure.*
>
> Yours,
> Thomas Walkeley.[1]

As another London bookseller acknowledged, 'the Preface of a Stationer [is] commonly interpreted no other then a slight to betray the Customer into the

55

buying of a Book'.[2] Thomas Walkeley, the stationer who addresses the reader, had published this first edition of *Othello*; you might be standing in his own shop, 'The Eagle and Child', but most copies of the book were sold in other retail bookshops, where Walkeley the wholesale distributor was not personally present to recommend it. So Walkeley writes his recommendation into the text; he identifies himself as a professional in the book trade ('The Stationer to the Reader'), but also as an individual, who has left you a note, as though you happened to step into the shop while he was out; he even appends a salutation and a signature – 'Yours, Thomas Walkeley' – transforming this paragraph into a personal letter, even though his roman 'signature' is as printed as the italic paragraph it underwrites.

In 2004 the book trade is dominated by national retail chains, selling books published by international publishing conglomerates. By contrast, *The Tragedy of Othello* was published by an identifiable individual, who put the name and address of his shop on the title page, and wrote a personal recommendation of the book on its first page. In 1622, what we grandly call 'the book trade' was a small group of individual enterpreneurs living and working within walking distance of one other, who all knew each other, and who knew most of their customers by name, and vice versa. Capitalism with a human face.

Walkeley's personal note to the reader takes for granted the 'bookscape' of early modern culture.[3] Between 1560 and 1666 a London bookshop was what Joseph Roach calls 'a vortex of behavior', a site which both attracts and structures reiterated social performances.[4] Bookshops were performance spaces, where individuals acted out socially scripted interactive rituals of self-fashioning. The central performer, in every shop, was the bookseller himself. 'If I were to paint Sloth', Thomas Nashe wrote in 1592,

> I would draw it like a Stationer that I knowe, with his thumb under his girdle, who if a man come to his stall to aske him for a Booke, never stirres his head, or looks upon him, but stands stone still, and speakes not a word, only with his little finger poynts backwards to his boy, who must be his interpreter, & so all the day gaping like a dumbe image he sits without motion, except at such times as hee goes to dinner or supper, for then he is as quicke as other three, eating six times everie day.[5]

It would be misleading to interpret this account as a description of a typical London bookseller of the 1590s; the characteristic wit of Nashe's prose depends upon its ability to translate an abstraction like 'Sloth' into the particularity of a recognizable individual, mercilessly mimicked by a master caricaturist.

There are three characters in Nashe's scene: the customer, the boy, and the bookseller. All three are male; bookshops were, if anything, even more exclusively homosocial spaces than theaters. Many contemporary sources refer to the presence of women in theatre audiences, but I have not found a single reference to women customers in a London bookshop before 1660. London theaters routinely contained males dressed as women; I have found no parallels for such transvestite behavior in the bookshops, and it was certainly not institutionalized there.

Let's begin with the customers. Nashe's 'man' comes to ask the bookseller for a particular book. This scenario gets repeated in many accounts of bookshops. In 1603 Dekker and Chettle say that a 'briske spa[n]gled' customer 'wil come into a Stationers shop, call for a stoole and a cushion, and then asking for some greeke Poet, to him he falles, and there he grumbles God knowes what, but Ile be sworne he knowes not so much as one Character of the tongue'.[6] Thomas Lodge in 1596 describes one who 'In the Stationers shop... sits dailie, Jibing and flearing over every pamphlet with Ironicall ieasts'.[7] Ben Jonson in 1601 describes a man who 'will sit you a whole afternoone sometimes, in a booke-sellers shop, reading in Greeke, Italian, and Spanish; when he vnderstands not a word of either'.[8]

That is, bookshops were not simply places where early modern Londoners bought books. Thomas Churchyard in 1594 recorded that 'Some reades awhile, but nothing buyes at all'.[9] Some men went to bookshops to read, or to be seen by other men to be reading (or pretending to read). They went to bookshops to sit, sometimes for the whole afternoon. They went there to smoke: Dekker in 1609 recommends that a would-be gallant should go to 'the Booke-sellers, where, if you cannot reade, exercise your smoake, and inquire who has writ against this divine weede'.[10] They went there, not to read silently, but to talk. In 1641 John Etherington wrote, 'I having heard that he had threatned me, spake to him at a Booksellers stall in Cheap-side',[11] and Arthur Hall in 1576 gives a detailed circumstantial account of such a hostile encounter in a bookshop, too long to quote here.[12] John Downe writes of 'An ancient friend of mine, and a worthy Scholler', who 'demanded in a Stationers shop in *Venice*... what was the difference betweene us here in *England* and the *Catholikes*'.[13] Above all, men went to bookshops to gossip with other men. Political historians have emphasized the importance of St Paul's, in the early seventeenth century, for the unregulated circulation of news, by word of mouth. But Paul's churchyard was also the center of the booktrade; it contained an extraordinary concentration of retail bookshops, and part of the news that men went to Paul's to pick up was the news about what was fresh off the presses. In George Ruggle's *Ignoramus* one scene begins with a bookseller crying his wares: 'Books, Books, who buyes my bookes, new books, witty books, witty and new, new and true, come who buyes my books, new books new!'[14] John Webster complained that most customers visited 'Stationers shops' 'not to inquire for good bookes, but new books'.[15]

Moreover, men did not come to Paul's simply to be passive recipients of the news, political and personal, oral and printed. They came to the bookshops to comment on what they heard or read. This is the most commonly described activity in bookshops: unregulated literary and political criticism. Thomas Adams in 1615 epitomizes 'The Envirous Man' as someone who spends his time 'in a Stationres shoppe geering at books'.[16] Dekker in 1609 sends a gallant 'to *Paules Church-yard*, where planting your selfe in a Stationers shop, many instructions are to bee given you, what bookes to call for, how to censure of new bookes, how to mew at the old'.[17] In 1606 he describes others who will 'stand somtimes at a Stationers stal, looking scurvily (like Mules champing upon Thistles) on the face of a new Booke'.[18] Jonson compares 'Booke-sellers stalls', to 'tauernes, two-penny roomes, tyring houses, noble-mens buttries, [and] puisne's chambers', these are all places where men 'maligne, traduce, or detract the person, or writings' of others.[19] Not only the writings, but also the person. The bookshop was the Elizabethan and Jacobean precursor of the Restoration coffee shop. The 'public sphere' analysed by Jürgen Habermas began in the male bookshops clustered in Paul's churchyard.

In Nashe's little dramatization of the early modern bookshop, the customer is one of the three characters, and the character with which he most directly interacts is 'the boy', who fetches the book he wants. Henry Parrot in 1615 categorizes various types of book customers. One 'asketh for' a particular book, by name, 'and the Boy showes it'. Another 'calls for new Bookes, heres one sayes the Boy'.[20] In this sense, every early modern quarto is what Jeffrey Masten calls a 'boy quarto', because it is the bookseller's apprentice, the 'boy' in the homosocial shop, who supplies the customer with his obscure object of desire.[21] In fact, the bookseller's boy could not only satisfy desire, but also create it. Robert Heath in 1650 describes a scam, where the bookseller 'bids [his] prentice read' a particular book in the shop, 'and admire' it, so 'That all i'th' shop may what he reads enquire'.[22] Like the customers satirized by Jonson and others, the boy not only reads in the shop, he performs the spectacle of reading: the boy makes desirable the book he displays.

In this anecdote, the boy's performance is staged by the bookseller. The apprentice learns through imitation of the bookseller's own performance. As an apprentice, the bookseller's boy always learns how to perform by taking direction from his master; like other London apprentices, if he did not perform well, he would have been beaten. Booksellers' boys were, like Lynn Enterline's schoolboys, participants in a pedagogical routine that involved imitation, reading, and beating. Moreover, at least some of them had, before being apprenticed, already endured a humanist education. Edward Blount, the chief publisher of the Shakespeare first folio, had a grammar school education, almost certainly at Merchant Taylors' school, before his ten year apprenticeship to William Ponsonby, the publisher of Spenser and Sidney. Blount learned literary publishing from his master, and it was probably as a 'boy' in Ponsonby's shop that he became friends with a notorious lover of boys, Christopher Marlowe. The bookseller displays the boy, displaying the book. The bookseller's art is, fundamentally, an art of display: he decides which books to display, and how to display them – and what to display besides books. Edward Blount had a prominent bookshop in Paul's churchyard: 13 feet, 3 inches wide fronting the churchyard; 39 feet 5 inches deep, for a ground floor total of between 522 and 542 square feet, not counting the stalls projecting out from the shop itself.[23] Blount was also a dealer in imported exotic seeds and plants and Italian paintings. In the late sixteenth and early seventeenth century books were still luxury commodities, displayed alongside other luxury commodities. Blount's shop also featured imported books, almost certainly in several European languages. Imports still constituted a large majority of the English book market, especially at the high end. Blount's bookshop, and others like it, were another example of the multilingual transnational contact zone described by Anston Bosman in his chapter.

The master of that contact zone is the bookseller; for him it is primarily an economic zone. He organizes that selling space, he situates himself and his books and his boy within it. Each bookseller was an individual, with his own performance style. In *The Fair Maid of the Inn* John Fletcher described one bookseller who 'look[s] as if butter would not melt in his mouth'.[24] John Davies writes an epitaph on a bookseller who had a stutter.[25] The stutter was so remarkable, for Davies, for the same reason that Nashe found remarkable the bookseller whose only response to a question was a motion of his little finger: because, in early modern London, bookselling was a conversational art; in the idiom of the period, a book when it was published or sold was said to be 'uttered'. John Eliot's transcription of a bookseller's dialogue begins with him saying 'Buy some new bookes sir, what bookes buy you, ... Honest man what book buy you'.[26] The bookseller initiates the conversation, solicits the customer as he passes by. According to Nashe, some booksellers were even more aggressive: they would 'plucke a man by the sleeve at everie third step in Paules Churchyard', to get him to come look at their wares.[27] Others took their books to the theaters: William Cartwright describes one who will 'Stand in a Play-house doore with thy long box, thy half-crown library, and cry small books'.[28] Henry Parrot says that books were 'at Playhouses' sold, alongside apples.

The bookseller could only satisfy the desire of his customers if he could antici-pate that desire. 'Sir', a bookseller says in Cosmo Manuche's play *The Loyal Lovers*, 'I know your mind, and shall endeavor to pleasure you presently'.[29] Henry Fitzgeffrey expected a stationer to warn customers against certain books in their own shops 'With a hand's off: it is not for your turn'.[30] Although some of my other customers might like this book, you would not. The successful bookseller reads books (otherwise he would not know their contents), but he also watches other men performing the act of reading; he is a good reader of other readers. Ben Jonson expected his bookseller to be his 'Bookes intelligencer, note / What each man sayes of it, and of what coat / His judgement is'.[31]

Booksellers needed to listen and observe the reading performances of their customers because, as Dekker noted in 1607, 'no one stationers stall can fit all customers with books to their diet'.[32] No shop can contain all books, not only because shelf space is limited but because investment capital is limited. So every bookseller had to decide which books to buy from the wholesalers, and every bookseller had to decide which, if any, books he should publish himself, by paying for their wholesale manufacture. Hence, the diversification of the book trade into different submarkets and specializations had already begun by the beginning of the seventeenth century, if not earlier. The iterated performances of the customer, the boy, and the bookseller took place on the stage of the book-shop, itself part of the larger stage of the street: when a bookseller opened his shop in the morning, he extended it into the street, by bringing out the 'stalls' on which he displayed the books he thought most likely to interest passersby. The stall is the 'thrust stage' of the bookshop. On it, different booksellers typically displayed different kinds of books.

Every wholesale publisher in early modern London was also a retail bookseller, and the art of retail display is inextricable from the art of wholesale display. The bookseller/publisher determines the material form in which an author's text will be displayed: what size, what kind and quality of paper, what typeface, what kind of title-page, what paratext intervenes between the title and the work. Thus, from our point of view the material forms of display chosen by the publisher tell us something about the bookseller's judgement of the potential market for the printed book of a play.

Unlike the customers of amazon.com or those who receive book catalogues in the mail, the casually browsing customers in Thomas Walkeley's shop in 1622, debating whether or not to buy *Othello*, could pick it up, open it, and be influenced by what Walkeley wrote on signature A2r. Walkeley assumed that potential customers might hesitate to buy a book if it did not contain an epistle of some sort: 'to set forth a book without an epistle' would be anomalous, would suggest that there was something wrong with this textual commodity. If Walkeley had published *Othello* in 1603, when it was brand-new, he would not have been so anxious because, until Ben Jonson's *Sejanus* in 1605 and *Volpone* in 1607, commercial plays had almost always been published without an epistle, or dedication, or front matter of any kind. In fact, only one of Shakespeare's plays published before Walkeley's edition of *Othello* – the 1609 edition of *Troilus and Cressida* – contained any prefatory matter at all. But by 1622 the buyers of printed plays were used to seeing *something* between the title page and the first entrance direction of the play; since Shakespeare was dead, and could not supply that something himself, Walkeley supplied it for him.

The very existence of Walkeley's epistle tells us something about the marketing of plays in London in 1622; so does what Walkeley actually wrote. Walkeley twice refers to 'the author', and once to 'his work'; thus, even before publication of the first folio, Shakespeare was recognized as an author, who had some singular proprietory pronomial relationship to 'his work'. This fact is itself rather surprising for those of us raised on the Gospel according to Saint Foucault. But Foucault's ignorance of the history of the book trade was as wide as it was deep. Authorship was not invented in the eighteenth century, and it was not a by-product of the state apparatus of censorship. For Walkeley, in 1622, the author-function is not political, but commercial. 'The author's name', Walkeley assures us, 'is sufficient to vent his work'.[33]

This is a claim modern Shakespeare enthusiasts will find gratifying and, at the same time, self-evident. But it is a claim contradicted by the epistle itself. If Shakespeare's name is sufficient, why does Walkeley need to print this epistle at all, or place it so conspicuously in the book? If the name is sufficient, why do readers need to be *told* that it is sufficient? If anything written by Shakespeare is guaranteed to sell, why does Walkeley write '*I have ventered to print this Play*'? Why '*ventered*'? If Shakespeare cannot fail to attract readers, why does Walkeley use the language of risk-taking to describe his decision to publish *Othello*? And why does the title-page need to advertise 'The Tragœdy of Othello, The Moore of Venice. As it hath beene diuerse times acted at the Globe, and at the Black-Friers, by his Maiesties Seruants'? The author's name is identified only after this evidence of the play's theatrical appeal, in both outdoor and indoor playhouses; the name of the acting company, the honorific title of its patron, come before the name of the author: 'Written by William Shakespeare'.

Obviously, in 1622, Shakespeare's name was *not* 'sufficient to vent his work'. If the self-contradicting rhetoric of the title page and epistle to Walkeley's 1622 edition of *Othello* does not convince you of that conclusion, perhaps you will be convinced by another kind of evidence.

The person who most heavily invested in William Shakespeare's name was not Thomas Walkeley but another London bookseller, Edward Blount, the dominant figure in the syndicate that published the famous first folio edition of Shakespeare's *Comedies, Histories, and Tragedies*. Between 1603 and the publication of the Shakespeare collection late in 1623, Edward Blount had published at least 72 titles, an average of 3.4 books per year. But from November 1623 until summer 1628 – that is, in the four and a half years immediately following publication of the Shakespeare folio – Blount did not publish a single book; in 1627 he lost his bookshop, which had been the foundation of his business for two decades.[34] Between 1624 and 1630, he sold off his copyrights in Marlowe's popular *Hero and Leander*, in Shakespeare's plays, and in at least four other books. Most shockingly, in 1627, and again in 1630, Blount was loaned £50 from a charitable fund, intended for the use of struggling young men just starting out in the book business;[35] Blount was, at the time, in his late sixties, and he had never needed a loan before.[36]

Of course, the apparent collapse of Blount's business immediately after publication of the Shakespeare folio may be a coincidence. Blount's account books have not survived, and without them it is impossible to prove a causal relationship between these two events: *post hoc* is not always *propter hoc*. But the only other established London bookseller who suffered a similar eclipse in these very years is William Aspley – another of the three booksellers who published the Folio. Aspley began publishing in 1599, and continued to do so in every subsequent year for 25 years. But he published nothing from November 1623 until 1629.

Finally, we know that the Shakespeare folio did not sell as well as other books published in 1623. We can measure sales of the Shakespeare collection easily if crudely enough, by looking at how many subsequent editions were published, and at the number of years between those reprints. The second edition did not appear until nine years later, in 1632. The list at the end of this chapter gives details of some of the other books, printed or reprinted in 1623, which outsold the Shakespeare folio. For instance, the 1623 reprint of Nicolas Themylthorp's *The Posie of godly prayers*, was only one of more than 29 editions from 1611 to 1640, and another five before 1676. Obviously, the name of Nicolas Themylthorpe was sufficient to vent *his* work.

From the perspective of the chief publisher of the Shakespeare folio, the most telling item on the list is Mateo Aleman's picaresque novel *The rogue; or, the life of Guzman de Alfarache*, a literary classic translated out of Spanish into English by James Mabbe, and published, in a folio edition, by Edward Blount, late in 1622 (some copies have 1623 on the title page). That literary folio was republished again in 1628, four years before the second edition of Shakespeare; it was published a third time in 1633. Aleman's novel sold faster than Shakespeare's plays, and it continued to outsell Shakespeare throughout the seventeenth century, accumulating seven editions by 1685, in contrast to Shakespeare's four. We can see here the rise of the novel, as a successful competitor to drama, long before our literary histories record its dominance of the reading market. More immediately and locally pertinent is the fact that *The Rogue* sold well enough to keep Edward Blount in business; something else on his list in 1623 must have been depressing his balance sheet.

In the early 1620s, Shakespeare's name was *not* sufficient to vent his work. That negative conclusion is important because it opens the door to a different kind of positive possibility. Anyone who believes that Shakespeare sells himself, who imagines that the intrinsic 'Genius of Shakespeare' is sufficient to account for his posthumous reputation, will have no incentive to examine who sold Shakespeare to the English public, or how the imperatives of the cultural marketplace re-packaged and transformed his work. In order to achieve and sustain canonical status, genius is a necessary, but not a sufficient condition. Genius is never enough, because genius is individual, and culture is collective. To transform the genius of the individual into the collective good we call culture requires a kind of work that genius cannot by itself perform. After all, geniuses, like other individuals, die. In *Cultural Selection*, I argued that culture, always and everywhere, begins with a death, and with the subsequent effort of survivors to preserve and transmit to others the memory of the deceased.[37] As Thomas Walkeley wrote, 'the author being dead, I thought good to take that piece of work upon me'.

So, what kind of work did they take upon themselves, the people who published the Shakespeare first folio? And why did they do it? These are big questions, and answering them would take more space than I have in this chapter. I can do no more, here, than sketch some of the relevant issues.

In trying to answer those questions, the first thing we have to do is familiarize ourselves with the booksellers' world that Blount knew so well, the wholesale and retail marketplaces in which he tried to sell Shakespeare's *Comedies, Histories, and Tragedies*.

In 1623, according to the revised Short Title Catalogue, 503 editions of separate works were published in England, or in English, for the British market. Of those, 356 (71 per cent) were new titles. Of those 356 titles, 15 were almanacs, 42 were official proclamations or petitions, 45 were numbered and dated newsbooks published by the news syndicate headed by Nathaniel Butter. All these texts clearly depend upon their timeliness; they satisfy curiosities and appetites specific to a particular week, month or year; they resemble the modern market for journalism, more than the modern market for books. Moreover, another 41 texts published in 1623 might be described as unnumbered, undated and occasional books of news: four single-sheet epitaphs, two accounts of spectacular crimes, separate accounts of decisions made by the Diet of Regensburg, of the martyrdom of five Persians, of a catastrophe which befell the Spanish bullion fleet from the New World, etc.[38] All these texts – together constituting 40 per cent of 1623's new titles – will either sell immediately or not at all.

The market for these designedly ephemeral texts clearly differs from the market for the Shakespeare folio, a book which took years to produce, and was clearly intended to last for years. But the more money reading people spend on printed ephemera, the less money they have left to spend on books like the folio. The same people bought both kinds of text. Earlier in 1623, Blount had written several surviving letters to Sir William Trumbull, the English ambassador in Brussels; Blount mentioned a number of new publications which he thought would particularly interest Trumbull, including two single-sheet proclamations and two big expensive folios, John Selden's critical edition of the medieval monk and historian Eadmer and J. Bingham's translation of Xenophon's *Anabasis*. The two proclamations were hot off the presses and dated, like Blount's own letters; the two folios resurrected texts originally written 500 or 2000 years earlier.

The market for venerable old texts was itself a venerable old institution. In Germany, Gutenberg began with a Bible; in Venice, Aldus Manutius specialized in Greek and Latin editions of classical authors; in England, Camden published Malory and Chaucer. But the market for printed news was itself new. The first dated English-language news sheets, called 'corantos', were printed in Amsterdam in December 1620; in September of the following year, Nathaniel Butter took over the trade, and began routinely publishing dated but unnumbered newsbooks in London; in mid-October 1622, Butter began publishing newsbooks that were not only dated, but numbered in sequence, thus enabling customers (and bibliographers) to know whether they had missed an issue. The Shakespeare folio, and other traditional books of 1623, had to compete with a whole new genre of printed commodity. That is perhaps why Ben Jonson specifically characterizes the contents of the Shakespeare folio as 'not of an age, but for all time'. In the 1620s Jonson repeatedly satirized the contemporary vogue for 'news', and Nathaniel Butter's 'Staple of News' in particular. His praise of Shakespeare belongs to the same ongoing struggle, within the marketplace of print, between the admittedly ephemeral and the allegedly eternal.

But which is which? Jonson's masque, *Time Vindicated to Himself*, performed once at court in the Christmas season of 1622, was published early in 1623; is that little quarto a newsbook, recording an ephemeral event at court, or is it literature? Is Thomas Middleton's *The Triumphs of Integrity. A Noble solemnity, at the establishment of M. Lumley, Lord Maior*, also published in 1623, news or art? Jonson considered Middleton 'a base fellow,' but *The Triumphs of Integrity* is as literary, or as ephemeral, as *Time Vindicated to Himself*: both memorialize the momentary. Both belong to the tradition described by Stephen Orgel, in which the printed texts of dramatic events advertise them as records of a singular event attended by Very Important People.

Shakespeare did not write court masques or civic entertainments; but plays could also be considered intrinsically ephemeral performances. As Natascha Wurzbach and Bruce Smith have shown, plays were often included in the same despised category as ballads. Standing room at the Globe could be purchased for a penny – the same price as a ballad broadsheet; the same Civil War Parliament that closed the theaters also criminalized the distribution of street ballads. Ballads thus constituted a genre then considered ephemeral, but which would later be celebrated as a genuinely popular literature, the voice of the 'folk' or the 'people' or the 'underclass', and therefore with its own claim to be 'not of an age, but for all time'. Certainly, from the perspective of historical bibliography, ballads are the very opposite of newsbooks, because they are usually impossible to pin down to a specific date. The *Short Title Catalogue* assigns seven ballads to 'c. 1623', but in fact they cannot be confidently assigned to that year or any other. Unlike a court masque, ballads were not designed for a single unique performance; instead, like commercial plays, they were made for iteration.[39] The ballad trade is the spectre that haunted a commercial playwright like Shakespeare, and which the 1623 folio was designed to exorcise. Shakespeare's *Comedies, Histories, and Tragedies* was the first English book which consisted entirely of a large collection of scripts commercially performed outdoors.[40] Ballads, of course, were also 'scripts commercially performed outdoors'.

And Shakespeare's plays were also, like ballads, performed repeatedly, and in different venues. In Jonson's *Works*, the plays, like the masques, are individually dated, like newsbooks; in Shakespeare's *Comedies, Histories, and Tragedies*, the plays are undated, and even after centuries of scholarship the exact date of the composition and first performance of many of them remains as disputable as the dates of ballads in the STC. Jonson provides a list, attached to each play, of the actors who performed it. This practice assumes that plays are like masques, performed only once; and although that may be true, or almost true, of a theatrical failure like *Catiline*, Jonson applies it even to his successful plays, thereby giving a special authority to the first performance of each play. But Shakespeare's *Comedies, Histories, and Tragedies* gives us, instead, only a single list of 'The Names of the Principal Actors in all these Plays'. Shakespeare's plays, unlike Jonson's, but like ballads, had been iterated and reiterated many times, by many different performers; the acting company does not want to insist on the authority of the first performance, or the first performer, because it wants spectators to keep coming to the theater, even though Richard Burbage and William Kemp are no longer available to play Hamlet and Dogberry. You may like 'You Can't Hurry Love', whether it's sung by the Supremes or by Phil Collins: songs, ballads, plays, can be sold to the same customer more than once.

The commercial success of Shakespeare's plays, which created the potential demand for printed texts of his work, had been based upon the structural similarities between plays and ballads, as iterable commercial outdoor performances; and the early octavo and quarto editions of the plays, from *Titus Andronicus* in 1594 to *Othello* in 1622, did not wander too far from the ballad paradigm, because someone willing to pay a penny for a single-sheet ballad text might well be willing to pay six pennies for a play text of seven to twelve sheets – especially since the printed play might be sold, with other small books, at the door of the playhouse. But copies of the 1623 *Comedies, Histories, and Tragedies* would have been hard to carry in a pedlar's basket. The folio attempted to move Shakespeare into an entirely different market, a market as indisputably elite as the market for ballads was indisputably populist. Jonson begins his praise of 'The AUTHOR, Master William Shakespeare, and what he hath left us', by acknowledging his 'writings to be such/As neither man nor muse can praise too much: /'Tis true, and all men's suffrage'.[41] But Jonson then quickly retracts this appeal to universal suffrage; this is a form of praise on which 'silliest ignorance' may alight, 'Which, when it sounds at best, but echoes right'. Anyone was entitled to an opinion about ballads; ballads could be enjoyed, and even performed, by the ignorant and the illiterate; ballads could be encountered anywhere, unexpectedly; as you walked down the street, you might 'alight' upon one being performed or peddled; ballads belonged to the ephemeral world of 'sound' and 'echo'.

By contrast, Shakespeare, like Jonson himself, created texts, not sounds, substantial material objects that are 'woven' and 'richly spun'; he 'casts' lines of verse which, like molten metal, are beaten into shape 'Upon the muses' anvil'. And these works of art were not random happenings on street corners; instead, Jonson testifies that Shakespeare's plays delighted 'Eliza, and our James', and the dedicatory epistle to the Earls of Pembroke and Montgomery informs us that they, too, saw and applauded performances of the plays. These are the sorts of people who truly appreciate Shakespeare, and who have the qualifications to pass judgement upon him. Having been praised by the rabble who praised ballads has not really enhanced Shakespeare's reputation; quite the reverse. 'These are as some infamous bawd or whore/Should praise a matron', Jonson indignantly asserts, and asks, 'what could hurt her more?' This unqualified praise has hurt Shakespeare, because it has treated him as though his work belonged in the realm of the ballad; Jonson wants to rescue him from his fans, by elevating him out of the bondage of balladry into the light of literature: 'Advanced, and made a constellation there; Shine forth, thou star of poets!'

Jonson is not alone in this work of transforming Shakespeare's plays into an elite commodity. As has often been remarked, the physical format of the book itself asserts its cultural legitimacy: the double-column folio format was strongly associated with serious and significant works. The first word of the first line of the 1623 title page, 'Mr. William Shakespeare', emphasizes his gentry status, a status reiterated in the title to every one of the four commendatory poems prefaced to the volume. Moreover, the engraved portrait on the title page dresses Shakespeare in the sartorial sign-system of an English gentleman. And, like Thomas Walkeley in 1622, Shakespeare's publishers in 1623 recognized the importance of appropriate prefatory matter: the book begins with a dedicatory epistle to the Earls of Pembroke and Montgomery, followed by an epistle 'To the Great Variety of Readers', followed by four commendatory poems and a table of contents.

By the 1620s, publishers simply had to supply a collection of commendatory poems for this kind of book. But the choice of authors for such dedicatory poems, and the specific terms of commendation, are much less predictable, and therefore much more interesting. Consider, for interest, who did *not* write commendatory verses for the Shakespeare folio. John Fletcher was the most successful playwright of the second and third decades of the seventeenth century; he had collaborated with Shakespeare on Shakespeare's last three plays; by the 1620s, he had succeeded Shakespeare as the chief dramatist of the King's Men; he had written commendatory verses for Jonson's *Volpone* and *Catiline*. He did not write commendatory verses for Shakespeare. Neither did Thomas Middleton. Middleton had collaborated with Shakespeare on *Timon of Athens*; the King's Men had hired Middleton to provide 'new additions' for *Macbeth* in 1616, and *Measure for Measure* in 1621; in 1623, Middleton wrote a poem 'Upon this masterpiece of Tragedy', prefaced to the first edition of Webster's *The Duchess of Malfi*. Why are Fletcher and Middleton not in the parade of praise which prefaces the first folio? Although Fletcher and Middleton both had their quarrels with Shakespeare, it is hard to believe that they could find nothing in his entire dramatic canon to admire. So why are they not here? Presumably because the publishers did not want them here.

Who did they want, instead? In the judgement of later centuries, Hugh Holland, Leonard Digges, and James Mabbe do not begin to compare with Fletcher or Middleton as imaginative writers or critics. But Holland, Digges, and Mabbe had a crucial advantage over Fletcher and Middleton from the perspective of the publishers. Holland, Digges, and Mabbe were not playwrights; they did not earn a living working for the iterable commercial outdoor entertainments. Holland, Digges, and Mabbe, like the Earls of Pembroke and Montgomery, were not playwrights, but exemplary spectators. The quality of their poetry in praise of Shakespeare matters, from the perspective of the publisher, rather less than their value as tokens of a class of potential readers and purchasers. Their presence in this book declares that these are works suitable for the leisure of a certain class of person.

Holland, Digges, and Mabbe were all university educated and widely travelled. Like Jonson, they were cosmopolitan intellectuals. Of course, Jonson was also a playwright – but (unlike Fletcher and Middleton) never prolific or very successful in the commercial theater. He had not written a play in seven years, and he was not in the habit of praising other men's plays. Wayne Chandler, in his book-length study of the genre of the commendatory poem, has pointed out that Jonson wrote more such poems than any other Englishman before 1650; indeed, Jonson wrote more than twice as many as the nearest contender. But the only play for which he wrote such a poem was Fletcher's *The Faithful Shepherdess* – which was, of course, a notorious failure. Thus, Jonson does not owe his prominence in the preliminaries of the Shakespeare folio to his status as a playwright, or a praiser of plays; he is there as a famous practitioner and critic of contemporary literature.

What do Jonson, Holland, Digges, and Mabbe have to say about Shakespeare? The one thing that their poems all emphasize – an emphasis also repeated in the two epistles by Heminges and Condell – is the fact that Shakespeare is dead. Since he had died seven years earlier, this hardly constitutes news. Nor does it consti-tute criticism, as we now practice it. But, as Laurie Maguire has pointed out, it does situate the *Comedies, Histories, and Tragedies* within the memorial and fune-real rituals of all human culture, and of early modern England in particular.[42] In her book, *Puzzling Shakespeare*, Leah Marcus meditated on what she considered the puzzling prominence of the engraved portrait on the folio title page; but that prominence is less puzzling if you compare it to something like William Swadon's 'Upon the Death of Queen Anne', reprinted in 1623, a single sheet folio which places funeral verses under a portrait of the deceased.[43] Jonson's little poem on the Shakespeare portrait represents it as a funeral effigy, sculpted 'in brass'.[44]

Marcus is right to notice that the Shakespeare portrait occupies more space than authorial portraits on other title-pages of the period, but I am not persuaded by her interpretation of that prominence, as evidence of the emergence of a new transcendental humanist poetics. After all, Shakespeare was not available to design a complex allegorical title-page and, even had he been inclined to do so, the publishers of the Shakespeare folio wanted to appeal to 'the great variety of readers', some of whom would be put off by the deliberately alienating effect of such conspicuous semiotic displays, which circle other title-pages like so much barbed wire, to ward off the unclean hands of the vulgar. The prominence of the portrait is thus, in part, a negative by-product of the partly deliberate, partly accidental absence of various signifying supplements. But the prominence of the portrait is also in part deliberately and specifically relevant. Shakespeare differed from other authors, including Jonson, in one crucial particular: Shakespeare was a working actor. Not a great actor, admittedly; but people who had seen his plays, the very people who might be most tempted to buy this book, had also probably seen *him*, acting in those plays and in other people's plays. Actors, unlike authors, live in large part through their faces. That is why the faces of Robert Armin, Thomas Greene, William Kemp, and Richard Tarlton had already appeared on title pages, and why the faces of Edward Alleyn, Richard Burbage, Nathan Field, and John Green had already been memorialized in contemporary paintings.[45] And that actorly emphasis upon the human face captures what was, for Shakespeare's contemporaries, the chief glory of his plays, his creation of a succession of remarkable individual characters. Shakespeare stares out of the folio title page, not only as an author, but as an actor, not only as himself, but as a character in his own plays – one of the many gentleman who appear in his plays, or even perhaps, since he is dressed in black, a prologue or a chorus.

Which brings us to a final question: why is the volume dedicated to the Earls of Pembroke and Montgomery? Montgomery had no real known connection with the drama generally, or Shakespeare specifically. Pembroke was, of course, Master of the Revels; but in the entire reign of James I he had only one play dedicated to him, Jonson's *Catiline*, a play which we know failed on the stage. Let me put this question another way: why was the Shakespeare folio not dedicated to King James? All the plays in the volume were performed by the King's Men; Heminges and Condell were liveried servants of the King; although the dedicatory epistle to William and Philip Herbert claims that Shakespeare was 'your servant', he was never technically a servant of either earl, but he was technically one of 'his Majesty's servants'. Alvin Kernan has described Shakespeare, in the last decade of his career, as 'the King's playwright', and many other critics and scholars have seen evidence that specific aspects of Shakespeare's Jacobean plays were written with the King's tastes in mind. Jonson's encomium specifically claims that James enjoyed Shakespeare's plays; indeed, given Jonson's position as poet laureate, his conspicuous presence in the folio itself testifies to Shakespeare's royal status. The publishers could not have been deterred by any undue sense of deference or decorum. From 1603 to 1623, James I had more than 350 books dedicated to him; in 1623 alone, he received 11 dedications, most of them by authors with far less claim to a relationship with the king. Edward Blount himself had published four books dedicated to the king. Why did the King's Men not dedicate their folio to their king?

I suspect that they had always intended to do so and that they changed their minds in October 1623, when Prince Charles and Buckingham returned from Madrid without the Infanta. James's entire foreign policy had been governed, for more than a decade, by the pursuit of a dynastic alliance with the Habsburgs – the kind of conflict resolution through dynastic marriage dramatized in *The Tempest*. In 1621, when *The Tempest* was set into print as the first play in the volume, its relevance to the foreign policy of the playwright's patron would have been obvious and unproblematic. And the conclusion of the volume, with *Cymbeline* – a play otherwise singularly inappropriately placed in the genre of Tragedies – would have closed the circle, representing the union of Britain and Rome. Both Digges and Mabbe, like the publisher Blount, were notorious hispanophiles; Hugh Holland was a Catholic; Jonson had been a Catholic and clearly hated the aggressive Calvinist wing of the English church. And Shakespeare himself, as I and others have argued, was probably a church papist and had certainly been called one in Speed's best-selling *History of Great Britain*. As originally planned, the Shakespeare folio would have been associated, very clearly, with the pacifist hispanophile and ecumenical policies of Shakespeare's final patron, King James.

But those Jacobean policies had become increasingly unpopular, in the early 1620s, as a series of military reversals on the continent seriously imperilled the Protestant cause. The rise of print journalism was itself directly related to English interest in, and concern about, the opening stages of the Thirty Years War. The return of Charles and Buckingham represented the complete collapse of James's foreign policy, and its repudiation by the heir to the throne and the king's own favorite. Moreover, the return of the prince, and the failure of his father's policy, was greeted, in early October 1623, with unparalleled outbursts of public jubilation throughout England. A week later the collapse of a private house in the Blackfriars district, killing dozens of Catholics who had secretly gathered there to attend mass, was taken as further evidence of the triumph of godly English protestantism over its Spanish Catholic adversaries. In this climate of triumphant xenophobia to dedicate the folio to King James would align it, unmistakably, with the unpopular policies of an old, ill king, rapidly losing power and authority to his son and favorite. Instead, the publishers dedicated the folio to the two Herbert brothers, who had been leaders of the anti-Spanish faction on the Privy council.

The publishers and printer of the folio could make this change because the preliminaries were not printed until just before the first issue of the book was published. The beginning of a book is almost always the last thing printed. In my beginning is my end. The 'end' of the 1623 publishers, their immediate objective, was an economic one: to sell the several hundred copies they had printed to other retail booksellers, and to the book-buying public more generally. But the preliminaries to the 1623 edition of Shakespeare's *Comedies, Histories, and Tragedies* were also, of course, preliminary in another sense. The 1623 edition was the first folio, not the last. Eventually, Edward Blount and his junior partners did succeed in creating a space for Shakespeare in the luxury book market. But those booksellers were not, as we tend to assume, satisfying an obvious, long-evident demand. They were not simply noticing, at last, the elephant in the room. They were, at great risk to their own livelihoods, carefully constructing a new niche in the public sphere constituted by the performance space of the bookshops around St Paul's churchyard.

I once said that Shakespeare had, by the late twentieth century, become a black hole. In the early seventeenth century Shakespeare's publishers were not simply filling a hole. They were creating one.

Best-sellers first printed in 1623

George Wither, *Hymns and Songs of the Church*, 9 editions 1623
Thomas Scott, *An experimental discovery of Spanish practices*, 4 editions 1623, a fifth in 1624
Richard Bernard, *Looke beyond Luther*, 4 editions 1623–24
John Sprint, *The Christian Sword and Buckler*, 6 editions, 1623–36
Thomas Playfere, Sermons, 6 editions, 1623–33
John Mayer, *Catechisme*, at least 7 editions, 1623–39
Ezekiel Culverwell, *A treatise of Faith*, 3 editions (1623), five more editions before 1648
Henry Cockeram, *The English dictionarie*, 12 editions 1623–72

Best-sellers reprinted in 1623

Nicolas Themylthorp, *Posie of godly prayers*, 29+ editions, 1611–40
Thomas Sorocold, *Supplications of Saints*, 26+ editions, 1612–40
John Speidell, *New Logarithmes*, 10 editions, 1619–28
Thomas Godwin, *Romanae historiae anthologia*, 9 editions, 1614–38
William Bradshaw, *A Direction for the Weaker sort of Christians*, 10 editions, 1609–36
Samuel Smith, *The Great Assize*, 10+ editions, 1617–38
John Willis, *The Art of Stenography*, 12+ editions, 1602–39
Claude Desainliens, *The French schoolemaister*, 16 editions, 1573–1636
Cicero, *De officiis*, 17 editions, 1606–39
Robert Openshaw, *Short questions and answeares*, 19+ editions, 1579–1639
Edward Dering, *Short catechism*, 27 editions, 1580–1634
Robert Record's arithmetic textbook, 28 editions, 1543–1640
Manual of Prayers (Roman Catholic) 29 editions, 1583–1640 (?)

Literary best-sellers reprinted in 1623

Samuel Rowlands, *Doctor Merryman*, 6 editions, 1614–26
Robert Speed, *The counter-scuffle*, 6 editions, 1621–37
Thomas Lodge, *Rosalynde*, 9 editions, 1590–1634
Thomas Heywood, *If you know not me*, 9 editions, 1605–39

Thomas Kyd, *The Spanish Tragedy*, 10 editions, 1592–1626
William Basse, *A Help to Discourse*, 17 editions, 1618–82
John Lyly, *Euphues*, 19 editions, 1578–1638

Best-selling folios reprinted or printed 1623

Bishop William Cowper, *Works*, 1623, 1628
John Speed, *The Theatre of the Empire of Great Britain* and *History of Great Britain*, 4 editions (each), 1611–31
Philip Sidney, *Arcadia*, at least 13 editions, 1590–1674
Mateo Aleman, *The rogue; or, the life of Guzman de Alfarache*, 7 editions, 1622/3–1685

Notes

Research on this project was supported in part by grants from the Hudson Strode endowment and the Guggenheim Foundation. I hope to publish a fuller and more satisfactory account of the matters discussed in this essay in a book, in progress, on Blount's career.

1. *The Tragedy of Othello, the Moore of Venice*, 'The Stationer to the Reader' (London, 1622), sig. A2r.
2. W. Sales, *Theophania: or Severall Modern Histories Represented by way of Romance: and Politickly Discours'd upon* (London, 1655), sig. A3r.
3. On 'the imagined, the remembered, and the actual' in what he calls a 'bookscape', see James Raven, 'Memorializing a London bookscape: the mapping and rating of Paternoster Row and St Paul's Churchyard, 1695–1814', in *Order and Connexion: Studies in Bibliography and Book History*, ed. R. C. Alston (Cambridge: D. S. Brewer, 1997), 177–200. The crucial dividing line here is the Great Fire of 1666, which destroyed the original book-complex around St Paul's, contributing to the rise of the coffee house as an alternative locus of the public sphere.
4. Joseph Roach, *Cities of the Dead: Circum-Atlantic Performance* (New York: Columbia University Press, 1996).
5. *The Works of Thomas Nashe*, ed. Ronald B. McKerrow, 5 vols, (London: A. H. Bullen, 1904), 1:208.
6. *The pleasant comodie of patient Grisill*, London, 1603, sig. C1r.
7. Thomas Lodge, *The Complete Works of Thomas Lodge*, 4 vols (New York: Russell and Russell, Inc., 1963), 4:15
8. Ben Jonson, *Every Man Out of His Humour*, in *Works*, ed. C. H. Herford and Percy and Evelyn Simpson (Oxford: Clarendon Press, 1925–52), 3:497 (3.1).
9. *A myrrour for man*, 'To the generall readers' (London, 1594).
10. Thomas Dekker, *The Guls Horne-booke* (London, 1609), 19.
11. *The defence of Iohn Etherington against Steven Denison and his witnesses* (London, 1641), 43.
12. See Arthur Hall, *A Letter Sent by F.A.* (London, 1576).
13. *Certaine treatises* (London, 1633), 61.
14. George Ruggle, *Ignoramus* (London, 1662), sig. F4r.
15. *The White Devil*, 'To the Reader' (London, 1612), sig. A2r.
16. *Mystical Bedlam* (London, 1615), 67.
17. *The Guls Horne-Booke*, 38.
18. *The Seuen Deadly Sinnes of London*, London, 1606, sig. π2a.
19. *Poetaster*, in Herford and Simpson, 4:315–6.
20. *The Mastive*, London, 1615, sigs. H4v, I1r.

21. 'My Two Dads: Collaboration and the Reproduction of Beaumont and Fletcher', in Jonathan Goldberg, ed., *Queering the Renaissance* (Durham: Duke University Press, 1994), 280–309.
22. *Clarastella*, (London, 1650), 36–7.
23. The exact dimensions of the shop in 1667–71 were 13′3″ (frontage), 14′4″ (back wall), 39′5″ (west wall), 37′10″ (east wall). See Peter W. M. Blayney, *The Bookshops in Paul's Cross Churchyard*, Occasional Papers of the Bibliographical Society, 5 (London, 1990), Figure 2.
24. *The Fair Maid of the Inn* (London, 1625), 44.
25. *Wits Bedlam*, (London, 1617), sig. L2r.
26. *Ortho-epia Gallica* (London, 1593), 67, 69.
27. *Pierce Penniless, The Works of Thomas Nashe*, 1:239.
28. *The Ordinary* in *Comedies, tragi-comedies, with other poems* (London, 1651), 52.
29. *The Loyal Lovers* (London, 1652), 1.
30. *Certain Elegies*, London, 1618, sig. H3v.
31. 'Epigram, to my bookseller', *Works*, 8:232.
32. *Iests to Make You Merry* (London, 1607), sig. A2r.
33. *The Tragedy of Othello, the Moore of Venice*, 'The Stationer to the Reader'.
34. Blayney, *The Bookshops in Paul's Cross Churchyard*, 27. Blayney's wording – 'Blount moved out when the property changed hands, and was succeeded by Robert Allot' – does not suggest any explanation for Blount's move; but the man who replaced him, Allot, also purchased from Blount his Shakespeare copyrights.
35. W. Craig Ferguson, *The Loan Book of the Stationers' Company with a List of Transactions, 1592–1692*, Occasional Papers of the Bibliographical Society, 4 (1989), p. 12. Ferguson attributes the loan to relief of Richard Bankworth's orphans, but this can only have been an excuse: Blount had been stepfather to those orphans for more than a decade at the time of the first loan.
36. In 1628, he published a little book, John Earle's *Microcosmography*, which became an immediate bestseller, and earned him enough money to capitalize the publication of a few more titles.
37. Gary Taylor, *Cultural Selection* (New York: Basic Books, 1996).
38. Other topics covered by such news-like pamphlets include: recent events in Virginia, of the travels of the son of the King of Bohemia, two accounts of French synods, two catalogues for the Frankfurt book fair, five pamphlets on the multiple fatalities caused by the collapse of a floor in a house filled with recusant Catholics, four accounts of the welcome Cambridge University gave to the Spanish ambassador, two accounts of the conversion back to Catholicism of Bishop MarcAntonio de Dominis, and 14 individual texts on different aspects of the visit by Prince Charles and the Duke of Buckingham to Spain, in pursuance of negotiations for the proposed marriage of Charles to the Spanish Infanta.
39. But unlike plays, ballads were not licensed by the Master of the Revels, and they were seldom even entered in the Stationers' Register; and each is so microscopically short that it hardly has room to betray internal evidence of its date of composition. So the seven ballads dated by the STC 'c. 1623' might not have been new titles in 1623; for all we know, there might have been no new ballads to compete for customers with the Shakespeare folio, or there might have been a hundred. In one sense, whether it was none or a hundred hardly matters, because the ballad business was a specialized sub-market: in the 1620s, the ballad trade, like the news trade, was being consolidated and effectively monopolized under a separate syndicate of stationers specializing in such commodities.
40. It is often said that the 1616 edition of Jonson's *Works* for the first time transformed scripts written for the vernacular commercial theatre into 'literature,' and that the 1623 *Comedies, Histories, and Tragedies* consolidated this transformation. This is one of those useful generalizations that saves us from the trouble of having actually to look at what is in front of our faces. Jonson's *Works* did contain seven plays, including some written for outdoor theaters, but it also included masques, pageants, and poems.

41. 'To the Memory of My Beloved, the Author, Mr. William Shakespeare,' in Herford and Simpson, 8:390–2.
42. *Shakespearean Suspect Texts: the 'Bad' Quartos and Their Contexts* (Cambridge: Cambridge University Press, 1996).
43. *Puzzling Shakespeare: Local Reading and its Discontents* (Berkeley: University of California Press, 1990).
44. 'To the Reader,' prefatory poem to the First Folio.
45. For images of actors' faces before 1623, see R. A. Foakes, *Illustrations of the English Stage 1580–1642* (London: Scolar, 1985), items 23 (Tarlton), 28 (John Green?), 40 (Armin), 43 (Thomas Greene), 66 (Kempe). The paintings of Alleyn, Burbage, and Field are all at Dulwich College.

3

From Print to Performance: Looking at the Masque in *Timon of Athens*

John Jowett

I

This chapter concerns the construction of sense-scape from the printed page.[1] My title reverses the trajectory of which we more usually speak, the phrase whose name appears in the title of this volume, 'from performance to print'. It recognizes, then, the backward-gazing processes of examining and interpreting printed artefacts as the route towards understanding the theatrical dimension of a play that survives only as a printed text. This chapter sharpens the issue by looking at a scene in *Timon of Athens*, a play that, for all we know, may well never have reached the early modern stage. The absence of any record of performance is a reminder of our precarious understanding of early staging. In other situations too we lack basic information: whether one play was performed, where another play was performed, and so on. How do we generate something that we may, perhaps over-optimistically, refer to as 'knowledge' of early modern performance? To what extent can this knowledge be grounded in the printed texts of plays? On what basis can we build an understanding of the aesthetic and ideological effects of the play as a theatre artwork?

Theatre as it arises from the text of an early modern play can be said to be 'of the mind' in two important respects. It is 'of the mind' in the sense that D.F. McKenzie used the phrase in referring to some of the conclusions of textual bibliographers.[2] That is to say, it involves constructs based on a present-day analysis that is all too dependent on the very assumptions that inform the analysis. At worst, as McKenzie showed in his sceptical dismantling of some of the earlier assumptions about seventeenth and eighteenth-century printers, the inferences might turn out to be groundless. The theatre, specifically of *Timon of Athens*, is also 'of the mind' in that the Folio text is understood to represent that play at a pre-theatrical stage. The performance, such as it is, to which the text bears witness can be securely attributed to no other locus than the minds of the authors. The plural should be noted: the hypothesis that Thomas Middleton shared with Shakespeare in the writing of *Timon of Athens* adds a further twist to the difficulty in locating performance in relation to the text in question.[3]

My discussion will focus on the masque in Sc. 2 of this play. As a script for performance this episode depends crucially on non-verbal elements, as signified verbally in printed and implied stage directions. It therefore demands a strong awareness of the semantics of theatre. However, the elements of stage signification are by no means straightforwardly derived from the printed text, which requires particularly careful negotiation on this account. As will be seen, the issue here is not particularly that the printed text falsifies the document on which it is based.

Performance is a sensory activity, appealing to a broader range of sensation than the verbal text as spoken, with the senses always variable, both from play to play and from moment to moment.[4] Yet in the sensory economy of the theatre – or at least of the stage – taste, touch, and smell are peripheral or irrelevant. Theatre concentrates on sight and hearing as the two senses through which it mainly communicates. Meaning is constituted within a complex dialogue between these two senses. The passage under discussion is critical in that it not only involves a heightened appeal to the senses, but also deals discursively with the semantic economy of the senses, giving a textual thematization of the theatrical experience offered to the audience's ears and eyes.

I will be concerned, therefore, with the play as a text, with the text as a script for a theatrical sense-scape that works with and against a binary opposition of the two senses of hearing and sight, and with sense-scape as a field of signification in its own right. I will highlight the contrast between theatrical sense-scape and the anaesthesia experienced by the reader of a play-text, and will deliberate on the role of the reader's assumptions in constructing a sense-scape. The thought of anaesthesia might lead to Pyrrhonian conclusions; but scripts enable real as well as imagined theatre. We may, after all, acceptingly embrace the idea of theatre as a realm of almost magical transformation, and we should know what we can say about it, as well as what we cannot say.

II

My starting point lies in the words that appear on the page, the part of one printed page of the First Folio as reproduced in the Appendix (pp. 88–9). In looking at this passage as printed we are immediately transported to a world of sound. The masque begins with a call for a '*Tucket*' or trumpet call. This is an immediate reminder of the aural division between non-verbal sounds and spoken words, the trumpet abrasively interrupting the social dialogue of banqueting. As the musician, or musicians, are specifically said to be out of sight 'within', the tucket lacks any visual preparation. The noise loudly and ceremonially punctuates the scene, setting a formal boundary on the masque episode that begins precisely here.

After the tucket the Folio indicates a movement into the masque itself with the direction '*Enter the Maskers of Amazons, with Lutes in their hands, dauncing and playing*'. Trumpets, which were associated with military as well as ceremonial contexts, are unusually relevant to the women as Amazons. But they are now replaced with non-aggressive amorous lutes, a transition that almost offers an aural equivalent to the opening soliloquy of *Richard III*, where the 'alarums' of 'Grim-visaged war' are suddenly translated into 'the lascivious pleasing of a lute'. The entry also injects new visual elements of fancy-dress costume and action, as a new group of figures performing in dance is added to those who are already on stage.

But to read the words of the stage direction thus as action and without attention to their position in the dialogue is to run ahead of the textual problem they present. The information in these words from the stage direction comes too early. The Amazons, having apparently come on stage dancing and playing, almost certainly have to be the same ladies who, a few lines later, are said to remain still 'Most desirous of admittance'. Of course one can try to be rigorous to the point of absurdity about retaining an open-minded scepticism: might the Ladies make a short appearance then retreat before entering formally? It seems most unlikely; if they are 'desirous of admittance' they surely cannot have already admitted themselves onto the stage dancing and playing. After Timon says 'I pray let them be admitted', in line with his words there is another entry for *'the Maske of Ladies'* to appear. They are now led in by a Cupid: *'Enter Cupid with the Maske of Ladies'*. The two stage directions provide two versions of the same entrance; the ladies are the same as the figures dressed as Amazons, and the dialogue provides for them to enter only once. Somehow the vagaries of inscription have produced a text that, taken at face value, is radically at odds with the very stage action it prescribes.

Here is a situation in which a textually minded critic will ask whether there might be a duplication resulting from co-authorship or some other form of secondary annotation. A distinct problem in allowing any degree of credence to this line of enquiry is that the two stage directions in question are both distinctive of the scene's author, who here has been firmly identified as Middleton. In particular, as R.V. Holdsworth first pointed out, the Folio stage directions share with a stage direction in Middleton's *The Nice Valour* at 2.1.147 a number of distinctive traits both in terms of both their overall concept as stage action and their precise wording; the equivalent phrases in that play are *'Enter . . . Cupid'*, *'women Maskers'*, and *'singing and playing'*; the action continues at 2.1.164 with *'A dance, Cupid leading'*.[5] It is the preliminary direction in *Timon of Athens*, the one that is placed too early, that contains most of the parallels with *Nice Valour*. The parallels meld together the verbal texture of the stage direction as writing with the conceptualization of stage action. Yet the Cupid's entry is also Middletonian as regards the latter, the stage action. There are Cupids in masques in *Dissemblers* and *Women Beware Women* as well as *Nice Valour*.[6]

There is, then, little possibility here of annotation by a second hand. Perhaps instead in the first direction the scripting of the action runs ahead of the dialogue, the action being more briefly and therefore quickly materialized as written words than the wordiness of speech. Strangely, even the second entry of the masquers is sent before its time. To judge by the dialogue, the ladies actually do not enter until after Timon says, in words that partly echo his earlier line, 'let 'em haue kind admittance. Musicke make their welcome'. This line falls some seven lines after the second entry direction. Timon's near-repetition before and after the Cupid's speech, 'I pray let them be admitted... let 'em haue kind admittance' is oddly consonant with the repetition in the stage directions, but presents no difficulty in its own right. The first simply leads to the 'fore-runner' Cupid entering as a prologue. Any precise connection between these two rhythms of repetition is hard to discern.

What is harder still to establish is the species of spectacle to which Timon's guests are treated. Is this a masque of Amazons, or a masque of 'the fiue best Sences' who 'acknowledge thee their Patron, and come freely to gratulate thy plentious bosome'? Or could it in some way be both? I wish to pursue this question in some detail, not least because I believe that I was initially misled in my own interpretation of the passage, which is testimony in itself to the uncertainty as to how the words can be interpreted as stage action. It also raises important theoretical issues as to the hermeneutics of reconstructed theatre action. The dilemma from an editor's point of view is this. Should the editorial resolution of F's repeated and excessive stage directions aim for the accommodation of as many details as possible, and so push towards an aesthetic of the parodic or the grotesque? Or, on the other hand, should it resist the potential excess on the assumption that F presents in a single textual sequence what is in fact a layering of different and partly irreconcilable intentions or versions? The interplay between assumptions about aesthetics and textual hypothesization is highly active in the instance before us, which writes large some issues that are more quietly at work in all translations from print to performance.

As noted already, dramatists' staging practices have offered valuable evidence in authorship attribution study; they are potentially a valid consideration here. Middleton's *Triumphs of Truth* describes a tableau of the five senses with their 'proper emblems' of an eagle for sight, a hart for hearing, a spider for touch, an ape for taste, and a dog for smell (ll. 354–8). This would appear to be a strong clue that the reference to 'the fiue best Sences' is a similar spectacle. And one then begins to postulate how such an episode might be staged. For example: might properties denoting the senses be carried? Might they perhaps be depicted on shields bearing emblematic motifs (as was the case in the 1578 Masque of Amazons performed for Queen Elizabeth and the French ambassador)? But the ladies carry '*Lutes in their hands*' and also dance, so it is hard to imagine how it would be at all possible to manage portable properties as well. Perhaps, then, the senses might instead be indicated by motifs on their costumes: either emblems, as with the actual properties in *Triumphs of Truth*, or the organs of the senses, as with Rumour '*painted full of tongues*' in the Induction to *2 Henry IV*.

The practicalities of staging a masque by Amazons of the five senses – as it were a masque within a masque – are probably manageable at a stretch. However, the text as it stands in the Folio can sustain a more literal reading that sets firm limits on such possibilities. This reading runs thus: 'There' at the banquet the senses 'rise' from the table in a purely figurative display of gratulation, whereas here and 'now' the Amazons 'come' to feast one sense exclusively, the 'eies'. The Amazons are materially there in order to be seen, as they will be once they are admitted.

Theatrically speaking, the lines contrast what is already on stage, the banquet, with what awaits entry within. This considerably eases the potential overloading of effect in the masque. The Amazons do not after all need to play the senses as well as themselves, for the senses are invoked as a verbal rather than visual conceit. This reading therefore bypasses any need to determine editorially between a flawed text that fails to reconcile two alternative stagings – the Amazons versus the five senses – and a physically and emblematically overloaded effect of masque-within-masque. It happens to reduce what would be an unusually high demand for six boy actors: the five senses plus Cupid.[7] And the postulated interpretation of the words and staging gives absolute priority to sight as the sense through which the masque entertains and signifies.

There is, however, another textual issue here that impinges on the passage's economy of the senses. The previous paragraph, while assuming that the stage directions require rationalization, has accepted the dialogue in the Folio text as it stands. By this reading of F, 'There' effectively fuses reference to the 'bosome' as the source of bounty with the 'Table' on which the effects are displayed. Hence the banqueting table is turned into an emblem of the plenteous bosom. By a long-established editorial tradition, however, 'There' might alternatively be an error for, or a misleading form of, 'Th'ear'. This emendation goes back as far as Lewis Theobald's edition of 1733. It is founded on an assumption of only slight error. 'Ere' was an acceptable spelling of *ear* until the sixteenth century at least, and spaces and apostrophes were not always indicated after 'th' for *the*. So if the reading were 'Th'ear', F would be only minimally corrupt.

The reading 'Th'ear' would increase the number of gratulating senses that are specifically identified from two to three, 'Th'ear, taste, touch', with sight reserved for its special role in the following line. With this reading, smell is all the more conspicuous by its absence. On this basis, a further emendation has been proposed and sometimes adopted. It is argued that 'all' reflects an accidental error whereby the sense of smell has been lost. Smell makes a vital contribution to the sensory pleasures of banqueting, and it is smell, of all the senses, that is the one that most appositely may be said to 'rise' from the table. In his 1747 edition, William Warburton made the double emendation of the Folio's 'There tast, touch all' to 'Th'ear, taste, touch, smell'. He noted that the passage was evidently adapted in Philip Massinger's *The Duke of Milan* (1621), where the reading includes both 'Th'ear' and 'smell': 'All that may be had / To please the eye, the eare, taste, touch, or smell / Are carefully prouided' (1.3.3-5).[8] *The Duke of Milan*, entered in the Stationers' Register on 20 January 1623, was written before the publication of the Folio and therefore without any possibility of Massinger's reading *Timon* in print; but Massinger, as regular dramatist for the King's Men, may have had opportunity to read *Timon* in manuscript. The influence seems likely – and an intriguing point in itself – but the wording of the two lines as a whole is not exact enough to bear reliable witness to the reading of individual words in the manuscript of *Timon*. For instance, any interpretation of F involves privileging the sight above the other senses mentioned, no matter how many they might be, whereas Massinger's 'All that may be had... Are carefully prouided' does not make this distinction. From the point of view of a textual editor, double emendation seems implausible, not least as 'smell' would not at all easily be corrupted to 'all'.

In their 1785 Variorum edition, George Steevens and Isaac Reed overcame this particular difficulty and added further sophistication to the editorial reworking of the passage. They introduced the alternative of inserting the word 'smell' as an addition, rather than substituting it for 'all', to give 'Th'ear, / Taste, touch, smell, all from thy table rise'. This assumes an easier error, and retains the word 'all' (which is found also in the Massinger passage, though not in the same position). But to the double error it adds a further difficulty with the metre, which then needs emending by taking back 'Th'ear' to the end of the previous line.

Reference back to the illustration of the passage will show that this relineation is in itself nonsensical, as F prints the previous lines as prose, not verse. The text put forward by Steevens and Reed therefore involves yet another change: that the first lines of the Cupid's speech should be rearranged as verse divided after 'all', 'senses', and 'freely'. This further emendation encourages Steevens and Reed's insertion of 'smell', because the editorially-constructed verse-line 'To gratulate thy plenteous bosom' is metrically defective, in that it lacks a final syllable. The insertion of 'smell' in the following line makes that line over-long. So 'Th'ear' becomes redundant to that line, and becomes available to make good the verse line that the editors have created. The logic based on metre that leads to turning F's prose setting to verse and the logic based on literary content that leads to adding smell to the list of senses are strongly complementary. One will conclude either that such is the nature of a corrupt text or such are the misguided but Siren-like charms of textual emendation as it emerged in the eighteenth century. I incline to the latter.

It can be recognized, I think, that the Cupid's first lines do have something of the rhythm of iambic pentameter. Yet here the authorial question comes once again into play. The intermixture of prose and verse, and the particular device of a single speech beginning in prose and ending in a rhyming couplet: these are both well-recognized features of Middleton's writing, as can be seen in this scene itself at 2.38–52. The passage may well appear to be suspect metrically from the perspective of Shakespeare's writing, but the Middleton perspective vindicates its unusual quality and so makes metrical emendation particularly unjustifiable.

The authorial factor decisively reverses the snowball effect in the Steevens–Reed treatment of the passage. If the lineation is acceptable and indeed characteristic of the author, there is no metrical basis for adding 'smell' to the senses, and the printing in the Folio immediately looks more justified in its own terms. So I return to the difficulty inherent in any reading that begins by emending 'There' to 'Th'ear'. How can the senses both rise from Timon's table *and* be identified with the masquers who have 'onely now' come to feast his eyes and require admittance? If, however, the other senses are 'There' at the banqueting table, their separation from the visual feast that 'now' awaits entry is straightforward enough.

This discussion of textual minutiae brings into focus the dilemma facing the editor of choosing between moderation and sensory overload. Just as I am intrigued by the possibility that an overdetermined masque of Amazons *and* of the senses might tilt interestingly towards parody, I am attracted by the strong emphasis on the senses that the eighteenth-century editors established. Yet, within the binary possibilities afforded by the stable and unitary edited text, with all the parsimony that implies, I reject both these options.[9] The grounds for this rejection lie in the difficulty of meaning in taking 'the fiue best Sences' as a reference to the masquers – an argument based on the dialogue that leads to emending the stage directions – and, quite simply, the coherence of the unemended Folio text of the dialogue, which therefore can stand intact. I therefore follow the usual editorial dispensation, with its preferences for economy of hypothesis, for avoiding emendation except where necessary. I accept too the usual procedure that privileges the textual status of dialogue over that of stage directions, recognizing the greater instability that is inherent in the latter. The passage illustrates clearly the need to rationalize the stage directions, but the dialogue itself can and should be treated with a higher degree of conservatism.

But I remain haunted by the thought that editing, through its alliance with philology and empirical lines of reasoning, and through its need to minimize the involvement of free interpretation in the procedures for establishing the text, might act as a puritanical restraint on the sensory potential of the passage. The editor's stage picture will almost always err on the side of plainness and fixity. In this respect, the masque's sensory aspect and its thematization of the senses can stand as an emblem of the tension between text-based editing and the potential of performance.

III

My discussion of the masque has so far attended to questions of its form, with some reference to its aesthetics. I turn now to questions centring on content and meaning, in so far as they are manifested visually as well as through spoken words. As we have seen, for readers the visual manifestation is itself problematic. Hence the spectacle that we as readers cannot see begins appropriately with the figure of Cupid. If he were to be represented as blindfolded on the stage this would add resonance to his announcement of a spectacle that will feast the eyes. Blind Cupid is itself, of course, in itself something of a reader's construct from a text that says merely '*Cupid*'. Both as an image and as a product of a reading practice it offers a fitting emblem of the position of the reader in relation to stage action. The Cupid takes the speaking part of the entertainment, and so his are the words from which we piece together some sense of sight.

The Cupid also emblematizes the relation between the public theatre of boy actors and the court masque where women appeared on stage. By the gender economy of the public theatre, Cupid is a role for a boy actor, but so too are the roles of the ladies. The masquers in this respect make up a homogeneous group that contrasts with their exclusively adult on-stage audience by way of age but not gender. Hence the Cupid, though a boy, represents the male professional performers of speaking roles as a whole. This actor stands apart from the '*Ladies*'. However, by the distribution of actors' roles within the masque the Amazons are played by '*Ladies*'. This reflects the gender and class economy of the court masque. In royal masques, exclusively male professional actors performed the speaking roles; aristocrats, including women, engaged in the physical display of costumes and bodies. In this respect the Cupid stands apart from the lady masquers. In a masque, a speaking Cupid would be a role for a professional boy actor, not an aristocratic lady.

It is therefore significant that one detail of the masque in *Timon* offends the decorum of court masque. There were only three masques performed before *Timon* was written in which ladies from the court appeared on the stage: *The Vision of Twelve Goddesses* (1604), *The Masque of Blackness* (1605), and (probably) *Hymenaei* (1606).[10] In none of these, nor as far as I am aware in any other court masque of the Jacobean period, do ladies play musical instruments. Having ladies appear on even the court stage, with its restricted and invited audience, stretched the limits of acceptability. Dudley Carleton noted in a letter to Sir Ralph Winwood that the ladies in Ben Jonson's *Masque of Blackness* wore apparel 'too light and Curtizan-like for such great ones'.[11] Later, in the Caroline period, there were partial exceptions in the entertainments put on by Queen Henrietta Maria ('partial' because they were not masques as such). The 1633 court production of Walter Montagu's pastoral *The Shepherd's Paradise* was performed entirely by Henrietta Maria and her ladies. Alison Findlay notes that, 'By staging *The Shepherd's Paradise*, Henrietta Maria was breaking every rule in the book'.[12] It was this production that prompted William Prynne provocatively to denounce Henrietta Maria and her fellow female masquers as 'notorious impudent, prostituted strumpets'. A year earlier, Aurelian Townshend's masque *Tempe Restored* had been, according to Clare McManus, the first instance of a noblewoman singing on stage in any public entertainment, masque or drama.[13] Women in the earlier Jacobean court masques did not go so far as to offer entertainment of a kind better left to paid professionals such as speaking, singing, and playing instruments.[14] In marked contrast, the ladies in *Timon*, described as '*with Lutes in their hands, dauncing and playing*', are there to be heard as well as seen.

This seems to me to be a provocative and significant detail, not least because it would be so much more straightforward in practical terms simply to avoid specifying that the ladies play lutes. In view of recent scholarship establishing women's participation in drama and theatrical activity of various kinds, it is important here both to affirm and to delimit the performance practice at issue. Our present view of masques as a whole is strongly skewed by the specific instance of the court masque, because these were regularly printed and so are known to us.[15] We remain more ignorant as to how far the same conventions applied to lost masques and other entertainments performed at the houses of aristocrats. Suzanne Westfall, reviewing entertainments in great households over the early modern period as a whole, writes that 'Denied acting roles in the civic and public theater, women sang, played musical instruments, spoke text, and danced in disguisings and masques' elsewhere. But the evidence remains sketchy and offers nothing to contradict the claim advanced above as to the playing conventions of Jacobean court masques.[16]

The example of *Comus* as a masque staged at the seat of a leading aristocrat is valuable, as Lady Alice Egerton played a role that involved both speaking and singing. Yet *Comus*, performed shortly after *Tempe Restored* and *The Shepherd's Paradise* in 1634, offers no counter-indication to the reading proposed here. Milton assumes that it is entirely proper for a young lady to perform, and indeed in his masque Alice Egerton's stage presence is designed to enhance its value as a celebration of sober female chastity. Yet this represents one aspect of Milton's critique of the masque as staged by Henrietta Maria at court. Despite their contrasting presentations of female performers, *Timon* and *Comus* share a similarity in that they both position themselves in relation to the court masque in a consciously extramural and critical fashion. It seems unlikely that either text presents female performers without pointed reference to what are understood to be the established conventions of court theatre. These practices would have been known to members of their audiences not least through circulation of the same printed texts of masques that are available to the modern reader, which would have been the core texts for the reproduction and imitation of masques in Jacobean culture.

One consequence of the cross-gender, inter-social, inter-theatrical presentation of the masquers in *Timon of Athens* is that it unsettles the ontological status of the *'Ladies'* themselves. This applies all the more in a culture where the very appearance of aristocratic women on stage readily led to accusations of whoredom. But at least in the court theatre the identity of the female actor was stable in that it was known to the audience and intrinsic to the meaning of the display, and the relation between actor and role was straightforward.[17] In the case of *Timon* as a play written for the public theatre, one might ask how the written term *'Ladies'* would have been manifested in performance in a situation where, taking the illusion back, they are performed by boys and, taking the illusion forward, they themselves represent Amazons. Can they securely be imagined as aristocratic ladies? The Cupid seems clear enough in declaring their status, but only at first glance: 'there are certain ladies / Most desirous of admittance'. 'Certain ladies' is an ambiguous phrase here: most straightforwardly it means 'a number of ladies', but *certain* might also suggest 'for sure', perhaps with ironic implication. Indeed, the ladies' certainty of decorously noble status is eroded by a string of words that are finely balanced between decorum and sexual innuendo: *desirous, admittance, wills, pleasures.* For us as readers today, knowledge of Middleton's authorship of the scene can only heighten our awareness that these are half-realized double entendres. Authorship does not usually signify in the theatre, but in the early modern theatre the rupture of court masquing conventions would so signify. This transgression can suggest that the women might be less socially elevated than ladies: performers who are, like actors, merely passing themselves off as ladies who perform in the masque.

Here, once again, suggestive comparisons can be made with other scenes by Middleton. One such is a comment on lady masquers made by the Passionate Lord in that very closely equivalent passage in *The Nice Valour* mentioned above. Inventing a wonderfully bizarre collective noun to describe the ladies, he says: 'what a felicity of whores is here'. In Middleton's *The Ant and the Nightingale*, the protagonist's 'most delicate drab' is described in these terms:

> Endued she was (as we heard) with some good qualities, though all were converted then but to flattering villainies. She could run upon the lute very well, which in others would have appeared virtuous but in her lascivious, for her running was rather jested at because she was a light runner besides. (ll. 565–71)

As this passage suggests, the Ladies' playing of lutes is in itself suggestive: David Munrow notes that in Renaissance illustrations 'The lute is often found in the hands of courtesans'.[18] In Middleton's comedy *Your Five Gallants*, written perhaps shortly after *Timon*, another group of 'ladies' play music in public. They are actually prostitutes in a brothel that passes itself off as a respectable music school for orphaned young gentlewomen. *Your Five Gallants* therefore shows a cross-over between genteel female musical entertainers and prostitutes. Something similar may be quietly insinuated to be the case in *Timon*. It is significant here that blind Cupid, 'the cause of most men's crests' according to the song in *More Dissemblers Besides Women* (1.4.93), was the usual sign for a brothel;[19] in other words the Cupid on stage may be a sign of the brothel-sign. Moreover, the boy actors who play two of the ladies would probably return later in the play as the whores accompanying Alcibiades. Perhaps nothing has changed and they play the same women; perhaps at any rate the boundary between the doubling of different roles and the reappearance of the same roles is blurred.

There are, moreover, suggestions that Timon himself treats the ladies as common entertainers. Following masque convention in the first instance, the emblematic pageant in the passage gives way to general dancing when the masquers take partners with members of the audience: '*The Lords rise from Table, with much adoring of Timon; and, to shew their loues, each single out an Amazon, and all Dance, men with women, a loftie straine or two to the Hoboyes*' (following 2.137). The ladies have presumably put their lutes down, and the sound timbre rises to something louder, more decorous, and more formal with the new instrument of the hautboys, an instrument of an arrestingly high-pitched sound that was used for ceremonial music in the theatre and at events such as banquets. But the effect of the dance is perhaps not simply exalting. The meaning and orientation of '*to shew their loues*' are both ambiguous. What is the value of this phrase to the realization of the scene in the theatre? What does it mean: to demonstrate their love towards Timon, or to identify their objects of desire, or partners, among the ladies? What sort of showing is to be shown on stage?

No matter how the words of the stage direction are translated into stage spectacle, the entertainment subtly diminishes the role accorded to the ladies by varying the conventions of masque. In a court masque it would be the masquing ladies who would 'take out' partners from the audience to dance. Here, conversely, the guests at Timon's table choose partners from the performing dancers, an eagerness on the part of the lords that deprives the ladies of initiative in constructing the dance as a vision of harmony between masquers and guests. More striking still is the demeaning treatment of the ladies at the end of the masque, when, far from installing themselves as the lords' partners and Timon's guests, they are ushered out of sight as quickly as is decently possible. After complimenting the ladies, Timon immediately invites them to an 'idle banquet' offstage, so that they take no further part in the homosocial scene.

By attending to the conventions of the court masque, and the aspects that are absorbed and the aspects that are resisted in this particular playhouse imitation of a masque, we become more aware that Timon treats the masquers in a way that would be consistent with them being whores, or at least being thought of as whores. What reality, or whose reality, does an imagined audience imagine it is looking at? Middleton described his *Masque of Heroes* in his rhyming headnote as 'made for ladies' and claimed that 'ladies understood' it (l. 8). *Masque of Heroes* was performed by male actors, and so offers a mirror to the masque in *Timon*, which, contrariwise, is performed by women, but made for and understood by men. Is this male-determined world one in which there are no women apart from whores, or one in which ladies cannot be seen other than as potential prostitutes? How do we relate these suggestions to Timon's claim that the ladies have 'entertain'd me with mine owne deuice'?

What Timon's enigmatic words mean as to the degree of responsibility he has for initiating or devising the masque remains uncertain. Yet they certainly indicate that the masque is emblematically appropriate to him. The play identifies Timon as the patriarchal 'Patron' of the five senses as presented in the masque. Thus far we are safely in a realm that is made for men. But Timon is also acknowledged as the maternal source of all bounties. As Coppélia Kahn and others have pointed out, Timon the gift-giver is figured as an unnatural breeder embodying both the male and female principles and bringing forth objects different in kind from himself.[20] In Renaissance terms he is a monster, a creature who defies nature's normal distributions and functions. His appropriation of the maternal principle connects intimately with the exclusion of women from the world in which he lives.

In this spirit the masque offers the audience a satirical commentary on Timon himself – and, by way of the allusion to court masque, on the vices of extravagant consumption and gift-giving embodied in King James. It presents an oblique and implicit commentary that unfolds in mime and communicates by way of inverted analogy. The maternal aspect, fleetingly attached to Timon in the dialogue, is demonstrated visually and in regendered terms with the Amazons. In *Troilus and Cressida* Troilus claims that 'In all Cupid's pageant there is presented no monster' (3.2.71-2), but this claim cannot be applied to the masque introduced by Cupid in *Timon of Athens*. The Amazons had been described by John Knox as 'monstrous women'. In so far as they were supposed traditionally to have seared off one breast so as to fight more effectively with bow and arrow, they contrast with Timon of the 'plentious bosome'.[21] Thus, mirroring Timon as he is presented in the banquet scene, they combined the attributes of both male and female. The appearance of Amazons often signified a threat to the cohesion of the patriarchal worldview, representing the intrusion, in Jeanne Addison Roberts's words, of 'a potentially unassimilable Wild'.[22] In his 'Life of Theseus' Plutarch records that the invading Amazons 'placed their camp within the very city of Athens'. This breach of the Athenian walls is echoed symbolically and ceremonially in the lady masquers' entry into Timon's banqueting hall – which is to say, in theatrical terms, the space of the stage. Trumpets were, after all, used in military as well as ceremonial contexts.

Masques were driven by the imperative to harmonize the potential for disorder as a sign of the patron's or dedicatee's power, beneficence and grace. So it is in *Timon of Athens*. There is an elaborate interplay between threat as represented by the Amazons and containment of threat within the complimentary artifice of the masque in which they are represented. The artificiality does not depend on elements of the incongruous or grotesque, although these would be appropriate enough as a way of highlighting it. Like Prospero's hasty dismissal of the masque in *The Tempest*, Timon's dismissal of the ladies expresses a failure to harmonize the masque with the world in which it is performed. Despite the dancing, this represents in turn a failure or refusal to integrate women into Timon's homosocial world. Timon will confront the female and the wild later, outside Athens, in the form of the 'Common mother' earth; then the visual theatre will have more to do with the elemental structure of the bare stage, unornamented with fancy costume, and with a trapdoor representing the hole that Timon digs. In contrast, the masquers' roles as Amazons is mentioned nowhere in the spoken dialogue and so is restricted to the visual. Articulation of this major thread in the play's imagery shifts to and fro between the iconographic and the verbal. The meaning of what is seen is vital.

IV

What, then, does the passage indicate about the role and relative importance of the different senses in this passage, as metonymic for the play and for early modern drama as a whole? The Cupid's reference to the 'fiue best Sences' suggests, presumably, that the senses share in an equal excellence and have no hierarchy. Yet, as we have seen, theatre inevitably creates a hierarchy in which sight and hearing are pre-eminent over the others. When the action leans towards spectacle, a contest potentially emerges between the aesthetic and significatory power of these senses. It is relevant to the treatment of this issue in *Timon of Athens* that the play was written during the period when Ben Jonson and Inigo Jones were developing their mutually contested practices and theories of court masque. The later hostility between these court masque-makers bears witness to a failure to make the visual and the verbal equally 'best'. The masque in *Timon* can be understood to embody elements of contest between sight and hearing, and elements of harmonization. It is an eruption of the visual as the primary signifying medium that transports the play into another mode of action. Taken literally, the masque is an element of Timon's lavish lifestyle. But as an unexpected and partly inexplicable interpolation into the main flow of verbally-driven drama, it claims the status of metatheatrical commentary.

However, speech is not reduced to silence. On the contrary: as the other guests do indeed lapse into spectatorial silence, Timon's critic Apemantus speaks out as critic and so enunciates commentary of another kind: explicit, verbal, and directed at the masque itself. He articulates how the masque signifies in relation to Timon's lifestyle, and he pushes his audience towards an ironized and Juvenalian reading of it. Taken simply as an entertainment, the masque is a gesture of compliment. Apemantus encourages a different reading. He speaks of the masque in a particular mode of satire that appropriates the masque to his own ends, so that it becomes, through his commentary, the visual element in his own moral emblem. Thus he generates an extramimetic dimension, turning the spectacle from a gesture of love to a gesture of dangerous hypocrisy.

The masque is, then, consistent with the main flow of dialogue and action at the level of mimesis as an act of elegant compliment, while it is also consistent with Apemantus' critique of it at a level closer to extramimetic commentary. It therefore might be said to parody itself as a mimetic event. This element of parody feeds into the larger flow of his critique of the goings-on in Timon's household. Ironically, then, the masque empowers Apemantus as critic. Readers of the masque of Cupid in *More Dissemblers Besides Women*, the wedding masque of the four elements in *No Wit/Help Like a Woman's*, or the banquet scene in *Women Beware Women* will recognize the technique, for it is highly characteristic of Middleton's dramaturgy. All of these scenes are satirical, and in all of them a disturbance in the co-ordination of the senses is a signal of a disturbance in the semantic economy and a shift towards a mode of drama that might be described as emblematic satire.

The emblem, in which the words make manifest the significance of the often cryptic visual image, provides an apposite, more general model for the relationship between the hearing and the sight in the theatre. That relationship is often enigmatic. In the scene under discussion there are suggestions of alienation between the senses even as their Platonic unity of purpose is celebrated in the masque's internal design. The Platonic and aristocratic harmony of the masque taken on its own terms is harshly contradicted in Apemantus' view of it as a 'sweepe of vanitie' performed at the furthest extreme from reason by 'madwomen'. The female, the visual, the sensual, and the insane are here opposed by the male, the aural, the critical, and the rational. But even here, there is no outright opposition between sight and hearing, for reasons that have been suggested. It is indeed the consistency between the masque as parodic spectacle and the satirical comments of Apemantus that generates a powerful emblematic extramimesis. Despite the contrasting modes of delivery, the same kinds of meaning and irony inhere in both.

Moreover, if Apemantus instructs us to read the masque as satire, the masque instructs us to read Apemantus, with his overpitched indignation, as part of the larger theatricalized emblem of folly. Apemantus is in this respect orchestrated within the masque episode. In Greg Doran's 1999 production by the Royal Shakespeare Company, Richard McCabe, playing Apemantus, began intoning the speech as a sermon, but he increasingly merged his words with the rhythms of

Duke Ellington's jazz music setting for the episode as the speech went on, and he took to the keyboard to accompany himself. His music supplemented and chimed in with the music of the masque. With his leather jacket and sunshades, he became a participant even as he was a critic. The effect was reminiscent more of the Blues Brothers than the early modern stage. McCabe's performance neverthe-less offers a useful reminder that the sound and music of the dancing sit alongside the words and rhythms of speech, all conveyed to the audience through the single organ of the ear. In such a situation, masculinist reason enjoys a precarious vantage. Even as the episode sternly foreshadows Timon's downfall, it invites its audience to enjoy its theatricality, its spectacle, and, perhaps above all, its mani-fest absurdity. The enhanced and redistributed appeal to the senses can even be taken as a metaphor for the enjoyably conflicted responses that the episode demands.

V

The interpretative issues raised by the masque scene are fully appropriate to a play that opens with a dialogue between a Poet and a Painter, the representatives of text and image, or perhaps one should say the representatives of hearing and sight in a performed artwork such as a play.[23] The positions of both figures are subsumed under the shared condition of patronage, and so the debate turns on the survival of truth-telling and 'free drift' in a world where the artist is as much dependent on Timon's favour as the flatterers he satirizes. The Poet defends the integrity of his art as a moral critique of its subject, whereas his response to the Painter's work suggests that the painting offers a flattering depiction of Timon. The masque scene will later polarize the same distinction more sharply. The word-less masque correlates with the art of the Painter. Apemantus assumes the role of Poet, issuing a verbal critique of what he sees.

Yet, as has been suggested, the case of Apemantus' commentary can also be seen to complicate the distinction between words and spectacle. It might there-fore be useful to highlight the limits that apply to the opposition between the two senses represented by Poet and Painter. Sight and hearing are both exploited in complex ways that relate both to semantics and to sensory effect. In the first instance, writing on the page is apprehended by way of the eye; in this respect it ironically shares with work such as the Painter does and with scene-painting as the visual aspect of stage presentation.[24] As for the ear, within the sensual economy of the theatre hearing plays a complex role. It is at this point in the text's transmission the means by which the verbal signifiers are apprehended, the words having been translated from one sense to another. And yet it is also an important sense in relation to non-verbal effects we have encountered in this passage such as music and sound effects. Recent developments in brain science refine our understanding of the relationship between the processing of language and of other sounds in ways that are valuable for our models and analysis of performance. It has long been recognized that the brain responds to spoken language more acutely than to other sounds. The complex mechanism by which this takes place is becoming apparent. Words as signifiers are processed by a different part of the brain from words as intonation, pitch, and the bearers of social information about the identity and orientation of the speaker. Brain scanning has shown that the brain has a speech-specific response whereby it 'takes speech and separates it into the words and "melody" – the varying intonation in speech that reveals mood, gender, and so on…words are then shunted over to the left temporal lobe for processing, while the melody is channelled to the right side of the brain, a region more stimulated by music'.[25] The brain itself therefore recognizes a distinction not simply between words and other sounds, but, within its processing of words, between verbal language as the mode of delivery of text and verbal language as part of the social and artistic sense-scape of the play. To use a formulation in use in the early modern period, one might say it is between the 'manner' that divulges the emotional temper of the language and the 'matter' of its verbal meaning.[26] Hence the brain responding to performance begins with a separation of text from the other elements of performance including the 'melodic' aspects of language (which are also in their own way significatory), before finally reintegrating the information from the two brain lobes into the impression of a single effect. This provides an interpretative tool for studying the sense-scape of the passage under examination, or, for that matter, any other. The words of the verbal poem exist as a separable entity within the event of performance as it is apprehended, as if their origin as text had not been forgotten.

Self-evidently, without the poem as printed in the 1623 Folio there is no performance, no painting. This nihilistic corollary to the very existence of theatre is especially pertinent to *Timon of Athens*, a play that perhaps was almost excluded from the 1623 Folio and so lost for ever, a play that may never have been performed in early modern England. *Timon* reaches towards its ending when Timon's own final utterance calls for an end to language itself: 'Lips let four words go by, and language end'. Timon goes on to say 'Sun, hide thy beams': thus the end of language leads on to the end of sight, or the end of poetry is the end of painting.

In absolute contrast, the opening lines that lead us into the play's world of activity exemplify the relationship between words and stage event by using the word *magic*. The Poet, the representative of words, observes figures passing over the stage to visit Timon. They are artisans and tradesmen – merchant, jeweller, mercer – those other makers of social theatre, those other makers of masque. Seeing them, the Poet invokes and brings focus to the sense of sight, and not only for the Painter. For the play's reader, his words speak thematically; for an audience they speak both thematically and as a literal injunction to use the eyes: 'See, /Magic of bounty, all these spirits thy power / Hath conjured to attend'. One aspect of the bounty to which the Poet refers is the metamorphosis of words – such as the Poet's very words in this very speech here and now – into imagined or potentially real theatrical event. The words of the text conjure the event; they translate the stage action into a meaningful social spectacle. We are invited to train our attention on the passing figures whose real or imagined presence testifies to Timon's richness. With that phrase 'Magic of bounty' the Poet has answered his own question about what is happening in the world out there when he asked, 'what particular rarity, what strange, / Which manifold record not matches'. The particular rarity is happening here and now. If only we could be sure whether the theatrical spectacle were indeed a vision of a particular rarity, or, for example, of some species of visual satire; if only we as readers could see.

Appendix: *Timon of Athens* Sc.2.109-53 (TLN 453-506), as printed in the 1623 First Folio

3.Lord. I promise you my Lord you mou'd me much.
Aper. Much.

> *Sound Tucket. Enter the Maskers of Amazons, with*
> *Lutes in their hands, dauncing and playing.*

Tim. What meanes that Trumpe? How now?

> *Enter Seruant.*

Ser. Please you my Lord, there are certaine Ladies
Most desirous of admittance.
Tim. Ladies? what are their wils?
Ser. There comes with them a fore-runner my Lord,
which beares that office, to signifie their pleasures.
Tim. I pray let them be admitted.

> *Enter Cupid with the Maske of Ladies.*

Cup. Haile to thee worthy Timon and to all that of his Bounties taste: the fiue best Sences acknowledge thee their Patron, and come freely to gratulate thy plentious bosome.
There tast, touch all, pleas'd from thy Table rise:
They onely now come but to Feast thine eies.
Timo. They'r welcome all, let 'em haue kind admittance. Musicke make their welcome.
Luc. You see my Lord, how ample y'are belou'd.
Aper. Hoyday,
What a sweepe of vanitie comes this way.
They daunce? They are madwomen,
Like Madnesse is the glory of this life,
As this pompe shewes to a little oyle and roote.
We make our selues Fooles, to disport our selues,
And spend our Flatteries, to drinke those men,
Vpon whose Age we voyde it vp agen
With poysonous Spight and Enuy.
Who liues, that's not depraued, or depraues;

Who dyes, that beares not one spurne to their graues
Of their Friends guift:
I should feare, those that dance before me now,
Would one day stampe vpon me: 'Tas bene done,
Men shut their doores against a setting Sunne.

> *The Lords rise from Table, with much adoring of Timon, and*
> *to shew their loues, each single out an Amazon, and all*
> *Dance, men with women, a loftie straine or two to the*
> *Hoboyes, and cease.*

Tim. You haue done our pleasures
Much grace (faire Ladies)
Set a faire fashion on our entertainment,
Which was not halfe so beautifull, and kinde:
You haue added worth vntoo't, and luster,
And entertain'd me with mine owne deuice.
I am to thanke you for't.
   1 Lord. My Lord you take vs euen at the best.
   Aper. Faith for the worst is filthy, and would not hold taking, I doubt me.
   Tim. Ladies, there is an idle banquet attends you,
Please you to dispose your selues.
   All La. Most thankfully, my Lord.   *Exeunt.*

Notes

1. The term 'sense-scape' is adapted from Bruce Smith's term 'soundscape', in *The Acoustic World of Early Modern England: Attending to the O Factor* (Chicago: University of Chicago Press, 1999). Smith's term derives from R. Murray Schafer, *The Soundscape: Our Sonic Environment and the Turning of the World* (Rochester, VT: Destiny, 1994).
2. D.F. McKenzie, 'Printers of the Mind: Some Notes on Bibliographical Theories and Printing-House Practices', *Studies in Bibliography* 12 (1969), 1–75.
3. For details of Middleton's hand, see John Jowett, ed., *Timon of Athens* (Oxford, 2004). References are to this edition, which uses through scene-numbering.
4. Some of these issues have been addressed with particular reference to hearing in Smith, *Accoustic World*, and Wes Folkerth, *The Sound of Shakespeare* (London and New York: Routledge, 2002), especially his comments on 'polythetic' meaning that 'allows us to conceive of meaning as a *process* that takes place within the experience of embodied consciousness' (p. 21).
5. R.V. Holdsworth, 'Middleton and Shakespeare', Ph.D. thesis, University of Manchester, 1982. Holdsworth's is the most comprehensive and persuasive demonstration of Middleton's hand in the play generally and in Sc. 2 in particular. The quotations are as in the 1647 Beaumont and Fletcher Folio; line references are from *Collected Works*, gen. ed. Gary Taylor and John Lavagnino (Oxford: Oxford University Press, forthcoming). Quotations and references to Middleton's works are from this edition unless otherwise stated.
6. The phrase 'masque of' followed by the role type is of course Jonsonian. But it is also found twice in Middleton's *Revenger's Tragedy*, written at about the same time as *Timon*

of Athens (following 5.3.40, '*the Maske of Reuengers*' and 5.3.48, '*the other Maske of entended murderers*'). It does not elsewhere appear in the plays of Shakespeare.

7. It should be noted, however, that here too *textual* assumptions based on economy of hypothesis lead towards an *aesthetics* of restraint.

8. Quoted from Philip Massinger, *Plays and Poems*, ed. Philip Edwards and Colin Gibson, 5 vols (Oxford: Oxford University Press, 1976), vol. 1.

9. See n. 3.

10. I date *Timon* at probably early 1606. See Jowett, ed., 3–9. I am grateful to Martin Wiggins for information from his work in progress on a database of English Renaissance drama.

11. In Ben Jonson, *Works*, ed. C.H.Herford, Percy Simpson and Evelyn Simpson, 11 vols (Oxford: Oxford University Press, 1925–50), 10.448. In another letter, to John Chamberlain, Carleton reported that there was actual misdemeanor: 'one woeman amongst the rest lost her honesty, for wch she was caried to the porters lodge being surprised at her busines on the top of the Taras'.

12. Alison Findlay, 'Gendering the Stage', in *A Companion to Renaissance Drama*, ed. Arthur F. Kinney (Oxford and Malden: Blackwell, 2002), 399–415 (411).

13. Clare McManus, *Women on the Renaissance Stage: Anna of Denmark and Female Masquing in the Stuart Court (1590–1619)* (Manchester: Manchester University Press, 2002), 185.

14. On women on stage, see also Stephanie Hodgson-Wright, 'Beauty, Chastity and Wit: Feminising the Centre-stage', in *Women and Dramatic Production, 1500–1700*, ed. Alison Findlay, Stephanie Hodgson-Wright, and Gweno Williams (Harlow: Longman, 2000), 42–67.

15. I am grateful to Stephen Orgel for this point.

16. Suzanne Westfall, 'Performances in the Great Households', in *A Companion to Renaissance Drama*, 266–80 (274).

17. On the distinction between the professional performers in masques whose identities 'were to be ignored' and the courtiers with whom 'the relationship between the reality and the symbol, the impersonators and the impersonation' was 'of crucial importance', see Orgel's edition of Jonson, *Complete Masques* (New Haven and London: Yale University Press, 1969), 5, and Suzanne Gossett, ' "Man-maid, begone!": Women in Masques', *ELR* 18 (1988), 96–113.

18. David Munrow, *Instruments of the Middle Ages and Renaissance* (London: Oxford University Press, 1976), 76. One could adduce a number of other references to lutes in Middleton with similar implications – and also the Shakespearian example already mentioned of 'the lascivious playing of a lute' in *Richard III* 1.1.13.

19. Middleton refers in *The Old Law* to a brothel as 'Cupid's scalding-house' (3.2.80).

20. Coppélia Kahn, ' "Magic of Bounty": *Timon of Athens*, Jacobean Patronage, and Maternal Power', *Shakespeare Quarterly* 38 (1987), 34–57. For the analogy with King James as, in his own words, 'nourish-father', see Curtis Perry, *The Making of Jacobean Culture* (Cambridge: Cambridge University Press, 1997), 115–24.

21. Details of Amazons from Simon Shepherd, *Amazons and Warrior Women* (Brighton: Harvester Wheatsheaf, 1981), 14–15. *Bosom* can denote both the breasts and the womb.

22. Jeanne Addison Roberts, *The Shakespearean Wild* (Lincoln, Nebr.: University of Nebraska, 1991), 125.

23. On Sc. 1 as a 'paragone', see A[nthony]. B[lunt]., 'An Echo of the "Paragone" in Shakespeare', *Journal of the Warburg Institute* 2 (1938–39), 260–61; John Dixon Hunt, 'Shakespeare and the Paragone: A Reading of *Timon of Athens*', in *Images of Shakespeare*, ed. Werner Habicht, D.J. Palmer, and Roger Pringle (Newark, Del., and London: Associated University Presses, 1988), 47–63.

24. The term 'scene-painting' refers to the composition of the stage picture in general terms, although of course it has a more literal application to the scenery of court masque.

25. Ian Sample, 'Brain scan sheds light on secrets of speech', summarizing research by Sophie Scott, University College London, in *The Guardian* 3.2.04. Scott has privately confirmed the accuracy of this summary. For full details, see Sophie K. Scott, C. Catrin Blank, Stuart Rosen, and Richard J.S. Wise, 'Identification of a Pathway for Intelligible Speech in the Left Temporal Lobe', in *Brain* 123 (2000), 2400–6.
26. The distinction is made in the 1604 edition of Thomas Wright's *The Passions of the Minde*, as cited in Folkerth, 59–60.

4

'As it was, is, or will be played': Title-pages and the Theatre Industry to 1610

Gabriel Egan

Whereas modern actors usually start with a printed text of some form, we are used to the idea that early modern actors started with manuscripts and that printing followed performance. Confirming this, the title-pages of printed plays refer back to past performance with such phrases as *'As it hath beene publikely acted by the right Honourable the Lorde Chamberlaine his Seruants'*[1] or *'As it was acted by the Kings Maiesties seruants at the Globe'*,[2] to take examples from two first printings of Shakespeare plays. These locutions promise the reader that the contents will be 'as' the play was acted, that the text captures something of the pleasure of performance, although my second example, the phrasing on the title-page of the first printing of *Troilus and Cressida*, comes from a book that survives in two states (Qa and Qb). Qb has a reset title-page that removes the reference to performance but adds that the lovers' 'history' is 'Famous'.[3] The necessity that this second state could not refer back to a performance – apparently because whoever printed it discovered that it had not been publicly performed – was made into virtue with an epistle that emphasizes the readerly benefits. At least, that is one way to read it. Alternatively, Gary Taylor's conjecture is that the epistle was written in 1603 when the play was surreptitiously obtained by a printer after the Inns of Court premiere. The printing was blocked, or not attempted, and the play went on to be performed at the Globe. When it came to be printed in 1609, the printers assumed that it had been played at the Globe and wrote the title-page to Qa, but towards the end of the printing they found the epistle, believed it, and so they set a new title-page and added the epistle.[4]

Even if, as Taylor reckons, the epistle is several years earlier than the printing it precedes, its phrasing is nonetheless caught between apologizing for the non-performance and making a virtue of it. Part of that virtue is its freshness ('you haue heere a new play, neuer stal'd with the Stage') and part is elitist access to something that 'the vulger' have not enjoyed. However, the epistle also claims that reading is an alternative route to Shakespeare's 'wit' (his attribute the epistle repeatedly stresses) and one that will endure long after the originating performances:

> *And had I time I would comment vpon it.... It deserues such a labour, as well as the best Commedy in Terence or Plautus. And beleeue this, that when hee [that is,*

Shakespeare] is gone, and his Commedies out of sale, you will scramble for them ... Take this for a warning, and at the perill of your pleasures losse, and Iudgements, refuse not, nor like this the lesse, for not being sullied, with the smoaky breath of the multitude; but thanke fortune for the scape it hath made amongst you.[5]

Just as Terence and Plautus are gone and their works must be enjoyed from print, so necessarily Shakespeare will go the same way. Of course, actors *can* put on the plays of Terence and Plautus afresh, but only from the printed texts that exist, so there is a backwards and forwards tension in printed play-texts: they preserve what was performed (and can give again something of the pleasure of those performances), and they can originate fresh performances.

Published the same year, 1609, the printed play-text of *Pericles* was indeed used to originate fresh performances, those of the company led by Richard and Christopher Simpson under the patronage of Richard Cholmley that played to Catholic audiences in Yorkshire, as described by C. J. Sisson,[6] G. W. Boddy,[7] and Peter Holland.[8] When tried for sedition these players insisted (falsely, it turned out) that they had not strayed from the printed texts, apparently thinking that this gave them a kind of surrogate licence from the Master of the Revels who had licensed the original manuscripts underlying the printing. One of the actors reported that at Candlemas 1609–10 they performed 'Perocles prince of Tire', which was undoubtedly the work of Shakespeare and Wilkins, and 'Kinge Lere' which might have been Shakespeare's (his quarto was the most recent) but equally might have been the old chronicle history of *King Leir* printed in 1605.[9] This chapter will survey how play printings' title-pages characterized their relationship to performance, from the early printed books to the Simpsons' use of *Pericles*, noting how that relationship changed over the period.

Title-pages, promotion, and the amateur-professional shift

The capacity of a printed play to originate fresh performances was something that the title-pages and the preliminary matter of the very first printings in the early sixteenth century made much of. Often the printings helped would-be performers by listing the parts to be assigned, indicating those that could be taken by a single actor, and even how to cut the text for a desired performance duration:

whiche interlude yf ye hole matter be playd wyl conteyne the space of an hour and a halfe | but yf ye lyst ye may leue out muche of the sad mater as the messengers p<ar>te | and some of the naturys parte and some of experyens p<ar>te & yet the matter wyl depend conuenytently | and than it wyll not be paste thre quarters of an hour of length[10]

The earliest extant printed play in English is Henry Medwall's *Fulgens and Lucrece*[11] but the tradition really begins with the printing of *Everyman* that W. W. Greg thought, on the evidence that four known copies belong to four distinct editions, must have appeared in at least ten early editions.[12] Then came *Mundus & Infans*[13] and then *The Nature of the Four Elements* just quoted. Thereafter in each decade from the 1520s to the 1570s somewhere between about a quarter to a half of all plays whose title-pages survive have on those title-pages a reference to potential future performance in the form of a list of parts or a statement of how easily a given number of actors may play it or a statement about the appropriate occasion for a performance such as 'to be played in Maye games'.[14] Specifically, the decade-by-decade proportions are 2/3, 2/9, 2/4, 1/3, 16/26, and 6/19, for the 1520s to the 1570s sequentially.

This trend abruptly ended with the first printed play of the next decade, *The Conflict of Conscience*, whose title-page featured a doubling chart 'most conuenient for such as be disposed, either to shew this Comedie in priuate houses, or otherwise'.[15] After *The Conflict of Conscience*, printed play title-pages acquired the now-familiar formulaic phrasing that described the contents being 'as it hath been played' (and variations thereon) rather than as material for new perform-ances, and title-page references to (and aids for) future performance stop. For the next two-and-a-half decades no first edition printed play refers or gives aid to future performance on its title-page, although a reprint such as the 1582 edition of Richard Edwards's *Damon and Pithias* might inherit such a reference ('the proper vse of them that hereafter shal haue occasion to play it') from its predecessor.[16] Over these two-and-a-half decades the printing of plays accelerated sharply: 15 plays were printed in the 1580s, 69 in the 1590s, and 124 in the first decade of the 1600s. (Occasionally a list of characters appears, as on the title-page of Marlowe's *Dido Queen of Carthage*,[17] but without guidance about how to distribute them among players; these appear to be readerly rather than performative aids.) In the great flourishing of play printing that forms the first third of the early modern dramatic canon (339 more plays were printed before the closure of 1642), title-pages almost always presented a book's contents as the opportunity to recover the pleasure of past performance rather than as a means to create new performances. The obvious explanation for this change happening in the early 1580s is the rise of the London professional theatre industry with the opening of permanent open-air amphitheatres in the suburbs: the Theatre in Shoreditch (1576) and its neighbour the Curtain (1577). From a marketing point of view, play printing became parasitic upon the professional stage, whose pleasures the book was advertised as recap-turing, rather than serving the (much smaller) demand for self-performable drama.

The same shift is detectable in what printed play books called their contents. The word 'play' itself was used on title-pages of sixteenth-century interludes by John Heywood – *The Playe Called the Foure PP*,[18] *A Play of Loue*,[19] and *The Play of the Wether*[20] – and in their reprintings these reach almost to the Shakespearian period. Likewise an anonymous verse jest about Robin Hood was reprinted several times in the early decades of the sixteenth century and for a printing around 1560 'a newe playe' of about 200 lines was added.[21] But just as references to potential future performances cease from 1581, so too does the use of the word 'play' on title-pages, and not until the 1609 printing of 'THE LATE, and much admired Play, Called Pericles, Prince of Tyre'[22] is a drama again called a 'play' on its title-page. And, by a suspiciously neat symmetry, searches of Chadwyck-Healey's Literature

Online database indicate that the word 'title-page' was not spoken in any drama before *Pericles*: Simonides's 'I place vpon the volume of your deedes, | As in a Title page, your worth in armes'[23] is the first usage.

One has to be careful with such claims about phrasing, because some title-pages just plain lie. Thomas Nashe's *Lenten Stuff* promises on its title-page 'a new Play neuer played before'[24] in praise of red herring, but is itself a red herring because it is wholly a non-dramatic prose satire. Despite its being a hoax, that Nashe's work purports to be an unperformed play (as does the epistle to *Troilus and Cressida*) hints at a bucking of the trend concerning references to past performance. Another hoax, and another rare use of the word 'play', is the printed description of Richard Vennard's entertainment called *England's Joy* that promises an extra-ordinary spectacle including the representation of the monarch on the stage and the enactment of her success in struggles with Spain and Ireland.[25] This is commonly called a playbill, and it certainly serves the playbill-like function of summarizing the performance: 'THE PLOT OF THE PLAY, CALLED *ENGLANDS JOY*. To be Playd at the Swan this 6. of Nouember. 1602'. In an article on playbills, Tiffany Stern pointed out that this is not a playbill at all but, as it says, a 'plot' of the kind

> handed out (when they were) to an audience already at the theatre. They were not, that is to say, hung up around London, but were, rather, 'gifts' for an established audience: something like a modern 'programme'. Usually, though, 'plots' were the preserve of court.... Indeed, Heironymo's gift of playbook and the 'Argument of that we show' to the King in *Spanish Tragedy*, is proof of the habit of giving plot-summaries out at court; the printed 'arguments' at the beginning of playbooks with literary pretensions probably reflect this habit.[26]

Like a playbill, such a document necessarily looks forward to future (indeed, imminent) performance rather than reflecting on past performance. Stern found similarities between the phrasing of playbills (as she inferred from indirect evidence) and the phrasing of title-pages in such things as naming the play, the players, and the venue, and providing a summary of the action. The likeness extends to their usage, for both were pasted up around London as advertisements. Stern gave the reasons for believing that this happened to title-pages and cited R. B. McKerrow's observation that that is why title-pages tell readers where to buy the book, some-thing that a customer would already know if he or she were reading the title-page in the bookshop itself.[27] However, Peter W. M. Blayney's assertion that the place of sale named in the imprint was the wholesaler from whom retailers could get the book wholesale[28] throws doubt on this point, since that information would presumably not interest most potential buyers.

The printing of playbills was a monopoly from 1587 and the successive holders were John Charlewood from 1587[29] to his death in 1593, James Roberts (by marrying Charlewood's widow) from 1594[30] to when he sold his business to William Jaggard in 1606 or 1608.[31] In 1615 Roberts formally transferred his right to print playbills to Jaggard,[32] who held the monopoly until his death in 1623, whereupon it passed to his son Isaac until his death in 1627,[33] and then via Isaac

Jaggard's widow Dorothy to Thomas and Richard Cotes from 1627[34] to the general closure of 1642. In 1582 a mass reassignment in the Stationers' Register[35] transferred from John (= Sampson) Awdely to Charlewood the right to print John Heywood's *The Playe of the Foure PP, The Play of the Wether*, and *A Play of Loue* – notable examples of the word 'play' in their previous printings – and, although there is no sign that he did publish those, Charlewood had published the occasional Tudor interlude, as when in 1566 he published *The Life and Repentaunce of Marie Magdelene* that was advertised on its title-page as being 'very delectable for those which shall heare or reade the same' and which came with a list of parts to how 'Foure may easely play' it.[36] An undated list of books that James Roberts had a right to print[37] includes a number that had been Charlewood's and were transferred to him with the playbills monopoly on 'ultimo maij [1594]',[38] but the list also shows that Roberts acquired the rights to Charlewood's former properties not mentioned in that transfer, namely *The Playe of the Foure PP, The Play of the Wether*, and *A Play of Loue*.

William Jaggard followed Roberts as the printer of playbills, getting the monopoly in 1606 (according to Katharine's F. Pantzer's index in the *Short Title Catalogue*) or in 1608 (according to McKerrow's *Dictionary of Printers*), and when he printed George Wilkins's *The Miseries of Inforst Mariage* for George Vincent, Jaggard produced a title-page claiming that the book represented the play '*As it is now playd by his Maiesties Seruants*' (see Figure 32).[39] Such a reference to ongoing performance at the time of printing was new, and it is tempting to wonder if Jaggard's experience of printing playbills had something to do with it. Although he had not yet the monopoly, since December 1602 Jaggard had been printing playbills for certain playing companies upon payment of monthly fees to monopoly holder James Roberts;[40] Jaggard had been seeking the right to print playbills as early as 23 April 1593.[41] Stern pointed out that a printed playbill would have provided ready copy for a play title-page, and wondered if the dramatist might not be expected to phrase such promotional material,[42] while Alan B. Farmer and Zachary Lesser noted that 'the ultimate decision lay with publishers, for they had all legal rights over the copy'.[43] A publisher who was producing playbills was likely to think of plays in the present and future tenses rather more strongly than one who was overtly presenting a post-performance text, and perhaps without consciously knowing it Jaggard started to phrase his title-pages to match this new conception of the relationship between book and performance. Whoever was responsible, the 'As it is now play[e]d' phrasing appeared in another play publication of 1607: John Day, William Rowley, and George Wilkins's *The Travailes of the Three English Brothers*,[44] printed by George Eld for John Wright (see Figure 33).

Another publisher's output here intersects with the change in how title-pages characterize their relation to performance around 1605–10. Nathaniel Butter achieved freedom of the Stationers' Company by patronage on 20 February 1604 and as Sidney Lee's entry for him in the old *Dictionary of National Biography* observed, Butter's early career was founded on sensational reports of various kinds, including one[45] that became the sole source for the apocryphal Shakespeare play *A Yorkshire Tragedy*,[46] and from 1622 he 'made journalism his chief business'.[47]

THE
Miſeries of Inforſt
MARIAGE.

As it is now playd by his Maieſlies
Seruants.

Qui Alios, (ſeipſum) docet.

By George Wilkins.

LONDON
Printed for George Vincent, and are to be ſold at his ſhop in
Woodſtreet.   1607.

Figure 32   Title-page of George Wilkins's *The Miseries of Inforst Mariage*, printed by William Jaggard for George Vincent in 1607. Reproduced by permission of The Huntington Library, San Marino, California

THE
TRAVAILES

Of

The three ENGLISH Brothers.

Sir THOMAS
Sir ANTHONY } SHIRLEY.
M.r ROBERT

As it is now play'd by her
MAIESTIES Seruants.
By J. Day, &c.

Printed at London for *Iohn Wright*, and are to bee fold at
his fhoppe neere Chrift-Church gate.
1 6 0 7.

Figure 33 Title-page of John Day, William Rowley, and George Wilkins's *The Travailes of the Three English Brothers*, printed by George Eld for John Wright in 1607. Reproduced by permission of The Huntington Library, San Marino, California

Butter's early work included anti-Catholic texts such as Thomas Bell's *The Downe-fall of Poperie*[48] and a prose treatise of 1607 called *The Jesuites Play at Lyons*.[49] This book claims to report a performance, but the report is so strange that we must doubt its veracity. Dramatizing the Christian day of judgement, French Jesuits apparently took the roles of God, Christ, and the virgin Mary, and commanding all the fiends of hell they 'seased on christian princes' including Henry VIII, Edward VI, and Elizabeth I and sent them to hell.[50] The text retains a narrative frame: the reporter tells us what happened in the performance, and hence this is a prose story of the performance rather than the raw material for the performance itself. The narrator wants to get so much of the script into the report that the framing device is something of an intrusion, and at one point[51] a 150-word speech is conveyed verbatim; one wonders if the narrator was tempted to dispense with it and simply give the alternating speeches with their speech prefixes.

One might say that any published playscript is a report of performance with the narrative frame dissolved and the words spoken presented as themselves. The anti-Catholic author of *The Jesuites Play at Lyons* uses the narrative frame to comment on the performance, and without it the raw material would be open to fresh interpretative possibilities and might even permit it to originate fresh performances, to the peril of unwitting actors and audiences. The following year, 1608, Butter published George Wilkins's prose novella *The Painfull Adventures of Pericles Prince of Tyre*, which stands in a similar relation to the King's Men's play about Pericles as the report stands to the putative performance at Lyons: the 'true History of the Play of *Pericles*, as it was lately presented by the worthy and ancient Poet *John Gower*'.[52] Thus Gower is cast as the medium of the presentation (and Wilkins himself as a subsequent medium) rather than a fictional character within the play. To this the titling of Henry Gosson's 1609 quarto of *Pericles* sounds like something of a response, calling itself 'THE LATE And much admired Play, Called Pericles, Prince of Tyre'.[53] This refers back to recent ('late') performance but also seems to insist that whereas the prose novella was a history of the play, here now *is* the play, unmediated: it is 'THE...Play'.

Butter had the previous year, 1608, published another Shakespeare play with a title-page that refers back to a past performance and to the same company's ongoing performances. The title-page of the Pide Bull quarto of *King Lear*, printed for Butter by Nicholas Okes, indicated that the contents represented the chronicle history '*As it was played before the Kings Maiestie at Whitehall vpon* | *S.* Stephens *night in Christmas Hollidayes.* | By his Maiesties seruants playing vsually at the Gloabe | on the Bancke-side'.[54] This phrasing was picked up by another stationer, Williams Jones, when publishing another King's men's play, the anonymous *Mucedorus* in 1610, as we shall shortly see. The title-page of the first printing of *Mucedorus* 12 years earlier refers to the contents as 'Very delectable and full of mirth' and refers back, somewhat vaguely, to past performance by claiming that it is 'Newly set foorth, as it hath bin | *sundrie times plaide in the ho* | *norable Cittie of London*'. On the reverse of the title-page is a doubling chart demonstrating that 'Eight persons may easily play it'.[55] This is the same advertising point – that fresh performances can originate from the printing – that we saw made on Tudor interludes' title-pages, although, being placed here on the reverse of the title-page, it would not have been visible in uncut copies of the book. If, however, extra copies of title-pages were printed for display on a bookseller's stall, as Alan B. Farmer and Zachary Lesser maintain,[56] it could presumably have worked as an added inducement to buy. Like many books, the title-page of *Mucedorus* begins with a gathering of four leaves made from one printed sheet, and in such cases it is hard to see how such extra copies of the title-page could have been printed without also printing the first few hundred lines of the play, unless the forme were remade to use half-sheet imposition, which would still produce two unwanted pages from the start of the play. Perhaps some kind of quarter-sheet imposition was employed; with no surviving examples of advertising title-pages we may never know how they were made.

Nor may we ever know whether the reverse of a title-page (which in complete books is often left blank) was also used for promotional purposes. In 1610 the stationer Williams Jones republished *Mucedorus* as 'Amplified with new additions' reflecting how it had recently been performed at Whitehall '*By his Highnes Seruantes vsually | playing at the Globe*',[57] which phrasing echoes the 'playing vsually at the Gloabe' of the Shakespeare *King Lear* quarto of 1608. The doubling chart moved from the reverse of the title-page to the reverse of the prologue on the next leaf, and showed that two more actors were now needed for the new parts of '*King Valencla*' and '*Anselmo*', so that 'Ten [formerly eight] persons may esily play it'. In the meantime – that is, between the 1598 and 1610 printings of *Mucedorus* – appeared a play perhaps written by Thomas Heywood called *The Fayre Mayde of the Exchange*. It too has a doubling chart, printed underneath the phrasing familiar from Tudor interludes that indicates the intention that the book originate fresh performances: 'Eleauen may easily acte this Comedie'.[58] Although the title-page makes no reference to past performance, it describes the contents as 'Very delectable, and full of mirth', the exact phrase used on the first edition of the period's only other play to be printed with a doubling chart, *Mucedorus*. It appears that something was happening in the second half of the first decade of the seventeenth century to make publishers think that it was worth describing their printed plays in terms that emphasized their capacity to originate fresh performances rather than reflect on past performances, although if we want to be sure that such developments were related to perceived promotional value we should confine ourselves to what is on the front of a title-page, not its reverse nor what appeared further inside the printed book.

Xylographic 'THE'

I mentioned that no play before *Pericles* is called a play on its title-page, which is true, but there had been a reference to *plays*, plural. *The Conspiracie, and Tragedie of Charles Duke of Byron* was the title of a printing of both parts of George Chapman's two-parter about the recent trial and execution of the Marshal of France. Its title-page claimed that the contents were 'Acted lately in two playes, at the Black-friers',[59] and these performances caused such grave offence that all the playhouses were for a time closed and Henry Evans, impresario of the Children of the Blackfriars, surrendered his lease to Richard Burbage in August 1608.[60] The wording of Thomas Thorpe's edition does not actually call the contents of his book the two plays – the *Pericles* quarto remains the first to do that since the Tudor interludes – but rather says that the book's contents were 'acted...in' two plays. But there is another curious connection between the printing and ones we have been considering that seem to show a growing sense of the printed text as a part of, rather than a recapturing of, the performance matrix. The first word on the title-page of the 1608 printing of *The Conspiracie, and Tragedie of Charles Duke of Byron* is a xylographic (that is, woodcut) *'THE'* that Greg labelled 'block 1', and in his reference list entry of Notabilia he recorded:

> xylographs (lettering cut on wood): 'The' block 1 [203(a-c), 242(a)], block 2 [148(b), 243(a), 264(b), 308], block 2* [249(b, c)], block 3 [256(a)]; 'Al Fooles' [219]; black-letter headings [412(c)]; and cf. woodcut in [414][61]

Greg died before completing this volume of his bibliography, and the index entry does not fully reflect what he knew and recorded in the preceding descriptions. For example, his descriptions of items 142e, 204a, 204c, 222, 274, 275 record use of the blocks but are not referred to in this index entry.

By his designations 'block 1', 'block 2', 'block 2*', and 'block 3' Greg appears to have meant that each is a particular design of woodcut letter, not particular pieces of wood reused in different printings. But in fact 'block 1' is a single piece of wood used in different printings by different printers. In 1604 Valentine Simmes printed John Marston's *The Malcontent* for William Aspley with 'block 1' on its title-page[62] and to within fractions of a millimetre (attributable to paper expansion or contraction, and the vagaries of inking) the internal and external dimensions of the xylograph in British Library copy C.34.e.17 match those of the same block design on the title-page of Simmes's 1604 printing of Thomas Dekker and Thomas Middleton's *The Honest Whore* for John Hodgets,[63] British Library copy at C.34.c.24. There are no obvious defects in the xylograph that one might use to determine with certainty that these two Simmes printings were made using the same piece of wood, but that is the obvious inference from the virtually identical dimensions.

No earlier play printing had such a xylographic *'THE'* on its title-page, but four others soon followed. In 1605 Thomas Creede printed *The London Prodigall* for Nathaniel Butter with the 'block 1' design on its title-page[64] and in the British Library copy at C.34.l.3 it has precisely the dimensions of the one on the Simmes title-pages for *The Malcontent* and *The Honest Whore*. Moreover, in this printing there are a number of defects visible in the woodcut that enable us to determine that the next three times it appeared on play title-pages the same piece of wood was used: the top right serif of the T has chipped, the right side of the central horizontal bar of the H has taken ink (become filled where it should be hollow), the outer edge of curve in the top left corner of the E has worn away (taken no ink) where it comes closest to the top-right corner of the H before it, and the bottom edge of the bottom horizontal bar of the E has a small chip that the serif of the central bar points to. Those next three times this xylographic *'THE'* appears on a play title-page are: Chapman's *The Gentleman Usher*[65] printed in 1606 by Valentine Simmes for Thomas Thorpe, Heywood's? *The Fayre Mayde of the Exchange*[66] printed by persons unknown in 1607 for Henry Rocket, and Chapman's *The Conspiracie, and Tragedie of Charles Duke of Byron*[67] printed in 1608 by George Eld for Thomas Thorpe. The British Library copies of these (at C.12.g.4 (5), C.57.e.27 and C.30.e.2 respectively) show identical defects to the *'THE'* on the title-page of *The London Prodigall*, so these four plays' title-pages at least were printed using the same piece of wood. The two title-pages of 1604 by Simmes were made either with the same woodcut before it started to show wear, or from a woodcut that was virtually identical to the one subsequently used by Simmes, Creede, Rocket's unnamed printer, and Eld. The obvious inference, made by Akihiro Yamada and by Paul Edmondson, is that Simmes lent his decorative xylograph to men with whom he shared printing, as Creede and Eld were.[68]

Whatever the explanation, putting a xylographic *'THE'* as the first word of a play title-page became quite a popular thing to do, as seen in Middleton's *The Phoenix*[69] in 1607, Dekker and John Webster's *The Famous History of Sir Thomas Wyat*[70] in 1607, Wilkins's *The Miseries of Inforst Mariage*[71] when reprinted in 1611 and 1629, the anonymous *The Merry Devill of Edmonton*[72] when reprinted in 1612, Elizabeth Carew's *The Tragedie of Mariam*[73] in 1613, and the anonymous *The Famous Victories of Henry the Fifth*[74] when reprinted in 1617. The size and unusual design of the xylograph might, as Edmondson put it, 'suggest that this play-text is the definitive article; the most longed for particular; the one and only'.[75] On the other hand Simmes's use of the xylograph on half a dozen non-dramatic printings supports Ferguson's suggestion that it was simply a convenient means to express the printer's preference for the first line of a title-page being a large *'THE'*.[76] Since over half the play titles in the period began with 'The', this decorative block was an economical way to embellish title-pages. The full list of publications in which Simmes used the xylograph was given by Ferguson[77] and includes the first edition of Michel de Montaigne's essays[78] and the second edition of Laurence Twine's version of the Apollonius of Tyre (= Pericles) story[79] that Wilkins plagiarized heavily to make his prose novella *The Painfull Adventures of Pericles Prince of Tyre*. Indeed whenever his memory of the play he had written with Shakespeare failed him, Wilkins simply copied from Twine's book.[80] There is no reason to suppose that this particular connection with Wilkins via the xylograph is anything but coincidence.

Let me review the narrative so far. Around 1600–10, the front matter of printed plays began to suggest a new way of thinking about the relationship between performance and printed book. Instead of only harking back to past performances, title-pages began to refer to ongoing performances – '*As it is now play[']d*' (*The Miseries of Inforst Marriage* 1607 and *The Travailes of the Three English Brothers* 1607) and '*playing vsually* [or *vsually playing*] *at the Glo*[a]*be*' (*King Lear* 1608 and *Mucedorus* 1610) – and referred to their own ability to generate new performances by printing doubling charts (*Mucedorus* 1598 and *The Fayre Mayde of the Exchange*

1607). Around the same time the word 'play' began to appear in the titles of textual versions of performances for the first time since the mid-sixteenth century, first in such misrepresentations as Nashe's *Lenten Stuffe* (1599), Vennard's *England's Joy* advertisement (1602), and R. S.'s *The Jesuites Play at Lyons* (1607), and then quite genuinely in the 1609 quarto of *Pericles*. At the same time, a xylographic '*THE*' began to appear on play title-pages, the first six examples being *The Malcontent* (1604) *The Honest Whore* (1604), *The London Prodigall* (1605), *The Gentleman Usher* (1606), *The Fayre Mayde of the Exchange* (1607) and *The Conspiracie, and Tragedie of Byron* (1607). As should now be apparent, much of this evidence can be linked to the King's Men: *The Miseries of Inforst Marriage, King Lear, Mucedorus, Pericles*, and *The London Prodigall* were written for them, *The Malcontent* was a Blackfriars boys' play that they stole, and *The Conspiracie, and Tragedie of Byron* got the Blackfriars boys out of the Burbages's indoor playhouse, allowing the King's Men to occupy it. These links may not be significant, for the King's Men were the most successful troupe and there was a great deal happening around them.

The Simpsons and the primordiality of text

What was happening around 1600–10 that might have caused this shift in the purported relation between performance and print? We may never know for sure, but certain coincidences present themselves. The 1590s had been the heyday of the open-air amphitheatres in London, with two companies (the Chamberlain's Men and the Admiral's Men) settled at two venues (the Theatre and the Rose) since 1594 and enjoying what Andrew Gurr characterized as settled practices made possible by their state-enforced duopoly of London playing.[81] Free of competition, these two companies developed enormous repertories, built a large customer base, earned vast quantities of money, and their star players acquired great personal fame. When James Burbage opened the Theatre in 1576 there had been competition of sorts from the semi-professional boys performing indoors at the Blackfriars and St Paul's, but the former ended in 1584,[82] and the latter in 1590.[83] Throughout the 1590s the professional adults had it all their own way, but at the turn of the century both boy companies started again.[84] Perhaps renewed interest in indoor playing by non-professionals – the mode of consumption that the Tudor interludes were marketed for – helped change readers' conception of the purpose of a printed play book.

Another possibility – an alternative or an addition to the one just offered – is a change regarding provincial touring. In a ground-breaking essay, Alan Somerset showed that far from being disconsolate meandering while barred from London during plague, provincial touring was highly organized, profitable, and attractive to the players.[85] Indeed, the King's Men toured more often and more widely under this name than they had as the Chamberlain's Men, even when there was no prohibition on playing in London and even though they were pre-eminent there. Somerset speculates that their licence (the patent issued to the company) not only allowed them but also to a degree commanded them to play throughout the realm.[86] One of the well-known effects of the arrival of travelling players is the renewal of interest in playing among those who are visited; Hamlet is typical in this regard. Travelling players might acquire their repertory by buying printed play texts, and in such a case the book would indeed precede rather than recapture a performance. For particular performances, the players or a patron (such as Hamlet) might insert additional material so that the performance exceeded the printed book on which it was based.

The matter of a performance exceeding print was of considerable importance to the playing company led by Robert and Christopher Simpson. Their patron Richard Cholmley was in London for the abortive Essex coup of 1601, for which he was imprisoned and fined; presumably it was to entertain such men that Essex's supporters paid the King's Men for a performance of *Richard II* at the Globe on 7 February 1601. Charles Forker thought that this performance must have included the deposition scene that was not printed until Q4 (1608), else 'the play could hardly have been thought to serve the rebels' political ends',[87] whereas David M. Bergeron long ago maintained that the scene probably did not yet exist and in any case it evokes so much sympathy for Richard that the rebels would have preferred the play without it.[88] Janet Clare pointed out that book censorship seems to have been no more severe than theatrical censorship, so the absence of the scene from the first three quartos strongly suggests that it was not performed else 'it would surely have been possible for the publisher, Matthew Lawe, to have obtained a fair copy prepared for stage use'.[89] There is ample evidence that a written text might contain more than was performed, whether because the actors cut what they did not want to use – as Humphrey Moseley claimed in the preliminaries of the Beaumont and Fletcher Folio[90] – or, to look at essentially the same phenomenon another way, because the company had a 'maximal' text authorized by the Master of the Revels but only ever played a subset of it, the 'minimal' text suited to the particularies of occasion and cast.[91]

The cutting of an allowed written text for performance is a practice that early modern theatre history can easily accommodate within its current set of working assumptions, but we have tended to draw a line regarding the writing of dramatic material solely for publication. Joseph Loewenstein argued that Ben Jonson is the central figure here, and that his carving out of an authorial identity for himself was 'a groping forward toward later authorial property rights within a bourgeois cultural marketplace, but modelled on the ethos of the classical *auctor* and the economics of patronage'.[92] Jonson certainly wrote and rewrote for publication, but Lukas Erne's suggestion that Shakespeare too deliberately wrote material intended for the printed page not the theatre stage would, if accepted, upturn many of our assumptions.[93] In Erne's explanation of the publication of Shakespeare's play a marked shift is discernible around the turn of the century (that is, coinciding with the shift we have been examining): the market for printed plays was glutted[94] and there was more live and printed drama available once the boy companies restarted and their plays were printed.[95] Broadening the appeal of printed plays – going beyond the simple recapture of open-air amphitheatre performance – might have been a marketing response to such pressure.

That a printed play contained no less than was performed was crucial to the defence mounted by the actors from the Simpsons company that were made to give an account of themselves at the trial of Sir John Yorke.[96] In Yorke's house on 2 February 1609 the company performed a play about Saint Christopher, which subject could offend no one had not the players inserted a interlude in which a Catholic priest disputed with and overcame a Protestant minister, and had him carried away amid theatrical thunder-and-lightning by a devil. (That this sounds much like the scene from *The Jesuites Play at Lyons* described above, which also used 'inuented Fyre-workes',[97] is itself a lesson in how similar narrative descriptions can derive from performances that present wildly different religious meanings.) The witnesses from the playing company knew that the charge against Yorke centred on this interpolated scene, and Richard Simpson insisted that 'That booke by which he and the other persons did act the said play...was a prynted book, And they onlie acted the same according to the contents...and not otherwise'.[98]

As well as the obvious perjury in this testimony – no authorized book about *Saint Christopher* could contain the scene described – we might suspect disingenuousness by Simpson: in all innocence, he seems to imply, we here in Yorkshire assumed that whatever was published in London must have been properly approved. Sisson even wondered if the company invented the book that they claimed to perform *Saint Christopher* from, 'of which no trace appears to remain',[99] but the other three printed playbooks cited by the players in their testimony are well known to us: *The Travailes of the Three English Brothers*,[100] called by them 'The Three Shirleys',[101] and 'Perocles, prince of Tire, And the other was Kinge Lere'.[102] No doubt 'Perocles' was *Pericles*[103] and 'Kinge Lere' was either the anonymous chronicle play[104] or Shakespeare's.[105]

If 'Kinge Lere' was Shakespeare's play, then all three plays we know this company performed from printed texts were among the first whose title-page show the shift from a backward-looking relationship with performance ('as it hath been acted') to a present-tense phrasing on its way to becoming the Janus-face relation that included the possibility of the printed book originating fresh performances. The title-page of Day, Rowley, and Wilkins's *The Travailes of the Three English Brothers*[106] was joint-first to use the '*As it is now play'd*' phrasing, the title-page of Shakespeare's *King Lear* was first to inform the reader that the actors could be found '*playing vsually at the Gloabe*'.[107] Before *Pericles* no one had thought to put 'THE...Play' on a printed drama's title-page[108] since the Tudor interlude printings that foregrounded their capacity to originate performance. Two people recur in this pattern: Wilkins as writer of two of the three plays (and of *The Miseries of Inforst Mariage*, the other joint-first to use '*As it is now played*' on its title-page), and Butter as publisher of *King Lear* and of Wilkins's prose novella version of the play *Pericles* called *The Painfull Adventures of Pericles Prince of Tyre*.[109]

In all likelihood there is an element of random coincidence at work here, and that if Wilkins and Butter were indeed responsible for these innovative phrasings, they were not conscious of the novelty. In their everday work of writing and publishing I do not suppose that these men thought terribly hard about the significance of present-tense and future-tense locutions, for they worked to produce and disseminate performances and books for money. But it would, I think, be stretching coincidence to say that the playing company in Yorkshire that bought these books and performed what was in them were unaffected by the new phrasing. It would be a remarkable coincidence indeed if the three plays that betray the new forward thinking were by chance the ones that the Simpsons' company happened upon. It seems more likely that the actors picked up what was implied by this shift in how title-pages characterized their relationship to performance, and when challenged they excused themselves with the assertion that the books, not the players, were the authors of their performances.

Notes

1. William Shakespeare, *[Richard 2] The Tragedie of King Richard the Second*, STC 22307 (Q1) BEPD 141a (London: Valentine Simmes for Andrew Wise, 1597), A1r.
2. William Shakespeare, *[Troilus and Cressida] The Historie of Troylus and Cresseida. As it Was Acted, Etcetera*, STC 22331 BEPD 279a1 (Qa) (London: George Eld for Richard Bonian and Henry Walley, 1609), A1r.
3. William Shakespeare, *[Troilus and Cressida] The Famous Historie of Troylus and Cresseid*, STC 22332 BEPD 279a2 (Qb) (London: George Eld for Richard Bonian and Henry Walley, 1609), ¶1r.
4. Gary Taylor, '*Troilus and Cressida*: Bibliography, Performance, and Interpretation', *Shakespeare Studies*, 15 (1982), 99–136 (pp. 118–21).
5. Shakespeare, *[Troilus and Cressida] The Famous Historie of Troylus and Cresseid*, ¶2v.
6. C. J. Sisson, 'Shakespeare Quartos as Prompt-copies', *Review of English Studies*, 18 (1942), 129–43.
7. G. W. Boddy, 'Players of Interludes in North Yorkshire in the Early Seventeenth Century', *North Yorkshire Country Records Office Journal*, 3 (1976), 95–130.
8. Peter Holland, 'Theatre Without Drama: Reading REED', in *From Script to Stage in Early Modern England*, ed. Peter Holland and Stephen Orgel (Basingstoke: Palgrave Macmillan, 2004), 43–67.
9. Anonymous, *The True Chronicle History of King Leir, and His Three Daughters*, STC 15343 BEPD 213 (London: Simon Stafford for John Wright, 1605).
10. John Rastell, *A New Iuterlude [Sic] and a Merry of the Nature of the Iiij Elements*, STC 20722 BEPD 6 (London: [John Rastell], 1520?), A1r.
11. Henry Medwall, *Here is Co[n]teyned a Godely Interlude of Fulgens Cenatoure of Rome*, STC 17778 BEPD 1, 2 (London: John Rastell, 1512–16).
12. W. W. Greg, *A Bibliography of the English Printed Drama to the Restoration*, 4 vols (London: Bibliographical Society, 1970), 1:82.
13. Anonymous, *Here Begynneth a Propre Newe Interlude of the Worlde and the Chylde, Otherwise Called [Mundus and Infans]*, STC 25982 BEPD 5 (London: Wynkun de Worde, 1522).
14. Anonymous, *[Little Gest of Robin Hood] A Mery Geste of Robyn Hoode and of His Lyfe, Wyth a Newe Playe for to be Plaied in May-games*, STC 13691 BEPD 32a (London: William Copland, 1560?), A1r.
15. Nathaniel Woodes, *An Excellent New Commedie, Intituled: The Conflict of Conscience. Contayninge, the Most Lamentable Hystorie, of the Desperation of Frauncis Spera*, STC 25966 BEPD 78A1 (London: Richard Bradock, 1581), A1r.
16. Richard Edwards, *Damon and Pithias*, STC 7514 BEPD 58a (London: [William Williamson for] Richard Jones, 1571), A1r; Richard Edwards, *Damon and Pithias*, STC 7515 BEPD 58b (London: Richard Jones, 1582), A1r.
17. Christopher Marlowe and Thomas Nashe, *The Tragedie of Dido Queene of Carthage*, STC 17441 BEPD 128 (London: The widow Orwin for Thomas Woodcocke, 1594), A1r.
18. John Heywood, *The Playe Called the Foure PP*, STC 13300 BEPD 21a (London: Wyllyam Myddylton, 1544?), A1r; John Heywood, *The Playe Called the Foure PP*, STC 13301 BEPD

21b (London: Wyllyam Copland, 1560?), A1r; John Heywood, *The Playe Called the Foure PP*, STC 13302 BEPD 21c (London: John Allde, 1569), A1r.

19. John Heywood, *A Play of Loue*, STC 13303 BEPD 16a (London: W[illiam] Rastell, 1534), A1r.

20. John Heywood, *The Play of the Wether*, STC 13305 BEPD 15a (London: William Rastell, 1533), A1r; John Heywood, *The Play of the Wether*, STC 13305.5 BEPD 15b (London: [William Middleton], 1544?), A1r; John Heywood, *The Play of the Wether*, STC 13306 BEPD 15c (London: [John Tisdale for] Anthony Kitson, c.1560), A1r; John Heywood, *The Play of the Wether*, STC 13307 BEPD 15d (London: John (=Sampson) Awdely, c.1573), A1r.

21. Anonymous, *[Little Gest of Robin Hood] A Mery Geste of Robyn Hoode and of His Lyfe, Wyth a Newe Playe for to be Plaied in May-games*, A1r.

22. William Shakespeare and George Wilkins, *[Pericles] The Late, and Much Admired Play Called Pericles, Prince of Tyre*, STC 22334 BEPD 284a (Q1) (London: [William White] for Henry Gosson, 1609), A1r.

23. Shakespeare & Wilkins, *[Pericles] The Late, and Much Admired Play Called Pericles, Prince of Tyre*, D1r.

24. Thomas Nash, *Nashes Lenten Stuffe, Containing, the Description of Great Yarmouth. With a New Playe of the Praise of the Red Herring*, STC 18370 (London: [Thomas Judson and Valentine Simmes] for Nicholas L[ing (Lyng)] and C[uthbert] B[urby], 1599), A1r.

25. Richard Vennard, *The Plot of the Play, Called Englands Joy. To be Playd at the Swan This 6 of November 1602*, STC 24636.7 (London: [John Windet], 1602).

26. Tiffany Stern, ' "On Each Wall / And Corner Poast": Playbills, Title-pages, and Advertising in Early Modern London', *English Literary Renaissance*, (forthcoming).

27. Stern, ' "On Each Wall / And Corner Poast": Playbills, Title-pages, and Advertising in Early Modern London'; R. B. McKerrow, 'Booksellers, Printers, and the Stationers' Trade', in *Shakespeare's England*, ed. Sidney Lee and C. T. Onions (Oxford: Clarendon Press, 1916), 2:212–39 (p. 232).

28. Peter W. M. Blayney, 'The Publication of Playbooks', in *A New History of Early English Drama*, ed. John D. Cox and David Scott Kastan (New York: Columbia University Press, 1997), 383–422 (p. 390).

29. Edward Arber, ed., *A Transcript of the Registers of the Company of Stationers of London 1554–1640*, 5 vols (London: Privately printed, 1875), II:477.

30. Arber, ed., *A Transcript of the Registers of the Company of Stationers of London 1554–1640*, 2:651–2.

31. A. W. Pollard and G. R. Redgrave, *A Short-title Catalogue of Books Printed in England, Scotland, Ireland and of English Books Printed Abroad 1475–1640*, 2nd edn, 3 vols (London: The Bibliographical Society, 1991), 3:145; Ronald B. McKerrow, ed., *A Dictionary of Printers and Booksellers in England, Scotland and Ireland, and of Foreign Printers of English Books 1557–1640* (London: The Bibliographical Society, 1910), 229.

32. Edward Arber, ed., *A Transcript of the Registers of the Company of Stationers of London 1554–1640 AD*, 5 vols (London: Privately Printed, 1876), 3:575.

33. Pollard & Redgrave, *A Short-title Catalogue*, 3:90–1.

34. Arber, ed., *A Transcript of the Registers of the Company of Stationers of London 1554–1640 AD*, 4:182.

35. Ibid., 2:405–6.

36. Lewis Wager, *Life and Repentance of Marie Magdalene*, STC 24932 BEPD 47A (London: John Charlewood, 1566), A1r.

37. William Herbert, *Typographical Antiquities, or an Historical Account of the Origin and Progress of Printing in Great Britain and Ireland: Containing Memoirs of Our Ancient Printers, and a Register of Book Printed By Them, from the Year 1471 to the Year 1600, Begun By the Late Joseph Ames*, 3 vols (London: Privately printed for the editor, 1786), 2:1032.

38. Arber, ed., *A Transcript of the Registers of the Company of Stationers of London 1554–1640*, 2:651.

39. George Wilkins, *The Miseries of Inforst Mariage. As it is Now Playd*, STC 25635 BEPD 249a (London: [William Jaggard] for George Vincent, 1607), A1r.

40. William A. Jackson, ed., *Records of the Court of the Stationers' Company 1602 to 1640* (London: The Bibliographical Society, 1957), 1–2, 6.

41. W. W. Greg and E. Boswell, eds., *Records of the Court of the Stationers' Company 1576 to 1602 from Register B* (London: The Bibliographical Society, 1930), 46.

42. Stern, ' "On Each Wall / And Corner Poast": Playbills, Title-pages, and Advertising in Early Modern London'.

43. Alan B. Farmer and Zachary Lesser, 'Vile Arts: The Marketing of English Printed Drama, 1512–1660', *Research Opportunities in Renaissance Drama*, 39 (2000), 77–165 (104n9).

44. John Day, William Rowley and George Wilkins, *The Travailes of the Three English Brothers: Sir Thomas, Sir Anthony, and Master Robert Shirley*, STC 6417 BEPD 248A1, A2 (London: [George Eld] for John Wright, 1607), A1r.

45. Anonymous, *Two Most Unnatural and Bloodie Murthers: the One By Maister Caverly, a Yorkshire Gentleman. The Other, By Mistris Browne*, STC 18288 (London: Valentine S[immes] for Nathaniel Butter, 1605).

46. William Shakespeare, *A Yorkshire Tragedy. Not so New as Lamentable and True . . . Written By W. Shakspeare*, STC 22340 BEPD 272a (London: R[ichard] B[raddock] for Thomas Pavier, 1608).

47. George Smith, Leslie Stephen and Sidney Lee, eds., *The Dictionary of National Biography: From the Earliest Times to 1900*, 22 vols (Oxford: Oxford University Press, 1937–38), III:547.

48. Thomas Bell, *The Downefall of Poperie: Proposed By Way of a New Challenge to English Jesuits*, STC 1818.5 (formerly 1817) (London: for Nathaniel Butter, 1604).

49. R. S, *The Jesuites Play at Lyons in France, as it Was There Presented*, STC 21513.5 (London: [William Jaggard and John Windet] for Nathaniel Butter, 1607).

50. Ibid., C4v.

51. Ibid., B3v.

52. George Wilkins, *The Painfull Adventures of Pericles Prince of Tyre. Being the True History of the Play of Pericles, as Presented By J. Gower*, STC 25638.5 [formerly 19628] (London: T[homas] P[urfoot] for Nat[haniel] Butter, 1608), A1r.

53. Shakespeare & Wilkins, *[Pericles] The Late, and Much Admired Play Called Pericles, Prince of Tyre*, A1r.

54. William Shakespeare, *[King Lear] M. William Shak-speare: His True Chronicle Historie of the Life and Death of King Lear and His Three Daughters*, STC 22292 BEPD 265a (Q1) (London: [Nicholas Okes] for Nathaniel Butter, 1608), A2r.

55. Anonymous, *A Most Pleasant Comedie of Mucedorus. Newly Set Foorth*, STC 18230 BEPD 151a (London: for William Jones, 1598).

56. Farmer & Lesser, 'Vile Arts: The Marketing of English Printed Drama, 1512–1660', 78.

57. Anonymous, *A Most Pleasant Comedie of Mucedorus. Amplified with New Additions*, STC 18232 BEPD 151c (London: [William White] for William Jones, 1610).

58. Anonymous [possibly Thomas Heywood], *The Fayre Mayde of the Exchange*, STC 13317 BEPD 242a (London: [Valentine Simmes for] Henry Rocket, 1607), A2r.

59. George Chapman, *The Conspiracie, and Tragedie of Charles Duke of Byron, Marshall of France. Acted Lately in Two Playes*, STC 4968 BEPD 274a, 275a (London: G[eorge] Eld for Thomas Thorpe, sold [by Laurence Lisle], 1608), A1r.

60. E. K. Chambers, *The Elizabethan Stage*, 4 vols (Oxford: Clarendon, 1923), 2:53–5.

61. W. W. Greg, *A Bibliography of the English Printed Drama to the Restoration*, 3:1642.

62. John Marston, *The Malcontent*, STC 17479 BEPD 203c (London: V[alentine] S[immes] for William Aspley, 1604), A1r.

63. Thomas Dekker and Thomas Middleton, *The Honest Whore, With, the Humours of the Patient Man, and the Longing Wife*, STC 6501 BEPD 204a (London: V[alentine] S[immes] for John Hodgets, 1604), A1r.

64. Anonymous, *The London Prodigall. As it Was Plaide By the Kings Majesties Servants. By W. Shakespeare*, STC 22333 BEPD 222a (London: T[homas] C[reede] for Nathaniel Butter, 1605), A1r.

65. George Chapman, *The Gentleman Usher*, STC 4978 BEPD 226 (London: V[alentine] S[immes] for Thomas Thorpe, 1606), A1r.

66. Anonymous [possibly Thomas Heywood], *The Fayre Mayde of the Exchange*, A1r.

67. Chapman, *The Conspiracie, and Tragedie of Charles Duke of Byron, Marshall of France. Acted Lately in Two Playes*, A1r.

68. Akihiro Yamada, *Thomas Creede: Printer to Shakespeare and His Contemporaries* (Tokyo: Meisei University Press, 1994), 72–3; Paul Edmondson, *A Critical Edition of* The London Prodigal, Unpublished Ph.D. thesis (Birmingham: University of Birmingham, 2001), 2, 22–3; W. Craig Ferguson, *Valentine Simmes: Printer to Drayton, Shakespeare, Chapman, Greene, Dekker, Middleton, Daniel, Jonson, Marlowe, Marston, Heywood, and Other Elizabethans* (Charlottesville VA: Bibliographical Society of the University of Virginia, 1968), 88.

69. Thomas Middleton, *The Phoenix, as it Hath Been Acted*, STC 17892 BEPD 243a (London: E[dward] A[llde] for A[rthur] J[ohnson], 1607), A1r.

70. Thomas Dekker and John Webster, *The Famous History of Sir Thomas Wyat. With the Coronation of Queen Mary. Written By Thomas Dickers, and John Webster*, STC 6537 BEPD 256a (London: E[dward] A[llde] for Thomas Archer, 1607), A1r.

71. George Wilkins, *The Miseries of Inforst Mariage*, STC 25636 BEPD 249b (London: [William White] for George Vincent, 1611), A1r; George Wilkins, *The Miseries of Inforst Mariage*, STC 25637 BEPD 249c (London: Aug[ustine] Mathewes for Richard Thrale, 1629), A1r.

72. Anonymous, *The Merry Devill of Edmonton*, STC 7494 BEPD 264b (London: Thomas Creede for Arthur Johnson, 1612), A2r.

73. Elizabeth Carew, *The Tragedie of Mariam, the Faire Queene of Jewry. Written By That Noble Ladie, E. C.*, STC 4613 BEPD 308A1, A2 (London: Thomas Creede for Richard Hawkins, 1613), π2r.

74. Anonymous, *The Famous Victories of Henry the Fifth*, STC 13073 BEPD 148b1 (London: Bernard Alsop, 1617), A1r.

75. Edmondson, *A Critical Edition of* The London Prodigal, 22–3.

76. Ferguson, *Valentine Simmes*, 79.

77. Ferguson, *Valentine Simmes*, 53.

78. Michel de Montaigne, *The Essays or Morall, Politike and Millitarie Discourses . . . Done Into English By . . . John Florio*, STC 18041 (London: Valentine Simmes for Edward Blount, 1603).

79. Apollonius of Tyre, *The Patterne of Painefull Aduentures: Containing the Most Excellent, Pleasant, and Variable Historie of the Strange Accidents That Befell Vnto Prince Apollonius . . . Gathered Into English By T. [Sic] Twine*, STC 710 (London: Valentine Simmes, 1607).

80. Stanley Wells, Gary Taylor, John Jowett and William Montgomery, *William Shakespeare: A Textual Companion* (Oxford: Oxford University Press, 1987), 557–8.

81. Andrew Gurr, *The Shakespearian Playing Companies* (Oxford: Clarendon Press, 1996), 78–104.

82. Irwin Smith, *Shakespeare's Blackfriars Playhouse: Its History and Its Design* (New York: New York University Press, 1964), 130–52.

83. Reavley Gair, *The Children of Paul's: The Story of a Theatre Company, 1553–1608* (Cambridge: Cambridge University Press, 1982), 112.

84. Smith, *Shakespeare's Blackfriars Playhouse*, 175–209; Gair, *The Children of Paul's*, 113–8.

85. Alan Somerset, 'How Chances it They Travel?': Provincial Touring, Playing Places, and the King's Men', *Shakespeare Survey 47* (Cambridge: Cambridge University Press, 1994), 45–60.

86. Somerset, 'How Chances it They Travel?', 53.

87. William Shakespeare, *King Richard II*, ed. Charles R. Forker, The Arden Shakespeare (London: Thomson Learning, 2002), 10n2.

88. David M. Bergeron, 'The Deposition Scene in *Richard II*', *Renaissance Papers* (1974), 31–7 (p. 34).

89. Janet Clare, 'The Censorship of the Deposition Scene in *Richard II*', *Review of English Studies*, 44 (1990), 89–94 (p. 89).

90. John Fletcher and Francis Beaumont, *Comedies and Tragedies*, Wing B1581 (London: For Humphrey Robinson, and Humphrey Mosely, 1647), A4r.

91. Andrew Gurr, 'Maximal and Minimal Texts: Shakespeare v. the Globe', *Shakespeare Survey 52*, (Cambridge: Cambridge University Press, 1999), 68–87.

92. Joseph Loewenstein, 'The Script in the Marketplace', *Representations*, 12 (1985), 101–14 (p. 109).

93. Lukas Erne, 'Shakespeare and the Publication of His Plays', *Shakespeare Quarterly*, 53 (2002), 1–20; Lukas Erne, *Shakespeare as Literary Dramatist* (Cambridge: Cambridge University Press, 2003).

94. Blayney, 'The Publication of Playbooks', 384–9.

95. Erne, 'Shakespeare and the Publication of His Plays', 16.

96. Boddy, 'Players of Interludes in North Yorkshire in the Early Seventeenth Century', 104–7.

97. R. S., *The Jesuites Play at Lyons in France, as it Was There Presented*, B1v.

98. Boddy, 'Players of Interludes in North Yorkshire in the Early Seventeenth Century', 106.

99. Sisson, 'Shakespeare Quartos as Prompt-copies', 142.

100. Day, Rowley & Wilkins, *The Travailes of the Three English Brothers: Sir Thomas, Sir Anthony, and Master Robert Shirley.*

101. Boddy, 'Players of Interludes in North Yorkshire in the Early Seventeenth Century', 104.

102. Boddy, 'Players of Interludes in North Yorkshire in the Early Seventeenth Century', 106.

103. Shakespeare & Wilkins, *[Pericles] The Late, and Much Admired Play Called Pericles, Prince of Tyre.*

104. Anonymous, *The True Chronicle History of King Leir, and His Three Daughters.*

105. Shakespeare, *[King Lear] M. William Shak-speare: His True Chronicle Historie of the Life and Death of King Lear and His Three Daughters.*

106. Day, Rowley & Wilkins, *The Travailes of the Three English Brothers: Sir Thomas, Sir Anthony, and Master Robert Shirley*, A1r.

107. Shakespeare, *[King Lear] M. William Shak-speare: His True Chronicle Historie of the Life and Death of King Lear and His Three Daughters*, A2r.

108. Shakespeare & Wilkins, *[Pericles] The Late, and Much Admired Play Called Pericles, Prince of Tyre*, A1r.

109. Wilkins, *The Painfull Adventures of Pericles Prince of Tyre. Being the True History of the Play of Pericles, as Presented By J. Gower.*

Part II
Editing and Performance

5
Editing Boys: the Performance of Genders in Print

Jeffrey Masten

For when yeares three times fiue and one he fully lyued had,
So that he seemde to stande betweene the state of man and Lad,
The hearts of diuers trim yong men his beautie gan to moue,
And many a Ladie fresh and faire was taken in his loue.

Ovid, Metamorphoses, trans. Golding[1]

Neither a borrower nor a lender boy.

Hamlet, 'Good Quarto,' (1604, sig. C4r)[2]

1. (or 'Why did the English stage take boys for boys?')

Or better yet, 'what did the English stage take boys for, as boys?' Here are some of the terms used to address and describe Viola when she becomes Cesario in *Twelfth Night*. Of course, to refer to this figure on stage as Viola is already to get ahead of ourselves, since, as is well known, Viola is not named in the dialogue as 'Viola' until 235 lines into Act 5 of the play; in her first scene, she is simply 'lady,' and 'madam.'[3] Like Violenta, the ghost-name of which she is apparently the subject in an entrance direction in the folio text, one might say, the name 'Viola' is an effect of print – of stage directions and speech prefixes and only eventually dialogue.[4] In performance, in her female gender, she has no name until the end of the play. Whatever we may make of this apparent lacuna, the terms of address and description are only more variable after her first appearance. Concealing herself, she becomes 'an eunuch' in 1.2, 'a gentleman' in 1.5, and self-addresses 'As I am a man' and 'As I am a woman' in 2.2. The dialogue first refers to this figure as Cesario in 1.4. He speaks of himself as part of the group 'We men' in 2.4 – which Orsino corrects or amends by addressing him as 'boy' almost immediately thereafter. He speaks as a 'friend' to the adult Feste in 3.1; swears by his 'youth' and is 'almost sick' for a beard in the same scene.

Orsino calls him 'good youth' (1.4.15), 'good Cesario' (2.4.2), and 'Dear lad'[5] – [not yet] 'a man' at 1.4.31. He often addresses him directly as 'boy': 'Come hither, boy' (2.4.14); 'Hath it not, boy?' (24, also 31); 'died thy sister of her love, my boy?' and then, threatening to kill him in act 5, 'Come, boy, with me, my thoughts are

113

ripe in mischief' (5.1.125).[6] Once Olivia has disclosed her marriage with (it seems) this boy, Orsino hails him as 'your minion' (5.1.121); he is also 'the lamb that I do love' (5.1.127). The diminutives continue with 'sirrah,' 5.1.140, and 'thou dissembling cub' shortly thereafter, 5.1.160.[7] Moments later, Orsino refers to him as 'My gentleman, Cesario' 5.1.177, and the play, of course, concludes with Orsino insisting on the future use of this name 'while [he is] a man' 5.1.375-6.

Olivia, for her part, calls him several times 'this youth' (1.5.286, 295), directly addresses him as 'youth,' and 'good youth' (3.1.129), but also 'The County's man' 1.5.290 – although in 3.1, she implies that he is not yet 'reaped' as 'a proper man' 3.1.131. Mistaking Sebastian, she addresses him as 'dear Cesario' (4.1.47) and 'gentle friend' (3.4.49). Later it is 'Cesario, husband,' 5.1.139, 140 – though just a few lines later 'this youth' (5.1.151, referring to Cesario, but mistaking for Sebastian). In the end, still called 'Cesario' while he is a man by Orsino, she is to Olivia 'A sister' 5.1.317.[8]

Who is Cesario, what is he, that all our swains commend him, and in such disparate terms? Man, boy, eunuch, youth; there is still more. Maria sees 'a young gentleman' (1.5.94), 'a fair young man' 1.5.97, but also 'the youth of the Count's' 2.3.124. Sir Toby sees 'A gentleman' 1.5.114f, but also 'the Count's youth' 3.2.31, 'the youth,' 3.2.56, 3.4.183, 3.4.186, and yet 'the gentleman' 3.4.186, 3.4.294 and 'the young gentleman' 3.4.179. Sir Toby refers obliquely to Cesario's 'manhood' 3.4.174, and in jest to 'such a virago' 3.4.265, but also to 'A very dishonest, paltry boy' 3.4.376. Fabian sees 'the youth' 3.2.60, as does Sir Andrew 3.1.84, who also sees 'the Count's servingman' 3.2.5, and later (mistaking Sebastian) 'The Count's gentleman, one Cesario' 5.1.175.[9]

Describing him initially as 'yon young fellow,' it is Malvolio of course who provides the most extensive gloss. Olivia asks, 'What kind o' man is he?' and Malvolio replies, 'Why, of mankind.' Like a man, of man's kind or likeness.

> *Olivia*: What manner of man?
> *Malvolio*: Of very ill manner: he'll speak with you, will you or no.

However frustrating to Olivia, Malvolio's semiotic riffs on her terms only further complicate any attempt firmly to distinguish or categorize Cesario. He is 'of mankind,' which is to say: like any man, but also, of a man's mere kind or likeness, perhaps a little less than kin. He is also a man who is of an ill manner: ill-mannered, certainly, but also perhaps only able to man, to be or play man, in an ill fashion. 'What manner of man?' The question may imply, after Malvolio's reply: how does one man (how does one manner, or play) a man? Undeterred, Olivia continues to refine her question: 'Of what personage and years is he?' Malvolio:

> Not yet old enough for a man, nor young enough for a boy: as a squash is before 'tis a peascod, or a codling when 'tis almost an apple. 'Tis with him in standing water between boy and man. He is very well-favoured, and he speaks very shrewishly. One would think his mother's milk were scarce out of him. (1.5.150-5)

Malvolio's analysis may be taken both to point attention to the proliferation of the list I have so far recited – that is, to the procession of conflicting, overlapping terms the play uses to refer to this figure in its male gender – but it also establishes a set of metaphoric associations for the boy or man or young fellow upon his second entrance in boy's, or man's, or youth's, or young fellow's clothes. On the one hand, the lines establish a developmental model of boyhood: not *yet* a man, though no longer a boy; a squash *before* it's a peascod, a codling *before* an apple; in 'standing water' – at the turning of the tide, say the glosses in almost all the editions – between boy and man. The tide will turn: boys will be men.

And yet, on the other hand, a hand that may seem more metonymic in its gestures than metaphoric, and potentially running athwart this developmental sense, Malvolio's lines – when lifted out of editorial attempts to pin them down and instead opened out into the context of other Renaissance discourses – set off a chain of associations that here only *intensify* the problematics of the figure he describes. The *OED*, for example, has no evidence, outside Shakespeare's own usage, for the typical gloss of 'squash' as 'undeveloped pea-pod (*peas-cod*)' (Oxford edn 110) – and thus for boy as not-yet-developed man (or more accurately, shell or husk of a man). The dictionary has no etymological explanation for why this sense developed, as it argues, 'Related to, or directly from,' the verb *to squash*, and this development apparently dies out with William Shakespeare in any event – if indeed it ever lived: one of the other Shakespearean uses of the term cited by the *OED*, in *A Midsummer Night's Dream*, sees the relation of squash to peascod as gendered, not developmental. 'I pray you commend mee to mistresse Squash, your mother, and to master Peascod your father.' Thus Malvolio's comment may gesture toward the gender instabilities I take to be axiomatic in the play's denotations of Cesario, a transitivity already well described in the play's criticism, especially in Greenblatt's, Howard's, and Orgel's formative works on the play.[10]

Stripped of an editorial desire to delimit and stabilize their meaning, the passage's other terms similarly ramify outward: *codling* seems to take off from *peas*cod and signifies not only an unripe apple, but also (as one might expect) a small fish, and also, since *cod* means 'bag' and thus 'scrotum,' 'a small bag, or testicles.' Denoting Cesario seems to require mixing apples and, well, apricocks.

A final example: as W. Roy Mackenzie pointed out in a 1926 note unregistered in recent editions of the play,[11] there is no period evidence for reading the line 'in standing water between boy and man' to mean (as the Arden edition glosses it) 'at the turn of the tide.' The line is much more likely to have meant a stagnant or standing pool or pond, a swamp between the states of land and water. In the use of the phrase Shakespeare, his fellow-actors, and his audiences were most likely to know, God in Psalm 107:33 'reduceth a wyldernes into a standing water: and a drye ground into water springes,'[12] and in Psalm 114:8, God is said to have 'turned the harde rocke into a standing water: and the flint stone into a springing well of waters' – translations that persist from the Bishops' Bible through the Authorized Version. 'Standing waters,' writes Burton in *The Anatomy of Melancholy*, thick and ill-coloured, such as come forth of pools, and moats, where hemp hath been steeped, or slimy fishes live, are most unwholesome, putrified, and full of mites, creepers, slimy, muddy, unclean, corrupt, impure, by reason of the sun's heat, and *still-standing.* . . .[13]

'The fattest standing water is always the best,' writes Harrison in the 1587 *Description of England*, 'whereon the sun lieth longest, and the fattest fish is bred.'[14] Clearly this phrase is part of Malvolio's vocabulary of derision, but it also suggests a Cesario between water and land, liquid and solid. In a pool not subject to tides or flow, he is *categorically*, not *temporally*, between boy and man. As the fish in these contextualizing quotations may also suggest, 'standing water' may, again, emerge into the text here not as yet another metaphor for developmental boyhood-as-incipient manhood, but as a metonymic connection to the codling – the little fish, the little testicle – above. If so, then we may also hear in this passage a further phallic insult in the oxymoronic sense of 'standing water.' Can standing water 'stand,' get it up?

I have gone pretty deep (as it were) into the text and what I take to be its attendant historical resonances here in part because I want to remind us that Cesario – this boy played by a woman played by a boy – is indicated in this play through a range of categories, from 'boy' to 'man' (including 'youth'), categories whose relation to each other is neither mutually exclusive, nor always logically developmental (boy *to* man), nor entirely systematic. The inability to categorize Cesario – or rather, the ability of this figure seemingly to call forth *repeated* and divergent categorizations – exceeds, I would want to argue, the often critically discussed gender transitivity of the figure (a 'fellow' who 'speaks shrewishly'; a 'lad' whose 'small pipe / Is as the maiden's organ' and 'semblative a woman's part'), since this bundle of categories is, as the play stresses, entirely and repeatedly also misrecognized, or simply *recognized*, as 'Sebastian.' Insofar as these multiple categorizations, recognitions, and hailings figure the responses of a variety of represented persons to this performing figure, I want to argue that they may also figure what an early modern audience saw, in all its multiplicity, when it saw boy actors playing women, sometimes playing boys and men.

My attention to these questions of categorization in part stems from a desire to historicize understandings of masculinity in early modern England, a critical project that has obviously been ongoing in the field for some time. But I am also suggesting that we need to pursue this project not only between genders (or within the one-sex model, to use Laqueur's terms),[15] but even more carefully *'within'* them. As Ilana Krausman Ben-Amos's book *Adolescence & Youth in Early Modern England* argues:

the boundaries between childhood and youth on the one hand and between youth and adulthood on the other could become extremely imprecise. Even in scientific theories which aimed at explaining the passage from childhood to old age, and which abounded in numeric divisions and categories, there was no universally accepted division between childhood, adolescence, youth, and so on.... a person might be considered mentally and emotionally mature for specific rights and obligations at different times during his teens, as well as legally mature at 21; but in terms of social experience, the requirements of some professions, or responsibility for a family, he could be considered, at 18, 20, or even 25, as still quite young.[16]

As Ben-Amos's work suggests, our modern Anglo-American default sense of something called adolescence is strongly inflected by our own institutionalized and routinized educational system, a set of transitions that the early modern system cuts across both in terms of age and in the variabilities in the system with regard to social class, geography, and other factors. In a culture where life-expectancy was, comparatively speaking, quite low and the mean age of marriage for men (one indicator of full entrance into adulthood) 'fluctuated between 27.6 and 29.3' (32), non-adulthood could in fact occupy the majority of a life. Further, as Bruce Smith has importantly shown, the range of reference for the term 'boy' was itself hugely elastic from our point of view, including, in one sodomy trial he analyses, following Jonathan Ned Katz, a 'boy' described as 'aged 29 years or thereabouts.'[17]

But my point is not only to ask that, in thinking about figures like Cesario and Sebastian in plays like *Twelfth Night*, we develop more subtle and historically appropriate ideas of masculinity, its ages and modes. For another aspect of what I seek to do here is to think about the relation of this definitional and categorical fluidity to the perceived erotic desirability of boys, youths, and men in this culture. As Stephen Orgel summarizes: 'boys were, like women – but unlike men – acknowledged objects of sexual attraction for men.... the homosexual, and particularly the pederastic component of the Elizabethan erotic imagination is both explicit and for the most part surprisingly unproblematic' (*Impersonations* 70). To press his point even further, a consensus of critics has begun to recognize the category of the boy or youth or young man as a 'universal object of desire' – a figure of erotic and affective attraction and availability for men and women alike.[18] Golding's Ovid's Narcissus is in this sense exemplary: at the age of 16, 'The hearts of diuers trim yong men his beautie gan to moue, / And many a Ladie fresh and faire was taken in his loue.' Standing water has its attractions for everyone, including, of course, Narcissus himself.

What might a renewed attention to the categories 'boy,' 'youth,' 'man' (and so forth) tell us about the erotic possibilities in early modern English culture? In his essay 'How to Do the History of Male Homosexuality,' David Halperin has brilliantly delineated a set of pre-homosexual discourses or structures that circulate from classical antiquity through the early modern period and into the present, representing structures or configurations of homoeroticism that contribute to, but are not the same as, the category of modern 'homosexuality.'[19] Several of these structures, including pederasty, are constituted through hierarchies of age, status, or gender-affinity. Building on Halperin's formulation, I want, in emphasizing the categorical unfixity of 'the boy,' both to highlight the complexity of a structure like pederasty as its attractions are enacted in plays like *Twelfth Night* (the way in which the 'ped' in 'pederasty' is a moving target, and thus the way in which the term, at least if understood in its modern self-evidentness is not precisely what we are seeing here), *and also* to indicate the ways in which pederasty overlaps with, slides into, sometimes becomes or comes from, other kinds of love, attraction, affection. To further explore these issues, and to consider how they might differently figure in performance and in print, I turn now to the roughly contemporaneous *Philaster, or Love Lies A-Bleeding*, another King's Men's play (written around 1609, acted at the Globe and the Blackfriars, and at court in 1612–13).

2.

'The love of boyes unto their Lords is strange,' Philaster says, near the beginning of act II of the play that bears his name. Speaking of Bellario, the boy '[s]ent by the gods' whom he found in the woods while hunting, Philaster enlarges on this strange boy-man love: 'I have read wonders of it, yet this boy / For my sake (if a man may judge by looks, / And speech) would outdo story' (2.2.615-18).[20] Philaster's speech both registers this structure as normative (a love whose name he has seen spoken before) and as (in this case) wilfully exceeding the wonder-full, outgoing the standard accounts. 'Strange,' but not unprecedented – and perhaps also strange because he is accustomed in the classical sources to seeing the affection flow in the other direction.

The boy Bellario is, in fact, the object of concerted erotic interest in *Philaster*, and not only *from* Philaster. Or more precisely (and this bears comparison with *Twelfth Night*), he functions as a figure for the possibility of eroticism, a figure always on the verge of eroticization. There is, first, the long pastoral monologue that interrupts the action, in which Philaster introduces Bellario – in Philaster's superlative terms, 'The trustiest, loving'st, and the gentlest boy, /That ever Master kept' (1.2.491-2). In fact, the boy's value in the play seems to be that he can, at whatever point, be invested with meaning; in the words of Dion (only one of many characters to dwell upon the word *boy* in Philaster), after Philaster has given Bellario to his beloved, the princess Arethusa, he is 'that boy, that Princess boy: that brave, chast, vertuous Ladies boy: and a fair boy, a well spoken boy' (2.4.1025-6). The courtesan Megra, however, invests the boy with less chaste erotic meaning: 'The princess,' she says, 'has a *Hilas*, an *Adonis*' (2.4.843), thus citing the boy's classical availability as the subject of erotic interest for both Hercules and Venus, men and women. Bellario himself cites another classical scene of erotic investment (the Ganymede myth, a figure hovering over the whole play), and thematizes his own tractability, when he notes to Philaster early on:

> Sir, you did take me up when I was nothing;
> And only yet am something, by being yours;
> You trusted me unknown.... (2.1.564-6)

Defined, constituted by, his relation to the master who has taken him up, Bellario emphasizes a few lines later his availability for pedagogic instruction and transformation:

> Sir, if I have made
> A fault of ignorance, instruct my youth;
> I shall be willing, if not apt to learn;
> Age and experience will adorn my mind
> With larger knowledge: And if I have done
> A wilful fault, think me not past all hope
> For once, what Master holds so strict a hand
> Over his boy, that he will part with him
> Without one warning? Let me be corrected.... (2.1.587-95)

As the work of Elizabeth Pittenger, Alan Stewart, and Wendy Wall on pedagogic beating has shown, this imagined scene of correction is itself not devoid of eroticism in this period.[21] Taking up Bellario's willful multi-valence, I want to argue that the play recognizes and records the erotic slippage available in the figure of the boy, the page, the servant, as the pedagogical scene and classical resonances that get attached to him begin to suggest. A Ganymede 'taken up,' a Hylas, an Adonis. This is so much the case that, when Megra finally articulates a specific erotic allegation against Bellario, the charge is immediately assimilable by other characters in the play: 'I know the boy/She keeps, a handsome boy, about eighteen:/Know what she does with him, where, and when' (2.4.991-3).

As I have already noted, the term *boy* has a capaciousness of reference in this period that may in fact bear some discursive responsibility for Bellario as a site of definitional struggle – denoting age (a *young* boy), but also often denoting servitude and/or social inferiority. Some of this breadth of reference may replay a more specific cultural ambiguity: in the Canons of 1604, proposals were made to change the age of consent for boys/men from 14 to 21 (the change was not in fact enacted until the eighteenth century).

Bellario's eroticization is not only the product of his age – though his age comes to function as a marker of his erotic availability – but also of his clothes. ''Tis a sweet boy' says Dion, 'How brave she keeps him!' (2.4.853). 'Where's the boy?' Arethusa says to her waiting-woman.

> *La*. Within Madam.
> *Are*. Gave you him gold to buy him cloaths?
> *La*. I did.   *Are*. And has he don't?
> *La*. Yes Madam
> *Are*. 'Tis a pretty sad talking boy, is it not?   (2.3.759-63)

Bellario becomes here a liveried servant of the princess – a point made emphatically at the beginning of a scene – and this 'brave' livery itself becomes a further mark of his eroticization, in a way that the text suggests as potentially excessive: 'She has made thee brave,' accuses Philaster (who has himself earlier made Bellario something out of nothing). 'My lord' Bellario replies, 'she has attired me past my wish, / Past my desert...' (3.1.1205-7). The liveried status of Bellario – his mark, badge, habit of service – becomes even more controversial, as the King's interrogation of Arethusa on the charge of boy-love hints:

> *King.* Tell me: have you not a boy? *Are.* Yes Sir.
> *King.* What kind of boy?
> *Are.* A Page, a waiting boy.
> *King.* A handsome boy?
> *Are.* I think he be not ugly:
> Well qualified, and dutiful, I know him,
> I took him not for beauty
> *King.* He speaks, and sings and plays?
> *Are.* Yes Sir. *King.* About Eighteen?
> *Are.* I never ask'd his age. *King.* Is he full of service?
> *Are.* By your pardon why do you ask?
> *King.* Put him away. *Are.* Sir?
> *King.* Put him away, h'as done you that good service,
> Shames me to speak of. (3.2.1358-71)

In this play, the erotic risk posed by Bellario's clothing here is a result of a gendered structure: to be the kept boy of Philaster – to be the 'trustiest, loving'st, and the gentlest boy / That ever master kept' – is to be endowed with affect apparently without risk, as Philaster's long introductory aria on Bellario suggests. But to be the kept-man (the 18-year-old liveried servant) of the princess is to open the possibility of multiple kinds of 'service,' and a service, as Philaster eventually jealously fantasizes, in which the servant may become a kind of master to the princess who is said to 'yield thee [Bellario] all delights / Naked, as to her bed: I took her oath,' [he lies], 'Thou should'st enjoy her.' (1250–1)

Fantasized here, and alluded to in *Twelfth Night*, in Orsino's sending his page to Olivia, this kind of erotic danger is what is in fact enacted in the Act IV hunting sequence of *Philaster*, a phantasmatically isolated forest space set up, in Arethusa's speech at the close of Act III. The forest and this speech explicitly ally the hunt with sexual desire, and wounding with penetration, as R. A. Foakes notes,[22] even as the speech encodes the prospective polymorphous perversity of the multiple woundings that will follow:

> I am in tune to hunt!
> *Diana* if thou canst rage with a maid,
> As with a man, let me discover thee
> Bathing, and turn me to a fearful Hind,
> That I may die pursu'd by cruel Hounds,
> And have my story written in my wounds. (3.2.1521-6)

The hunt imagined here by Arethusa is multi-valent and multi-directional. Like Orsino in the first scene of *Twelfth Night*, Arethusa writes herself as Actaeon, and thus, if only in the conditional ('*if* thou canst rage with a maid'), within a scene of self-endangering female–female voyeurism and desire. This is a scene in which, moreover, she imagines viewing the bathing Diana – to whom Arethusa's classical namesake was originally bound in service, before Arethusa was herself hunted by Alpheus and turned into a fountain. The passage is explicit in linking desire with unsafe hunting practices, and suggests that the resulting wounds themselves will become the text of the tragedy the play at this point threatens to unfold.

Let me then quickly recount the woundings of Act IV of *Philaster*. Philaster wounds Arethusa. 'A Country Fellow,' whom the wounded Arethusa accuses of 'intruding [him]self / Upon our private sports, our recreations' (4.5.1840–1), then wounds Philaster. Philaster, fleeing, finds Bellario asleep, and, in an attempt to thrust guilt for Arethusa's wounding upon him, wounds *him* by replicating his own wounds: 'Sword, print my wounds / Upon this sleeping boy' (4.6.1918-19). To use the words of the play's subtitle, all 'loves' lie 'a Bleeding' in Act IV of this play.

The end of *Philaster*, of course, binds up these wounds, and in doing so reintegrates Bellario, the figure of the 'boy,' into the combined household of the betrothed Philaster and Arethusa.[23] The text is careful to make prophylactic at least some of the eroticism it had earlier worried about, by disclosing that Bellario is 'really' Euphrasia, a maiden apparently chastely devoted to Philaster. If the play has, in other words, significantly expanded the erotic availability and meaning of 'the boy' over the course of the play, it seems here largely to shut down that experimentation by the last-minute disclosure – news to everyone but herself, including the audience – that Bellario is in fact Euphrasia.

3.

That is at least one of the stories one might derive from *Philaster*, although one might notice that the play also simultaneously leaves open some of the possibilities it had earlier exhibited. The disclosure of the truth of Euphrasia's gender is for example greeted with significant ambiguity:

> *Di.* Why my shame, it is a woman, let her speak the rest.
> *Phi.* How! that again.   *Di.* It is a woman....
> *Phi.* It is a woman Sir, hark Gentlemen!
> It is a woman...
> It is a woman...
>   But Bellario
> (For I must call thee still so) tell me why
> Thou didst conceal thy Sex....   (5.5.2595-2613)

Philaster's request ('tell me why...') in turn produces another narrative which is *simultaneously* a genealogy of his/her true gender *and* a version of Philaster's earlier speech explaining the love of boys unto their lords, with Euphrasia's now 'female' version of her story nevertheless still structured by the rhetoric of 'taking up' associated with the shepherd Ganymede:

> I saw a God,
> I thought (but it was you) enter our Gates,
> My bloud flew out, and back again, . . .
> . . . then was I call'd away in hast
> To entertain you. Never was a man
> Heav'd from a Sheep-coat to a Scepter rais'd
> So high in thoughts as I. . . .   (2626-33)

Her story, ostensibly the back-story of her true gender, simultaneously restages Ganymede's flight, legible, as Leonard Barkan has pointed out, as his ravishment or his education: the story of awakened desire here is also the story of rising thoughts. Having dressed herself 'in habit of a boy,' Euphrasia continues, she sat 'by the Fount / Where first you *took me up.*'

But *why* must Philaster 'call [Bellario] still so'? Is it the persistence of the boy-clothing that she still wears – the force of 'habit'?[24] Or what Orgel describes as her 'deci[sion] to remain permanently in drag'?[25] Even to ignore these ambiguities, to ignore the persistence of Bellario's boy-ness, and concentrate on Euphrasia, is not to arrive at an ending without eroticism. In the shared household, the threesome with which it concludes, the play supplies an ongoing man-boy relationship (Philaster still calls this girl 'Bellario'; she still tells that story), as well as what we might see – following Valerie Traub's foundational work – as a relationship of 'chaste-femme' love between Arethusa and her former boy, now a girl, Euphrasia.[26] But that relationship is itself a mirror image of Arethusa's speech before the hunt, as we've already noticed: the servant girl viewing her naked, bathing mistress, who is imagined, at least, to rage with maid as well as man. 'Oh, never,' says Arethusa, earlier in the play, 'never such a boy again, as my Bellario.' As if noting that this excess might eventually be read as a different story, Philaster responds: 'all this passion for a boy?' (3.2.1428, 1434).

4.

Thus far, in thinking about the figure of the boy in *Philaster*, I have been working in a relatively familiar interpretive vein: noting the play's emphasis on the figure of the boy, Bellario; noting the text's seeming offering of non-heteronormative erotic possibilities; then noting the foreclosure of those possibilities by the exposure of the boy's 'real' gender as a woman; then noting the way in which that foreclosure is itself not closed, and in a number of directions – the residual of a man-boy attraction at the end of the play; the possibility of female–female eroticism broached by Arethusa persisting in the play's ending; the unresolved erotic triangle in the household the play sets up at its end. (In this sense, my general approach is like any number of readings of *As You Like It* that emphasize the space of erotic play in the Rosalind as Ganymede scenes, the seeming foreclosure of these possibilities in heterosexual marriage at play's end, the persistence of Rosalind's boy gender and what, homoerotically, it may represent, even – as Orgel and I have both argued – in the wedding scene of the play, and the erotic multivalence that many critics have located in the play's epilogue.) In doing so, I have been relying implicitly on a model of what may have been visible and audible in a *performance of Philaster*, even saving my reminder that Bellario is 'really' a woman, within the representation, until late in my discussion.

I have chosen the example of *Philaster*, however, because it differs from the usual suspects in discussions of cross-dressing boys in both performance and, significantly, in print. First – unlike the usual Shakespearean examples, *Philaster* presents (and as I have suggested, eroticizes) a boy who is, throughout, a boy, until the last lines of the play. There is no initial scene establishing the boy actor as a woman who then dresses up; thus, in its eroticization and argument over the erotic meaning and function of the boy, this play lacks the potential prophylaxis (a protection in advance) with which plays like *As You Like It* and *Twelfth Night* present their audience (however briefly, in the latter case) – an audience that knows, yes, that this is a boy actor (and thus a Ganymede or Cesario) and simultaneously that, within the representation, he is 'really' a woman. *Philaster* provides such an out only in retrospect, and it presses this possibility to the very limit of theatrical titillation in performance by emphasizing, describing, and finally threatening to reveal the body of the boy actor and boy Bellario before apparently resolving the problem. That is: the disjuntion between the boy-gender Bellario has embodied throughout the play and his 'real' female gender only emerges in the last scene of the play as the King, first, conjures up the image of an offstage torture and further wounding of Bellario ('Bear away the boy / To torture' [5.5.2829-30]). (Wounding, recall, has already been set by the play within a context of Ovidian sexuality, and torture itself has been glossed elsewhere in the play as 'ravishment.') A few moments later, the King then proceeds to order the performance of this torture onstage, and commands, 'strip that boy,' an imperative that proposes to reveal an erotic possibility the play has held out from the beginning. In its threat to strip both the livery of Bellario and the costume of the boy actor, the play emphasizes its absolute equation, to this point, of the player-apprentice and the liveried servant.[27] Unlike the Shakespearean examples often adduced, then, a performance of *Philaster* might be said to reiterate the boyness of the boy actor (whatever that may be) from beginning to end.

But what about *Philaster* in print? First, there is a lot of it, and a quick review of the terrain is perhaps in order: there are ten quartos and an appearance in the second Beaumont and Fletcher Folio between the play's first appearance in 1620, and the end of the seventeenth century. Since Kirschbaum's 1938 census of bad quartos, the 1620 first quarto has usually been considered one. 'Comparison of Q1 and Q2 reveals in the former,' Kirschbaum writes, 'all the phenomena of bad quartos: ... "mishearings" ..., addition, omission, substitution, restatement, transposition, mislining, corrupt blank verse, and the giving of speeches to the wrong characters.'[28] Q2 has been taken as the good and authoritative text, and, in the usual construal of things, according to Robert K. Turner, the editor who has studied the texts most minutely, writing in the Bowers edition of the Beaumont and Fletcher canon, 'A comparison of [the later] editions reveals little more than the progressive degeneration of the text that is inevitable in a long series of reprints' (371). These views are shared by Dora Jean Ashe in her Regents edition of 1971 and Andrew Gurr in his Revels edition of 1969 (recently republished); Gurr calls the first quarto 'botched' and 'inferior,' 'with nonce-constructions and variants that are evident misreadings of the Q2 text's readings on an average of one line in four' (lxxv-lxxvi).

It is not my purpose in this essay to save a 'bad' quarto (as much fun as that can be); it is true that Q1 is a tough read and rather less tidy than certainly a modern reader might prefer, though it should also be noted that Q2 has its own extensive share of what is taken to be mislineation, a number of speeches attributed to what seem like the wrong characters, and so forth. Instead, I want to suggest that one person's textual corruption and 'progressive degeneration' may be another person's history of sexuality. It might be argued that this has been the case since 1622, when, in the striking and familiar address to the reader of the second quarto, Thomas Walkeley, the publisher of first two quartos, wrote that '*Philaster*, and *Arethusa* his loue, haue laine so long a bleeding, by reason of some dangerous and gaping wounds, which they receiued in the first Impression....' (A2). Walkeley, deploying the language of wounding, in other words, inserts the text very early in its history into a discourse of eroticism employed by the play itself; if editorial work on this play (including editorial work over the course of its printing in the seventeenth century) has seen itself as following the less wounded text, it may well also have been led, through Walkeley's anti-wounding rhetoric (which is to say, in this context, anti-Ovidian-erotic rhetoric), to look away from other eroticisms.

I propose, then, at least provisionally, to rename the 1620 first text of Philaster from 'the Bad Quarto' to 'the Boy Quarto.'[29] (Following Kirschbaum, this may entail a subsequent 'Census of Boy Quartos,' but I leave that for another time.) For, though this text features, as he notes 'addition, omission, substitution, restatement, transposition,...and the giving of speeches to [different, if not exactly] the wrong characters,' what may be most striking about this text is the way in which some of these additions and restatements (which are, of course, actually differences and *pre*statements) figure the character I have been calling Bellario, but who is most often figured in Q1, the Boy Quarto, simply as 'boy.' The first description of him, in all the texts, as I have already mentioned, occurs in Philaster's speech beginning 'I haue a boy, sent by the gods' (Q1, C2v), and the presentation of this figure throughout the Q1 text emphasizes this generic quality. This is the case in the dialogue I've already discussed that Q1 predominantly shares with Q2, from which I quoted above, but it's even more emphatically the case in the Q1 apparatus. Where, with this figure's first entrance in 2.1, Q2 has '*Enter Philaster* and *Bellario*' (Q2 D1 17), Q1 has '*Enter* PHYLASTER, *and his boy, called* BELLARIO' (C3v 14). Where Q2 thereafter begins its practice of using the speech prefixes '*Bell.*' and sometimes '*Bel.*' throughout, the boy called Bellario in Q1 speaks through the speech-prefix 'BOY,' in small caps, until a moment in the last scene (to which we will return). Hailed and described in the dialogue as 'boy' throughout, he is likewise 'boy,' generic boy, throughout the stage directions, appearing there by name only in his first and last entrance indications. Thus, the text is (at the level of its dialogue and its paratext) a litany of summonses to a generic boy: '*Exit boy*,' at end of this scene, followed immediately by 'The loue of boyes vnto their Lords is strange' (C4v, 16). '*Enter boy*.' (38), '*ExitBOY*.' [sic] 39; '*Enter* BOY.' (42); '*Exit* BOY.' ([4]3); '*She sits downe, Enter* BOY.' (45); '*Exit* BOY.' (64 [46]); '*Enter the* BOY.' (49); '*Boy falls downe*.' (50). '*Enter* PHYLASTER, *Princesse*, BOY, *in prison*.' (53). '*Enter* PHI. *Princesse*, BOY, *with a garland of flowers on's head*.' (55). And so forth.

The love of this text unto this *term* seems strange, from this vantage point, but I hope I have begun to suggest the way in which the Boy Quarto seems, in print, to maintain and even to amplify some aspects of the play that, as I have argued above, would have been central to a performance of this play. The one departure from this rule is the list of '*The Actors Names*' which prefaces the Q1 text; there, this character is figured as 'BELLARIO a Page, LEONS daughter.' This entry may well depict the emerging difference between *Philaster* in performance and *Philaster* in print (or rather, *Philaster* and what it further performs in print), for, unlike what may have been the performance experience for either of these texts in the theatre, this moment in the printed text attempts to insert into the otherwise resolutely 'boy' quarto, a pre-history for the character Bellario's 'true' gender that the Boy Quarto does not otherwise share. (To put this another way: 'The Actors Names' here acts the function of Rosalind before the forest, or the unnamed lady Viola emerging from the shipwreck – the establishment of a gender that is then thrown off or covered over for the bulk of the play.)

In the Boy Quarto of *Philaster*, Bellario as daughter emerges in the last three pages of the play, but her gender (disclosed by her kneeling to Leon and the stage direction '*discouers her haire*') is accompanied *not* by her emergence from the speech prefix 'BOY' into a named female identity (she has no female name in this text), but by her taking on, for the first time in this text, the speech prefix 'BEL.' for Bellario. For a reader of this quarto, this text maintains or performs a persistent ambiguity around this figure: *he* is a daughter in a list at the outset; *she* goes by her male name when she 'turn[s] woman.' 'How, our sometime Page, *Bellario*, turn'd woman?' asks the Princesse; 'I doe beleeue thee,' the Princesse says a moment later; and then (simultaneously disbelieving) '*Bellario* I shall call thee still' (pp. 64, 65). (Here again the play both makes impossible and practices a same-sex female eroticism, to use Traub's terms, since its impossibility both absolves the Princess from the accusation of having slept with a boy, and remains present in her affection for her page turned woman.)

The second quarto (let's call it the Bellario Quarto) maintains a similar ambiguity throughout, though differently articulated: there is no list of the actor's names, but Bellario remains Bellario consistently throughout (in stage directions, speech prefixes, before and after his/her gender transformation); for a reader of the Bellario Quarto, this dissonance or ambiguity emerges perhaps most visibly at the moment Bellario speaks his/her (other name): the speech prefix announces italicized Bellario, and Bellario announces italicized *'Euphrasia.'* 'What's thy name?': *'Bel. Euphrasia.'*

It's perhaps useful for me to pause here in this history that attempts to avert corruption and degeneration to comment on my reconfiguring of the first two texts of Philaster. I bother to think about this at all because I think that, even with several pretty good twentieth century editions of the play available, based on the Good (or Bellario) Quarto, there is a way in which these editions fail to register aspects of the ostensibly bad text, the boy text, that nevertheless disclose something crucial about *Philaster* as it is registered even in the good text and, as I have suggested, in early-seventeenth-century performance practice. (This is only more the case when one registers the fact that the middle sections of these texts are, in the dialogue they register, more or less identical, with only parts of the first and last acts showing marked divergence.[30]) It should be clear that I *don't* call these texts the Boy Quarto and the Woman Quarto, for neither of these texts fully begins with or restores a female Euphrasia even in the ambiguated ways that (say) Rosalind and Viola end their plays. Neither do these texts map easily onto something that might look like 'pederasty' vs. heteronormativity, since the Boy Quarto of 1620 is, if anything, more resolute in marrying Bellario-turned-woman off to Trasiline at the last moment (thus both evacuating and repeating the love of this woman still dressed as a boy unto a lord), and the Bellario Quarto of 1622 (still harping on boys in its dialogue if not in its stage and speech directions[31]) leaves Euphrasia (called still Bellario) unmarried but as a chaste servant to the Princess and Philaster.

For a Euphrasia Quarto, we might well turn to the 1628 third quarto, which begins with a list of *'The persons presented'* followed in all subsequent texts, a list that for the first time divides the characters by gender as well as class, moving Euphrasia to the bottom of the group of women characters: 'EVPHRASIA, Daughter of *Dion*, but disguised like a Page, and called *Bellario*.' Here we have the girlhood of Beaumont and Fletcher's boy-heroine set out, although again, still, I would want to notice that a reader would have confronted a hybrid text, or a hybrid approach to this figure. Even as the dramatis personae list marks the arrival here of a notion of gender-stabilized character that seems to precede, govern, and potentially outlast the fiction, it sits in considerable dissonance with the text itself as a reader must have experienced it, for this 'person presented' continues in all other respects to be presented by the text as 'Bellario' (in dialogue, speech, and stage directions): not only is Euphrasia 'called *Bellario*' by the play's characters; she/he is also consistently called Bellario *by the edition*, including (again, still) at and after the moment of her disclosure as Euphrasia.

The folio of 1679 and all but the last of the subsequent quartos (1634, 1639, 1652, 1661, 1661, 1687[32]) follow this hybrid or dissonant presentation of the character. Even as Turner saw the 'inevitable' 'progressive degeneration of the text' in these editions, we would have to say that, at least with regard to this figure of the boy/woman, that something more complicated is going on: on the one hand, something that, in the dramatis personae lists, looks like a straightening out of gender and the idea of character across the texts, and thus *potentially* of the erotic plot of this play; and, on the other, the persistence of a boy-centered eroticism that has extended well past the modes of production in the early seventeenth-century theatre that it may have emerged from and in part represented.

It may not be beside the point at all that the text in which Euphrasia first appears in a dramatis personae list, the third quarto of 1628, is also a quarto that begins to acknowledge, however tentatively, a difference between a reading public and plays in print, and a performance audience and plays in the theatre – something set out in a new preface, 'THE STATIONER *TO* THE VNDERSTANDING GENTRIE' (A2r):

> THis Play so affectionately taken, and approoued by the Seeing Auditors, or Hearing Spectators, . . . hath receiued (as appeares by the copious vent of two Editions,) no lesse acceptance with improouement of you likewise the Readers . . . (A2r).[33]

One might then hypothesize, however tentatively, the linking here of 1) a more literate idea of the playtext quarto, related to but increasingly separable from the playhouse; 2) the straightening out, however rudimentary, of character gender and erotic trajectories in ways that depart from the ways of or available in performance; and 3) the persistence of and tolerance for those erotic possibilities, such that they did not appear to require the fullscale re-editing or re-configuration of the text. (It's worth recalling, as I've noted elsewhere, that, in the last scene of *As You Like It*, Rosalind is still joining 'his hand' with Orlando's until the third folio edits out the remaining boy in 1664.[34]) The next step on this route, which I will not take up in detail here, would be the last seventeenth-century quarto, in 1695, which, as it says on its title page, is 'Revis'd, and the Two last Acts new Written,' and has a dramatis personae list which perhaps clarifies, which is to say, reconstitutes under a new regime of production in the Restoration, the relationship of the actor and the boy the play represents. It reads, quite simply:

> *Bellario.*   *Mrs. Rogers.*

To recast Turner's 'progressive degeneration' this way – that is to say, as a movement toward a more modern sense of gender normativity, never of course fully accomplished (or at least here's hoping), and as a movement toward a straightening out, in the modern sense, of man-boy, woman-boy love – is also to remind ourselves that these things we tend to speak of as 'shifts' in the history of sexuality and of British theatre are incremental rather than instantaneous or immediately realized. There are, that is to say, persons whose experience included two different sets of performance practices in *Philaster* (the unknown, earliest, boy-acted Bellarios, through Mrs. Rogers) and who experienced as well a reading practice that confronted various of the hybrid or dissonant texts that I've examined. Take Samuel Pepys for example, contemporaneous with quartos 4–10 of *Philaster*, who notes on 30 May 1668, after a performance of the play, that

> it is pretty to see how I could remember almost all along, ever since I was a boy, Arethusa's part which I was to have acted at Sir Rob. Cooke's; and it was very

pleasant to me, but more to think what a ridiculous thing it would have been for me to have acted a beautiful woman.[35]

Here we might see even in Pepys (who seems in some other ways the very model of a modern, privatized heterosexual subject) the conflict between the nostalgic pleasure he takes in remembering an earlier moment of theatrical cross-gendering, and the self-discipline he enacts in finding this memory now ridiculous.

5. (Boys in Print)

Thinking about boys in British theater history, I've been considering printed versions of texts originating in performance. But, in considering the meaning of boys on stage, which has, for a variety of reasons within theatrical history, feminist scholarship, and more recently queer studies, been an important concern, I think we might usefully broaden our view to think about the category of the boy and the erotic energies that category sometimes engages in this culture in specifically print contexts, and not just as print products of the stage. I want to cast the net somewhat widely here, and suggest what will have to be a somewhat telegraphic prolegomenon for considering Boys in Print.

First, we might think of the overlapping structures of familial structure and affect that may have attended master and/or mistress and apprentice relations in the printing house as well as the playhouse. I'm on record as deeply skeptical of the secret lives sometimes generated for the compositors of Shakespeare first folio, but one might pause to notice the relation sometimes assigned to Compositor E and Compositor B.[36] E has 'imitative tendencies' and is said to 'follow copy closely,' and he thus recapitulates some of the pedagogic structures noted above. The education and relations of apprentice compositors are worth examining in greater detail.

Second, I would want to consider the proliferation of other signs of boys in print culture. By this I mean to consider, as I've mentioned elsewhere, that the first two editions of *Philaster*, strangely enough, were printed 'for *Thomas Walkley*, and [were] to be sold at his shop at the *Eagle and Child* in Brittaines Bursse' (1620, also 1622).[37] The Boy Quarto and the Bellario Quarto, that is, were sold at what must have resonated as the sign of the Rape of Ganymede, this story of both pedagogical uplift and homoerotic ravishment and adoption. In the 1620s and early 1630s, Walkeley sells at the sign of the Eagle and Child in or near the New Exchange (*Othello* is among his wares, as are catalogues of nobility, the masque *Loves Triumph Through Callipolis*, some other plays by Beaumont and Fletcher, and Massinger), but this is not an unfamiliar sign either before or after him: there are several imprints of Thomas Creede printing and selling at this sign in 1600, 'in the Old Change...neare Old Fish-streete'; there's a golden eagle and child in Pater Noster Row in 1590; Jasper Emery sells books at the Eagle and Child located in Paul's Churchyard near Watling St. in the 1630s at least through 1642; Thomas Thornicroft sells under this sign 'near the little north door' in the 1660s.[38] Given the variety of texts printed and sold at this Ganymedic sign, my point is not that there is some necessary thematic connection or causal relation between the printed text and the sign, though of course the connection in the case of *Philaster* is a tantalizing one. Rather, I want to gesture toward the ubiquity of this sign of the Ganymedic child (sign in all the senses of that word) in this culture – the everydayness of this image, which we, visiting from our very different culture, may have trouble reckoning. To expand the field of early modern vision and ubiquity even further, we could notice that another Boy in Print is the Black Boy, under which sign (near Paul's) a number of imprints are sold in the latter half of the sixteenth century, and then, notably, a flurry of texts in 1660s–90s and thereafter.

Finally, I want to consider another set of 'boys in print,' the archive of images of male children and adolescents that decorate Renaissance printed texts. I hardly need to point out the swarms of *putti* that adorn a wide range of Renaissance visual materials. But the larger point is to think about the implications of an emergent print culture that thinks of unclothed boys, youths, and sometimes men not only as decorative (though this in itself is not inconsequential) but also as framing, presenting, and emblematizing a wide variety of texts – on title pages, in printed borders, in printers' ornaments, in decorative capitals, in grotesques used as page borders, and so forth. The merest glance through McKerrow and Ferguson's lists of printing images – which is in fact all I am going to do in this essay – may begin to remind us both of the range of uses of boys in these contexts *and*, just as I began in *Twelfth Night*, the range of figures that might be included in this category. Here are five examples, which is of course only a small sampling of the possibilities, but it may help us to think about what play-readers and other book-readers saw when they saw boys in print:

- First, naked boys reading in the uppers margins of the title page of the 1559 edition of Elyot's Dictionary (Figure 34), along with bare-breasted women.[39] This is a book border that, in other contexts, continues to be used through 1579.
- Second, a somewhat older (and buffer) selection of boys (the lower set with wings) framing – playing musical instruments in the margins of – the title page of the 1565 edition of Golding's partial translation of Ovid's *Metamorphoses* (Figure 35), a border that has continued use through at least 1615, where it is used for a psalter.[40]
- Third, an ornament with motto of a boy and dolphin (Figure 36),[41] which again brings together the ideas of boys and education, the motto reading 'IMMORTALITY IS GOTTEN BY THE STVDY OF LETTERS.'
- And then two different versions of a similar printers' ornament (Figures 37 and 38), depicting a boy or youth with one winged arm, while the other arm is weighted down.[42] (The younger of these boys appears, late in his printed career, on the title page of the 1604 *Dr. Faustus*). The god who summons from above in these ornaments suggests to me a resonance with the Eagle and Child, but I leave that open to further investigation.

These images we conventionally think of as 'ornaments,' 'devices,' mere 'borders' to the texts proper, but part of my point here is to think about the ways in which

Figure 34   Border first used for Sir Thomas Elyot's *Dictionarie*, 1559

they visualize, connect with, and re-articulate the signifiers in moveable type (e.g. 'BOY') that have occupied the latter part of this chapter. Part of the job, in other words, is to pull these graphics back from their separate McKerrow entries and put them back in conversation with the texts from which they have been excerpted, and the texts among which they circulated, including plays. Working this way – bringing these materials together, and I mean the larger range of materials in this chapter – may allow us to think more specifically about the contours, activities, identifications, desires, aspirations, and so forth of readerships in print culture, a readership that intersects with, is sometimes informed by, but is not identical with, the audiences for these plays in the theaters. Emblematic printers' ornaments are not simply ornamental; as emblems, they seek to inspire emulation and identification. Both adult readers and boys are, as the dolphin ornament

Figure 35   Border first used for William Golding's translation of Ovid's *First Fower Bookes of Metamorphosis*, 1565

suggests, within the circuit of letters. In Ovid's *Metamorphosis*, a text relevant to several of the texts and signs in this paper, desired boys are at both the centers and the margins; from the upper right margin of Elyot's Dictionary, a boy looks out engagingly toward the reader (almost like a boy player, you might say). He is performing, among other things, learning to read and reading.

Figure 36   Printer's device of a boy seated on a dolphin, first used in England in 1571

Figure 37   Printer's device of a boy with one arm winged and the other weighted down, first used in England in 1563

Figure 38   Another version of the device in Figure 37, first used in England in 1619

Notes

1. Ovid, *Metamorphoses*, trans. Arthur Golding, in *Shakespeare's Ovid*, ed. W. H. D. Rouse (Carbondale: Southern Illinois University Press, 1961), 71, Book 3, lines 437–40.
2. I am grateful to Coleman Hutchison, who first brought the sense-making possibilities of this line to my attention.

3. All references are to the Oxford text, ed. Roger Warren and Stanley Wells (Oxford: Clarendon Press, 1994).
4. In the folio text of 1.5, Viola is apparently the subject of the stage direction 'Enter Uiolenta.' On this crux see Laurie E. Osborne, *The Trick of Singularity: Twelfth Night and the Performance Editions* (Iowa City: University of Iowa Press, 1996), 17.
5. 1.4.29.
6. 5.1.125 (when Orsino is about to kill him), and 5.1.261, still, after the disclosure about 'his' woman's clothing.
7. Note the connection with the name 'Orsino,' although edited texts typically gloss the animal as a 'fox' cub.
8. On the name Cesario (as 'belonging to Caesar,' and thus 'cut'), see Stephen Orgel, *Impersonations* (Cambridge: Cambridge University Press, 1996), 53–4.
9. See also 3.4.54–5.
10. Stephen Greenblatt, 'Fiction and Friction', in Thomas C. Heller et al. (eds), *Reconstructing Individualism: Autonomy, Individuality and Self in Western Thought* (Stanford: Stanford University Press, 1986), 30–52; Jean Howard, 'Crossdressing, the Theatre, and Gender Struggle in Early Modern England,' *Shakespeare Quarterly* 39 (1988), 418–40; and Orgel, *Impersonations*. For additional revisionary treatments of gender in the play, see Valerie Traub, *Desire and Anxiety: Circulations of Sexuality in Shakespearean Drama* (London and New York: Routledge, 1992), and Laurie Shannon, 'Nature's Bias', *Modern Philology* 98 (2000), 183–210.
11. W. Roy Mackenzie, 'Standing Water,' *Modern Language Notes* 41 (1926), 283–93.
12. Thus the Bishops' Bible, substantially the same in the Authorized Version; the Geneva Bible has 'still pools.'
13. Quoted by Mackenzie, 290.
14. Quoted by Mackenzie, 289; see *OED* under fat.
15. Thomas Laqueur, *Making Sex* (Cambridge, Mass.: Harvard University Press, 1990).
16. Ilana Krausman Ben-Amos, *Adolescence & Youth in Early Modern England* (New Haven: Yale University Press,1994), 36.
17. Bruce Smith, *Homosexual Desire in Shakespeare's England: a Cultural Poetics* (Chicago: University of Chicago Press, 1991), 194–5.
18. See for example Wendy Wall's chapter on *The Knight of the Burning Pestle* in *Staging Domesticity* (Cambridge: Cambridge University Press, 2002), Chapter 5.
19. David Halperin, *How to Do the History of Homosexuality* (Chicago: University of Chicago Press, 2002).
20. All quotations from *Philaster* are taken from the folio text available online at www.uq.edu.au, unless otherwise noted. Act and scene divisions are included here for convenience; the online text has through-line numbering. As this essay will suggest below, there are a number of reasons to resist modern editions' privileging of the second quarto text of the play, and implications to the quarantining of the first quarto's first and last scenes to an appendix.
21. See Elizabeth Pittenger, 'Dispatch Quickly: The Mechanical Reproduction of Pages,' *Shakespeare Quarterly* 42 (1991), 389–408; Alan Stewart, *Close Readers* (Princeton, 1993), chapter 3; Wendy Wall, *The Imprint of Gender* (1993), esp. chapters 3 and 4; also Mario DiGangi, 'Queering the Shakespearean Family,' *Shakespeare Quarterly* 47 (1996), 269–90, expanded upon in his *The Homoeroticism of Early Modern Drama* (Cambridge: Cambridge University Press, 1997).
22. R. A. Foakes, 'Tragicomedy and Comic Form,' in A. R. Braunmuller and J. C. Bulman (eds), *Comedy from Shakespeare to Sheridan: Change and Continuity in the English and European Dramatic Tradition* (Newark: University of Delaware Press, 1986) 74–88, at 83.
23. In Di Gangi's terms, he has become an outsider inside the family. See Orgel's comment on this passage; whether Bellario/Euphrasia 'decides' that this will be his/her ultimate position is, I think, unclear (*Impersonations*, 163n8). See below on the difference in the gender discovery in the first and second quartos.

24. On the 'force of habit' – the power of clothes to determine gender in the theatre at any particular moment, despite what we might consider evidence to the contrary – see Orgel, *Impersonations*, 32–5.
25. *Impersonations*, 163n8.
26. Valerie Traub, *The Renaissance of Lesbianism* (Cambridge: Cambridge University Press, 2002).
27. On this, see Peter Stallybrass, 'Transvestism and the "body beneath": speculating on the boy actor,' in Susan Zimmerman, ed., *Erotic Politics: Desire on the Renaissance Stage* (New York: Routledge, 1992), 64–83. Also Ann Rosalind Jones and Peter Stallybrass, *Renaissance Clothing and the Materials of Memory* (Cambridge: Cambridge Univesity Press, 2003).
28. Leo Kirschbaum, 'A Census of Bad Quartos,' *Review of English Studies*, 14 (1938), 20–43 (43).
29. This is the place to note the influence on this essay more generally of the work of Randall McLeod, here in particular his essay (under the name Random Cloud) 'The Marriage of Good and Bad Quartos,' *Shakespeare Quarterly* 33 (1982), 421–31.
30. One might argue that this quarto may represent a version of either a text used in performance or a transcript/representation of what one person or more saw in performance.
31. There are several interesting emphases of 'Boy' in the dialogue via capitalization: 74, '*Ki.* Beare away that Boy / To torture,' and 77 [Bel:] 'drest my selfe / In habit of a Boy.' Cf. 'Maid.'
32. 1695 gives a simplified cast list for this revised text; see below.
33. This is also the first edition to describe Beaumont and Fletcher as '*The Authors*' on its title page.
34. Jeffrey Masten, 'Textual Deviance: Ganymede's Hand in *As You Like It*', in Marjorie Garber et al., (eds), *Field Work: Sites in Literary and Cultural Studies* (New York: Routledge, 1996), 153–63.
35. Robert Latham and William Matthews, eds, *The Diary of Samuel Pepys*, Vol. 9 (Berkeley: University of California Press, 1995), 217–18. 218n suggests that the earlier episode must have taken place between 1639 and 1653 (Pepys would have been between 6 and 20).
36. Jeffrey Masten, 'Pressing Subjects; Or, the Secret Lives of Shakespeare's Compositors' in *Language Machines*, (eds) Jeffrey Masten et al. (New York: Routledge, 1997), 75–107.
37. Jeffrey Masten, 'Ben Jonson's Head,' *Shakespeare Studies* 28 (2000), 160–8.
38. See Peter Blayney, *The Bookshops in Paul's Cross Churchyard* (London: The Bibliographical Society, 1990).
39. R. B. McKerrow and F. S. Ferguson, *Title-page Borders* (London: The Bibliographical Society, 1932), #98.
40. McKerrow and Ferguson, *Title-page Borders*, #121.
41. R. B. McKerrow, *Printers' and Publishers' Devices* (London: The Bibliographical Society, 1913), #166.
42. McKerrow, *Printers' and Publishers' Devices*, #142 and #393.

6

On Not Looking Back: Sight and Sound and Text

A. R. Braunmuller

> Warburton: Who does not see that the integrity of the metaphor requires
> we should read. . . .
> Johnson: Who does not see that upon such principles there is no end of
> correction?[1]

Perhaps I should explain my title, which has, conveniently, two halves. The first
half alludes to a wise man, a sage of baseball rather than of British theater. The
wonderful and perdurable pitcher Satchel Paige allegedly said, 'Don't look back.
Something might be gaining on you.' I hope to look forward in discussing editorial
protocols and theatrical performance, although some glances back will be necessary, and I hope that a fair reading will not convict me of having always already
been gained upon. My title's second half describes the editor's task when she or
he is asked to record and/or to imagine how a playscript is made physical, is
sounded and seen onstage.[2] Sixth and lastly, let me say, defensively, that I am an
eager, frequent theater-goer in both hemispheres, a friend of actors and of
performance and of the criticism that arises from performance. I am also an editor
of playscripts, a person who turns the printed possibilities for, or remnants of,
performances into new, or renewed, proto-remnants of performances for scripts
400 years old.

Recently, there has indeed arisen a 'performance-based scholarship in the study
of Shakespeare,'[3] and one wonders, with others, if and how a printed edition of
Shakespeare might respond to this development. Though I must say that when
the same critic describes 'Shakespearian editing' as being 'long conducted in a
quiet intellectual backwater, undisturbed by larger cultural wars,' he is tactless,
and his claim false.[4] Tactless because insult – 'quiet intellectual backwater' – is a
poor stimulus to reasoned debate. False because untrue: past and on-going work
by – to name alphabetically three scholars almost at random – Peter Blayney, Gary
Taylor, and Paul Werstine refutes the claim; for at least three decades, these
scholars and many others have placed editorial theory and the editions that
theory might mandate at the heart of Shakespearean critical discussion.
Even longer ago, almost a century now, the 'new bibliography' began to make

and continued to make intentionality and all its discontents central to informed critical debate.[5]

Further, recent editions of Shakespeare undeniably respond, or seek to respond, to 'larger cultural wars,' for instance with those editions' concern for multi-cultural, multi-ethnic, and non-Anglophone audiences,[6] but these salutary and enlightening editorial developments are tangential to my topic here. Rather, I want to discuss how editors have tried – consciously or unconsciously, with or without good warrant – to shape the look and the sound of the performed Shakespearean text. That is, how have editors and their editions responded to calls, from Barbara Hodgdon and Michael Cordner among others, now and earlier, for differently conceived or newly reconceived editions of Shakespeare?[7] Or have editors in fact sometimes anticipated what's being asked for?[8]

Most of these critics of editors and editions set their scene in the same way, so I may be brief in re-setting it here. Each of the main current series of Shakespearean editions, the Oxford, the New Cambridge, the Arden 3, makes some variant on the following claim, quoted here from early volumes in the New Cambridge series: 'While offering ample academic guidance, it [the new edition] reflects current critical interests and is more attentive than some earlier editions have been to the realisation of the plays on the stage, and to their social and cultural settings.'[9] So set, the scene is promptly (or not so promptly) dismantled through a series of textual examples, each usually no more than a few lines long, for which the editorial annotation is held to be imperceptive of or inattentive to various theatrical possibilities of sound, dialogue, posture, and so forth – all, that is, that constitutes the actor's craft and the director's skill.

Let me be clear: I could not agree more that editors are usually neither adept actors nor skillful directors, and editors have not been adept or skillful in fulfilling what their theatrically imaginative critics wish. With some distinguished exceptions, editors are (only, solely) editors, and they are *a fortiori* unlikely to be either skilled actors or successful directors.[10] Editors produce texts with various features and for various audiences. Hodgdon proposes the term 'textual-users' as a way of including such audiences as the beginning student of a Shakespearean text, an advanced one, a scholar, an actor studying a role, and a director studying a text-for-performance.[11] Further, and contradistinctively, I suggest that those theatrically imaginative and theatrically sensitive critics ask for editions unimaginable both practically and ideally.

Be that as it may, and I will return to the issue.

My first task, however, is to show the ways, or some of the ways, that editors have in fact sought to direct or control the performance of dramatic texts. That is, editors, whatever their limitations, are indeed seeking to be actors and theatrical directors of the texts they edit. Or at least editors try to be actors and directors. My tale here is a sad one or a laughable one or a frustrating one because it is a tale of editors trying to be what their performance-sensitive critics want them to be and, alas, what editors frequently are not.

I begin with the least mark on the page, the mark of punctuation. Since I am both defending and criticizing editors of Shakespearean texts, it is only just that I begin with an anecdote against myself. When I told my distinguished colleague R. A. Foakes that I had that long-ago day sent off my first edition of a Shakespearean play, he asked, 'Are you satisfied with the punctuation?' A cruelly apt question, because, of course, I was not satisfied. I had agonized over many such marks because I believed they would direct, or at least might help, an actor's speaking of a line. Whether ultimately ignored or overturned by an actor's performance, editorial punctuation receives a lot of attention in rehearsal. A second personal example comes from a recent post-play discussion of the Odyssey Theatre's 2004 production of *Macbeth* when Jake Stehlin (Macbeth) asked me – I speak truth – 'You heard the Arden punctuation, didn't you?'[12] I had. The company used Kenneth Muir's Arden edition (1954 and later revisions), and Muir's punctuation had been regularly debated in rehearsal and had indeed influenced the actors' preparation and their on-stage speaking.

In the very edition (*King John* [Oxford: Oxford University Press, 1989]) Reg Foakes skewered post-postally, I campaigned against the exclamation point.[13] It is a mark of high importance to the reader, to the actor conceiving a speech, and to the director imagining a performance, but it is also, of course, a mark that hardly appears in the First Folio or in many quartos of Shakespearean texts. And it is a mark that would have been unfamiliar to most literate early modern English-speaking persons – a small group that included the actors of the Lord Chamberlain's and King's Men. In the Tudor–Stuart era, compositors' cases rarely included a sort for the exclamation point. What does appear in the cases is what we call the question mark, a symbol that had not yet been consistently differentiated from the exclamation point. It's not hard to understand how exclamation and question could be represented by the same sign. Robert Pinsky observes:

> Every speaker, intuitively and accurately, courses gracefully through immensely subtle manipulations of sound. We not only indicate, for example, where the accent is in a word like 'question,' but also preserve that accent while adding the difference between 'Was that a question?' and 'Yes, that was a question.'[14]

My 'point,' my punctuation, in editing *King John* was that editors resorted to punctuation – or re-punctuation – as a way of directing the actor in how to enunciate a line or sentence. You must now be anticipating my next example, the most notorious Shakespearean example of the dilemma over the question mark/exclamation point/other mark of punctuation: Lady Macbeth's reply to her Lord when he asks 'If we should fail?' and she replies 'We fail?' The Lady excoriates her Lord for cowardice and unmanliness, emphasizing her dedication to Duncan's death:

> I have given Sucke, and know
> How tender 'tis to love the Babe that milkes me,
> I would, while it was smyling in my Face,
> Have pluckt my Nipple from his Bonelesse Gummes,
> And dasht the Braines out, had I so sworne

> As you have done to do this.
>   *Macb*. If we should faile?
>   *Lady*. We faile?
> But screw your courage to the sticking place,
> And wee'le not fayle.... (TLN 533–42)

How Lady Macbeth inflects this line has been endlessly debated, and actors have taken every editorially imagined and theatrically recorded choice. Editors have made their punctuational choices, and some have been theatrically sensitive enough to write notes on the choices and the problem.[15] Here, of course, it could be argued that either the early modern question mark or the modern exclamation point cannot really control meaning at all and simply throws the problem back at the actor. Is that temporizing conclusion really so bad? Does not the editor fulfill an assumed duty by noting and explaining the possibilities rather than leaving the chosen and historically variable punctuation mark listlessly on the page? The moment's meaning for its audience will grow not from an editorial decision but from an actor's, a company's, plethora of choices – ones that might well change from performance to performance. And of course 'the moment's meaning' will ultimately lie with the beholders, who also change from moment to moment and performance to performance.

Since we're looking at *Macbeth*, I might note that it has yet another one of the tidiest typographical conundrums in the canon. Macbeth returns from killing Duncan and reports to his Lady on what he experienced:

>   *Macb*. Me thought I heard a voyce cry, Sleep no more:
> *Macbeth* does murther Sleepe, the innocent Sleepe,
> Sleepe that knits up the ravel'd Sleeve of Care.
> The death of each dayes Life, sore Labors Bath,
> Balme of hurt Mindes, great Natures second Course,
> Chiefe nourisher in Life's Feast.
>   *Lady*. What doe you meane?
>   *Macb*. Still it cry'd, Sleepe no more to all the House:
> *Glamis* hath murther'd Sleepe, and therefore *Cawdor*
> Shall sleepe no more: *Macbeth* shall sleepe no more. (TLN 691–700)

There's no certain way to tell how much of this first Folio text is what Macbeth says he heard and how much is his commentary on what he heard and how he reacted to what he says he heard.[16] Edited texts make their choices manifest through added quotation marks, italics, or other historically inflected print conventions to mark reported speech. Doctor Johnson established the commonest choice that 'Sleep no more: / Macbeth doth murder sleep' and 'Sleep no more' and 'Glamis hath murdered sleep' are the quoted words, the rest Macbeth's comment. Other editors, mostly eighteenth-century tinkerers like Hanmer, have made other choices, and the choices – especially enlarging the voice's part and reducing Macbeth's responses – subtly but substantially affect how we understand the scene and Macbeth at this crucial moment. And the editorial choices also affect, or could affect, how the actor speaks these lines and how the audience understands them.

With this example of Macbeth and the voice he says he heard and the necessary, ineluctable but also unenviable, editorial decisions about how to represent his speech and the voice's speech, let me digress for a moment to Shakespeare's non-dramatic texts, where editorial quotation marks have also played their part. As endlessly debatable as the mark that ends 'We fail' and the exclamation points inserted by editors to stress certain lines or words are the quotation marks that surround many words and lines in modern editions of Shakespeare's texts. The simple question is 'what is quoted speech?' Or, further, what speech is being quoted as spoken by another voice and what is being quoted as *hypothetical* speech by another imagined speaker? Presumably, a recent editor of *Venus and Adonis* does not insert quotation marks for direct speech when Venus indirectly describes sexual satisfaction as 'balm' because when Venus 'trembling in her passion, calls it balm, / Earth's sovereign salve, to do a goddess good'[17] the lines are spoken/ written/heard/read in the narrators' voice or one of the narrator's voices or in one of the plural narrators' voices. Yet why does the same editor insert quotation marks in a line from *Lucrece*, 'Haply that name of "chaste" unhapp'ly set' (*Lucrece* 8)?[18]

In his 1790 edition, Edmond Malone inserted a colon after 'But be contented' at the beginning of Sonnet 74 ('But be contented when that fell arrest...'); since then, every word that follows has been understood, or has had to be understood, as dramatized speech. Similarly, Sonnet 99, 'The forward violet thus did I chide,' went unmodified (except for orthographic modernization) until 1855 when an editor, Robert Bell, added quotation marks to indicate what 'I' said when 'I' chided the violet, 'Sweet theefe whence did thou steale....' One could spend a long time worrying the question of who or what the 'I' of Shakespeare's sonnets is, or the question of who or what the narrator(s) of *Venus and Adonis* and of *Lucrece* is or are. Many have done so. Pertinent here is the wide gap of time between Malone's added quotation marks in 1790 and Bell's in 1855.[19] Does that gap mean that sonnet-readers and sonnet-imaginers in the theaters of their minds needed certain editorial assistance in 1790 for Sonnet 73 that they did not need for Sonnet 99 until about six decades later? Perhaps we are simply observing a shift in printing conventions, but I would suggest that what changed over those six-plus decades was an understanding, right or wrong, editorial or cultural or typographical,[20] of what was considered quoted speech and what was not.

I return to playscripts with a brief example from a recent editorial version of Orlando's opening speech to Adam in *As You Like It*:

For my part, he [Oliver] keeps me rustically at home or, to speak more prop-erly, stays me at home unkept – for call you that 'keeping' for a gentleman of my birth, that differs not from the stalling of an ox?

Why has the editor – alone among recent ones of this play so far as I can find – placed quotation marks around *keeping*? Because the speaker emphasizes that *keeping* in this case is not keeping, because oxen are kept, not gentlemen. Yet Betite Vinklers, a scrupulous professional copy-editor of my acquaintance, avers that the modern convention holds that a phrase such as 'call you that' in itself constitutes a signal to the reader/listener/speaker that the word *keeping* is at issue as a word and does not require further typographical designation. (Hence, for example, when one describes another person as a 'so-called Puritan' the phrase 'so-called' is sufficient to indicate emphasis on the word *Puritan* and no further typographical distinction is needed.)[21]

A rudimentary 1580s and 1590s way of writing a soliloquy was to people, Richard II-like, the small world of the speaker's head with still-breeding thoughts, that is, to invent one or more imaginary interlocutors and give them dialogue. A good example is the Bastard's reflection on his rising status:

> *Bast.* A foot of Honor better then I was,
> But many a many foot of Land the worse.
> Well, now can I make any *Joane* a Lady,
> Good den Sir *Richard*, Godamercy fellow,
> And if his name be *George*, Ile call him *Peter*,
> For new made honor doth forget mens names:
> 'Tis two respective, and too sociable
> For your conversation, now your traveller,
> Hee and his tooth-picke at my worships messe,
> And when my knightly stomacke is suffis'd,
> Why then I sucke my teeth, and catechize
> My picked man of Countries: my deare sir,
> Thus leaning on mine elbow I begin,
> I shall beseech you; that is the question now,
> And then comes answer like an Absey booke:
> O sir, sayes answer, at your best command,
> At your employment, at your service sir:
> No sir, saies question, I sweet sir at yours,
> And so ere answer knowes what question would,
> Saving in Dialogue of Complement,
> And talking of the Alpes and Appenines,
> The Perennean and the river *Poe*,
> It drawes toward supper in conclusion so.   (*King John*, TLN 192–214)

Here it is fairly obvious what text should be modernized with quotation marks and what capitalized to make Question and Answer into personifications, but not entirely so, and different editors have made different choices and thereby have affected both how an actor might speak the lines and the inferences actor and director might make about the Bastard's social place or placelessness, his attitudes towards rank and status, and so on.

A more difficult question, I have always thought, concerns a similar soliloquy from *Richard III*, perhaps Richard of Gloucester's second most famous after the opening one:

What? do I feare my Selfe? There's none else by,
Richard loves *Richard*, that is, I am I.
Is there a Murtherer heere? No; Yes, I am:
Then flye; What from my Selfe? Great reason: why?
Lest I Revenge. What? my Selfe upon my Selfe?
Alacke, I love my Selfe. Wherefore? For any good
That I my Selfe, have done unto my Selfe?
O no. Alas, I rather hate my Selfe,
For hatefull Deeds committed by my Selfe.
I am a Villaine: yet I Lye, I am not.
Foole, of thy Selfe speake well: Foole, do not flatter.
My Conscience hath a thousand severall Tongues,
And every Tongue brings in a several Tale,
And every Tale condemnes me for a Villaine;
Perjurie, in the high'st Degree,
Murther, sterne murther, in the dry'st degree,
All severall sinnes, all us'd in each degree,
Throng all to'th' Barre, crying all, Guilty, Guilty.   (*Richard III*, TLN 3644–61)

Unlike the Bastard's creation of imaginary abstractions he then puts in dialogue with an hypothecated version of himself and for his own entertainment, the self-division here is just that: Richard divides himself into a series of opposites to his proclaimed 'self' and various threats which he attempts to deny or repel through appealing to that 'self' which he loves, does not fear, etc.[22] As the tongues of his conscience multiple so does my restiveness about whether there is quoted albeit hypothetical speech here. If an editor places quotation marks around 'Guilty, guilty,' as editors do in all the recent editions I have consulted, then why not put quotation marks around 'Fool, of thyself speak well' and 'fool, do not flatter,' since these fragments even come equipped with vocatives? And, again, a straightforward case could be made that these quotation marks, present *or* absent but especially if present, significantly affect performance and its reception.

The word *or* in the last sentence was italicized because from marks of punctuation I want to turn briefly to fonts. A strange if intermittent malady seems to have struck some recent editions of Shakespearean texts, and that malady is italics.[23] By the end of the sixteenth century, the modern convention that prints the spoken text of a play in roman and the didiscalia – the unspoken writing meant to regulate the performance (stage directions, speech prefixes, etc. including *etc.* itself) – had appeared, and this text generally went into italic. As my examples from folio *Macbeth*, *King John*, and *Richard III* show, italic does appear in early modern theatrical texts for English or Scottish proper names – *Glamis, Cawdor, Joane, Richard, George* – most foreign names, especially classical ones, and geographical names (*Poe*), and sometimes a few other fairly inferrable categories. The same conventions are visible in some manuscript plays since most writers and scribes commanded several hands, including italic and secretary. What early modern printing and writing largely lacked, however, was what we call 'emphasis-italic' – italicized text that thus indicates verbal and/or rhetorical stress.

Hence, the following piece of edited text betrays printing history as well as an odd editorial desire to interfere where no interference is needed:

> THIRD PLEBIAN Your name, sir, truly.
> CINNA Truly, my name is Cinna –
> FIRST PLEBIAN Tear him to pieces! He's a conspirator.
> CINNA I am Cinna the *poet*! I am Cinna the *poet*!
> FOURTH PLEBIAN Tear him for his bad verses, tear him for his bad
> verses.   (*Julius Caesar*, 3.3)

Funny, no doubt, though not for poets, and always a big hit with students, but the italics – 'I am Cinna the *poet*! I am Cinna the *poet*!' – raise several questions. What actorly, readerly, or directorial problem is solved by these italics? What misunderstanding or incomprehension is the editor helping any likely reading or acting constituency to avoid? The editor might defend the italics by pointing to the fact that the Folio capitalizes 'Poet' and the capitalization is sometimes, or is sometimes thought to be, one way the folio's compositors drew attention to a word. Unfortunately, in the folio the last word of the preceding line, 'Conspirator,' is also capitalized. Thus, on the theory – not proven – that Folio compositors some-times used capitalization as *emphasis*, the edited text should read

> FIRST PLEBIAN Tear him to pieces! He's a *conspirator*.

Even more puzzling is the following editorial imposition of italics where none are needed:

FESTE Now Jove in his next commodity of hair send thee a beard.
VIOLA By by troth I'll tell thee, I am almost sick for one, though I would not have it grow on *my* chin. Is thy lady within?   (*Twelfth Night*, 3.1)

Same question: what do these italics seek to do, to expound, in the text or how do they assist the performers? Is the editor worried that we – readers, actors, directors – have forgotten the Viola beneath Cesario's disguise? or that we have forgotten that Cesario is not to be imagined as a male? or are these italics meant to alert us to the fact that the late-Elizabethan boy actor playing Viola/Cesario will, when she/he does have a beard on his/her chin, have to cease playing women's roles?[24] None of these erroneous possibilities seems very likely to me, and I do not under-stand the italics. Given my interest in beards and boy actors, though, I entertain the possibility that these italics appeared to prevent some smutty Viola (or his/her director) placing an emphasis on *chin* and thereby remind us of another 'beard,' one shared by female role and boy actor, but not on the chin. Again, though that possibility would delight this critic, I do not hold out much hope it explains the editorial italics, which, finally, I find incomprehensible.[25]

These examples from *Julius Caesar* and *Twelfth Night* illustrate editors trying to harness plural signification and wrestle it to the ground of singular signification; they intervene to rule some meanings in, some out. Yet, one supposes that Shakespeare could and often did out-think, out-imagine, out-create his editors. One of the special pleasures of attending a performance of a Shakespearean play is watching and hearing a new group of theatrically skilled minds and bodies find yet another of the embedded possibilities in a word, line, scene, and – if one is especially lucky – the entire performed play.[26] Here, in this instant of performance – in this word, sound, inflection, movement – the editors we have read and imagined as we read have not respected the possible plural signification of the text but have sought to make it singular. They have most certainly not respected, or even allowed, *jouissance*.

So far we have looked at various forms of punctuation and a little at fonts. With this discussion of italics, we verge on what most people, including editors, think editors do and that is to emend, because that's what the added italics are, they are emendations. Indeed, I often worry that many people go to editing school so that when they graduate they may emend officially, or licentiously. Two categories have proved especially worrying to those who worry about emendation – Shakespeare's foreign languages, especially his characters' French, Spanish, and Welsh – and his characters' malapropisms. Tidying up the foreign languages so they become correct or more correct and modernized so we can understand them risks, of course, missing the point – that they *are* incorrect or that correctness did not matter to Shakespeare, or to his audience and actors, or to his printers.

Malapropism poses a related problem, specifically, when does it exist and how should the editor treat it? Consider the classic example in R. B. Sheridan's *The Rivals* when Mrs Malaprop describes Lydia; she is 'as headstrong as an allegory on the banks of Nile' (Act 3, scene 3). Presumably, the alert audience understands Mrs Malaprop to have mistaken 'allegory' for 'alligator,' though why alligators should be notably or popularly headstrong escapes me – violent, dangerous, predatory, yes, but why 'headstrong'? How many members of the audience will reach another level of error? It is crocodiles, a European-Asiatic reptile, not alligators, a new world creature, that lie on the banks of Nile. And if an alert audience does see or hear that next level of error, so what? Are we to infer a deep cleverness in Sheridan? A multi-layered ignorance in the represented character of Mrs Malaprop? What does an editor do? Obviously, the text cannot be emended to fix the so-called errors because at least one of the errors – allegory/alligator – is the required joke. And what does the glum editor write for a note, grimly correcting Malaprop's or Sheridan's zoological 'error,' or confessing (with me) befuddlement over 'headstrong'?

A malapropism is a pun gone bad, and puns good or bad make for bad or ridiculous editorial notes.

In the abstract, a *malapropos* word has to be close enough to the expected, *àpropos*, word to be both itself and that other word; the distance between them semantically has to be great enough to cause pleased surprise, usually because the 'wrong' word has an inappropriate signification in its verbal context, and both right and wrong words have to be available almost instantly in the audience's perception. The problem for the writer and, later, for the editor, is that the closer the words are in sound, the more likely the audience will themselves be unable to make the discrimination that leads to pleasure. When the two words, one wanted and correct, the other unwanted and humorous, are too close they do not produce pleasure and when they are too far apart they risk causing incredulity or the suspicion that the malapropist is actually in control of the spoken language. From an editorial viewpoint, there's a fine example in *Much Ado*. The Watch are discussing whether they have the authority to 'stay' a man. Verges thinks not. Dogberry disagrees: 'Five shillings to one on't with any man that knows the statutes he may stay him' (*Much Ado*, 3.3). So the quarto. The Folio reads the same except that 'statutes' is printed as 'statues.' The Folio reading, 'statues,' is a respectable Dogberryism, especially since the Watch is soon confused by 'fashion' and 'one Deformed' – they are having a semiotic meltdown: what represents what? On the other hand, 'statues' might have been introduced by a slip *currente calamo* – author's or copyist's or compositor's – in the chain of transmission leading to the printed folio text. Or someone involved with the quarto's printing might have missed the joke – if it is one – and corrected manuscript 'statutes' to 'statues.' One can never solve the crux.

It is worth further noting that another celebrated mis-speaker, Constable Elbow in *Measure for Measure* Act 2, scene 1, might not be so celebrated were it not for Pompey's relentless ridicule of the constable's speech in asides (?) to Escalus. In fact, editors have been rightly puzzled over at least some examples of Elbow's supposed mis-speaking, and on the principle (which I hanker after) that an editor should first try to understand what is printed before emending it, some of Elbow's supposed mistakes do make a kind of sense, lunatic or otherwise. They therefore do not require emendation to make them ridiculous, for they are not ridiculous, or not unequivocally so. Finally, note that on at least one occasion (*Measure*, TLN 545), Pompey himself seems to 'misplace' words when he says 'distant,' apparently an error for 'instant.' That is, Pompey, notable for mocking another character, Elbow, for mis-speaking here seems to himself mis-speak. Or does he? It's an editorial problem.

Thus far, I have concentrated on the ways an editor might seek to regulate the speaking of a text through punctuation, choice of fonts, and emendation, and the way the text might resist such regulation or offer, unamended, alternatives that such regulation rules out. With *Much Ado* still before us, I turn now to the rather grosser ways an editor may intervene to specify a script's performance and hence the way it is perceived and received by its audience. I mean, of course, editorially added stage directions, and I reckon this is where you might have thought I would begin my argument. From sound to, coarsely put, sight. *Ado* has a little scene, the second of Act 1, where Leonato's household prepares to celebrate the return of Don Pedro & Co. from the war. Antonio has relayed the overheard word that Claudio might be interested in Hero, Leonato has ordered that the news be relayed to Hero. Then, at the scene's very end:

Cousins, you know what you have to do. – O, I cry you mercy, friend.
Go you with me and I will use your skill. – Good cousin, have a care this
busy time.   *Exeunt*

This version of this moment is an editor's, Sheldon Zitner's, and is preceded by
the interpolated stage direction *Enter attendants*. As Zitner notes, 'Some editions
have Antonio exit after [line] 21 and specify the entrance of Antonio's son, of
Balthasar, or of a musician. The text requires only bustle here, and such directions
seem both literal-minded and pre-emptive of directorial decisions.'[27] This note
seems exemplary to me, acknowledging the 'bustle' (wonderful word) and not
trying to control actors and director, as numerous earlier editors had done.

The literal-mindedness of interpolated editorial directions or of editors' interpretations are a special target of those critics who charge Shakespeare's editors
with erroneous, limited, or non-existent sensitivities to the performance of the
texts they edit. And there's little question that the critics' arrows sometimes hit
their targets. One popular target has been George Steevens. Writing about
Measure, Act 1, scene 2, the scene in which Claudio is being taken to prison and
the visibly pregnant Juliet is also on stage, Steevens is anxious about impropriety
and wants to get Juliet off-stage so she (or he, that is, the actor who originally
played the part) does not have to hear Claudio's powerful speech on having
lawfully gained Juliet's bed and regretting that their mutual pleasure is with
character too gross written on her body.

Steevens remarks:

> This speech is surely too indelicate to be spoken concerning Juliet, before her face,
> for she appears to be brought in with the rest, tho' she has nothing to say....[28]

Many editors have agreed, if not with the sentiment then at least with the interpolated stage directions that remove Juliet from supposed embarrassment. It is
undoubtedly difficult to imagine (and also to edit or to produce on stage) this
scene from the printed traces in the Folio; there seems, for instance, to be some
repeated information (*Measure*, TLN 153–64 and 183–94) about Angelo's plans for
dismantling brothels that might indicate revision incompletely carried through.
Yet, Steevens's note manifests cultural attitudes about female–male verbal relations
appropriate to the later eighteenth century, but perhaps not so certainly the
attitudes of the early seventeenth. For instance, pre-marital pregnancy was
common in Shakespeare's day, indeed in his own life, and *Measure* makes much of
its plot from a socially conflicted and socially inflected conception of what
constituted a legally and ecclesiastically valid contract or marriage.[29]

Even if we recall E. P. Thompson's withering remark about the condescension
of the present to the past,[30] Steevens's note is easy to mock, and Joseph Ritson's
later reply even more so (Ritson thought the provost's men took Juliet off-stage
as the offending speech was spoken). Poor man, poor editor, Steevens did not
know enough, did not empathize enough. And, be it noted, editors and their

performance-minded critics also do not know enough. It's impossible not to be temporally culture-bound, and impossible not to be ignorant, or both at the same time. Even Doctor Johnson did not know or recall enough about past popular culture to escape a culture-bound error.[31]

I have a few more examples of to interpolate or not to interpolate. One of the most famous moments – for theater practitioner and editor – occurs as Duncan's murder is revealed, and Macbeth justifies killing the grooms who alive might have been witnesses of their own innocence:

> *Macb.*   . . . who could refraine,
> That had a heart to love; and in that heart,
> Courage, to make's love knowne?
> *Lady*. Helpe me hence, hoa.
> *Macd*. Looke to the Lady. (*Macbeth*, TLN 881–5)

Since the 1709 edition by the playwright Nicholas Rowe, editors have thought that Macduff's 'Looke to the Lady' must be spoken in response to *something* the actor playing Lady Macbeth does since 'Helpe me hence, hoa' is a strong request for physical assistance. Rowe responded with *Seeming to faint* and a few lines later, *Lady Macbeth is carried out*. I do not recall that any editor since has been able to resist writing and interpolating a direction or directions, but does the Lady faint or does she feign a faint or does 'Look to the lady' mean something else altogether?[32] It's a major decision for actor and director – what does the Lady do here? Is the Lady overcome by what she and her husband have done? Is she drawing attention away from a Macbeth who might reveal his guilt or horror at what she and/or he has done? Is she drawing attention away from what she or he did or might be suspected to have done? Does the editor need to add a direction here? And this editorial direction, if one is added, is a minor (or major?) decision for the editor who chooses to provide a stage direction – *She faints* or *She pretends to faint*? – and those choices then generate others, such as how does an actor pretend to faint? I have seen it claimed that Adelaide Ristori did manage this latter feat, but how she did it I do not know.[33]

One response to the problem might please those performance critics dissatisfied with current editorial practice. An editor might write a note canvassing the possibilities as that editor understood them and leave the text as is. This choice is utopian because nobody reads notes, and without a visible sign in the text, the line will remain extremely puzzling. And when I say 'nobody reads notes,' I especially do not mean undergraduate students or novice Shakespeareans. I mean 'nobody.' It may perchance be the case that 'editors are primarily speaking to themselves,' as some performance-minded critics have claimed,[34] but editors – like the rest of us – want to be read, considered, even cited, and passed through communal memory to the future. Editors, like the rest of us, are not doing what they do for their health.

Finally, two examples from a recent edition of *Troilus and Cressida*:

Enter THERSITES, [*followed by*] AJAX. [*Ajax is having trouble getting the attention of Thersites, who is no doubt pretending not to hear.*]

(*Troilus and Cressida*, 2.1, opening stage direction)

PATROCLUS [*to Thersites, as though addressing Ajax*] Jove bless great Ajax!
THERSITES [*Mimics Ajax' manner*] H'm!   (*Troilus and Cressida*, 3.3)

The first of these directions is questionable because the situation so elaborately described – note *described* – and the theatrical effect of the interpolated direction either emerges from the dialogue or does not. My own bet is that many readers, actors, and directors will imagine exactly what the direction says, though *no doubt* is a bit strong, and no imaginable audience needs the direction to understand the immediate situation. The second stage direction really stipulates what the actor must do and *Mimics* is only one possibility, though it is clear from 'Do this' that Achilles has asked for the Patroclus-and-Thersites-show to 'do,' that is to perform, one of Shakespeare's characteristic inset-plays *ex tempore*. Be it noted that another current edition, also one that strives to be theatrically informed and performance-friendly, has no added directions in either place.

So, there you have it: a miscellaneous collection of editorial interventions in both how a play sounds and how it looks; in the last few cases editors have even given gestural and postural hints. In most of the examples, I think the intervention unnecessary or excessive, though always the consequence of an honest, laudable desire to imagine the plays in performance and to help readers – undergraduate students, mostly, if truth be told about most editors' ambitions, and perhaps graduate students – visualize performance. (Trying to impress another audience – one's scholarly colleagues – in an edition risks catastrophic commercial neglect and press complaints about length. And one's colleagues are sadly hard to impress.)

Most of these editorial interventions fail, though they fail in different ways – hence the miscellany. Yet the performance-critics unhappy with current editions (and I have said that there is great variety out there and many differences of accomplishment) want editors to do more of at least some of these things in addition to what editors have always done, more or less, for better or worse. Editors are rarely good at imagining multiple performance possibilities in the plays they edit, witness my miscellany, and that's why good editors have recourse to performance history to guide them to the problems and solutions that up to 400+ years have identified as cruxes for performers. Let us imagine that every academic editor of Shakespeare is accompanied by Harry Berger or Deborah Warner or Jonathan Miller or Julie Taymor and that those luminaries illuminate the theatrical aspects of the text, and the editor writes it all down and purveys it in the edition, which also includes her own editorial contributions – introduction, performance and critical history, annotation, collation, textual discussion. What do you achieve? You achieve *a very large book*, which few would undertake to publish and which quite possibly none, or few, or some would read as anything but a reference work.[35]

Make no mistake, though I quarrel with some of the performance critics' views, I find their theatrical imaginings stimulating and sometimes – even often – with editorial consequences. My contention here is (a) persons equipped to make good editions of old plays are (b) rarely equipped (or at best only intermittently equipped) to understand matters of performance to the same standard[36] and (c) if performance exploration for an entire Shakespearean play were added to the still-necessary apparatus already there in present editions, the book would balloon and fail commercially, if it finds a publisher, and fail any other of its possible audiences.[37]

One other proposal comes to mind, and it's not a good one. Just as the Shakespeare in Production series (originally published by Bristol Classical Press, now by Cambridge University Press under the general editorship of J. S. Bratton and Julie Hankey) publishes running performance history annotations opposite an unglossed text,[38] so too could a third style of annotated but unglossed text arise, this time annotated with performance possibilities in mind – and here I mean possibilities for a variety of stages and casts, some perhaps historical, others hypothetical – stages round, square, thrust, proscenium, interior, exterior, formal or *ad hoc*, casts small, large, uni- or heterosexual, uni- or multilingual, with or without costumes, props, sets, sound design or music.

Though I seek no compassion or pity – critics typically make only a few noticed errors, editors (who are critics *and* editors, after all) make many – I end with a plangent lament for the editor, any editor:

> What makes editing such a near-impossible task is the many-armed Briareus of a thing it has become. Before [F. W.] Bateson's time [and the Longman Annotated English Poets series he inaugurated], editors mostly aimed to know their Golden Age *auctores* and perhaps the Church Fathers. But he showed literature's whole context to be potentially relevant, and no one can now catch all the associations so considered.[39]

The same critic quotes Bateson, who 'wanted an altogether different sort of editing, concerned "primarily with the *meaning* of the extant texts in their various contexts..."' and, this critic says, Bateson wished the editor would '"provide the reader in assimilable form with the information accumulated by recent scholarship and criticism on the meaning and occasion of the individual poems."'

This view of editing and of literary criticism is an *ignis fatui*. It is also a dearly-to-be-desired goal, but it is a goal no edition, no piece of editing, could ever achieve, just as no imaginable edition of a Shakespearean text can, or could, ever achieve the form(s) all its critics desire.

Notes

1. Samuel Johnson replies to William Warburton's remark on 'Who falling in the flawes of her owne youth, / Hath blisterd her report,' lines in *Measure for Measure*, here quoted from the first Folio, T[hrough] L[ine] N[umbers] 964–5, as lined by Charlton Hinman in

the Norton facsimile of the first Folio (New York: W. W. Norton, 1968) with i/j, u/v, 'long' *s* modernized and spacing normalized; later quotations from the Folio are similarly modified and cited with TLN parenthetically in my text. Warburton and Johnson are cited from *Johnson on Shakespeare*, ed. Arthur Sherbo, in the Yale Edition of Samuel Johnson, 16 vols (New Haven: Yale University Press, 1968), 7: 186. My epigraph begs the reader's patience: my tale is one where there is no end of correction, but also a tale that hopes for an end, or at least begs thoughts about why there is no such end. Subsequently, place of publication is London unless otherwise indicated.

2. Even this early, I warn the reader that things are not so simple as they might appear. As my argument evolves, it will become clear that the editor imagined by her critics is required, or may be required, to record past performance choices as well as possible ones – history, practice, possible practice, in short. Stephen Orgel's written comments and Peter Holland's verbal ones improved this chapter, although, alas, they are not responsible for its flaws. Many thanks, too, to Barbara Hodgdon, who shared both her pre-publication writings and her good thoughts.

   Two volumes will be referred to here by short-titles: Ann Thompson and Gordon McMullan, eds, *In Arden: Editing Shakespeare: Essays in Honour of Richard Proudfoot* (Arden Shakespeare/Thomson Learning, 2003), hereafter cited as *In Arden*, and Lukas Erne and Margaret Jane Kidnie, eds, *Textual Performances: the Modern Reproduction of Shakespeare's Drama* (Cambridge: Cambridge University Press, 2004), hereafter cited as *Textual Performances*. These two volumes have many essays that develop and deepen points I make; they are strongly recommended.

3. Michael Cordner, 'Annotation and Performance in Shakespeare,' *Essays in Criticism* 46 (1996), 289–301, from p. 289. See also George Walton Williams: 'We stand now at a point of transition in the editing of Shakespeare's plays...I argue that every editor should be a director, whose page is his stage' ('To edit? to direct? – ay, there's the rub' in *In Arden*, 111–12). There have been, too, sound objections. Reviewing various Shakespeare titles, James Fenton touches on the critical trend in which '[p]erformance itself became the criterion for interpretation' and comments, 'This seems to derive from a stage-struck scholarship, or from a critical orthodoxy that conveniently forgets how much a modern production of Shakespeare depends on scholarly and critical guidance.... it remains true that without scholarly editions neither actor nor director would have the foggiest notion of what crucial passages in the plays mean' (*New York Review of Books*, 8 April 2004, 56).

4. Michael Cordner, 'Actors, editors, and the annotation of Shakespearian playscripts,' *Shakespeare Survey* 55 (Cambridge: Cambridge University Press, 2002), 181–98, from p. 181; for a similarly equivocal remark, see 'All of these editions offer exemplary scholarship... with elegantly conceived annotative apparatuses designed to alert readers to matters etymological, literary, historical, sociological (in a veritable host of Polonian combinations)...' (Barbara Hodgdon, 'New Collaborations...' in *Textual Performances*, 211).

5. Essays documenting and attacking the new bibliographers' idealization of intentionality appear in Laurie Maguire and Thomas Berger, eds., *Textual Formations and Reformations* (Newark: University of Delaware Press, 1998). See also Laurie Maguire, *Shakespearean Suspect Texts* (Cambridge: Cambridge University Press, 1996), chapters 1 and 2 (where the joking Freudian allusion also appears) and Ernst Honigmann, 'The New Bibliography and its critics' in *Textual Performances*, 77–93.

6. See, e.g., Helen Wilcox, 'The Character of a footnote... or, annotation revisited' in *In Arden*, 205, and consult the editorial guidelines for the Oxford, New Cambridge, and Arden 3 editions, respectively.

7. In addition to the essays cited in notes 2 and 3 above, see Barbara Hodgdon, 'New collaborations with old plays: the (textual) politics of performance commentary' in *Textual Performances*, 210–23, for instance.

8. See, *inter alia*, the essays by Barbara Hodgdon, George Walton Williams, Lynette Hunter and Peter Lichtenfels, and John Russell Brown in *In Arden*.

9. This sentence and indeed the entire prefatory text it once inhabited have vanished from recent volumes, presumably because the original writer and general editor, Philip Brockbank, has died and because the now-established series no longer needs a preface or introduction *per se*.

10. Among the exceptions: Nicholas Rowe in the eighteenth century and Henry Irving (with Frank Marshall) in the nineteenth are, respectively, a playwright and a distinguished actor who published theatrically sensitive editions of Shakespeare's plays.

11. Barbara Hodgdon, 'New collaborations,' in *Textual Performances*, 212.

12. Odyssey Theatre, Los Angeles, California, 21 March 2004.

13. See Barbara Hodgdon's remarks about exclamation points, 'Who is performing "in" these text(s)?; or, *Shrew*-ing around' in *In Arden*, 99 and Cordner, 'The Annotation...', 191.

14. Robert Pinsky, *The Sounds of Poetry: A Brief Guide* (N.Y.: Farrar, Straus, and Giroux, 1998), 3.

15. See, e.g., the relevant note in A. R. Braunmuller, ed., *Macbeth*, New Cambridge Shakespeare (Cambridge: Cambridge University Press, 1997): 'F's question mark...can represent either interrogation (sincere or scornful) or exclamation (surprised, scornful, or resigned).' I now recognize that this note is too dichotmous (note the *or*s), but it is a start.

16. The recession of hearing and speaking here is a classic, but unusual, example of free indirect discourse in drama.

17. Shakespeare, *Venus and Adonis*, lines 27–8 in *Complete Sonnets and Poems*, ed. Colin Burrow, The Oxford Shakespeare (Oxford: Oxford University Press, 2002).

18. Ibid.

19. Let me be explicit and complimentary that the data on Malone's and Bell's changes derive from Colin Burrow's collation to his thoughtful edition of the non-dramatic poems and sonnets of Shakespeare, cited in n. 17.

20. These three words – editorial, cultural, typographical – are, of course, mutually dependent, not exclusive; each is the others.

21. Private correspondence, B. Vinklers, 16 February 2004, citing *Chicago Manual of Style*, 14th edition (Chicago: University of Chicago Press, 1993), 6.80, and *Words into Type*, 3rd edition (Engelwood Cliffs, N.J.: Prentice-hall, 1974), 217. Neither authority quotes the phrase 'call you that' *As You Like It*, but do cite 'so-called,' 'termed,' 'called,' and 'known as.'

22. Note the superb ambiguity of *fear* in 'do I feare my Selfe' (TLN 3644): do I frighten myself? am I afraid of myself? Further, the thorough capitalization of *self* and its separation from the possessive *my* are noteworthy; the latter – 'my Self' rather than *myself* is not especially unusual in the Folio, where no conventional spacing (*myself* or *my self*) seems to prevail, but combined with the capitalization of *self* seems a deliberate attempt to represent typographically a specific psychic and verbal situation.

23. In the following examples from recent editions, I attempt to represent the edited texts accurately, but I have usually not specified the editor and source of each example. My point is not to quibble with individual editors but to show a range of editorial practice (my own included) as a category.

24. See Flute's complaint or worry: 'Nay faith, let not mee play a woman, I have a beard comming' (*Midsummer Night's Dream*, TLN 309–10).

25. Editors of Shakespeare are not alone in such editorial-directorial-actorly italicizing. J. S. Cunningham's excellent Revels Plays edition of *Tamburlaine the Great* (Manchester: Manchester University Press, 1981) twice introduces italics, once collated, once not: see *Tamburlaine the Great, Part II*, 2.4.90 (collated) – 'Her name had been in every line he wrote' – and 4.1.51 (not) – 'I go into the field before I need?', respectively.

26. For example, Roger Allam's pause before 'stuff' in a difficult line from *Macbeth* – 'Cleanse the stuffed bosom of that perilous stuff' – at the RSC in 1996, where the pause indicated (to me) the character's fatigued inability to discover an appropriate or more precise word. Editors have been much bothered by the repetition, and much emendatious.

27. Sheldon Zitner, ed., *Much Ado About Nothing*, Oxford Shakespeare (Oxford: Oxford University Press, 1993) 1.2.22, 24n.

28. Quoted from Mark Eccles, ed., William Shakespeare, *Measure for Measure*, a new variorum edition (N.Y.: Modern Language Association, 1980).

29. The literature is immense; see Victoria Hayne, 'Performing social practice: the example of *Measure for Measure*,' *Shakespeare Quarterly* 44 (1993), 1–29, for instance, and, more generally, B. J. Sokol and Mary Sokol, *Shakespeare, Law, and Marriage* (Cambridge: Cambridge University Press, 2003).

30. 'I am seeking to rescue the poor stockinger ... the "obsolete" hand-loom weaver, the "utopian" artisan ... from the enormous condescension of posterity.' See E. P. Thompson, *The Making of the English Working Class* (1963), 12.

31. Commenting on 'Standing on slippers, which his nimble haste / Had falsely thrust upon contrary feet' (*King John*, ed. A. R. Braunmuller, Oxford Shakespeare [Oxford: Oxford University Press, 1987], 4.2.197–98), Johnson wrote, 'Shakespeare seems to have confounded a man's shoes with his gloves. He that is frighted or hurried may put his hand into the wrong glove, but either shoe will equally admit either foot. The authour seems to be disturbed by the disorder which he describes.' See *Johnson on Shakespeare*, 7:425. 'Hippoclides' cites a letter from Thomas Seccombe to argue that Johnson's note is confusing because he does not make clear the distinction between slippers (which were interchangeable left-to-right in Johnson's day) and shoes (which in most styles were not and never had been); see 'Dr. Johnson's Boots,' *Notes & Queries*, 5 March 1910, 184–5.

32. A hinted suspicion of the Lady's complicity, perhaps? This possible performance might be conveyed by a calm or meditative, reflective or puzzled, rather than an excited or exclamatory delivery.

33. See 2.3.112 n. in Braunmuller, ed., *Macbeth*.

34. Hodgdon, 'New Collaborations', *Textual Performances*, 212.

35. You might achieve an online edition, but I now agree, though I didn't once, with John Lavagnino that 'It's not a straightforward task to make something digital that is easier to use than a book for this kind of thing [edited dramatic text with commentary]' ('Two varieties of digital commentary' in *Textual Performances*, 194–209; from p. 200). See also n. 37 below.

36. I include myself, alas.

37. As Barbara Hodgdon and Peter Holland (the latter privately) have noted (in Hodgdon's words), 'Several projects designed to present commentary attuned to performance have been mounted or proposed – among them Ardenonline's performance site and the Arden 3 *Complete Performance Edition*, the one defunct, the other withdrawn' (Hodgdon, 'New Collaborations,' *Textual Performances*, 219). I submit that such an edition as the latter might be compact enough for commercial success, but at the expense of omitting all or most of the Arden 3 commentary as currently conceived if the performance commentary were of the same standard.

38. What does 'unglossed' mean? It means that these volumes print an edited text that offers the reader or 'text-user' no information about obsolete or archaic words, biblical or classical allusions, nor other helps to interpretation and aids to reflection. At least some critics of current annotative styles apparently think verbal annotation impedes or ignores theatrical imaginings. Michael Cordner reports that his 'confidence dwindles' after he reads 'that the Arden 3 notes "will offer glossarial and other explication of verbal difficulties"' because '[r]endering our Shakespeare editions convincingly performance-friendly must entail recognizing that "the explication of verbal difficulties" is itself frequently bound to raise ... issues of "theatrical interpretation"' (Cordner, 'Actors, editors ...,' 182). This is not new *news*: old words need explication, and actors' understanding of old words will, doubtless and with or without help from critics of editions or editors, affect performance (see also ibid., 187).

39. Frank Kermode, review of Nigel Smith's edition of Andrew Marvell, [London] *Times Literary Supplement*, 12 December 2003, 7.

7

De-generation: Editions, Offspring, and *Romeo and Juliet*

Wendy Wall

> O thou untaught, what manners is in this,
> To presse before thy Father to a grave.
>
>

Romeo and Juliet[1]

I. Slouching towards Bethlehem

In 1933 Ronald B. McKerrow lectured the British Academy in an ambitious attempt to rehabilitate eighteenth-century editors of Shakespeare. Rather than dismissing these practitioners as quacks, McKerrow carefully outlined the assumptions and blindspots of their work. In doing so, he constructed a generational line of both editors and of texts, assessing work in part by looking to an editor's grasp of textual lineage: did he or did he not understand the basic point that earlier, parent texts had authority that their belated textual children lacked? Speaking specifically about Edward Capell, who had labored to transcribe Shakespeare's earliest quartos in preparation for his 1768 edition, McKerrow writes:

> Unfortunately having got together this magnificent collection of material for editing Shakespeare, Capell, did not know, any better than his *predecessors*, how to use it. That he was perfectly capable of working out the relationships of the texts seems obvious.... He saw quite clearly that *editions tend to degenerate with each reprint*, but he seems never to have drawn the inference that Johnson did, that readings in a late text which differed from those of an earlier one from which it had itself been printed could not possibly be of any authority.[2]

For McKerrow, this was simply an obvious and logical issue: a text set from a previous one could not introduce an authoritative difference. This tenet makes sense, for editions reset and published over time do alter. McKerrow's foundational schema, as outlined here, however, raises one important question: can it always be determined which text was set from which?[3] Is there one evident grandfather playscript that bears final authority? And do subsequent editions then necessarily 'tend to degenerate' within a conceptual schema where differences are equated with 'errors'? What does it mean to impose a diachronic model structured on biological generations on the transmission of texts, a structuring lens so powerful that it is used even to map similarities and differences among individual editors? What information gets pushed to the side if an editor approaches textual issues using the lens of family?

McKerrow's assumption is so common – and so obviously open to ideological critique – that it slips under the radar of what needs consideration today.[4] Leading editorial practitioners this century, including Alfred Pollard, simply assumed the importance of establishing the Shakespearean text's proper genealogy. When W. W. Greg qualified the established paradigm, he did so by differentiating between 'substantive' and 'derivative' editions, with substantive defined as the 'first of [a] line of descent.'[5] If Pollard created, and Greg refined, the guidelines that McKerrow elaborated, neither extensively highlighted metaphors of family association. McKerrow, that is, put a fine point on an *implicit* new bibliographical structure designed to establish priority, and he did so by figuring it in terms of generations. The year before McKerrow's lecture, the British Academy had strikingly heard Sir Arthur Quiller-Couch argue that Shakespeare's plays gradually accentuated 'higher strain[s] of paternal feeling and of correspondent filial affection.'[6] His lecture, entitled 'Paternity in Shakespeare,' worked from the assumption that there was a gradual loosening of the Father's absolute command over persons and property in Shakespeare's works, and a correspondent strengthening of the patriarch's rightful respect. McKerrow's essay is prominently now bound for posterity along with Quiller-Couch's previous annual talk in volumes of the *Proceedings of the British Academy*; that is, the material form of McKerrow's address about bibliographical practice notably displays ways in which he took prevalent *thematic* considerations of Shakespearean filiation into the register of editing.

Margreta de Grazia's work has addressed the broader issue of why modern methods were not obvious at all to eighteenth-century editors. In her account, Edmond Malone's decision to turn consistently to original editions marks a moment in which conceptions of literary property, individuation, and authenticity were altered.[7] Previous editors had consulted early versions of Shakespeare's plays, but they usually only did so when a problem with a later and preferred edition arose. In such instances editors then grouped the earliest texts into a hodgepodge with later editions. It was precisely the editors' decisions not to seek a single original base text that so bothered McKerrow. It was not really apparent to eighteenth-century editors, that is, that texts de-generated over time. It took modern bibliographers to create the framework that made this assessment possible. Before they did so, texts seemed to move unevenly, neither spiraling toward perfection nor slouching towards Bethlehem.

McKerrow used 'degenerate' to mean a general decline in value. If we look to the most common definition of 'degenerate,' as expressed in early modern bilingual and hard-word dictionaries, we find that its meaning derives from *genus*: 'to grow out of kinde: to be or become unlike his ancestours in manners or conditions.'[8] McKerrow's choice of phrase is haunted by its historical root meanings, a semantic pressure evident throughout his discussion of bibliographical method.

Playscripts need to be established only by creating proper filiation, McKerrow argued:

> if we want Shakespeare's original text the only place where we have any chance of finding it is in a quarto or folio which is at the head of *a line of descent*, and... if *descendants* of such a quarto or folio have different readings from their *ancestor*, those readings must be either accidental corruptions or deliberate alterations by compositors or proof-readers, and in no case have an authority superior to, or even as great as, the readings of the text from which they differ.[9]

Editorial work requires patiently tracking 'a line of descent,' with descent implying both spatial and temporal movement – to come after, derive from, but also to flow downwardly, fall, or sink. Bad editions are faulty precisely because they include legitimate heirs between their covers, blended indiscriminately with their ancestors. Good editions recognize the absolute sterility of the original. Once determined, the ur-text exists in categorical separation from the line of descent it engenders. Establishing a genealogy allows editors to isolate the source and then to map the concomitant process of falling as that source devolves. The textual family lineage thus has clear valences: being outside the family line or at its head designates a text as 'substantive'; being included snugly within the family makes one a poorly reproduced and 'derivative' beneficiary. For McKerrow, only a systematic rather than eclectic comparison of texts might illuminate the lines of descent that travel back – upwardly – to the author-forebear. His goal was the creation of a hereditarily faithful edition, one true, to take early modern definitions, to the manners of the progenitor text rather than to its diminished descendants, and one constructed by those who had a clear retrospective view of the family line. Editorial work today, however nuanced and qualified in its terminology, finds itself often retracking a genealogical quest activated by new bibliographers, attempting to detach the original that spawned imperfect and belated descendants.

The association of degradation with a familial uprooting is evident everywhere in early modern usage. 'Degenerates' in Shakespearean vocabulary typically fracture the family, un-making lineage by introducing a troublesome difference. When Lear calls Goneril a 'Degenerate bastard,' we see that what functions as a handy all-purpose moral slur today – ('you degenerate you!') – was deep-structurally embedded in conceptions of the early modern family.[10] As Lear metaphorically un-fathers his daughter, he means assuredly to denounce her character, but Goneril's sin is expressed as a rupture of pedigree, the child's manners severing her claim to the father she has wrongly attempted to rule. As the fool has just commented in this scene, the cart draws the horse. So Lear sees his daughter as 'debased,' a reversal or setback lowering the degree of humanity as she corrupts the family. Shakespeare's Henry IV sees his self-consciously wayward son Hal in comparable terms; his 'near'st and dearest enemy' becomes 'degenerate' because capable, the king imagines, of plotting patricide with the Percys (3.2.123; 128). 'Degenerate...ingrate rebels' are said to rip up the womb of 'dear mother

England' in *King John* (5.2.151; 153). And Lucrece sees her rapist Tarquin's moral bankruptcy as amplified by his now tainted but prestigious bloodline: 'The baser is he, coming from a king,/To shame his hope with deeds degenerate' (ll. 1002-3). It seems a common discursive slide, in the Shakespearean text, to move from accusations of degeneracy to assertions of familial fracture or generational violence; moral failures, that is, are commonly read as signs of either sterility, family obliteration, or de-evolution.

Later editors are not of course bound by Renaissance meanings for their terms. But, as we've seen, the notion that degeneration implied 'a fall away from ancestral excellence; a decline in character' (*OED*) still haunts McKerrow's usage centuries later, saturated as it is with concern for the erosions of temporal reprintings. That McKerrow's schema implies a teleology privileging origins is obvious. That he sees genealogy as the structure best figuring the transmission of Renaissance play-texts is obvious as well. But in this chapter, I think it important to dwell on the obvious, in part because there's still much to mine in the specific case of *Romeo and Juliet*, a play commonly touted as investigating the formative power of the family and a play whose specific textual history presents problems for a lineage model. Scholarship on the play shows that it *hasn't* been obvious that the kinship structure imposed on the text's bibliographical history might bear on questions routinely asked of it by readers and critics. While the very early texts of this play at hand have something useful to say to editors who grapple with their confusing status, I concentrate centrally on another question: how does an analysis of the play's earliest forms, freed from the organizational straitjacket of a bibliographic family tree, complicate the stories that literary critics tell?

I should qualify: new bibliographers clearly theoretically understood the ambiguity of the 'original,' as do modern editors. Greg allowed for two substantive semi-parents with divided authority and he acknowledged that derivative texts could become substantive if much altered; that is, texts could be 'mixed,' or could work themselves in and out of a bloodline, an event rather more difficult to accomplish within biological families.[11] Rather than beholding a tidy lineage, editors sometimes encountered a polygenous tree, with sprouting bastard kin in disarray. But, to Greg's thinking, this disorder only provoked a more intensified search for a pattern of resemblances to a mythologized and textual father rather than prompting a look at other, horizontal, perhaps less causal, less organic, or less definitive models. Editors after the new bibliographers inherited a directive: you have to fashion the father's image out of blemished progeny. All you've got, at first, however, are unruly textual adolescents. Just kids.

II. A poxed play-text a both your houses

It's standard wisdom that *Romeo and Juliet* scrutinizes the power of family identification in relation to phantasmatic desires and social anomie. In all early play-texts, the lovers disavow an identity grounded in familial origin. 'Denie thy Father, and refuse thy name, / Or if thou wilt not be but sworne my loue, / And il'e no longer be a *Capulet*,' croons Juliet on the balcony, imagining a feverish erotic connection predicated on the repudiation of family ties.[12] Romeo later imagines radically and violently amputating his ancestral marker: 'Ah tell me holy Fryer,/ In what vile part of this Anatomy/Doth my name lye? Tell me, that I may sacke/The hatefull mansion?'[13] Renouncing the family name while remaking one's self *sui genesis* is the utopian erotic fantasy that ignites and binds the lovers, tied as it is to what Jonathan Goldberg calls a 'powerful utopian sense of an identity that is separable from its verbal representation.'[14] The yearning to be freed from the grip of inherited determination coincides with a craving for liberty from a fixed 'name.' This desire – as well as the intense fear that the possibility arouses – is something that McKerrow would want to put in check so as to reinstate the play, if not its characters, to a rightful and stable lineage; textual progeny, in his paradigm, should bear the imprint and name of the parent text, or else risk being dismissed as having no independent authority.

Yet plotting family relationships between the early texts of *Romeo and Juliet* isn't an easy task. To use McKerrow's approach requires that one identify the genetic trajectory of the play's earliest editions. Since all Folios and seventeenth-century quartos derive ultimately from the quarto published in 1599 by Thomas Creede, it's uncontroversial to establish it – hereafter called Q2 – at the head of one family line. Once named as such, Q2's heirs thus become irrelevant because they are impure copies of their superior predecessor. But a baffling situation arises when we turn to the other extant substantive text, the much shorter quarto published in 1597 by John Danter and Edward Allde (Q1). According to McKerrow, we need to know which quarto was set from which. Largely assumed in the eighteenth and nineteenth centuries to demonstrate authorial revision of playscripts, twentieth-century editors explained these double texts by calling forth the story of pirates and forgetful reporters. New bibliographers were quick to argue that Q1 was one of those naughty quartos that degenerated from the family line; it descended through the memory and hands of reporters, actors, and perhaps the playwright Henry Chettle.[15] Because the 'good' Q2 was first advertised as 'corrected and amended,' it is said to supplant a previous corrupt form of itself. So the later text is really a version of a prior one, and the earlier one an abridged, reassembled stab at the manuscript on which the later one is more accurately based. To create a stemma, editors must posit a chronology that is, on the face of it, *preposterous*, in the Renaissance use of the term (*prae* meant 'in front of' and *posterus* 'behind'). The 'heir' is really the ancestor; the *seeming* ancestor a degenerate, something altered in manners and conditions from its (later) precursor. Such has been the standard story repeated by editors throughout much of the twentieth century.

But even with such an ingenious inversion, editors remain faced with puzzling arrangements of sequencing, for Q1 cannot be dismissed as a text merely set badly from Q2 in the printshop. Q2 came later than Q1 except in some posited ideal form, a textual Romeo without a name. More importantly, editors can't simply tell the story that would, in their schema, solve the textual problem in expected familial terms. They cannot declare that Q2 was set from a better source than Q1 altogether and thus that Q2 exists in a completely separate line of descent. Why not? Because at least one long passage, and perhaps more, from Q2 are lifted directly from the printed 'bad' quarto, as typographical peculiarities such as italics, punctuation, and speech prefix abbreviations evidence. Editors agree that Q2 inherited *something* directly from the physical layout of Q1.[16] Thus the standard claim is that Q2 was printed from authorial foul papers or from a promptbook marked up with confusing interlining and annotation, one that required that the compositor look in places at Q1 but not when setting the whole text. Q2 thus becomes an odd descendant re-evaluated as an *ascendant*, a forebear who came after, and therefore a text both substantive and partially derivative. What this means is that Q2 is said to come before Q1 in its platonic manuscript form, but to *follow* Q1 in its printed material incarnation. This theory necessarily makes Q1 a 'tainted' forerunner to Q2 but *only sometimes*. According to this line of thinking, both early editions of the play appear to be a little bit bad, a little bit degenerate, and a little bit original. If Q1 is an edited version of some form of Q2, or, as Goldberg argues, Q2 is an anthology of performance options or a text revised over time, then we have a game of mutual citation and derivation that makes absolute priority impossible to determine. The two quartos simply mutually begat each other in peculiar ways.

Even editors satisfied with the unusual provenance of these quartos don't feel at liberty to declare the second quarto authoritative and move out of the textual quagmire that becomes apparent in editors' accounts. Because of Q2's famous 'false starts' (repetitions that put forth double versions of some of its lines), the text itself seems to be temporally divided internally; it bears within it its own descendant, its fallen shadow. This feature, according to some editors, proves the text's authenticity because it reveals characteristic signs of a messy authorial manuscript complete with first attempts and trial formulations. Such an air-tight, if circular, argument leaves the editor with the prerogative, or rather the imperative, to alter Q2 to make it more singular. One standard way of cleaning it up is by consulting Q1 for a reference point, the very text that standard wisdom accounts a bastard progeny. Whether Q2's superfluity bears signs of authorial revision (as Grace Ioppolo suggests[17]) or simply puts forth a plentitude of performance options (as argued by Goldberg and Steven Urkowitz[18]), its multiplicity eventually presents the problem of the text's relationship to Q1: from what did they descend? Is each relatively corrupt or relatively reliable? And how would such *relatives* be tailored to fit a paradigmatic line of descent? As double step-parents? Incestuously intermingled generations? Kissing cousins?

Since the exact relationship of these texts remains unsure and, to my mind, insoluble, all theories, however informed and researched, must remain speculative. The model of vertical biological generations that tends to underpin editorial practice, however, tends to naturalize knowledge and fails to reflect the doubt at its core. The family model, that is, forces the texts into a reductive paradigm that can't allow for the interconnections between the texts that editors freely admit. What is definite is that two published substantive texts reached readers in the period. An eighteenth-century editor who consulted multiple quartos without being fully assured of which should have the worst seat at the family gathering was hardly as misguided as the new bibliographers assumed. In fact, these early editors only did freely what modern editors do occasionally and surreptitiously, since current editors emend Q2 sometimes by reference to her estranged sibling who is also her bad parent at moments but not at others.[19] Without disavowing the 'obvious' principle that McKerrow outlined, editors today necessarily have recourse to a synchronic, somewhat confused, family tree, a queer one, one might say, despite a commitment to principles resting elsewhere.

In the *Textual Companion* to the Oxford edition of Shakespeare's works, John Jowett helpfully attempts to map the complicated textual genealogy of the earliest editions of *Romeo and Juliet* in diagram form (see Figure 39).[20] This project involved slotting the texts into a family tree in which generations are expectedly

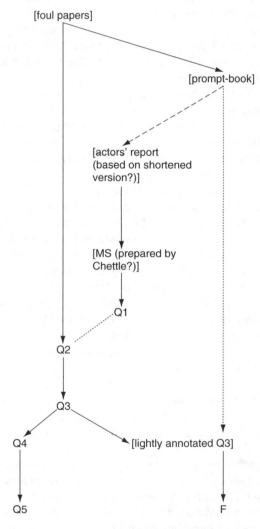

Figure 39   The family tree of the *Romeo and Juliet* text. Reprinted from *William Shakespeare: A Textual Companion*, by Stanley Wells and Gary Taylor, with John Jowett and William Montgomery (Oxford: Clarendon Press, 1987), 288

signaled vertically. Stemming from Shakespeare's hypothetical foul papers are two lines of descent, one leading to the prompt book and the other leading to the second quarto. As such, the diagram suggests a clear bond between the author's original draft and Q2, with Q2 begetting three subsequent quarto editions. But the diagram boasts features that indicate how precarious the relationships among the texts remain: dotted lines, broken lines, and question marks indicate uncertainty about various paths of transmission, foregrounding the editor's necessary speculation about the origins and causality, and sometimes indicating a questionable route for Q1's path in particular (that is, the text became corrupted precisely by following the lines that remain provisional, and thus the lines are 'questionable' in many senses of the word). For my purposes, it's striking that the text of Q1 doesn't remain firmly fixed in any one vertically-aligned generation, but occupies instead an in-between position, hovering in the air between generations, as both sibling and parent to Q2. The broken line descending down from Q1 to Q2 points to the 'bad' quarto's odd place as corrupting precisely in its capacity to be generative. Modern editions based on these models are cross-fertilized in ways that make a normative family model hard to maintain.

When Goldberg describes Q1 as the unacknowledged 'legitimating ancestor for any edited *Romeo and Juliet*,' he uses 'ancestor' in a curious and revisionary fashion to indicate its secret prominence for editorial projects disavowing its authority: it's the 'dark specter' haunting an editor's job, a parent text retrospectively nominated as such because *verifying* habits of offspring.[21] As such, Goldberg elasticizes the family model that binds the texts in restrictive ways. His chief assumption, that *Romeo and Juliet*'s textual properties are steeped in issues taken up by the play-texts themselves, is a point that I want to re-elaborate in a different register. How do the texts, taken in their multiplicity, shed light on one familiar – or perhaps I should say familial – phantasmatic infrastructure of bibliographical practice?

III. Cutting him out in little stars

> *Ro.*: O teach me how I should forget to thinke.
> *Ben.*: By giving libertie unto thine eyes/Examine other bewties[22]

If the earliest texts of *Romeo and Juliet* are viewed as what Leah Marcus calls 'troublesome doubles' rather than as parent and progeny, what might critics gain?[23] I explore this inquiry by focusing on the plays' endings, the famed scenes of collective grieving, memorialization, and civic reconciliation that name this tragedy as legendary. In both quartos, surviving families and state work to translate events into a meaningful 'story of woe.' Both endings toy with temporal order, casting a look backwards to grasp and solidify horrific events that then are made contingent on future narrations. But on what do these future representations depend? What inheres in and secures closure? Is the family rehabilitated as a viable institution in Verona, emerging from its pathological tie to fated death? Or do we see staged the feudal family's limitations? Such questions, regularly asked by critics, can't be answered definitively, in part because the earliest play-texts offer subtly different answers. These 'troublesome doubles,' I suggest, trouble at least three issues that arise in criticism of the play: the final authority of the state; the reconciliation of the feud; and the play's famed self-referentiality.

First, let's examine the status of the prince at the end. Declaring everyone chastised, Q2 Prince includes himself in those suffering divine retribution: 'See what a scourge is laide upon your hate?' he asks, 'That heaven finds means to kil your joyes with love; / And I for winking at your discords too,/Have lost a brace of kinsmen, all are punisht.'[24] 'Eskales,' the character formerly known only as 'prince' in Q1 and identified here only in print, then witnesses the fathers' agreement to join hands and create a collaborative memorial. He responds by separating himself from his ruled subjects (and perhaps from the audience as well): 'Go hence to have more talke of these sad things,/Some shall be pardoned, and some punished. For never was a Storie of more wo, / Then this of *Juliet* and her *Romeo*' (M2r). The effect is to have the city-state distinguish itself from within Verona's competitive political scene. The Prince issues directives to the fathers, and emphasizes his juridical role in assigning blame. All are emotionally punished but only some will be singled out for discipline at his discretion. Capulet's and Montague's agreement to reconcile, he implies, isn't tantamount to closure, nor do family heads have the right to arbitrate the social calamity or to determine the course of events. Whatever their authority in buying conspicuous funeral monuments and attempting to value their children, they need to talk some more and await punishments handed down from on high. The superlative story of woe – however seemingly 'closed' the formal final couplet implies – is still in the process of being shaped.

Now let's turn to Q1 Prince, who draws the families into a collaborative conversation, even while establishing a measure of authority over them. Almost inviting the patriarchs to pitch in and make sense of baffling matters, he exhorts them: 'Come *Capolet*, and come, olde *Montagewe*. / Where are these enemies? See what hate hath done' (K4r).[25] The Prince's directive, 'Come,' is then taken up by Capulet, who imagines a single family unit formed of two enemies. 'Come, brother *Montague*, give me thy hand,' he commands, replicating the Prince's verb in his marriage-like proposal. This repetition aligns state and domestic authorities rhetorically, an effect enhanced by the Prince's closing response to the fathers: '*Come*, let us hence / To have more talke of these sad things. / Some shall be pardoned and some punished' (K4r, my emphasis). Through this formulation ('come' rather than 'go'), the Prince obviously wrests back discursive control from Capulet, but he does so while simultaneously incorporating the families into official deliberations. It is tempting to see the text as offering here a cue for blocking in performance (or, to imagine the text as following the performance, as recording a memorable gesture), one in which the actor playing the Prince puts a hand on each of the patriarch's shoulders and draws them toward him. Whether or not this physical gesture accompanied the text in its earliest productions, the words suggest a mutual joining of authorities rather than an insistent differentiation. Readers of the first quarto or witnesses of any performance of which it is a record see at the finale a weakly united social group, likely to make a muddle out of things just as they have done previously but nevertheless combining forces to reflect upon this exceptional and sorrowful story.

Imagining the texts as non-identical twins complicates readings of any one single play's particular representation of desire, state, and family in the closure. Dympna Callaghan, for instance, maintains that *Romeo and Juliet* enacts an emergent ideology of romantic love that transfers power from feudal family to centralized state. In her reading, the play lauds the seemingly individualized and universalizing eroticism that, in fact, fits the needs of an emergent and oppressive state and nuclear family.[26] Escalus's appropriation of power from friar and father require a mode of desire severed from the confines of the feudal family. Callaghan's compelling argument, however, only truly pertains to Q2. Since Q1 displays the Prince's collective and weak power, and since it downplays conflict between family and state, no one singular 'play' can be cited as synecdochal evidence of an historical shift in ideology. In fact, choosing Q2 as the basis for an edition or for commentary unwittingly commits one to a text embedded more fully in the ideology that Callaghan helpfully articulates. Reading Q1 along with Q2, however, fractures the confidence of any one single narrative about how the state is presented and allows critics instead to see multiple political and stylistic options available in the 1590s.

The family reconciliation is also inflected differently in the two quartos, as Capulet describes his proffered handshake as a *dowry* in one text, a *jointure* in the other.

> *Cap*: Come brother *Mountague* give me thy hand,
> There is my daughters dowry: for now no more
> Can I bestowe on her, thats all I haue.

> *Moun*: But I will giue them more, I will erect
> Her statue of pure golde:
> That while *Verona* by that name is knowne.
> There shall no statue of such price be set,
> As that of *Romeos* loued *Iuliet*.

> *Cap*: As rich shall *Romeo* by his Lady lie,
> Poore Sacrifices to our Enmitie.   (K4r)

In this exchange, Q1 Capulet initiates a penitent handshake with Montague as the marital gift bestowed on his daughter (perhaps because he feels guilty for forcing her marriage to Paris), and he freely describes himself as spent, evacuated ('thats all I haue'). In his formulation, Juliet becomes almost momentarily alive to receive the dowry as it transfers through her to her husband. Montague responds by upping the ante, promising to provide for 'them' (that is, for both children) a durable legacy, a statue to commemorate his son's choice, 'Romeo's loved Juliet.' Montague thus extends, enlarges, and creates symmetry from Capulet's initial tribute. Capulet counters by competitively matching this gift (he does have more, after all, it seems!) – and through this exchange they fashion the story of heroic sacrifice that the statues will commemorate for all eternity, or for as long as Verona is known by its name. The first quarto thus stages a conversation in which Capulet sets the terms of a joint gift, with his new kin Montague supporting and increasing its meaning. They form a tense, rivalrous, and aggrieved but unified front.

In the text with which modern readers are familiar, however, Capulet does not offer a gift to his daughter or to Montague. He instead broaches the subject of reconciliation by casting it as a 'demand,' asking his new kin for the groom's guaranteed annuity, the jointure or lands held in tail for the wife upon her husband's death, expressed and cancelled as a handshake:

> *Cap.* O brother *Mountague*, give me thy hand,
> This is my daughters ioynture, for no more
> Can I demand.
>
> *Moun.* But I can give thee more,
> For I will raie her statue in pure gold,
> That whiles Verona by that name is knowne,
> There shall be figure at such rate be set,
> As that of true and faithfull *Juliet.*   (M2r)

In this version, it is Montague's bright idea to change the terms that Capulet offers, replacing an order for 'joining' with a generous offer to 'give' more than Capulet has sought. In this version Montague is also asked to bestow a gift to Capulet, rather than to their children. Though Capulet is generous in making the first move toward harmony, his discourse is pointedly not that of free expenditure; he figures the exchange as a *claim*, an exacting of what is due to him (for going out a limb to put aside the feud, perhaps). Therefore Montague's response reprimands his new kin for not knowing the properly magnanimous language to use in creating feudal bonds. The appropriate vocabulary is a freely offered 'gift.' Any good aristocrat should know this practice. Capulet had, in fact, acknowledged that he understood the importance of the gift earlier in the play when he threatened to disinherit Juliet: 'If you be mine, Ile give you to my frend: / If not, hang, drowne, starve, beg,/ Dye in the streetes.'[27] Possession rests, he suggests, in the right to give. Montague's rebuke for forgetting such a basic point is evident at the play's end, and Capulet's fierce worry about social standing once more exposed. Q2 Montague then further embarrasses Capulet by offering lavish praise for the other patriarch's child, something that Capulet has not thought to do. Gift giving is pointedly a weighty social practice carried out between dads, not primarily a legacy for offspring.

This textual difference might seem slight, for each passage concerns competitive expenditure, each ratifies the protagonists' marriage after the fact, and each asserts fatherly control in a moment of grieving chaos. In each, the fathers turn to the task of rehabilitating *degenerates*, those unruly teens refusing to bear the proper marker of the ancestral mold. Not only have they attempted to shake off their names, but even their deaths form a 'preposterous inversion' of sorts. 'O thou untaught,' exclaims Montague upon hearing of his son's death, 'what manners is in this,/To presse before thy Father to a grave?' (Q1, K3r) For Montague (in both quartos), admittedly shocked with grief, the son's failure to be 'taught,' to take the imprint of family manners, has made him 'degenerate'; Romeo has altered in kind from his predecessor by 'press[ing]' before when he should go behind. The fashioning of artificial statue-children thus allows the fathers to right this inversion and author meaning for the tragedy; it will direct people to memorialize the worth of the lovers by making them reflect and thus become akin again to their families ('poor sacrifices to/of *our* enmity'). The fathers thus hope to control the legacy of a seemingly heir-less family, making it all of one kind once again. But since Q2 makes the story of Capulet's ongoing thwarted attempts to take charge of his world central to this gesture, it foregrounds a serious fissure in patriarchal power and its unifying effects. Q2 Capulet attempts an alliance that will restore to heads of family the authority they have lost. We aren't surprised to witness Capulet's social anxiety in the closing scene. Always nostalgic for a past when he fantasizes himself virile, Capulet has, throughout the play, belied insecurities. He says, for example, that decorum dictates that he invite only 'one or two' friends to his daughter's wedding, since held so soon after Tybalt's funeral, but Falstaff-like, he ups it to six guests in the same speech. Soon he's asking for twenty cooks to prepare a lavish feast with banqueting dishes. Capulet just cannot seem to control his boundless desire to move up in the world.

While keeping firmly in mind the dangers of flattening out contradictions *within* each individual quarto, I think it possible to argue generally that parental, church, and state authority are more lavishly displayed in Q2 than in Q1. Q2 Lady Capulet is imperious to Juliet about marriage as seen in their first exchange where she issues a flat directive about Juliet's future plans ('well thinke of marriage now'). In keeping, Q2 Juliet thinks to be deferential to the Friar when she rushes into church to get married ('good even to my ghostly confessor' she says politely upon entering the room and seeing her beloved with the priest); and Q2 Capulet flaunts control over his daughter to Paris, speaking confidently of her state of mind and issuing 'decrees' to her (Juliet 'will be rulde / In all respects by me nay more I doubt it not', he says[28]). In Q1, by contrast, Lady Capulet solicits Juliet's opinions about marriage rather than ordering her simply to comply with her parents' wishes; Juliet thinks of the friar only after speaking lovingly to her fiancé in the wedding scene; and Q1 Capulet is hesitant to claim too much knowledge about his daughter to others, even suggesting at key moments that managing Juliet is Lady Capulet's domain. Q2 Capulet's nervous attempt to control the play's resolution thus continues a pattern in this text whereby strategic moves to establish authority are revealed only then to bring about more crisis. Q2 Capulet exits the stage at the end of the play still ferociously preoccupied with orchestrating social networks, and still not quite able to accomplish this task effectively, as Montague pointedly makes clear. Q1 exposes what is at stake in this alternate rendition, in its pointed *lack* of interest in the internal problems of family, in distinguishing personalized foibles, or airing a competition between family and state. It instead highlights the 'gloomie' peace held in place by weak collaborative institutions working on a proper memorialization and course of action.

Yet critics tend to assess, cite, and thus re-produce just one form of the reconciliation in the kinship system. Readings such as Robert Applebaum's astute investigation of the imperfect masculinities dispersed throughout the play, for instance, might find welcome refinement in a comparison of its earliest texts. Applebaum identifies internal contradictions in the play's conception of gender, fissures that expose gender as a system of compulsive desires for which there is no final goal, fulfillment, or escape.[29] He notes how 'the regime of masculinity seems to have a doubleness that is all but insoluable' (252). In his reading, the ending, however, offers Romeo an unproblematic escape out of unstable masculinity. Though dead and unable to enjoy it, Romeo is swallowed into a stable civic order that empties out the problems of gender. Yet the double endings of Q1 and Q2 stage competing ways of imagining homosocial faultlines and failures – one locked in contestatory feudal exchange in which there is one would-be and one knowing elite, the other displaying an indiscriminate rivalrous legacy to be channeled into joint decision making. It is not that there are two competing masculinities that critics such as Applebaum should cite (e.g., some distinct Q1 and Q2 'gendering'). To my mind, the significance lies in the possibilities of optional masculinities circulating through the same materials simultaneously in 1590s performances and/or editions. Criticism attentive to the prosthetic nature of gender and sexuality might thus usefully be supplemented by an awareness of the incompletion and substitution going on at the level of the text.

Finally, we turn to the fact that the father's strategy for closure rests on managing a *story* of woe and, as such, the ending bears on what Goldberg terms the plays' 'self remarking textuality.'[30] Arthur Brooke's previous poetic account ends by lauding the superlative quality of the built artifact which will memorialize the lovers: 'Ther is no monument / more worthy of the sight:/Then is the tombe of Juliet / and Romeus her Knight.'[31] Shakespeare's retelling conspicuously shifts the memorialization so that it rests on discourse, on a *tale*. As Catherine Belsey notes, the play in general 'puts on display the hopeless longing to escape the confines of the signifier, to encounter directly, immediately, the rose that exists beyond its name. And to this extent *Romeo and Juliet* suggests the degree to which the named, differentiated love is always only a stand-in for something which cannot be embraced.'[32] Belsey's claim can be refined, split, in a sense, and expanded to take into account the diverse textual forms that constitute but divide the stand-in that we call 'the play.' For instance, Q1's collaborative social structures seem markedly more tolerant of being anchored to plural and diffuse authorities. When the prince seeks to sift evidence, he calls for written documents as well as witnesses. Instead of being given Romeo's single letter as guarantor of the truth, Q1 litters the stage with missives. Q2 Escalus looks to a single letter for proof of the Friar's testimony while Q1 Prince holds in his hand multiple letters that authenticate the story told to him. One version hints at a single written corroborating document; another allows for disparate narratives that nevertheless are confirmed as reliable. In a McKerrow-like vein, Q2 Prince imagines his project as one of establishing proper lineage: 'Seale up the mouth of outrage for a while,/Till we can cleare these ambiguities,/And know their spring, their head, *their true discent*.'[33] What is being verified is a truth with its regrettable downward fall – or descent – into error. For Q2 Prince, uncertainties necessarily signal an unfortunate rupture from origin. But Q1 Prince is not invested in clearing away a degenerative tree of error to find its single ur-root. Instead he uses textual figures to search for plural sources: 'Come seale your mouthes of outrage for a while, / And let us seeke to finde the *Authors* out/ Of such a hainous and seld seene mischaunce.'[34] The play's acknowledgement of itself – as incomplete, split and a substitution for a story not yet completely ever told – is clear in both versions, but Q1 embraces its multiple and proliferating textual and social authorities.

Certainly both endings return to the issue of the name and worry about the fate of the story. Capulet and Montague's validation of the importance of kinship turns the Prince's juridical findings, so fully played out in his sorting of evidence, comparing of witnesses with documents, and promise of a deliberate ruling, into a memorial. Each father has seen his child 'degenerate'; Romeo has become absent from social life and from himself, while Juliet has rebelliously refused her dynastic responsibility. The fathers' collective response is to rehabilitate the children by creating an orderly artifact representing their offspring. But because they do so by nominating themselves as custodians for a *legend*, their concerns run up against the play's scrutiny of itself as a famed tale clearly extending beyond the confines of any one account or text. Here we find Q2's investment in isolating a single pre-eminent authority undercut by the indeterminacy of the narrative it so fully displays. The two quartos compel a closure that will secure fixed meanings but raise the possibility of incommensurable interpretations. After all, the heirs have remade, in some yet unknowable way, their ancestor-survivors; they have generated a story that bears their imprint as they have pressed before their fathers to the grave. The Prince's shift of attention from the family monument to *discourse* thus appropriately presents a tale in process, one contested and set to be remade in future conversation and one perhaps subject to a generative de-generation. As a person living in the future imagined in these final speeches, I might ask: what is the name that stands in for the legend to be memorialized? *The Excellent conceited Tragedy of Romeo and Juliet* (1597)? Or, as the running titles sometimes say 'the most excellent Tragedie'? Or *The Most Excellent and Lamentable Tragedie of Romeo and Juliet* (1599)?

What is past and what is prologue remain uncertain, not simply within the texts but in the interplay between them. The *Romeo and Juliets* that persist in material form, it seems, resist a clear model of generation; their unstable and plural existence embodies nicely their thematic refusal to secure sovereign power for inheritance and heritage.

IV. Coda: sweet discourses

> All this woe (Q1) / these woes (Q2) shall serve
> For sweete discourses in the time (Q1) / our times (Q2) to come.

It is apparent now that I am following the lead of others, including Randall McLeod, Jill Levenson, Steven Urkowitz and Jonathan Goldberg, in welcoming the division of the kingdoms, that has been more fully accepted for other early modern plays, to *Romeo and Juliet* (perhaps more appropriately termed the 'divorce of the families,' or the 'unmaking of the kinship system').[35] Despite sophisticated recent historical inquiries into the early modern conditions of playwrighting and the materiality of the book, work that has usefully opened the door for reconceiving dramatic works in many ways, most critics and readers still encounter *Romeo and Juliet* as an unambiguously single play.[36] All available modern editions tell some version of the narrative of the quarto's unfortunate textual descent while fitfully relying upon a degenerate Q1. The exception in print to date, Jill Levenson's Oxford edition, presents both quartos in their entirety. Levenson's attempt to save Q1 from descending below the critical radar, however, is still inscribed with the sense of Q1's belatedness. Q1, printed with minimal apparatus, tags along after the well-annotated Q2, like a poor relative without proper attire. Although she lays out the case for textual multiplicity adeptly, Levenson cites only passages from Q2 in offering an interpretation of 'the text' in the introduction. Perhaps this deep-rooted inscription of Q1 as secondary has prevented critics from seizing the opportunities opened up by textual revolutions of the 1980s and 1990s, steering scholars to imagine a single and stable Q2 *Romeo and Juliet* rather than to draw on new resources available on the web which highlight the play's original multiplicity. If parthenogenetic lineage is an implicit structure underwriting the practices through which editors create a play for readers (present in the assumption that there is a single original, with imperfectly reproduced followers), the logical outcome of using this model might be to raise the prospect of the early texts as step-sibling, adopted, multigenerational, incestuous, twinned, and/or queer quartos.

To do so, editors and critics might take a page from the play's performance history, where family positions have historically been queered. Stage versions of the play in the last 400 years have readily tinged the mythic story of heterosexual passion with hints of gender-trouble, incest, and, notably, cross-generational romance. Let me just list some such performances. In one 1660s restoration version produced by William Davenant's company, Mary Saunderson played Juliet with her real life lover Thomas Betterton playing not Romeo but Mercutio. In 1744, Theophilus Cibber played Romeo passionately in love with his fourteen-year-old daughter, with the prologue advertising this family romance to audiences in print. Young Jane (called Jenny) 'full of modest terror, dreads t'appear / But trembling begs a father's fate to share,' the text reads. Several contemporary commentators, including David Garrick, snickered at the incestuous feature created by this casting.[37] In 1789, Sarah Siddons took the stage as Juliet besotted with a Romeo played by her brother John Philip Kemble. Fanny Kemble first starred as Juliet at Covent Garden, with her father Charles playing the role of Mercutio and her mother appearing as her fictional mother Lady Capulet. Fanny Kemble later starred opposite her father as Romeo on tour in the United States. In the theater scene in the eighteenth century, the picture emerges of an ever shifting star-crossed family romance within the Kemble family, one that fueled the heterosexual tale of passion with a certain celebrity aura.[38]

The nineteenth-century English stage undercut the normative ordering of the family primarily rearranging the gender of one of its principal actors. It was perhaps because several major actors, including Edmund Kean, William Macready and Henry Irving, failed disastrously in their attempts to play Romeo that several cross-dressed actresses (including Caroline Rankley, Fanny Vining and Ellen Tree) took to the stage as the titled hero passionately wooing female Juliets. The most famous of these actresses was Charlotte Cushmann whose Romeo died in the arms of a Juliet played by her sister Susan in the 1840s and 1850s. The erotic fervor of this incestuous, female–female legendary romance did not go unnoticed by at least one commentator, though the performance was largely approved and celebrated.[39]

The text of the play itself, by this point, had undergone many changes on the stage: James Howard's comedy version in the restoration played alongside a revived tragic one, so that Lazarus-like, the lovers could die one night and live the next.[40] A few years later, Thomas Otway sandwiched the story of Romeo and Juliet into a Plutarchan Roman context in his 1679 *Caius Marius*, adding dialogue in which the lovers converse before dying at the end of the play. Otway's emendation was so popular that this added scene was kept in important and different 1740s adaptations, including those by Cibber, Thomas Sheridan, and David Garrick. Garrick's production included many alterations; for instance, he omitted rhymed verse, changed Juliet's age, and dignified Mercutio's bawdy language. The added tomb dialogue between the lovers persisted well into the nineteenth century when Cushman restored much of Shakespeare's 'original' version. In performance, the family and its foundational bi-gendered core, seemed as variable as the text itself.

Importing the flexibility evidenced in this proliferation of roles into the framework editors use to conceptualize textual families would be impractical and perhaps perverse. I raise the prospect, however, as a way of foregrounding potential fault-lines in the received generational model, in hopes of exploring ways in which readers might be cued to be more self-conscious about editorial practice and its valencies. As well as reconceptualizing the 'work' and 'text' historically, as Peter Stallybrass, Margreta de Grazia, and Stephen Orgel have urged us to do in recent years,[41] that is, scholars might acknowledge more fully a point so obvious that it seems to be forgotten at times: the *performative* nature of any edition, its ability to call into being the text to which it seemingly refers by citing it within present regimes of knowledge and present paradigms. Since this formulation insists on the shared citational practices that saturate both editorial and interpretive work, it prompts critics to take account of the ever-changing systems organizing material forms, the edition's necessarily conditional reframing and reconstitution of the text and the valences attached to those ever-shifting frames. In doing so, critics might take their cue from the lessons of the play itself, which, as Peter Holland observes, shows 'a tension between the possibilities of patterning and order and the recognition of the temporary and evanescent nature of such possibilities.'[42] It is that tension that scholars might keep in focus when searching for a text to read, something so obvious that it has not mattered much in recent scholarship of *Romeo and Juliet*.

I close by calling to mind Lord Capulet and Lord Montague's grieving attempt to solidify a dynastic past in a shaky future citation of an unfixable present story. Their drive to *generate* a line of descent referring back readily to its origins is mockingly concretized when translated into perdurable gold, for the broader context of the play makes clear that this heartfelt attempt at solidification is, in fact, sure to be ephemeral, resting lightly on the breath of princes, storytellers and actors as well as inscribed in the different inky marks of type manipulated by compositors and editors. With a knowing glance, the quartos close by *inhabiting* the inconclusive nature of the legend they revisit belatedly, exposing its protean – or perhaps I should say its re-generate – character.

Notes

1. William Shakespeare, *The Most Excellent Tragedy of Romeo and Juliet* (London: John Danter, 1597), K3^r. This passage has the same wording in the earliest two editions (1597 and 1599), and appears in a modern edition based on the 1599 text (*The Most Excellent and Lamentable Tragedy of Romeo and Juliet*) in *Romeo and Juliet*, ed. Jill L. Levenson (Oxford: Oxford University Press, 2000) at 5.3.214-15. Since the issues that I take up explicitly complicate the question of how to cite a text that is, in fact, a moving target, my citations might appear cumbersome. I will generally cite passages from *Romeo and Juliet* to the 1597 edition, noting textual differences with the 1599 edition if necessary, and providing act, scene, and line number in a modern edition when it seems useful.
2. Ronald B. McKerrow, 'The Treatment of Shakespeare's Text by his Earlier Editors, 1709–1768' *Proceedings of the British Academy* 19 (1933), 29, my emphasis.
3. W. W. Greg notes that McKerrow's formulation of guidelines fails to take into account cases where there isn't one clear original but two authoritative texts independently derived from a lost original. See Greg, Preface, *The Editorial Problem in Shakespeare* (Oxford: Clarendon Press, 1951), v.
4. Margreta de Grazia writes, 'Although genealogical accounts appear as natural as growth itself, they are strongly biased against difference and change. In order to chart progression towards an end, they must postulate a single objective through time. A genealogical account of Shakespeare's texts takes the desire for authenticity as axiomatic.' *Shakespeare Verbatim: The Reproduction of Authenticity and the 1790 Apparatus* (Oxford: Clarendon Press, 1991), 4.
5. Greg, *Editorial Problem*, xiv–xv.
6. Arthur Quiller-Couch, *Proceedings of the British Academy* 18 (1932), 3–20.
7. De Grazia, *Shakespeare Verbatim*, esp. 132–220. De Grazia specifically comments on why modern practices were not 'obvious' to eighteenth-century editors (57–9).
8. Thomas Thomas, *Dictionarium Linguae Latinae et Anglicanae* (London: R. Boyle. 1587) offers this definition; In *The English Schoole-maister*, Edmund Coote similarly defines 'degenerate' as 'to be unlike his ancestors (London: Widow Orwin, 1596), a definition echoed in dictionaries by John Florio and Robert Cawdrey.
9. McKerrow, 'The Treatment of Shakespeare's Text,' 21, my emphasis. See also McKerrow, *Prolegomena for the Oxford Shakespeare: A Study in Editorial Method* (Oxford: Clarendon Press, 1939), appendix B entitled 'The Descent of Editions,' which elaborates the importance of the textual genetic line.

10. William Shakespeare, *King Lear,* in *The Norton Shakespeare, Based on the Oxford Edition,* ed. Stephen Greenblatt et al. (New York: W. W. Norton and Co., 1997). *King Lear* is printed in two editions in this volume, on facing pages. In the Quarto, this line is found at 1.4. 232; in the Folio at 1.4.215. Citations to Shakespeare's other texts in this paragraph are from the Norton edition.

11. Greg, *Editorial Problem,* xiv–xv.

12. Shakespeare, *The Most Excellent Tragedy of Romeo and Juliet* (London: John Danter, 1597), D1v. These lines can be found in a modern edition based on the 1599 edition in *Romeo and Juliet,* ed. Levenson, 2.1.77-9.

13. Shakespeare, *The Most Excellent Tragedy of Romeo and Juliet* (London, 1597), G1^v. A modern edition based on the 1599 text reads: 'O tell me, Friar, tell me, / In what vile part of this anatomy / Doth my name lodge? Tell me, that I may sack / The hateful mansion' (Levenson, 3.3.104-7).

14. Jonathan Goldberg, 'What? in a names that which we calls Rose: The Desired Texts of *Romeo and Juliet,*' in *Crisis in Editing: Texts of the English Renaissance,* ed. Randall McLeod (New York: AMS Press, Inc., 1988), 190.

15. David Farley-Hills argues that Q1 is a version of Q2 that the troupe adapted for traveling (see 'Bad Quarto'); Hoppe and Irace argue that the Q1 was memorially reconstructed by actors (Kathleen Irace, *Reforming the 'Bad' Quartos: Performance and Provenance of Six Shakespearean First Editions* (Newark: University of Delaware Press, 1994); Harry Hoppe, *The Bad Quarto of 'Romeo and Juliet'* (Ithaca: Cornell University Press, 1948). John Jowett proposes that Q1 was shaped primarily in the printshop, through Henry Chettle's interventions. See Jowett, 'Henry Chettle and the First Quarto of *Romeo and Juliet,*' *Papers of the Bibliographical Society of America,* 92 (1998), 53–74. The best critique of memorial reconstruction as a theory is launched by Paul Werstine, 'A Century of "Bad" Shakespeare Quartos,' *Shakespeare Quarterly* 50 (1999), 310–33.

16. Editors agree that one long passage in Q2 was directly set from Q1. In Levenson's edition, this passage is found in Q2 at 1.2.53-1.3.36.

17. Grace Ioppolo, *Revising Shakespeare* (Cambridge, Mass.: Harvard University Press, 1991), 89–93.

18. Goldberg, 'What?'; Steven Urkowitz, 'Two Versions of *Romeo and Juliet* 2.6 and *Merry Wives of Windsor* 5.5.215-45: An Invitation to the Pleasures of Textual/Sexual Di(Per)versity,' in *Elizabethan Theater: Essays in Honor of S. Schoenbaum,* ed. R. B. Parker and S. P. Zitner (Newark: University of Delaware Press, 1996), 222–38.

19. The Arden edition of *Romeo and Juliet* includes 100 variants from Q1, collated into its copytext of Q2; the Riverside edition includes over 60.

20. Stanley Wells and Gary Taylor, with John Jowett and William Montgomery, *William Shakespeare: A Textual Companion* (Oxford: Clarendon Press, 1987), 288.

21. Goldberg, 'What?' 185.

22. *The Most Excellent and Lamentable Tragedie, of Romeo and Juliet* (London: Thomas Creede, for Cuthbert Burby, 1599), B2r. This passage appears in Levenson's edition in 1.1.223-4.

23. Leah Marcus, *Unediting the Renaissance: Shakespeare, Marlowe, Milton* (New York: Routledge, 1996), 129.

24. *The Most Excellent and Lamentable Tragedie, of Romeo and Juliet* (London: Thomas Creede, for Cuthbert Burby, 1599), M2r.

25. *An Excellent conceited Tragedie of Romeo and Juliet* (London: John Danter, 1597), K4r.

26. Dympna C. Callaghan, in *The Weyward Sisters: Shakespeare and Feminist Politics,* ed. Dympna C. Callaghan, Lorraine Helms, and Jyotsna Singh (Cambridge, Mass: B. Blackwell, 1994), 59–101.

27. *An Excellent conceited Tragedie of Romeo and Juliet* (London: John Danter, 1597), H1v. These lines appear in variant form in 1599; see Levenson's edition, 3.5.191-2.

28. See *The Most Excellent and Lamentable Tragedie, of Romeo and Juliet* (London: Thomas Creede, for Cuthbert Burby, 1599), B4v, F2r and H2r. These passages can be found in modernized language in Levenson, Q2, 1.3.71; 2.5.21; and 3.4.13-14.

29. Robert Applebaum, 'Standing to the Wall': The Pressures of Masculinity in *Romeo and Juliet*,' *Shakespeare Quarterly*, 48 (1997), 251–72.
30. Goldberg uses this phrase to describe a speech by Juliet 'consonant with the play's theatricality' ('What?' 191).
31. Arthur Brooke, *The Tragicall Historie of Romeus and Juliet* (London: Richard Tottel, 1567), fol. 84.
32. Catherine Belsey, 'The Name of the Rose in *Romeo and Juliet*,' in *Critical Essays on Shakespeare's* Romeo and Juliet, ed. Joseph Porter (New York: G. K. Hall, 1997), 79.
33. *The Most Excellent and Lamentable Tragedie, of Romeo and Juliet* (London: Thomas Creede, for Cuthbert Burby, 1599), L4v-M1r, my emphasis. In modernized form in Levenson, 5.3.216-18.
34. *An Excellent conceited Tragedie of Romeo and Juliet* (London: John Danter, 1597), K3r, my emphasis.
35. This phrase, now synonymous with the practice of presenting multiple distinct versions of Shakespearean texts rather than conflating different versions, comes from the pioneering work, *The Division of the Kingdoms: Shakespeare's Two Versions of King Lear*, eds Gary Taylor and Michael Warren (New York: Oxford University Press, 1983). Those arguing to 'divide' *Romeo and Juliet* in order to respect the qualities of each individual early text include Random Cloud (Randall McLeod), 'The Marriage of Good and Bad Quartos,' *Shakespeare Quarterly* 33 (1982), 421–31; Jill Levenson, introduction to the Oxford *Romeo and Juliet*; Steven Urkowitz, 'Two Versions of *Romeo and Juliet* 2.6 and *Merry Wives of Windsor* 5.5.21545: An Invitation to the Pleasures of Textual/Sexual Di(Per)versity'; and Goldberg, 'What?'
36. The editors of the current Riverside edition of Shakespeare's works announce, without qualification, that *Romeo and Juliet* Q1 is 'generally agreed' to be a memorial reconstruction, but they then acknowledge that 'the ultimate authority of Q2, however, is also ambiguous'; there is 'an uncomfortable uncertainty about the final authority of the Q2 text in those passages which it shares more or less in common with Q1' ('Notes on the Text,' 1139). William Shakespeare, *The Riverside Shakespeare*, ed. G. Blakemore Evans, 2nd edn (Boston: Houghton Mifflin Co., 1997).
37. On the Cibber production, see James N. Loehlin, 'Introduction' to William Shakespeare, *Romeo and Juliet*, ed. Loehlin (Cambridge: Cambridge University Press, 2002), 10–11.
38. My information about the Kemble family's participation in theater comes from Loehlin, 20, 23 and 28.
39. Loehlin, 27–8.
40. Ibid., 7.
41. Peter Stallybrass and Margreta de Grazia, 'The Materiality of the Shakespearean Text,' *Shakespeare Quarterly* 44 (1993), 255–83; Stephen Orgel, 'The Authentic Shakespeare,' *Representations* 21 (1988), 1–25.
42. Peter Holland, introduction to *Romeo and Juliet* in William Shakespeare, *The Complete Works*, gen. ed., Stephen Orgel and A. R. Braunmuller (New York: Penguin, 2002), 1252.

Part III
Living Theatre

8
Rhetoric, Discipline, and the Theatricality of Everyday Life in Elizabethan Grammar Schools

Lynn Enterline

In sixteenth-century English grammar schools, the theory and practice of imitation slowly replaced older methods of learning Latin by precept. Juan Luis Vives claimed that humanist training would turn a 'beast' into a 'man' and virtually every pedagogue who commented on the matter claimed that instruction in grammar and rhetoric directly benefited the English commonwealth.[1] Critics in the 1940s and 1950s demonstrated the profound impact of humanist pedagogy on England's literary Renaissance, but in the last 15 years, scholars have been far more interested in the school's participation in the process of social reproduction.[2] My investigation draws on both traditions, expanding the first by taking archival evidence about the school's material practices into account when analysing subsequent literary history and the second by bringing psychoanalytic questions about subjectivity, language, and sexuality to bear on the texts its schoolboy subjects produced. I examine several kinds of archival evidence about grammar school training and discipline in conjunction with one former schoolboy's exercise in classical imitation (a poem better known by the title, *Venus and Adonis*).

This juxtaposition of archive and canon, institutional training and literary production, allows me to develop three, related, arguments about the school's social and literary effects. First, close attention to matters usually deemed strictly literary – rhetorical tropes, choice of genre, techniques of imitation – affords a properly historical understanding of this institution's impact on early modern masculinity. Second, the way Shakespeare represents character and emotion has much to tell us about both his indebtedness and resistance to the theatricality of the institution that gave him his 'cultural capital' as an early modern 'gentleman'.[3] And third, far from the minor genre they are often taken to be, Ovidian epyllia like *Venus and Adonis* are far more revealing about sixteenth-century theater history than we have yet to acknowledge.

I will begin with a brief outline of the rhetorical, gendered, and erotic issues in *Venus and Adonis* that inform my reading of the poem as well as my investigation of the humanist institution and classical curriculum that made it possible. A dramatist well-known for his fascination with the erotic possibilities of theatrical cross-dressing wrote two narrative poems in the Ovidian art of cross-voicing.[4] An accomplished female impersonator, Shakespeare gives voice to Venus's desire while at the same time satirizing her frustrations, excesses, and absurdities. Critics often note that the poem's joke on Venus stems from the fact that she is trapped by Petrarchan rhetoric ill-suited to the occasion. But they have not adequately addressed another aspect of her predicament: not only does Venus adopt a traditionally male position – a 'bold-faced suitor' wooing a reluctant object – but her rhetorical exuberance shapes her desire for a boy to the extent that he *isn't* one, to the extent that he resembles a woman:

> 'Thrice fairer than myself,' thus she began,
> 'The field's chief flower, sweet above compare,
> Stain to all nymphs, more lovely than a man,
> More white and red than doves or roses are...'[5]

And Venus is off – busily turning Adonis into Laura in clichés of 'beyond compare.'

I called Venus's Petrarchan rhetoric 'ill-suited to the occasion,' by which I mean that a literary mode founded on unrequitedness presumes the speaker's disappointment. That Venus will remain unsatisfied is never in doubt. The phrase has limitations, however, if it suggests a heteronormative frame of analysis for a poem that works to exploit and explode such assumptions.[6] Reaching beyond Petrarch, Shakespeare draws on the polymorphous sexuality of Ovid's *Metamorphoses* – a poem that, as I argued elsewhere, anticipates Freud's *Three Essays* by separating desire from object choice and stressing the sheer force of *amor* without regard to its end.[7] Joining Petrarch's binary code of address to Ovid's penchant for cross-voicing and polymorphous perversity, Shakespeare reinvents the story of Venus and Adonis in such a way that the poem's plot, tension, and humor rely on the difference between male and female bodies and desires while also undermining those distinctions at every turn.

Shakespeare's narrator, moreoever, draws on yet another classical text – the virtually taboo *Ars Amatoria* – to cast Venus in yet another role: that of Ovid's rhetorically capable 'master of love' (*magister amoris*). The word 'master' generates a complex set of meanings in Shakespearean poetry and drama; such complexity is due, in part, to the long shadow the grammar school cast over his career. But one of the most important affective words attached to 'master' and 'mastery' in Shakespeare's texts is 'love.' To Bianca's query about what text he is reading, Lucentio disguised as Latin pedagogue also recalls the *Ars*: 'I read that I profess, the Art to Love' (4.3.8). To Prospero, the island pedagogue who shares a grammar schoolmaster's penchant for instructing (and dominating) pupils by way of question and answer, Ariel similarly understands his relation to 'mastery' as one of love: 'Do you love me, master?' (4.1.48). Adonis, for his part, rejects his would-be master's erotic lesson by declaring himself an 'orator too green' to follow the 'treatise' and 'old...text' of love she offers (806 and 774). When Adonis dismisses Venus's lesson twice as an 'idle, overhandled theme' (422 and 770), he uses school terminology for precisely the kinds of exercises masters used to develop skills in oratory.[8] True to her literary genealogy, Venus reads the world as a re-enactment of Ovid's *Ars* and like any good grammar school teacher, begs her pupil to learn from classical precedent:

> Let me excuse thy courser, gentle boy,
> And learn of him, I heartily beseech thee,
> To take advantage on presented joy;
> Though I were dumb, yet his proceedings teach thee.
> O, learn to love, the lesson is but plain,
> And once made perfect, never lost again.   (403–8)

Fond as he is of turning pedagogical relationships into sexual predicaments, teaching's affective and potentially erotic charge is not exclusive to Shakespeare. Schoolmasters regularly portray themselves as fathers who love and hate, who demand love and obedience in return. In Lily's Latin grammar – a text Shakespeare quotes often and Henry VIII authorized for 'all teachers of grammar within this realm' – the first lesson is how to decline *magister*. 'The accusative case followeth the verb, and answereth to this question, whom or what? As, *Amo Magistrum*, I love the master.'[9] Lily's first lesson is one Venus would happily to teach.

I will return to *Venus and Adonis* in the final section. But first, I am going to examine several texts from the institution in which boys like Shakespeare first encountered schoolmasters and Ovid's poetry. A word about methodology. Language training in the grammar school embodied two branches of rhetoric that continuously interact: tropological (requiring formal, literary analysis) and transactional (requiring social and historical analysis).[10] This argument will move between both precisely because schoolmasters are extremely consistent about linking formal concerns directly to social experience. Nor am I the first to notice that the school's founding belief in language's productive force invites comparison with psychoanalytic theory. Schoolmasters and Lacan agree on at least one thing: language precedes and shapes character rather than the other way around.[11] When I invoke psychoanalytic theory here, it is in light of its leavening proximity to rhetoric. Moreover, Lacan's claim that the subject is an *effect of signification*, as well as his corollary critique of mastery, is particularly apt for an institution devoted to the cultivation of character by means of submission to – indeed 'love' for – a master of grammar and rhetoric.[12] My invocation of Lacan's critique of mastery, in short, means that I recognize the school's extraordinary cultural reach while also keeping an eye out for its immanent contradictions.

I. Imitate and punish

Some years ago, Richard Halpern observed that 'imitation is a principle that animates not only humanist stylistics but also humanist pedagogy.'[13] His formulation captures two important strands of school practice. Contemporary satire best captures the shift to imitation that followed the grammarians' war. The *Parnassus* trilogy derides teaching as 'interpreting' a common schooltext 'to a companie of seaven-yeare-olde apes.' Skelton is rather more succinct: 'Speak, Parrot!'[14] Alongside the new pedagogy of imitation, however, almost every school ordinance required the master to provide an exemplary character for his students. The ideal of imitating authoritative examples therefore structured the school's hierarchy of personal relations as much as its language lessons: a teacher is 'such one as the child by imitation following may grow excellent.'[15]

But imitation was also intrinsic to the school's more overt disciplinary strategies. A scholar from the seventh form at the Westminster school wrote a detailed account of daily life – the only extant account of its kind written by a student rather than an adult. He details how profoundly imitation operated in his school's daily theater of judgment:

> *they were all of them* (or such as were picked out, of whom the Mr made choice by the feare or confidence in their lookes) to repeat and pronounce distinctlie without booke some piece of an author that had been learnt the day before. Betwixt 9 and 11 those exercises were reade which had been enjoyned *us* overnight (one day in prose, the next day in verse); which were selected by the Mr; *some to be examined and punished, others to be commended and proposed to imitation.* (Emphasis mine)[16]

A Westminster boy's choice is stark: imitate well or be beaten. He could, in fact, look forward to the exact hour of potential punishment. The account reads like a book of hours: 'Betwixt 9 and 11 ... Betwixt 3 and 4 they had a little respite.'[17]

Imitation also shaped Westminster's hierarchical apparatus for supervising and controlling acceptable (i.e. Latin) speech. The master appointed older boys as surrogates to 'monitor' and reprimand the younger boys' linguistic performance in his absence. These monitors, in turn, were required to give a weekly public accounting:

> These Monitors kept them strictly to speaking of Latine in theyr several commands; and withall they presented their complaints or accusations (as we called them) everie Friday morn: when the punishments were often redeemed by exercises or favours shewed to Boyes of extraordinarie merite, who had the honor (by the *Monitor monitorum*) manie times *to begge and prevaile for such remissions.* And so (at other times) other faultes were often punished by scholastic tasks, as repeating whole orations out of Tullie, Isoc.; Demosth ...

Imitation (in the narrow linguistic sense) and corporal punishment are equivalent: 'punishment' is 'redeemed by exercises,' 'remission' for whipping is 'repeating whole orations out of Tullie.' The chance to perform rhetorically – by 'begging and prevailing' for exemption from flogging – becomes an 'honor' for boys of 'merit.' Once set in motion, imitation (in the broader sense of one person copying another's example) proliferated: *magister, monitor, Monitor monitorum*. This elaborate hierarchy of imitation was devoted to the hourly regulation of verbal facility: translation exercises, cases brought against, pleas advanced, and the 'repeating' of 'whole orations.'

One telling phrase – 'By the feare or confidence in their lookes' – attests to a diffuse, yet still daunting, attempt to discipline socially acceptable affect. Schoolmasters claimed to teach proper 'behavior,' and a text like this one tells us that the school's discipline extended to gestural, expressive, and bodily performance as much as verbal (*actio*, of course, being an important aspect of an orator's training). At the same time, the phrase also reveals the young *monitor*'s identification with his master. Writing about '*their* lookes' rather than 'our lookes,' the young writer separates himself from his now former classmates by means of a hierarchy of imitation that moves him up the ranks from the supervised to the supervisor or *monitor*. Psychoanalytically speaking, the phrase suggests the student's identification with, or desire for, access to the place from which he is seen – also the place from which he is judged and loved[18] – as well as the attending divisions of self-surveillance in Freud's topographic description of the fractured psyche.[19] In other words, the *Consuetudinarium* indicates how the school might establish within each student a division between being monitored and being the *monitor*, speaking and watching, being looked at and looking. In such a disciplinary setting, successfully performing a socially sanctioned emotion means learning to imitate another while also *learning how to monitor oneself* in the act of imitation. This student's testimony describes a self-reflexive turn that Harry Berger might call the 'internal *monitor*' within each schoolboy.[20] '*Monitor monitorum:*' Westminster's hierarchy for regulating the performance of Latin eloquence pushes Berger's meta-theatrical definition of Shakespearean subjectivity – the constant activity of an internal auditor – in the direction of socially inflected judgment and censorship implicit in the psychoanalytic model of a divided, self-admonishing subject.

This disciplinary scene, in other words, is deeply theatrical. The boys are engaged in the daily performance of Latinity and affect for their masters, their peers, and, eventually, themselves. Still other school activities allied discipline very closely to theatricality. The ordinances of the Shrewsbury school mandate that upon a master's election, he 'shall make a Latin oration; one of the best scholars shall welcome him with a congratulatory Latin oration, promising obedience on behalf of the school.'[21] The titlepage to one schooltext, *Catechismus paruus* (1573) (see Figure 40), shows a scholar gesturing and declaiming before the master. A birch sits prominently by his side; the rest of the class sits around the young orator who performs his speech 'without book.'[22] Both this woodcut and the *Consuetudinarium* attest to intensive training in public performance from memory. So it can hardly surprise that many of the child actors impressed into service at Blackfriars were grammar school boys. (The most minutely recorded case, of course, was the complaint brought by Thomas Clifton's father against those from the Chapel Royal theater who 'carried off' his son on his way to school and made him learn their 'sayd playes or enterludes . . . by harte').[23]

Because of our own anachronistic distinction between rhetoric and drama, moreover, we have not attended as carefully as we might to the school's habitual association between declamation and acting: schoolmasters thought *both* were good training in eloquence and gentlemanly behavior. Several school ordinances use the verbs 'declame' and 'play' as virtual synonyms.[24] A Merchant Taylors' student

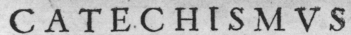

Figure 40 Title-page to *Catechismus paruus pueris primum Latine...proponendus in scholis* (London: John Day, 1573). Reproduced by permission of the Folger Shakespeare Library

described the stage as a 'means' to teach 'good behaviour and audacitye,' while John Bale praised the headmaster of the grammar school in Hitchin for building a large, permanent stage 'to train the young and babbling mouths of his students... to speak clearly and elegantly.'[25] Charles Hoole is particularly keen: acting prepares boys 'to pronounce orations' well and thereby expels 'that subrustic bashfulness and unresistible timorousness which some children are naturally possessed withal.'[26]

In such a setting, the presence of an actual stage was hardly necessary. The Westminster account of carefully monitored speech – of begging, prevailing, delivering orations – indicates that a theatrical *habitus* shaped the school's language training and forms of discipline, its real and phantasmatic hierarchies, its expectations for the performance of eloquence and of feeling.[27] What concerns me here is not simply that humanist schools made language training an increasingly public activity. Rather, the form this increasingly public education took became, thanks to the concentration on rhetoric, a matter of staging: performances and spectacles of imitation and punishment turned the school into a kind of *daily theater for Latin learning*. Far from consolidating schoolboy subjects as it claimed to do, early modern pedagogy would tend rather to produce divided, rhetorically capable, yet emotionally labile speakers for whom self-representation entailed the incessant dislocations of the theater. By 'dislocations' I mean not simply the activity of bilingual translation (an early lesson in language's incessant slippage about which Shakespeare's Mechanicals are perhaps most eloquent, running in terror as they do from Bottom's Ovidian 'translation'). I also mean something quite familiar to Shakespeareans: the constant internal movement in his characters between seeming and being, *persona* and person, address and self-representation; between assuming, whether successively or simultaneously, the positions of writer, actor, and audience. English schoolmasters announced themselves to be in the business of consolidating rhetorical mastery and, thereby, proper English gentlemen. But I would argue that their practice pulled against the drive to verbal, gestural, visual, and affective self-mastery because of their profound indebtedness to the theatricality of the very rhetorical tradition they taught.

II. A gentleman is being beaten

The affect performed in the Westminster *Consuetudinarium* is fear or confidence, but in other texts it could also be fear and desire. In this regard, Alan Stewart examines a remarkable passage in John Stanbridge's 1520 *Vulgaria* and an equally remarkable anecdote about Richard Mulcaster; both reveal what Stewart calls an 'erotic economy.' Precisely *what kind* of erotic economy is rather hard to determine and requires, I think, a closer look. In the *Vulgaria*, the master 'hath taught me a lesson' is a euphemism for beating: 'my buttockes deth swete a blody sweat.' And 'marrying the master's daughter' refers to the moment of stinging connection between the rod and buttocks. In the St Paul's anecdote, Mulcaster is said to have paused before striking a boy's naked backside due to a 'merry conceyt taking him.' Instead of whipping, Mulcaster intoned, 'I aske the banes of matrimony between this boy his buttockes, of such a parish, on the one side, and Lady Burch, of this parish on the other side.' But the boy got off without a stripe when a second scholar in the audience watching this disciplinary performance objected: 'all partyes are not agreed.' The master 'spared the one's fault and th' other's presumption' because he liked the 'witty answer.'[28]

The erotic charge attached to both flogging and rhetorical performance in these stories was hardly momentary or fleeting. A ubiquitous trope in sixteenth-century school texts – Lily's Grammar describes Latin as a lesson 'well-beaten into a student' and vulgaria frequently invoke the birch in sentences for translation – flogging appears again in a remarkable poem written by an 11-year-old scholar at Merchant Taylors' in 1696. One of a collection of poems written by the first scholars and 'spoken upon public days of Examination or Election,' 'The Birch' was declaimed in the voice of the master's rod. It tells us that over the next century, the erotic connection between flogging and rhetorical facility became, if anything, quotidian and institutionalized:

> 'Tis true I us'd like tortur'd Martyrs
> And lay'd about your hinder quarters,
> When finding an unlucky Urchin,
> (Whose Bum's in cue for putting birch in
> Down went his Breeches, up his jerking,
> And strait the Whipster fell to forking)
> Be sworn I'le soundly make you smart it,
> And suffer too, as many have done.
> The laying of a whipping on,
> *Whipping that's Virtues Governess*
> *Tutress of Arts and Sciences;*
> *That mends the gross mistakes of Nature*
> *And putts new life into dull matter;*
> That lays foundation for Renown
> And all the honors of the Gown:
> But one wou'd think there's nothing sillyer
> Than with back-side to be familiar,
> Tho' I confess my conversation
> *My wonders working virtue spread*
> *Itself up strait from Tail to Head,*
> Thus the ablest disputant and wit
> Has by my Influence been bit,
> So by my power their learned store
> *Goes in behind and out before.*
> My dispensations are effectual
> I grant to help the Intellectual,
> Duly apply'd sance too much vigour
> *When whipping's us'd in mood & figure.*
> Thus spiritual mortification
> As well as flesh is in fashion,
> Further'd by my all powerfull charm

> Both to inform and reform
> And in this practise there is sense
> Confirmed by long experience;
> For commonly by whom I cant mend
> The Sea, the Camp, or Gallows end.[29]

Inscribed alongside other, less startling poems, in an annual record of declamations, 'The Birch' takes the homoerotic and sexual aspects of flogging to be, at best, an open secret. Only the slightest of euphemisms is required to evoke a connection between whipping, student nakedness, and a masterful 'forking.' The poem's anal conceits (knowledge being something that 'Goes in behind and out before' or spreads 'From tail to Head') give plenty of time to homoerotic fantasy. But the poem's 'erotic economy' continues to expand in other directions as well: whipping, we learn, 'mends the gross mistakes of Nature/And putts new life into dull matter.' Such a phrase feminizes a boy's buttocks (and, eventually, mouth and head) along conventional Aristotelian lines: a master's whip becomes the 'informing' (or inseminating) principle of a student's new born 'wit.' 'Both to *in*form and *re*form': Latin rhetorical training is at once sexual, punitive, and socially efficacious.

All of these texts – school exercise, anecdote, declamation – return historical weight and complexity to our own nearly evacuated cliché, 'I'll teach you a lesson.' They remind us of the phrase's institutional, yet at the same time deeply ambiguous, erotic and disciplinary origins. The 'marriage' scene between the master's 'daughter' and a boy's buttocks and the phallic intrusion of 'The Birch's' 'working virtue' – the violent impregnation of a boy's 'dull matter' – are fantasies that both deploy and exceed such reductive, binary taxonomies as male/female, sadistic/masochistic, homo-/hetero-erotic. All three scenes *provoke* rather than answer questions. Nor do I mean that these questions are posed simply for us. The boys represented in these texts, who are asked under threat of punishment to imitate them – and their masters – or *to witness the spectacle of punishment* before them, were between 7 and 12 years old.[30] Staged, public flogging may signify an 'erotic economy,' but erotic for whom? With what object or aim? With what impact on gender difference? What, if any, coherence pertains to such tropes as 'marrying the master's daughter' or giving birth to a 'learned store'?

To answer such questions – or rather, since answering them involves the disappointing act of naming of a fantasy, to take stock of the effect that humanist discipline had on contemporary experiences of 'masculinity' – means accounting for yet one more kind of dislocation implicit in the school's daily practice. Whether we call it latency or trauma, such internal dislocation designates the unpredictable intersection between a culture's structuring narratives and the accidents of personal history, an intersection that distances subjects from access to their own experience in both language and time. For Freud, Lacan, and Laplanche, 'latency' refers to the incommensurable relation between the time required to reach biological sexual maturity and the time required not simply to acquire a language, but to grasp a culture's full range of sexual meanings. 'Latency' signifies an unpredictable and historically variable misfire between the temporality of human biology and a subject's belated understanding of the social codes that give bodies, actions, and desires their culturally specific significance.[31]

Laplanche contends that sexuality is inherently traumatic for speaking beings: we are born too early and understand too late. But his emphasis on speech means that the particular color and texture of sexuality's traumas are subject to the vagaries of history, transpersonal as well as personal. If I recall his double focus on the temporal and semiotic dimension of sexuality's dislocations in connection with the school's disciplinary theater, it is because this linguistic understanding of puberty suggests how profoundly 'all parties' in these flogging scenes are 'not agreed.' The exact significance of flogging fantasies – which might remain indecipherable even to adult minds – is not equally available, or legible, to all. The extreme (to us) yet clearly familiar (to them) trope of a flogging as a marriage ceremony or the forced impregnation of 'wit' in the 'Intellectual' are vivid examples of a difficulty in sexuality that Laplanche addresses directly: sexuality emerges in a series of missed encounters with the unanticipated 'intrusions' of adult fantasy – a fantasy that, because undecipherable at the moment of its occurrence, remains an 'alien internal entity.'[32] Such a claim reminds us that there is a significant difference, *for sexuality*, between being taught a lesson and learning it. That difference is the temporality of trauma – and also the space of fantasy. To my meta-theatrical account of the school's training, then, it is crucial to add the uneven temporality and semiotic disjunctions attending a child's subjection to language and sexuality. Taken together, such performative, temporal, and semiotic dislocations suggest how *unpredictable* gender and desire might become in grammar school training – despite (or indeed, because of) the overt efforts of school authorities to direct it.

For the early modern schoolboys represented in these texts, writing them, or reading them, 'whipping's us'd in mood & figure': the proto-eroticized threat of punishment is directly and systematically linked to verbal skill – be it an exercise in imitation, a 'merry conceyt,' or a 'witty answer.' All three texts testify to the affective and libidinal complexity of grammar school training while also linking matters of sex and affect directly to rhetorical performance. My final section therefore examines the impact of humanist training on the experience of masculinity by asking what two formal concerns – genre and trope – can tell us about the connection between gender and rhetorical training while taking a close look at a classical lesson gone terribly awry in *Venus and Adonis*.

III. The art of loving mastery

I'll begin with genre. Humanists made enormous claims for the political and moral efficacy of a classical education. Mulcaster says he wrote *Positions* out of 'a great good will towards this my cuntrie' so that he might 'train up' rhetorically capable gentlemen and help England become 'the best of common weales.' The most extended equation of rhetorical power with good governance is Kempe's *Education of Children*: 'great Magistrates' in ancient 'common-wealths' captured 'the examples and rules of eloquence.' We learn that 'it is reported' of Virgil that 'when he did reade some part of his booke in the assemblie, the people did no lesse reuerence unto him, then if it had been to the Emperour himselfe' and that 'Ouids learning, like Orpheus musicke, perswaded euen the Getes, a wilde and barbarous people, to use great humanitie towards him while he liued, and afterwards to burie him with great pompe.' Rhetoric's civic benefits, moreover, stem directly from epic: Homer is 'the prince of all poets,' because his 'precepts' made 'Solon' a 'good Lawmaker'; Virgil and Ovid are 'the only Latin schoolmaisters to all good students.'[33]

Latin textbooks and the curricula of individual schools bear out Kempe's belief in epic's moral and political efficacy. Lily's grammar quotes numerous authors, but most frequently cites Virgil, Ovid, Terence, and Cicero. The lesson on the impersonal verb is typical: *Oportet me legere Virgilium*, 'it is good for me to read Virgil.' Curricula vary, but nearly every school built toward reading epic as a culminating achievement in the fifth and sixth forms.[34] Given the school's interest in the good of the 'commonweal,' epic's pride of place cannot surprise. Then again, this is true only if one thinks of epic in its Virgilian mode – and especially, as Heather James points out, the anodyne *reading* of Virgil as encomiast of empire that emerged from the habit of appropriating the *Aeneid*'s translation of empire to legitimize state authority.[35] Ovid's satire of the *pax romana* in the last books of his *Metamorphoses*, as well as his fascination with what Virgil represents as the politically damaging *furor* of desire, fit less happily into the school's ideological program. Masters betray some nervousness about Ovid's 'unwholesome' content, but the epic that has its hero abandon Dido for the sake of his nation escaped censure.[36] A collection of verses by the headmaster and several scholars of the St Paul's school indicates how the preference for Virgil worked in practice. Presented to Elizabeth in 1573, the volume opens with the master's poem, setting out the theme of *translatio imperii* for his boys' imitation: first Malim, then several of his scholars, praise Elizabeth for bringing a 'second Rome' to England.[37]

Subject to Lily's maxim, 'it is good for me to read Virgil,' schoolboys were drilled in imitation and imbibed a system of rhetorical training built around an ideal of devotion to nation like that of Aeneas. Given the resonance between Virgilian civic duty and the school's announced goal of fashioning gentlemen by bringing Rome to England, there is something puzzling about the results of its training: poems written by former schoolboys rarely followed *anything like* the model of the *Aeneid*. Rather, as poetry in the 1590s indicates, school training encouraged an outpouring not of epic poetry, but of epyllia – and epyllia of a distinctly Ovidian, erotic cast. Before I return to *Venus and Adonis*, one ostensibly Virgilian imitation is instructive: Thomas Heywood's *Troia Britannica*.[38] The preface refers to Britain as 'Troy-novant' and cites Virgil as one who 'redeemd olde Troy from fire.' Heywood thereby invites expectation that something of the *Aeneid*'s form, structure, hero, or plot will inform the poem. Instead, *Troia Britannica* swerves from Virgil to Ovid: canto 1 begins not with arms and the man but with 'The Worlds Creation' and descent from a Golden age. The connection to Britain remains as loose as the one in Ovid between the world's creation and Rome: only the last two of 17 arrives in Britain. Nor does Heywood ever create a hero anything like Aeneas. The preface professing the allegiance to Virgil the poem fails to deliver is written in the so-called

'Venus and Adonis' stanza characteristic of Ovidian epyllia. Heywood used this verse for 'Oenone and Paris,' as had Lodge and Marston in their epyllia. Even when invoked in its most recognizable trope of *translatio imperii*, in other words, the *Aeneid* did not guide invention in nearly the way its position in the Elizabethan curriculum, or resonance with the school's ideological purposes, suggest it might have done.

The best explanation for generic experiments by former grammar schoolboys is Halpern's argument that training in rhetorical *copia* 'atomized larger structures of meaning and ideological content,' dissolving texts 'into generative strategies of style.' A blissful disregard for ideological content does reign over hybrid generic forms in the period.[39] This argument explains why Ovid's skeptical critique of Roman rule, never mind his sexual content, sat side by side with the *Aeneid* without provoking much anxiety among teachers. But it does not sufficiently answer why the poems and plays of former schoolboys show a decided, specific preference for Ovidian eroticism over Virgilian *pietas*. Or why former schoolboys turn epic convention away from the national, political, and moral themes into investigations of character, emotion, and desire.

My second formal concern – trope – indicates that the vogue for Ovidian imper-sonation derives fairly directly from school training. When poets in the 1590s imitate characters from the *Metamorphoses*, they are practicing the inherently dramatic art that Quintilian calls *prosopopoeia*. A trope that pervades the *Metamorphoses*, *prosopopoeia* began in Roman rhetorical training as the art of personifying historical, imagined, and mythological characters. It was one of the chief reasons Ovid was renowned in the art of declamation[40] and is, of course, the central trope of *Venus and Adonis*. Shakespeare's impersonation, in other words, derives from an institutional as much as a literary tradition: schoolmasters revived the Roman practice of decla-mation, and with it *prosopopoeia*, in year-end examinations and public orations.

Prosopopoeia informed beginning language lessons as well: *vulgaria* from the Magdalen school – an institution strongly associated with humanist reform – stand apart from precursors by making impersonation the *foundation* for language-learning. Passages offered for double translation are either dialogues or monologues; and the characters are two – a schoolboy or his master.[41] Bringing mythological *prosopopoeia* home, the *vulgaria* put *personae* in place of persons. The also establish a decentering kind of imaginary practice: for schoolboys using such a volume, assuming a Latin *ego* meant putting such an 'ego' in quotation marks from the beginning – and sometimes, it meant speaking in the voice of the other, the master, monitoring that 'ego's' progress.

Other school texts suggest, however, that learning to impersonate the role of a Latin-speaking *puer* could take unexpected turns. In 1565, an 11-year-old student at Winchester school, William Badger, wrote a poem entitled 'Sylvia loquitur.' In it, he speaks in the voice of a 'trembling' and 'terrified' Sylvia and calls his schoolmates an 'unhappy throng of boy-girls' whose complaints rise to the stars. The word he coins for his peers is neither *pueri* nor *puellae* but *puelli*.[42] Transgendered *prosopopoeiae* were commonplace at Eton: Udall celebrated Anne Boleyn's coronation by declaiming in the voice of each muse; the annual custom of writing as a muse began at Eton not long after he became headmaster.[43] A detailed record of an oration at Shrewsbury school in 1591 tells us that in a ceremony of farewell for their patron, Henry Sidney, the boys gathered on a riverbank, 'apparelyd in greene' with 'greene wyllows uppon theire heades,' and bid farewell by impersonating the voices of nymphs. As Sidney sailed by, the boys '[made] lamentable orac'ons sorrowinge hys departure.'

> *Four boys appear in green singing –*
> O woefull wretched tyme, oh doleful day and houre
> Lament we may the loss we have, and floods of tears out poure.
> Come nymphs of woods and hilles, come help us moane we pray,
> The water nymphes our sisters dear, doe take our Lord away.
> Bewayle we may our wrongs, revenge we cannot take.
> O that the gods would bring him back, our sorrows for to shake.
>
> *One alone with musick –*
>
> O pinching payne, that gripes my hart, O thrice unhappy wight
> O sillie soule, what hap have I to see this woful sighte,
> Shall I now leave my lovinge Lord, shall he now from me goe,
> Why will he Salop nowe foresake alas why will he so!
> Alas my sorrowe doe increase, my hart doth rent in twayne,
> For that my Lord doth hence depart, and will not here remayne.

A witness writes that 'so pytyfully and of sutche excellency' was the nymphs' performance that 'it made many bothe [those] in the bardge upon the water as also people upon land to weepe and my Lorde hym selffe to changde countenance.'[44]

Such a moving rhetorical performance was clearly worthy of the inventive, pleading nymphs and goddesses in Elizabethan epyllia: Shakespeare's Venus, Heywood's Oenone, Beaumont's Salmacis. Avoiding the epic their masters admired, poets in the 1590s preferred, like Mr. Badger and the Shrewsbury boys, to adopt the voices of nymphs, women, and goddesses complaining. (On the few occasions when poets do invoke the *Aeneid*, the voice they recall is Dido's, the woman whose passion interfered with Aeneas's duty to Rome). Literary history, in short, suggests that school training in personification may have released identifications and emotions in students that were at some distance from their masters' declared purpose. I've already characterized the school as a daily theater for Latin learning. If I draw attention to the many women and nymphs complaining in the epyllia of former schoolboys, it is to suggest that the logical extension of the grammar school's training in how to be an English 'gentleman' was, in fact, a transvestite theater.

In *Venus and Adonis*, a former schoolboy carries on his classical lesson by fragmenting epic form, personifying its characters, borrowing from two of the Ovidian texts that were off-limits at school,[45] and imitating a passion at some distance from the social definition of the body he actually inhabited. Ventriloquizing the emotions of an aggressive, feminized *magister* as well as a reluctant, pretty *puellus*, Shakespeare takes aim at the institution in which he learned the art of *imitatio*. But over the course of this satiric performance, the narrator also moves through a shifting array of emotions, identifications, tones, and fantasies that exceed the gender distinctions – as well as preference for civic duty over eros – that schoolmasters claimed their curriculum would impart. Indeed, it (famously) ends by switching gears, inviting momentary sympathy for Venus's considerable grief over the death of her beloved. Such a poem betrays signs of resistance to grammar school teaching even when most profiting from its training.

Like other epyllia from the 1590s, *Venus and Adonis* does more than unsettle normative gender categories. The poem turns rhetoric itself, as trope and as trans-action, into an erotic event. The well-known ekphrasis on painted grapes as a metaphor for Adonis – grapes that 'surfeit the eye and pine the maw' – derives Venus's desire from representation by way of an ancient *exemplum* for rhetorical power.[46] At the same time, the poem equates persuasion with seduction when an eroticized teacher urges her pupil to take a lesson from Ovid's *Ars Amatoria*. Because the poem makes rhetoric as such an erotic event, I remember the disciplinary regime under which its author learned the art of classical imitation. In it I hear a schoolboy still grappling with the contradictory significance of such deceptively simple words as 'master/magister,' 'boy/*puer*,' and 'gentleman' – and with the equally contradictory mix of pleasure and pain that constituted Latin instruction.

Schoolmasters promulgated a myth of consolidation, and contemporary critics often echo that myth. William Kerrigan applauds that the conversion of the English 'I' into the Latin ego 'was a wholly male achievement.' Both Shakespeare's Venus and his Adonis – the aggressive *magister amoris* and pouting *puellus* – tell us that the word 'male' is somewhat less transparent than Kerrigan would have us believe. In a similar vein, Lisa Jardine and Anthony Grafton write that humanist pedagogy successfully 'fostered in its initiates a properly docile attitude toward authority.' To counter that claim, I'm going to give the last word to Adonis, that ambiguously gendered boy who is less than persuaded by his lesson in classical desire.

The passage I quoted at the beginning of this paper – 'O learn to love' – follows hard on the heels of the ekphrasis to Adonis's lusty horse that Shakespeare imitates directly from the *Ars Amatoria*. Notice that the 'old text' Venus wants Adonis to imitate is *already an imitation*, not the thing itself ('Look when a painter would surpass the life'). At least two layers of imitation mediate Adonis's feelings – we learn what he wants, or doesn't want, by contrast to an exemplary classical authority. It may be an oblique way to capture emotion, but it is consonant with school training: in this poem, as at school, representation precedes and shapes character rather than the other way around. If Adonis reveals his feelings in relation to classical imitation, however, he does so in the mode of resistance – flatly refusing the place in gender and desire Venus's 'old text' offers. Shakespeare's lovely *puellus* does something more than fail to adopt an understanding of 'natural' love – the 'well-proportioned' stallion who 'welcomes the warm approach of sweet desire.' Worse than that, he won't learn to imitate the *representation* of masculinity his master offers him as 'natural.' A *prosopopoeia* from a Latin text, Adonis becomes an animated principle of refusal, declining to play the part already written for him. Perhaps he is simply bettering his lesson, overgoing Ovid by derailing one of the *Metamorphoses*'s few stories of happy heterosexual love ('I know not loue... nor will not know it,/

Unlesse it be a Boare, and then I chase it'). Or perhaps Adonis's painful death is a kind of payment for his refusal – a fantasy that testifies to the violence of the institution in which Shakespeare learned what it meant to be a Latin-speaking gentleman. Of the poem's abrupt shift of tone and mood at Adonis's castration and death, then, I'll venture one last observation. If a gentleman is being punished in this poem, there is also someone mourning the inevitable violence of that event.

Notes

1. 'Pater: hunc filiolum meum ad te adduco, ut ex belua hominem facias (Juan Luis Vives, *Linguae latinae exercitatio*, A6r). Henry VIII's primer, authorized for 'the good of the schools,' phrases this claim about pedagogy in a monarchical way: it will teach 'the better bringing up of youth' in 'knowledge of duty' toward God, prince, and 'all others in their degree' (as quoted in Jo Ann Hoeppner Moran, *The Growth of English Schooling, 1340–1548* [Princeton: Princeton University Press, 1985], 45).
2. T. W. Baldwin, *Shakespeare's Small Latine and Less Greek* (Urbana: University of Illinois Press, 1944); Donald Lemen Clark, *John Milton at St. Paul's School, a Study of Ancient Rhetoric in English Renaissance Education* (New York: Columbia Univeristy Press, 1948); R. R. Bolgar, *The Classical Heritage and its Beneficiaries* (Cambridge: Cambridge University Press, 1954).
3. I rely on John Guillory's discussion of canon formation and schooling in *Cultural Capital: The Problem of Literary Canon Formation* (Chicago: University of Chicago Press, 1993).
4. For a related discussion of Shakespeare's ventriloquism in *The Rape of Lucrece*, see my *The Rhetoric of the Body from Ovid to Shakespeare* (Cambridge: Cambridge University Press, 2000).
5. *Venus and Adonis*, lines 7–11 in *The Riverside Shakespeare*, 2nd edn, ed. G. Blakemore Evans (New York: Houghton Mifflin, 1997). All subsequent quotations from this edition.
6. For a critique of the way such assumptions have informed criticism of the poem, see Richard Rambuss, 'What It Feels Like for a Boy: Shakespeare's *Venus and Adonis*,' in *A Companion to Shakespeare's Works, Volume IV, The Poems, Problem Comedies, Late Plays*, ed. Richard Dutton and Jean Howard (Blackwell, 2003), 240–58.
7. See *The Rhetoric of the Body*, chapter 1.
8. First set out by Erasmus in *Copia* and often adapted to the themes of Aphthonius, themes were preliminary to full-fledged orations. Baldwin points out that Venus's first argument is a version of the same school theme important to the narrator of the sonnets: 'motiues to procreation as ye way to outliue time' (1:186).
9. William Lily's *A Short Introduction of Grammar, Compiled and set forth for the bringing up of all those that intend to attain the knowledge of the Latin Tongue*. Compiled in 1512 for the St Paul's School and printed shortly after, it remained in print and in school use for the next 150 years. As J. Howard Brown notes, ordinary editions of books ran to 1250 copies, while Lily's Grammar had a print run of 10,000 (*Elizabethan Schooldays* [Oxford: Blackwell, 1933], 42).
10. I borrow Harry Berger's insight in 'Narrative as Rhetoric in *The Faerie Queene*,' *ELR* 21 (1991), 3–48.
11. See William Kerrigan, 'The Articulation of the Ego in the English Renaissance,' in Joseph H. Smith, *The Literary Freud: Mechanisms of Defense and Poetic Will* (New Haven: Yale University Press, 1980), 261–308. My understanding of psychoanalytic theory, as well as what that theory means for social reproduction, differs considerably from his.
12. See Barbara Freedman's account of the difference that psychoanalytic thinking introduces into the scene of pedagogy ('Pedagogy, Psychoanalysis, Theatre: Interrogating the Scene of Learning,' *Shakespeare Quarterly*, 41 (1990), 174–86).
13. Richard Halpern, *The Poetics of Primitive Accumulation: English Renaissance Culture and the Genealogy of Capital* (Ithaca: Cornell University Press, 1991), 29.

14. Erasmus's position on imitation became standard. In *The Education of Children* (1588), Kempe writes that students 'obseru[e] examples . . . in other mens workes' and make 'somewhat of [their] owne . . . first by imitation, and at length without imitation' (F1v-F3v).

15. Thomas Elyot, *Boke Named the Governour* (New York: Garland Press, 1992), 19. Dean Colet wrote that 'the master of the grammar school . . . shall be a good and honest man, and of much and well attested learning. Let him teach the boys, especially those belonging to the cathedral, grammar, and at the same time show them an example of good living. Let him take great heed that he cause no offence to their tender minds by any pollution of word or deed. Nay, more, along with the chaste literature let him imbue them with holy morals, and be to them a master, not of grammar only, but of virtue.' As quoted in Michael F. J. McDonnell, *A History of St. Paul's School* (London: Chapman Hall, 1909), 20.

16. John Sergeaunt, *Annals of Westminster School*, 279–82. *Etoniana*, no. 10, July 15, 1907, records a consuetudinarium written by William Malim, headmaster at Eton c. 1560, for the Royal Commissioners who visited Eton in 1561. (Malim was Udall's student and also renowned for beating; the pupils who escaped Malim's flogging prompted the dinner conversation about flogging recorded in Ascham's *Scholemaster*). Malim also elaborates the hierarchy of surrogate monitoring; there seem to have been at least two in each form. At least two other schools (at Cuckfield in Sussex and at Saffron Walden in Essex) explicitly modeled their disciplinary practice on that of Eton.

17. The ordinances at the Shrewsbury school describe punishment as a timed, daily public spectacle: 'The Second Schoolmaster shall comme to the schoole everie morning for the space of one weke before the bell cease, to th' intent to see the schollers singe and saie the nowe usuall praiers there reverentlie upon their knees, the which praier beinge ended, he shall orderlie call the Rolles for absents of the hole schoole, and punyshe them for negligence according to his discression and their deserts' (*A History of the Shrewsbury School from the Blakeway Mss., and Many Other Sources* [Shrewsbury and London: Adnitt & Naunton, 1899], 46–52). Apparently Friday was the day at Eton and Winchester when 'all the offences committed during the week past were enumerated and culprits punished' (*Etoniana*, 10 (1907), 139–40).

18. My formulation relies on Slavoj Žižek's description of 'symbolic identification' in *The Sublime Object of Ideology* (London: Verso, 1989).

19. Laplanche's description of Freud's topographical and dynamic model is suggestive for this schoolroom scene: 'This approach does not merely set up an interplay between the . . . agencies . . . . Special importance comes to be assigned to the 'relations of dependence' obtaining between the various systems . . . *the intrasubjective field tends to be conceived of after the fashion of intersubjective relations*, and the systems are pictured as relatively autonomous persons-within-the person . . .' (*The Language of Psychoanalysis*, J. Laplanche and J.-B. Pontalis, translated by Donald Nicholson-Smith [New York: Norton, 1973], 452, emphasis mine).

20. *Imaginary Audition: Shakespeare on Stage and Page* (Berkeley: University of California Press, 1989), 74–104. See his development of this conception of Shakespearean subjectivity – the way characters' acts of persuasion are simultaneously acts of self-persuasion and judgment – in *Making Trifles of Terrors: Redistributing Complicities in Shakespeare* (Stanford: Stanford University Press, 1997).

21. *A History of the Shrewsbury School*, 46–52.

22. *Catechismus paruus pueris primum Latine . . . proponendus in scholis* (London: John Day, 1573).

23. As recorded in David Baldwin, *The Chapel Royal: Ancient and Modern* (London: Duckworth, 1990), 117–18.

24. *A History of the Shrewsbury School*, 315. St Saviour's Grammar School in Southward required in 1614 that 'on play days the highest Form shall *declaim* and some of the inferior Forms *act* a scene of Terence or some dialogue.'

25. The student was Sir James Whitelocke, who entered Merchant Taylors' in 1585. He was commenting on the frequency with which Mulcaster's boys acted at court (quoted in

E. K. Chambers, *The Elizabethan Stage* [Oxford: Clarendon Press, 1923], 2.76). Bale, *Scriptorum Illustrium Maioris Brytannie...Catalogus*, 1577, as cited in Hillebrand, 700: 'ad formandum os tenerum & balbutiens, quo clarè, eleganter, & distinctè uerba eloqui & effari con-suesceret. Plurimas in eius museo uidi ac legi tragoedias & comoedias, epistolas, orationes, congratulationes'.

26. Malim as quoted in *Etoniana*, 10, 1907, 159. Translation of Hoole's comment is Watson's, *English Grammar Schools*, 316.

27. I borrow Pierre Bourdieu's term from *The Logic of Practice* (Stanford: Stanford University Press), 56.

28. As quoted in Stewart, *Close Readers*, 98–9. The anecdote appears in McDonnell, *A History of St. Paul's School* and Foster Watson, *Richard Mulcaster and his 'Elementarie'* (London, 1893), 5. Mulcaster refers, in *Positions*, to his rod as 'my lady birchely' (274).

29. 'A Collection of Verses, Orations, &c, Compos'd & Spoken by the eight upper Boys of Merchant Taylors' School, in London, upon certain public days of Examination or Election' (no publisher).

30. The seal of Louth Grammar School (1552) depicts a master with a boy on his knee, birch poised mid-air: six other boys watch the performance as the master pronounces a Latin lesson that informs all viewers, whether inside and outside the picture, that loving and flogging are one: 'He who spares the rod, hates his son.' As depicted in N. Carlisle, *Concise Description of the Endowed Grammar Schools of England and Wales.* 2 vols (London: 1818).

31. These questions arise from my understanding of retrospection and trauma as outlined by Jean Laplanche in *Life and Death in Psychoanalysis* (Baltimore: Johns Hopkins University Press).

32. Clearly a significant location for grammar school attention, the boy's buttocks in these and other stories might be read in relation to Laplanche's discussion of 'zones of exchange' that 'attract the first erotogenic maneuvers from the adult. An even more significant factor, if we introduce the subjectivity of the first 'partner': these zones focalize parental fantasies.... So that we may say, in what is barely a metaphor, that they are the points through which is introduced into the child that alien internal entity which is, properly speaking, the sexual excitation' (24). An important difference, of course, is that Laplanche calls these the 'marks of *maternal* care' because of modern parenting practices. But in the Tudor period, the grammar school intervened in the parenting function (indeed, masters portrayed themselves as paternal but occasionally as maternal too), so that the gender of the parental figure who attends to certain zones of the body, thereby lending those zones significance, fluctuates. This institutional intervention in child-rearing means that disciplinary or parental figures could be deeply ambivalent – as ambivalent as the fantasy of the 'phallic mother' in psychoanalytic discourse.

33. William Kempe, *The Education of Children in Learning: Declared by the Dignitie, Vtilitie, and Method thereof* (London: Thomas Orwin, 1588), C2v, D1v.

34. I draw on J. Howard Brown, *Elizabethan Schooldays*; T. W. Baldwin, *William Shakespeare's Petty School* (Urbana: University of Illinois Press, 1943) and *Shakespeare's Small Latine and Less Greek*; and several histories of particular schools, including Sir H. C. Maxwell-Lyte, *A History of Eton College* (London: Macmillan and Co., 1911); Michael F. J. McDonnell, *A History of St. Paul's School* (London: Chapman Hall, 1909); the anonymous *History of the Shrewsbury School*; and the anonymous issue of *Etoniana*, 10 (1907), which gives a detailed account of daily life at that institution.

35. *Shakespeare's Troy: Drama, politics, and the translation of Empire* (Cambridge: Cambridge University Press, 1997), 1–18. Virgil's reputation as a counselor of political order in the state was further consolidated by the immense popularity of his allegory of the bees from the fourth book of the *Georgics*. As Baldwin once observed, 'probably no Elizabethan schoolboy escaped those bees' (*Small Latine*, 1.327).

36. In *The Governour*, Elyot recommends imitating Virgil, but Ovid is a necessary evil: he helps 'for understanding other authors' but has 'little other learning concerning virtuous

manners of policy.' Wolsey recommends imitating Virgil, 'the first among all poets,' because the 'dignity of his song, conducted with sonorous voice' will 'give shape to tender mouths' and promote 'the most elegant of pronunciation' (Thomas Wolsey, *Rudimenta grammatices* [London 1536]).

37. British Library, Royal ms. 12 A.LXVII. One of Malim's verses reads, 'Tullius altisonis [...] dum scripta Maronis / Intonuit subito, o magnae spes altera Romae.' A verse from one 'Ioannes Pratt' then refers to 'Haec noua Trois super reliquas caput eriget omnes' while 'Richardus Clercus' writes a brief poem in which Elizabeth's reign surpasses all others, particularly Troy and Rome: 'not ita... non ita... non ita.... Non ita Troia potens Priamo celebrata potenti / Non ita Caesareo numine Roma fuit....' 'Edmundus Winchus' and 'Thomas Sandersonus,' clearly younger Latin students, continue the theme in much shorter poems.

38. *Troia Britanica: or, Great Britaines Troy* (London: W. Iaggard, 1609).

39. *Primitive Accumulation*, 45–56.

40. For Ovid's training in declamation, as well as the impact of the retreat of Roman rhetoric from its public role on his representation of embodied subjectivity, see *The Rhetoric of the Body*, chapter 2.

41. William Nelson, *A Fifteenth Century School Book* (Oxford: Clarendon Press, 1956) and Nicholas Orme, *Education and Society in Medieval and Renaissance England* (London and Ronceverte: Hambledon Press, 1989) provide modern editions of the English sentences of both *vulgaria* but, with the exception of a few examples, the Latin part of the text is preserved only in manuscript. Three examples will give a sense of the kinds of familiar voices through which schoolboys conducted their first language lessons: 'For nowe at fyve of the clocke by the monelyght I most go to my booke and lete sleepe and slouthe alon. And yff oure maister hape to awake us, he bryngeth a rode stede of a candle.... here is nought els preferryde but monyshynge and strypys'; 'Me semeth I ame more bownd to my maisters than to my father or my mother, for as for my father and mother to se as sent bornard seid make me as a damnyd body or y was borne in-to the world' and 'I hade leuer teche in any place in the worlde then her at oxford, wher I can teche nothyng that I thanke profitable for my scolares bot sum be agenst yt; I can consell nothyng but the consele the contrarie...'

42. British Library, Additional Ms. 4379.

43. Udall began with 'Apollo loquitur,' then declaimed nine more poems in the voice of each muse. The titles were like Badger's, i.e. 'Calliope Loquitur' and his performance was followed by verses declaimed 'by an othir child.' See British Library Royal Ms. 18 A.LXIV. For the tradition at Eton, see Michael Meredith, *Five Hundred Years of Eton Theater* (Eton College, 2001).

44. *A History of the Shrewsbury School*, 65–6.

45. The epigram is from the *Amores* – the Ovidian text that had Patrick Cheney reminds us had the 'dubious distinction' of being a 'cultural taboo' – and Venus's precursor the Ars amatoria's *praeceptor amoris*. Following Ovid rather than Virgil, Shakespeare embellishes the *Metamorphoses*' story with the two Ovidian texts that schoolmasters carefully kept out of the curriculum. On Marlowe's transgressive use of the *Amores* to define his own career, see Patrick Cheney, *Marlowe's Counterfeit Profession: Ovid, Spenser, Counter-Nationhood* (Toronto: University of Toronto Press, 1997), 31–67.

46. Both Halpern and Belsey devote much of their analysis of *Venus and Adonis* to understanding the relationship between this ekphrasis and desire.

9

History Between Theaters

Anston Bosman

The theaters of my title are both buildings and books, and my subject is the history of the relation between performance and print; but I will also concern myself with another, grander history, namely that of the relation between certain national cultures which playhouses and publications have enabled and sustained. The more carefully we trace these histories, the more we will notice a dynamic reciprocity not only between theatrical printing and practice, but also among the various territories and polities upon which the discrete narratives of traditional theater history are based. Without obliterating areas of distinction among, first, the cultural practices and, second, the national models according to which we reconstruct the history of theater, we may still come to recognize how often and how boldly those areas are criss-crossed, even trespassed, and how texts, performances and cultures are less isolated, less integral, and above all less inert than we tend to imagine.

I begin with two artifacts from theater history. One object comes from a building, the other from a book, yet paradoxically both are monuments to mobility. The first is a copy of a theater curtain designed for one of the first commercial playhouses in eighteenth-century Germany, the Theater auf der Ranstädter Bastei in Leipzig. Before the actor-manager Heinrich Koch opened the house in 1766, he commissioned Adam Friedrich Oeser, the Austrian artist and founding director of the Leipzig academy of art, to paint its curtain and ceiling; neither decoration survives, but we do have a picture of the curtain by one of Oeser's students (Figure 41). The *Vorhang* is an allegory of the history of drama. It shows a colonnaded forecourt to what the original festival brochure calls the Temple of Truth, but an eminent observer elsewhere describes as the Temple of Fame. (Both interpretations are feasible: in the distance, the temple goddess stands nude and open-armed like an icon of Truth, while from above putti swoop down bearing the laurel wreaths and garlands of Fame.) On either side of the forecourt entrance are statues of Sophocles and Aristophanes, attended by the tragic and comic muse respectively. Beside Tragedy sits History, who turns away from her opened book to behold the mask and buskin being shown to her by Aeschylus; this presumably is History torn between printed chronicle and

Figure 41 Christian Friedrich Wiegand, after Adam Friedrich Oeser, Curtain for the Theater auf der Ranstädter Bastei (1819, original 1766). Reproduced by permission of the Stadtgeschichtliche Museum, Leipzig

performed drama. Behind her the brochure identifies Socrates, Euripides, other Greek poets, and nameless German and French followers. On the other side of the vestibule, beside festooned Aristophanes, we find Menander reading, Plautus leaning on his staff to study the writings of his predecessors, and Terence accepting the torch of Cupid. As a whole, the composition has a pleasing symmetry: three statues, three muses, three named ancients on each side, and up in the clouds the embraced and hovering trinity of the Graces.

But now comes the odd part – 'das Wunderliche,' to quote our eminent observer, who is the painter's sometime pupil and later close friend, J. W. von Goethe. In the eighth book of *Dichtung und Wahrheit* Goethe describes the shadowy figure at the curtain's center left, a person whom the artist has chosen to depict from behind:

> Through the open center was seen the portal of the distant temple, and a man was making his way between the two above-mentioned groups, without troubling himself about them, directly towards the temple; it was therefore that his back was seen, and there was nothing particularly striking about the figure. Now this man was to represent Shakespeare, who, without predecessors or followers, unconcerned as to models, pursued his own way [auf seine eigne Hand] to immortality.[1]

If Goethe is right to identify the temple as that of Fame, then Oeser has justly painted Shakespeare as still en route. In the Germany of the 1760s Shakespeare was only beginning to be widely read and was very rarely produced on stage. Literary interest had begun in the 1730s with translations of Addison's *Spectator* and intensified with the Berlin essayists of the 1750s, who sought to impress English drama into a new and bourgeois German culture independent of the French-oriented courts; their manifesto was G. E. Lessing's seventeenth *Literaturbrief*, which insisted that the future of German drama lay in the English past. Calling for a transitional stage between national theaters, Lessing wished that 'the masterpieces of Shakespeare had been translated, with modest changes, for our Germans,' and in the half-dozen years between his essay and Oeser's curtain, the wish was granted.[2] Between 1762 and 1766 22 plays appeared in the translations of the poet Christoph Martin Wieland; the number, completeness and sophistication of these versions was without precedent, and they would grow more popular than any other published drama in Germany. But for some time their impact was on the reading rather than the theater-going public. It would be another decade before Friedrich Schröder, reworking Wieland's translations, produced his acclaimed *Hamlet* and eight other Shakespeare plays, lodging them firmly, albeit in adapted form, in the standard German repertoire. The canonization proper dates from 1786, when Berlin's Royal National Theatre opened with an allegorical ballet on the German art of acting, featuring busts of Euripides, Sophocles, Plautus, Terence, Shakespeare and Lessing; this is the beginning of the national myth of 'unser Shakespeare.'

Oeser's curtain painting, then, has proved not only allegorical but prophetic. That no French dramatist is recognizably foregrounded; that any English author at all appears in the pantheon; that Shakespeare is represented as unexampled and in closest proximity, depending on one's interpretation, to truth or to fame: these are not present realities in the Leipzig of 1766, but more like projections into the future. (On the theater's opening night, by contrast, the curtain rose on a wholly traditional program: a tragedy from Germanic legend, a ballet, and a French comedy based on Plautus.) When Shakespeare finally did enter the house of fame it was certainly not, as Goethe words it, 'by his own hand,' but rather thanks to the zealous imitation and advocacy of many others, notably the *Sturm und Drang* writers whose leading spokesman was Goethe himself. Nor did Shakespeare abandon his books at the temple gate; on the contrary, his access was gained through writing rather than playing. When Goethe likened him to Prometheus, it was divine poetry, not the secret of performance, that Shakespeare was understood to have stolen.

I turn now to my second theatrical artifact, which at once complements and contradicts the first. If the first was a stage decoration that revealed, even as it mystified, a moment in the history of literary production, then the second is printed evidence, a textual capture, of an episode in the history of performance. So much for the complementarity; the contradiction is that whereas the curtain depicts Shakespeare taking his first steps towards fame in Leipzig in the 1760s, this page represents a primordial footprint on that journey, set down in the same country and perhaps in the same city but a whole century and a half earlier (Figure 42). It is the title-page of a 1620 collection of plays performed on the continent by the strolling troupes generally called 'the English comedians.' The volume is an octavo of 384 unnumbered pages, and the title page translates thus:

> English Comedies and Tragedies, that is, very beautiful, excellent and select, sacred and worldly comic and tragic plays, together with Pickle-herring, which on account of their fanciful inventions, entertaining and partly true stories, have been acted and presented by the English in Germany at royal, electoral, and princely courts, as well as in the foremost imperial, coastal, and commercial towns; never before printed, but now published to please all lovers of comedies and tragedies, and others, and in such a manner as to be easily performed in turn, and presented for the delight and invigoration of the spirit. Printed in the year 1620.

There is a good deal of information on this page, but let us begin with what it does *not* tell us. No author, editor or publisher is recorded; nor for that matter is the place of publication (the widespread assumption that the volume was printed in Leipzig lacks conclusive evidence). We are given no clues as to what party or parties provided what sort of manuscripts to whom. All that seems safe to deduce is that, in this transaction, the actors and their performing scripts were English, and the printers and their copy texts were German. This is in fact the current critical view: the leading scholar on the subject refers to the compilation as 'the first anthology of English drama in German prose translations.'[3]

Yet even these deductions are far from secure. To appreciate this it will be necessary to step away from our document for a moment and consider its larger context. First of all, who exactly were 'the English in Germany' invoked here, and what was the 'English drama' they so deftly imported to the continent? These questions are invariably answered with lists of actors (Browne, Green, Sackville, Jolly) and authors (Marlowe, Dekker, Kyd, Shakespeare), but as a guide to the actual performers and their productions, such lists are misleading. As I have argued elsewhere, if the players and their plays were exclusively English in the 1580s, they did not long remain so; on the contrary, that the former became multinational and the latter polyglot is easily demonstrated.[4] To begin with the nationality of the performers, it is clear that the title 'English comedians' lost descriptive accuracy over time, for the simple reason that the strolling companies began in their early days to augment their numbers by hiring foreign players. By the seventeenth century, while managers or leading players still tended to be English, most of the troupes active on the Continent were in fact mixed. The lucrative association with England was often retained (even in the eighteenth century, wholly continental groups continued to bill themselves as English), but players could also choose to adopt the name of the country they were in or had just passed through: having traveled to Germany via the Low Countries, for instance, the same company could variously style itself 'englische,' 'niederländische,' or 'hochdeutsche Komödianten,' and in a mixed company all three epithets

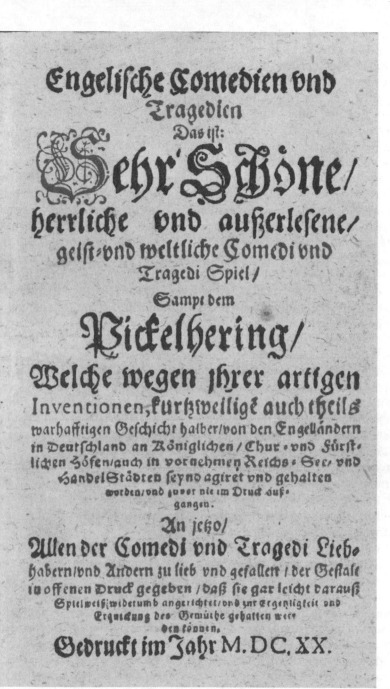

Figure 42   Title-page to *Engelische Comedien und Tragedien* (1620). Reproduced by permission of the Folger Shakespeare Library

might be true. In their time the troupes were most accurately described with composite names like 'comedians from England and the Netherlands' or 'English and Cologne comedians'; it will therefore be observed that to refer, as our title-page does, to 'the English in Germany' is not to offer a solution to the actors' identities, but only to restate the problem.

Nor does the phrase 'English drama' do justice to their repertoire. The players' intercultural context would have further unsettled the already complex relationship between text and performance in early modernity. We cannot say, for example, whether a given play would have begun its continental run as a printed edition, prompt-book, touring abridgement or memorial reconstruction, but we can be sure that any script would have been transformed in the staging process, and that this transformation would have intensified as the company traveled on. A crucial index here is the language of the performances – or rather, the *languages*, since only one did not suffice for long. On their first excursions the actors typically engaged a guide or interpreter and in the 1590s productions were still in English, leading Fynes Moryson to sneer that 'the people not understanding what [the players] said, only for their action followed them with wonderful concourse.'[5] By the turn of the century, however, the situation had begun to change. In 1602 a troupe of 11 Englishmen visiting Münster performed 'on five successive days five different comedies in their English tongue' but 'were accompanied by a clown, who, when a new act had to commence and when they had to change their costume, performed many antics and pranks in German during the performance, which amused the audience.'[6] What started as a chorus gradually saturated the whole action: as more Englishmen acquired German and more Germans joined the English comedians, the local language seems to have gained the upper hand. After 1606 we have no definite records of performances in English, and in 1613 at Nuremberg a company is praised for its 'guter teutscher Sprach.'[7] This hardly proves that by the second decade of the century a transition from English to German was complete, but it does suggest varying linguistic and cultural competencies within and among companies, and shows that the German translation of English drama was a lengthy, uneven and collaborative process in which performers and printers alike had roles to play.

If we now return to the 1620 title-page, we will find an instance of this transitional theater ready at hand. The volume, we read, consists in English comedies and tragedies 'together with Pickle-herring'; but who was this character and what is his relationship to the plays? Pickle-herring descends from the clown who amused the crowd at Münster; he is a jig-making jokester who pops up between the acts of full-length dramas and also stars in his own playlets. In this volume, he first appears at five break points in the *Comoedia von Fortunato*, where he has no set dialogue, only improvisations cued with the direction 'Here Pickle-herring performs.' Next, the volume adds to its six comedies and two tragedies a couple of two-act farces labeled 'Pickelherings Spiele' and five untitled verse interludes or 'Engelische Aufzüge' complete with music, four of which feature the clown. Now it ought to follow from the identification of the actors, plays and interludes as English that Pickle-herring was drawn from England's stage, but this is not the case; in fact, the role seems to have been created by one or more of the players in the course of their travels. Thus the *OED* not only cites the very document before us as the first printing of the word to denote a 'clown, a buffoon, a merry-andrew,' but states explicitly that 'this application of the term originated in German.' The standard theater histories maintain that Pickle-herring was an invention of the actor Robert Reynolds, who arrived on the continent in 1618 and eventually became the leader of a troupe using the moniker 'bieklingherings compagnia'; more recent research has corrected this by finding in a court account-book an earlier reference to another player by the title, but there is still no evidence of it in England.[8] And yet 1621, the year after our volume, saw the publication of two topical broadsides entitled 'Engelländischer Pickelhäring' and 'Englische Pickelhäring'! The name has a kind of looking-glass logic to it, like a word that speakers of one language imagine as belonging to another whose speakers would, however, never recognize it as such (the modern German 'Handy,' meaning a mobile phone, comes to mind). Nor should we hesitate to name this logic: it is the process by which we say languages and cultures 'meet' – a process, that is, of mutual incomprehension, interference, and invention. It is the logic of the contact zone.

To invoke the contact zone in discussing early modern European theater is to recall the origins of the concept – now a staple of anthropological discourse – in the field of linguistics, where the term 'contact language' refers to improvised codes that develop among speakers of different native languages who need to communicate with each other consistently, usually in contexts of trade.[9] Such languages, which typically begin as pidgins and become creoles when they have native speakers of their own, were long regarded as chaotic, barbarous or lacking in structure. In time, however, scholars of language acquisition began observing that the process of language learning seemed to involve not only two linguistic systems but three: not only, in formal terms, a native language and a target language, but an in-between language or grammar as well. This third system had been invisible to earlier linguists, who saw language acquisition as a transfer from one monolingual situation to another, and could therefore perceive intermediate linguistic phenomena only as a random collection of errors, as deviances from or approximations of some other system, never as themselves constituting a system apart. The important shift from this purely transitional notion of language transfer to a theory granting a measure of autonomy and coherence to a third interlocking system required the introduction of a new term, which is now established as 'interlanguage.'[10] Based on the intermediary data observable at a single stage of language contact, linguists treat interlanguage as having a grammar distinct from that of the native and target languages, but one open to constant extension and amendment. Systematic, permeable, and dynamic, the interlanguage concept has more recently been broadened by cultural theory to the term 'intersystem,' which is used to describe the interactions of colonial encounters or polyethnic societies.[11]

A theory of intersystems has much to offer a revised history of Europe's traveling players, their translated and adapted texts, and improvised characters of the Pickle-herring type; the theory may bring into focus features of early modern theater that traditional nation-based accounts have rendered marginal or even invisible. Until now the international and multilingual qualities of the itinerant companies' legacy in performance and print have been downplayed because scholars have preferred to cast the theater as merely transitional, the decline of one form or the rise of another rather than a form in its own right. An exemplary study traces the 'process of decomposition' to which English drama was subjected by the troupes, then their 'thorough Germanization', but scarcely pauses to consider what this intermediate theater might actually have been.[12] In other accounts the tendency is to undersell the phenomenon as little more than the 'activities of the English players on the Continent' or to oversell it as a 'collective transference' from one nation to another; again, the resistance is to naming and analysing a theater in between.[13]

There are at least two reasons, one specific and one general, for this elision. In specific, the scholarship must confront the differences in theatrical infrastructure separating early modern England, which had fixed scenic spaces and widely circulated playbooks by the late 1500s, from Germany, where even in the 1650s local actors were still barred from performing in theaters (court venues reserved for Italian opera and the occasional French troupe) and forced perpetually to tour, and where the managers of those actors defensively opposed the printing of play-texts. When these differences are allowed to harden into a dichotomy, the result is not inclusive theater history but exclusive theater histories. Consider, for example, two accounts of how the 1620 anthology under discussion came to be printed. Here is how the authoritative English scholar in the field judges the question:

> [The] volume of *Engelische Comedien und Tragedien*...probably represents an attempt of Browne and Green to turn to profit with the printers their repertory of 1618–20, now rendered useless by their return to England.[14]

And here is his distinguished German counterpart:

> We have to do here with the adaptations of uneducated speculators, whose object was to spoil the market for the English, and to appropriate their subjects for the benefit of German companies, who had begun to compete with the English at an early period. It is impossible to imagine for a moment that the English actors themselves made this collection.[15]

The two explanations contrast starkly in argument – they remind us that theater histories are also stories, that is, patterns of affect as well as fact – but they agree in interpreting the volume as an episode in one distinct national narrative. Both the comedy of English enterprise and the tragedy of German piracy foreclose the complex collaboration of actors, managers, scribes, and printers that was necessary for the anthology to be produced at all.

The second, more general, difficulty in describing this theatrical intersystem goes beyond the relationship of seventeenth-century Germany and England. It is the difficulty of trying to write *any* theater history in terms other than the national. Can it be that theater history is in this regard moving more slowly than literary or cultural history in general?[16] The question does not imply that nation-based accounts of the theater are inherently reactionary or simple-minded; on the contrary, some brilliant and progressive work has been done in this vein. But on occasion one feels that the terms of the debate have simply been reversed: that the same texts and performances once used to aggrandize nations are now being used to denounce them, while still treating nation-formation as organic and inevitable. Though no longer celebratory but critical, too many accounts of theater as national allegory risk reduplicating the discourses of otherness, the local divisions of the world, they were first concerned to expose. We may, in other words, have dispensed with the tone adopted by the critics of the strolling players I have just cited, but much of their method remains.

How then might one go about reworking theater history as a contact zone? Recent critical interventions hold out great promise, and I will note three examples ranging from the abstract to the empirical. First, Stephen Greenblatt has sounded a cautionary note about the national model of literary history and its 'illusion of sedentary, indigenous literary cultures making sporadic and half-hearted ventures towards the margins' (a paraphrase of views on traveling theater if ever there was one). 'The reality,' he says, 'for most of the past as once again for the present, is more about nomads than natives.' Greenblatt ends with a call for 'mobility studies,' his term for inquiry into the movements and disruptions making up global culture.[17] Second, narrowing the focus to early modern Europe, Richard Helgerson has argued that humanist ideals of imitation rendered the Renaissance dream of a national literature compatible with cross-cultural identification and mimicry rather than isolation in uniqueness; contrary to the post-Romantic assumptions of modern literary history, he asserts, the sixteenth-century English, French and Spanish 'could readily embrace, even celebrate, their hybridity.'[18] Finally, on the subject of theater, Julie Stone Peters has challenged, in a remarkable conspectus of four centuries of 'European theatre's resistance to and continual refashioning of itself in the world of print,' the traditional 'contrasts between north and south, Italy and England,' deeming these 'misleading given the variation of traditions within nations and the strong and rapid trafficking in ideas and aesthetics that characterizes European theatrical culture.'[19] These and similar revisionist perspectives will surely make it harder for theater historians to return to business as usual.

Yet none of these arguments addresses the particular problem of the contact zone with which I am concerned. That problem, to recall the artifacts with which I began, is how we are to trace in print and performance the hybridizing process that connects the 1620 title page with the 1766 stage curtain, leading from the first encounters between theaters through their production of composite and unpredictable new forms. I am urging us not to view these objects as evidence of either English or German theater history alone, but rather as interstitial and developing phenomena, as stages of contact in a theater no longer English and not yet contrastively European, assimilable neither to a unidirectional model of cultural transference nor to a strictly reciprocal one of cultural exchange. To describe this theater will require vocabulary that acknowledges both the continuum of transculturation across which it moves and the temporary stable configurations in which it can legitimately be examined. Drawing on the afore-mentioned research in linguistics, I hope to adapt the concept of interlanguage to this purpose, and therefore propose for the intermediary theatrical system we have hitherto been approaching the name of *intertheater*.

The concept of intertheater makes several claims. First and foremost, it takes the sum of textual representations and embodied performances of the strolling troupes seriously as a distinctive form of theater. Second, intertheater draws atten-tion to processes of interaction and interference between two cultural systems as well as to the production of third intermediary phenomena. Last, intertheater calls for empirical studies and composite theories of its cognitive and affective dimensions; we should ask both how and why intertheater developed, exploring its assembly and its motivation. On these three points intertheater differs from the notion of 'intercultural theater' circulating in performance studies. First, intercultural theater does not posit a separate theater system, but rather names a trend in the European avant-garde, from the late eighteenth century through today, toward adopting foreign elements into established traditions. Second, work in this area avoids specifying the interface of theater systems by shifting attention to universal principles underlying or overlaying theater as a whole, such as the nostalgia of Eugenio Barba's theater anthropology or the utopia of the great human vocabulary by which Peter Brook imagines uniting the world on stage. Third, research on interculturalism has tended to privilege gesture and image over language and text, so that intercultural theater mostly means intercultural performance, with an implicit bias against literacy and, at times, representation itself. My argument, by contrast, is that an investigation of the drama of the early modern traveling companies should no more be confined to text or performance than to England or Germany. Against the isolated national theaters of *or*, the players counterposed an intertheater of *and*. This is their challenge to literary history and performance studies alike.

What most prevents us from taking up this challenge, I suspect, is the matter of authorship, which remains the organizing principle of national canons of theater notwithstanding the recent critical emphasis on collaboration in early modern playwriting, staging, and bookmaking. Anonymity is still anathema, it seems, even when the concept is perfectly compatible with a critic's broader argument. Thus, while one understands the anxiety of earlier scholars to settle the prove-nance of the 1620 anthology, it is odd that Julie Stone Peters, who includes the volume in a discussion on the public nature of both acting and printing plays, cites the work under 'Green, John [pseud.], and Robert Browne, eds.'[20] Peters repeats an unverifiable attribution even though she might quite consistently and persuasively have argued that the volume's anonymity conforms to the logic of its 'publication,' its becoming fully public. The same problem has obstructed inter-pretation of the plays collected in the book, again, even when anonymity is both the form and the theme of the work. The best example among the comedies is

Eine schöne lustige Comoedia von Jemand und Niemand [A beautiful and merry comedy of Somebody and Nobody], which recasts the Elizabethan hybrid play *Nobody and Somebody* – a play not only anonymous but centered around a character called Nobody. Writing of the English play, Muriel Bradbrook noted its 'frame at once familiar and exciting, into which any local characters might be inserted at will,' and Luke Wilson has recently read the Nobody character as a metaphor for symbolic exchange in fiction; neither scholar, however, has observed the redoubtable intercultural legacy of this adaptability.[21] And yet the play is a virtual template for intertheater, as is proven by its vivid continental applications in several languages for over a century.

We confront *Nobody and Somebody*'s checkered past each time we see the famous watercolor of John Green in balloon pants (Figure 43), but do we really notice that history? That the drawing graces the cover of R. A. Foakes's *Illustrations of the English Stage* seems to me ironic, since while it most likely depicts an English actor it does so in a German manuscript commemorating an Austrian perform-ance and is titled in Latin. We think of the sketch as the portrait of John Green as Nobody, but this thought may be wrong in every respect. Foakes cautions that the figure is 'probably' Green; indeed, the evidence for such an identification – the date and place of the performance and the dedication by 'Joannes Grün Nob. Anglus' – is suggestive but circumstantial.[22] Nor can we be sure that this is a portrait, in the sense of a representation of a person made from life, since, as Stephen Orgel observes, 'the picture alludes only to the character' and not to an actor in a role.[23] Finally, and crucial to our purpose, as the figure's exchange of an original scroll for a missal and a rosary certify, this is no longer a depiction of Nobody, the English character, but rather of his transformation into a new delocalized and intertheatrical persona. If the 1606 English dramatic text tells the story of Nobody and the 1620 German one tells that of Niemand, then this manuscript from 1608 shows a character between them, one who belongs nowhere – which, as the play's pronominal reversals remind us, is to say anywhere. The drawing's motto, after all, reads '*Neminis virtus ubiq[ue] laudabilis*'; 'Nobody's virtue is everywhere praiseworthy.' Of course to translate this sentence into English is crudely to repatriate it; on the contrary, the key to the sketch lies in the figure's being named, in both the heading and the caption, in Latin. For in our determination to find an English or German actor or character, it is the pan-European *Nemo* we have always missed.

Such is our resistance to intertheater in the case of anonymous texts and images; but the stakes rise immeasurably when canonical authors are in ques-tion. A pertinent case unfolded in the pages of *Shakespeare Quarterly* over another illustration, the pen-and-ink drawing on the top part of Longleat manuscript, possibly by Henry Peacham and probably depicting a scene from some version of *Titus Andronicus*. These qualifications indicate how baffled scholars still are by each part of the manuscript – a drawing, a textual excerpt, a signature and date, and a separate endorsement in a different hand. Light glim-mered at the tunnel's end when June Schlueter proposed that the drawing depicts a scene not from Shakespeare but from *Eine sehr klägliche Tragaedia von*

Figure 43   Illustration to the manuscript *Jemand and Niemand* (1608). Reproduced by permission of the Bibliothek des Zisterzienstiftes, Rein

Tito Andronico und der hoffertigen Käyserin [A very lamentable tragedy of Titus Andronicus and the haughty empress], the second of two tragedies in the 1620 *Engelische Comedien und Tragedien*.[24] More heat than light, however, was Richard Levin's verdict on Schlueter's argument, as he read the German play in translation and refuted the case point for point.[25] Though Schleuter's evidence is plainly not conclusive, I find it more promising than does Levin, and I am puzzled by occasional circularity in his rebuttal. In one instance we are asked to reconnect the scene with Shakespeare rather than the German play because the Moorish villain cannot be delivering his soliloquy with other characters on stage – and the clincher is that 'Shakespeare usually avoids the situation'![26]

Where precisely *is* 'Shakespeare' in the passages below the drawing, which splice separate scenes from the master text, have Tamora plead for several sons at the beginning of her speech and only one at the end, and close with a speech prefix for a character who has no lines in Shakespeare's play? One notes, moreover, that an authorial conundrum has here quite occluded a discussion of the *Tragaedia von Tito Andronico* in its own right.

This has also been the fate of the most provocative text in early modern inter-theater, the German version of the *Hamlet* story entitled *Der bestrafte Brudermord*. In 1781 a German theater journal published the first full text of a manuscript which has since disappeared, entitled *Der bestrafte Brudermord, oder Prinz Hamlet aus Dännemark* (often rendered in English as *Fratricide Punished*). Dated 27 October 1710, the manuscript had long lain dormant in the private hands of a celebrated family of actor-managers; nor did its publication arouse much public interest until it was reprinted in 1865 in a landmark German study together with an English translation.[27] This version and later translations encouraged investigation of the manuscript's relation with early sources, texts, and performances of Shakepeare's *Hamlet*. In the century after 1865, *Der bestrafte Brudermord* was tied to either the First Quarto or the Second or both, and even to the First Folio, but most scholars judged it to be based on the lost *Ur-Hamlet* supposed to have served as Shakespeare's source. That consensus has since been overturned. Now the Arden editor disposes of what he calls the 'mirage' of the *Ur-Hamlet* by asserting that *Der bestrafte Brudermord* 'seems to preserve a few pre-Shakespearean strands, but for the most part it originates in Shakespeare'; and the Oxford editor contends that 'there is no need to drag in the *Ur-Hamlet*,' since 'the German play is an adaptation of the abridged version of *Hamlet* that lies behind the First Quarto,' that is to say, an adaptation of a memorial reconstruction of an acting version of the Folio text.[28] In both editions there is a sense of relief that *Der bestrafte Brudermord* has been proved to follow rather than precede Shakespeare: 'Mercifully,' the Arden sighs, 'the difficulty of the problem is in excess of its importance'; the Oxford likewise dismisses 'the interest this version of *Hamlet* has excited, an interest out of all proportion to any intrinsic value it may have.'[29] The study of Shakespeare, the editors agree, is best disentangled from the problem of this play.

Now this may well be the case – and not just for Shakespeare's sake. Regrettably the business of discovering the master's source, demonizing his bad quarto, and demonstrating the superiority of his authentic version to other texts or perform-ances has left little room for an appraisal of *Der bestrafte Brudermord* itself. Indeed, the most illuminating treatment of the play has not been a monograph but a production. In 1924 William Poel staged first at Oxford and then in London an English version of *Fratricide Punished* based largely on an amalgam of two existing translations. Forty years earlier Poel had produced an experimental *Hamlet* with no scenery, a thrust platform, an Ophelia played by a boy, Elizabethan costumes and the text of the First Quarto. His *Fratricide Punished*, the prompt-book of which was later edited and published, was equally innovative. Read today against academic critiques of the German play, Poel appears marvelously positive and pragmatic, concerned not with textual deficiencies but with performing possibilities. Still, his trust in his source material does falter, and this leads to disappointing emenda-tions. Consider, appropriately enough, the arrival of the traveling players. In *Der bestrafte Brudermord*, the principal actor Carl announces his troupe as 'foreign High-German players' [fremde hochteutsche Comödianten] whom Hamlet has previously seen at Wittenberg.[30] The key word is 'fremde': unlike Shakespeare's players, 'the tragedians of the city,' these Germans in Denmark are unambigu-ously foreign.[31] Hamlet proceeds to ask Carl whether his troupe still includes 'the three females who acted so well.' Only two of them, answers Carl; the third 'remained behind with her husband at the Court of Saxony.'[32] We are here reminded that the inclusion of women in strolling companies was a controversial but common feature of theatrical life in the Northern European Renaissance.[33] It is unfortunate, then, that Poel should have altered Hamlet's question to 'Have you still all three *Boys* with you?'[34] In his production, moreover, where the Queen and Ophelia were played by women, it comes off little short of absurd. Such are the perils of hypercorrection with the yardstick of the Elizabethan stage.

Above all, Poel was anxious to tone down the rambunctious physicality of the play. In *Der bestrafte Brudermord* the Ghost keeps opening its jaws in an apparent effort to speak, the Lord Chamberlain Corambus has a coughing fit behind the arras, and the court fool Phantasmo responds to Hamlet's suggestion that it is cold by chattering his teeth; but *Fratricide Punished* will have none of this. In German the Ghost boxes the sentinel's ears; in English it merely taps him on the shoulder. What assumptions underlie such emendations? First, there is an ideal of the original text, of which the foreign version must be a crude, degenerate travesty. Second, there is a revulsion at the body itself, a sense that actions are inferior substitutes for words, to which foreign audiences must surely have been deaf. Yet scrutiny of the above instances makes either assumption hard to sustain. Consider the point just before the final duel in *Der bestrafte Brudermord* at which Hamlet has a nose-bleed:

> Now come, Horatio. No matter what, I shall go and present myself to the King. But oh! What does this mean? Drops of blood fall from my nose; my whole body is trembling! Alas, what is happening to me? (*Faints.*)[35]

At the corresponding moment in *Fratricide Punished*, Hamlet weakens and swoons, but neither nose nor blood is mentioned. Now why should a play that contains stabbing, poisoning and shooting not be allowed to show a nose-bleed? The answer cannot be that such a thing is a Teutonic barbarity: Launcelot Gobbo in *The Merchant of Venice* refers to a past nose-bleed, and Antonio Bologna in *The Duchess of Malfi* has one all over his paperwork. On the contrary, the incident and Hamlet's subsequent dismissal of it strike me as convincing analogues for his defiance of augury in Shakespeare – a rejection of the visceral evidence of his own body so muted in the Folio text (compared with Q1's 'heart is on the sudden very sore,' and Q2's 'how ill all's here about my heart') here forces itself vividly on our attention. *Der bestrafte Brudermord* does not merely transpose verbal apprehension into physical dysfunction, but threatens a rupture between Hamlet's rational

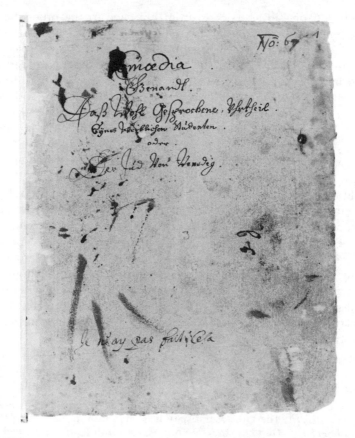

Figure 44 Title-page to the manuscript *Comoedia Benandt Daß Wohl Gesprochene Uhrtheil Eynes Weiblichen Studenten oder Der Jud von Venedig* (n.d.). Reproduced by permission of the österreichische Nationalbibliothek, Vienna

speech and his symptomatic body, an epitome of theater's division between language and the event.

We may resume the intertheatrical motifs of displacement, fragmentation and anonymity in a final example from a seventeenth-century manuscript. The *Comoedia Benandt Daß Wohl Gesprochene Uhrtheil Eynes Weiblichen Studenten oder Der Jud Von Venedig* (that is, the comedy called *The Well-Spoken Judgment of a Female Student, or The Jew of Venice*) survives at Vienna in a late seventeenth-century hand, and probably represents the text used by English players at the Dresden court theater in the 1680s. The play is a kaleidoscopic patterning of four dramatic elements: themes from Marlowe's *Jew of Malta*, adaptations of Shakespeare's *Merchant of Venice*, a disguised courtship of Greek or Roman derivation, and intrusive antics by Pickle-herring the clown. Indeed, the modern reader's disorientation before this text resembles the plight of Pickle-herring, who complains of sea-sickness en route from Cyprus to Venice, whining that the boat's motion 'on and on, up and down, from one side to the other' has left his intestines, lungs, liver and spleen 'all jumbled up together like buttermilk and sauerkraut.'[36] As the scene progresses, however, it turns out that Pickle-herring has eaten and drunk himself sick and is blaming the voyage in order to get his debts paid by his master. The clown's metaphors of consumption, indigestion, purgation, and compensation are visceral but wholly consonant with the play's composition and themes. Commenting on this play in his variorum *Merchant*, the younger Dr Furness called Pickle-herring 'not fun but filth': 'It is inconceivable,' he sniffed, 'that such language and actions could ever have been tolerated in public.'[37] This is manifest nonsense, but also echoes countless milder dismissals, in the name of propriety, integrity and authority, of what I am calling intertheater. Nor should we imagine such disavowals as exclusive to Victorian sensibilities. For if we examine the title-page of *Der Jud Von Venedig* we read, in the same hand as the text, a peculiar motto by which the scribe appears to disclaim any responsibility for the work (Figure 44). At the bottom of the page stand the words 'Je ne'ay pas fait Cela.' That the disclaimer is in French, which is not the language of the play or any of its sources, at once allows this writer to take maximum distance from the text and broadly underscores the macaronic diffusion of authorship in the theatrical culture of the age. Of course the scribe is not ultimately responsible for this play – but is anyone? Or when we track the strolling players to their Temple of Truth, will we find Nobody at home?

Notes

1. J. W. von Goethe, *Aus Meinem Leben: Dichtung und Wahrheit* (Berlin: Akademie-Verlag, 1970), 261. The English translation is cited from J. W. von Goethe, *Poetry and Truth: From My Own Life*, trans. Minna Steele Smith (London: G. Bell and Sons, 1930), 278.
2. Gotthold Ephraim Lessing, *Werke* (Munich: Carl Hanser Verlag, 1973), 5:72. All translations are mine unless otherwise noted.
3. Jerzy Limon, *Gentlemen of a Company: English Players in Central and Eastern Europe, 1590–1660* (Cambridge: Cambridge University Press, 1985), 22.
4. See my essay 'Renaissance Intertheatre and the Staging of Nobody,' *ELH* 71 (2004), 559–85.
5. *Shakespeare's Europe: Being unpublished chapters of Fynes Moryson's Itinerary*, ed. Charles Hughes (New York: Benjamin Blom, 1967), 373.
6. Albert Cohn, *Shakespeare in Germany in the Sixteenth and Seventeenth Centuries* (London: Asher & Co., 1865), cxxxiv–cxxxv. E. K. Chambers disputes Cohn's dating of 1599, suggesting 1602; see Chambers, *The Elizabethan Stage* (Oxford: Clarendon Press, 1923), 2: 273 n. 2.
7. Rudolf Genée, *Geschichte der Shakespeareschen Dramen in Deutschland* (Leipzig: Wilhelm Engelmann, 1870), 19.
8. See Willem Schrickx, *Foreign Envoys and Travelling Players in the Age of Shakespeare and Jonson* (Wetteren: Universa, 1986), 220–39.
9. See Mary Louise Pratt, 'Arts of the Contact Zone,' *Profession* (1991), 33–40; and Pratt, *Imperial Eyes: Travel Writing and Transculturation* (London: Routledge, 1992), 6–7.
10. The term was introduced in Larry Selinker, 'Language Transfer,' *General Linguistics* 9 (1969), 67–92, and elaborated in Selinker, 'Interlanguage,' *International Review of Applied Linguistics* 10 (1972), 209–31.

11. See Lee Drummond, 'The Cultural Continuum: A Theory of Intersystems,' *Man* 15 (1980), 352–74. Drummond turns to anthropological ends the linguistic research in Derek Bickerton, *Dynamics of a Creole System* (Cambridge: Cambridge University Press, 1975).

12. Friedrich Gundolf, *Shakespeare und der Deutsche Geist* (Berlin: Georg Bondi, 1918), 19, 43.

13. Limon, *Gentlemen of a Company*, 7; Heinz Kindermann, *Theatergeschichte Europas* (Salzburg: Otto Müller, 1959), 3:366.

14. Chambers, *Elizabethan Stage*, 2: 285.

15. Cohn, *Shakespeare in Germany*, civ.

16. A recent leap forward is Dennis Kennedy's decision in the *Oxford Encyclopedia of Theatre and Performance* (2003) to eliminate summary articles on national theatre traditions, replacing them with entries on regional centers and linguistic traditions. See Dennis Kennedy, 'Confessions of an Encyclopedist' in W. B. Worthen with Peter Holland, eds, *Theorizing Practice: Redefining Theatre History* (Basingstoke: Palgrave Macmillan, 2003), 30–46.

17. Stephen Greenblatt, 'Racial Memory and Literary History,' *PMLA*, 116 (2001), 59–60.

18. Richard Helgerson, 'Before National Literary History,' *MLQ*, 64 (2003), 178.

19. Julie Stone Peters, *Theatre of the Book, 1480–1880: Print, Text, and Performance in Europe* (Oxford: Oxford University Press, 2000), 3–4.

20. Peters, *Theatre of the Book*, 238, 459.

21. Muriel Bradbrook, 'When every one is Nobody . . .' in *KM 80: A Birthday Album for Kenneth Muir* (Liverpool: Liverpool University Press, 1987), 16; Luke Wilson, *Theaters of Intention: Drama and the Law in Early Modern England* (Stanford: Stanford University Press, 2000), 216–62.

22. R. A Foakes, *Illustrations of the English Stage, 1580–1642* (Stanford: Stanford University Press, 1985), 62.

23. Stephen Orgel, *Imagining Shakespeare: A History of Texts and Visions* (New York: Palgrave Macmillan, 2003), 32.

24. June Schlueter, 'Rereading the Peacham Drawing,' *Shakespeare Quarterly*, 50 (1999), 171–84.

25. Richard Levin, 'The Longleat Manuscript and *Titus Andronicus*,' *Shakespeare Quarterly*, 53 (2002), 323–40.

26. Levin, 'The Longleat Manuscript', 326 n.10.

27. The text, with translation by Georgina Archer, appears in Cohn, *Shakespeare in Germany*, 236–303.

28. William Shakespeare, *Hamlet*, ed. Harold Jenkins (London: Methuen, 1982), 122; Shakespeare, *Hamlet*, ed. G. R. Hibbard (Oxford: Clarendon Press, 1987), 378.

29. Shakespeare, *Hamlet* ed. Jenkins, 112; Shakespeare, *Hamlet*, ed. Hibbard, 373.

30. *Der bestrafte Brudermord* is quoted from Cohn, *Shakespeare in Germany*, 263. The English translation as *Fratricide Punished* is quoted from Ernest Brennecke, *Shakespeare in Germany, 1590–1700* (Chicago: University of Chicago Press, 1964), 267.

31. Shakespeare, *Hamlet*, ed. Jenkins, 2.2.327.

32. *Fratricide Punished*, trans. Brennecke, 268.

33. See Hans-Joachim Kurtz and Bärbel Rudin, 'Pickelhering, rechte Frauenzimmer, berühmte Autoren,' in Bärbel Rudin, ed., *Wanderbühne: Theaterkunst als fahrendes Gewerbe* (Berlin: Gesellschaft für Theatergeschichte, 1988), 29–60; and Claudia Puschmann, *Fahrende Frauenzimmer: Zur Geschichte der Frauen an deutschen Wanderbühnen* (Herbolzheim: Centaurus Verlag, 2000), 19–45.

34. *William Poel's Prompt-Book of* Fratricide Punished, ed. J. Isaacs (London: Society for Theatre Research, 1956), 17. Emphasis original.

35. *Fratricide Punished*, trans. Brennecke, 286.

36. The translation of *Daß Wohl Gesprochene Uhrtheil* as *The Well-Spoke Judgment* is quoted from Brennecke, *Shakespeare in Germany*, 129.

37. *The Merchant of Venice*, ed. H. H. Furness, 7th edn (Philadelphia: J. P. Lipincott Company, 1888), 326.

10
Robert Armin Do the Police in Different Voices

Richard Preiss

At the still heart of a morbidly introspective play we find the remains of a clown, and they make the speaker want to vomit.

> Alas, poor Yorick. I knew him, Horatio, a fellow of infinite jest, of most excellent fancy. He hath borne me on his back a thousand times, and now how abhorred in my imagination it is! My gorge rises at it.[1]

Hamlet is not alone in capturing an institutional moment when clowns are the object of both nostalgia and repudiation. Marston's *Antonio's Revenge*, an exact contemporary, features a cry under the stage that turns out to be the entombed buffoon Balurdo, who claws his way up through the trap toward freedom and, of course, food.[2] But *Hamlet* is unique in the degree to which it thematizes this comic repression and return – not least in the Prince himself, who frustrates his own edicts on theatrical decorum while 'some necessary question of the play' remains to be considered, and who delivers his eulogy for the impertinent lords of misrule with one of them still very much in evidence. I will come to the Gravedigger shortly, but I begin with this ambivalent tableau – the clown both timeless and obsolete, both 'old mole' and '*hic et ubique*,' moribund yet indestructible – because it has inspired two incompatible accounts of popular performance in the early modern theater. Since this chapter attempts to mediate between them, they warrant a brief exposition.

For the first, the clown is the functional residue of the communal festivity out of which professional theater grows, a heteroglossic avatar of the urban playhouse's conditions. In his rustic garb and country disposition, he is all peasants and migrants; in his mistaking of words, his pratfalls, and his obliviousness to rank, he deflates the pretensions of dramatic mimesis, reducing literary language and affect to their material and corporeal substrata. For C.L. Barber, this element of Carnival serves as a Saturnalian release from the rhythm of labor so that the social order may be reaffirmed.[3] For Bakhtinian critics like Michael Bristol and Robert Weimann, clowning creates more radical openings in the social text – a self-criticism intrinsic to theater's subversive power.[4] Vice, devil, and clown all designate a principle of pluralism in the play, interrogating its ideologies of domination from a skepticism

208

aligned with the disenfranchised audience, with whom the player cultivates a bond. The multiplicity he subtends is thus tied to the stability of his identity: because Dick Tarlton or Will Kemp is always Dick Tarlton or Will Kemp, spurning the confines of his role to speak as himself, the crowd vicariously does the same. Issuing commentary within character and soliciting it from without, triumphantly retaking the stage at play's end for the jig or to spar extemporaneously with the spectators, the very substance of his performance is survival, his improvisations instantiating an 'authorless' theater of collective experience rooted in mutual contest and defiant individuality. For Weimann, such techniques actually enable modes of verismilitude as they undermine it, creating multi-dimensional characters who enlist us in their arbitration of competing values.[5] Like Richard III before him or Iago after him, Hamlet represents the apotheosis of the clown, the elevation of 'infinite jest' to the centrality of tragic anti-hero.

For another strain of analysis, however, this same dramatic figure is subjected to a poetics not of synthesis but of purgation; Hamlet's *ubi sunt* is merely one in a series of death knells for popular performance on the stage, acts of renunciation along which a counterpart narrative of institutional development can also be strung. How, Richard Helgerson asks, did this static 'players' theater' by 1600 give way to an 'authors' theater' that conditioned the reception of plays as products of a singular agency?[6] The opening of the Globe and Fortune, the revival of the private halls, the rise of city satire, the dissection into 'rival traditions' of high and low, the nationalization of patronage with the accession of James – for Helgerson, building on work by Alfred Harbage and Colin MacCabe, all these milestones in professional legitimation are anticipated by a dramaturgy of subtle divisiveness in the preceding decade.[7] Marlowe's juxtaposition of 'high astounding terms' to 'riming mother-wits' heralded a new generation of educated poets, employed in an artisanal theater of and for their inferiors, who sought to ennoble their 'base trade' by stressing difference rather than the class fluidity that theater represented. The class fluidity it actually presented, then, in its 'mingling of kings and clowns,' thus became a target of reform. Rather than dissever them, dramatists devised ways of engaging popular culture that facilitated a withdrawal from it. This self-consuming vehicle was the history play: from *Jack Straw* to the May Day riots in *Sir Thomas More* to Falconbridge in *Edward IV*, depictions of populist revolt were thoroughly carnivalized so as to discredit its utopian goals and make its leaders self-defeating. Such parodies of rebellion not only barred commoners from a national vision, but reciprocally pejoratized the clown, internalizing the hierarchy his performance disrupted. Once linked with rebellion, the festive inversions of the jig could be condemned, improvisation censured, the *platea* of the platform stage rendered an illicit space that violated the sovereign *locus* of a playwright allied with censor and crown.

This strategy, Helgerson argues, played out acutely in the case of Shakespeare, whose career epitomized his company's gentrification. Having made sedition comically licentious in Jack Cade, he proceeded to make comic license seditious and to punish it accordingly – most memorably with Falstaff, whose banishment in *2 Henry IV* (upheld by the poet in *Henry V*) inaugurates Hal's Lenten civil policy. Hamlet and Richard are, ultimately, losers, usurped by governors with a more refined grasp of political theater. These staged exclusions culminated, finally, with the literal defection of Will Kemp from the Chamberlain's Men in late 1599, and the abolition of the jig from the Globe. Helgerson thus offers a bootstrap model of how the centralized 'author's theater' unfolded according to a kind of self-fulfilling determinism, in which the reiterated symbolic eventually becomes fact. In this stunted dialectic, Shakespeare unilaterally shaped the dramatic conditions that would predispose his textual reception as a writing subject and as a canonical author. By equating the order of the state with the order of the theatrical event, the clown was made the scapegoat for a popular performance tradition whose disgorgement became the signature digestive ritual of a professional theater intent on describing its cultural production as labor rather than as holiday, as work rather than play.

Despite its theoretical elegance, there is a tautology here. Helgerson concedes the clown a role in the discursive shift toward dramatic authorship, but that role remains entirely penal: he is inscribed into this developmental narrative only insofar as he is programmatically written out of it. We thus have a narrative in which playwrights beget themselves, when the engine of that parthenogenesis – their authority to determine performance – was precisely at issue. By setting as an approximate endpoint for this process the institutional upheavals circa 1600, furthermore, the purgation argument neglects a major complication – persistence. The clown did what he does best: survive. And he did so across theatrical stratifications. For the Admiral's Men, royal favor portended no significant shift in personnel. Upon the death of their clown John Singer that same year, they replaced him with the comedian John Shanke – just as Worcester's Men, becoming Queen Anne's Men, promptly replaced the fading Will Kemp with a carbon-copy, Thomas Greene.[8] And while both companies, at the Fortune and Red Bull respectively, later became part of the stalwart 'citizens' theater' whose violent jigs the Middlesex Sessions tried to ban in 1612, the absence of jigs on the Globe and Blackfriars stages did not prevent the King's Men from acquiring Shanke for themselves in 1613.[9] If the ambitions of playwrights continued to operate through a tension with the clown, they did not show it, at least not enough for him utterly to disappear. Whatever complicity he had in the emergence of the author, it was constrained not by his termination but by his continuity.

Robert Armin was the King's man whom John Shanke succeeded, and the one who had succeeded Kemp in 1599.[10] Nevertheless, thanks to the cathartic stress laid on Kemp's departure, Armin's career has been compressed into an afterthought conforming exactly to this rupture, a submission to the hegemony of the playwright preserved in a qualitatively new 'line' of comic character, 'the fool.' The transgressive gadfly of the clown is exchanged for a comedian who is now wholly the author's creature. For Helgerson, as for Leslie Hotson, the distinguishing trait of Armin's parts is that they are socially unmarked – the fool's motley signifying, unlike the russet jerkin, liminality rather than class-specificity – and also courtly, the jester drawn from the world of *noblesse oblige*.[11] Witty and learned, unlike the vulgar and witless clown, the fool speaks truth confusingly where the other spoke confusion truthfully; his ridicule is directed not at his superiors but at the universality of folly, a mockery steeped in philosophical tradition rather than plebeian protest. The fool is thus a mimic, performing not himself but others. Whether dressed as a prince like Cloten and Autolycus or stripped like Thersites and Caliban, whether aping the courtier like Touchstone or the drunkard like Carlo Buffone, he grotesques humanity itself, deforming all values but introducing none of his own. Foremost among those he imitates, then, is the poet, who dictates to this empty vessel his abstruse railing; after 1600, for David Wiles, 'there is no longer a dichotomy of poetic and extemporal styles.'[12] The 'fool's privilege' that, as Charles Felver puts it, is both 'his passport and his license' also marks his subjugation – he is free to say anything only because it has already been 'allowed' by the playwright, and at the end of that leash lies the whip.[13] In place of the exiled clown, runs the Armin footnote, Shakespeare created a puppet, an extension of his textual will and a rehabilitated asset to his social and aesthetic interests.

This is a remarkable reversal, but one distorted to supply the strong authorial agency an 'expulsion' narrative seemingly demands. 'The fool' no more emerged as a discrete theatrical entity with Armin's rise in the Chamberlain's Men than did 'the clown' vanish from them with Kemp's exit; if anything, their fortunes appear intertwined. Though Armin is a court fool in *As You Like It* and *Twelfth Night*, he is 'clown' in speech prefixes and stage directions; in his consistent pairing with genuinely rustic antagonists, indeed, like Sogliardo in *Every Man Out* or Corin and William in the Forests of Arden, all the way to the *Winter's Tale*'s Shepherd and 'Clown,' there seems a conscious effort to dislodge a comic function from its customary social signifiers. Meanwhile, however, those significations were being perpetuated in stock peasants like *Hamlet*'s Gravedigger, *Macbeth*'s Porter, *Measure for Measure*'s Pompey, and the nameless walk-ons in *Othello* and *Antony and Cleopatra*. Since the repertory already entailed Armin's inheritance of Kemp's characters, Shakespeare's ongoing provision of these broad comic parts indicates an investment in sustaining convention as much as changing it.[14] As reductive categories for the fictive roles a leading comedian took, the terms 'clown' and 'fool' have little bearing on his larger theatrical identity, determined by playhouse practices that escape what the text records. But their respective associations obviously mattered, and in Armin's case their alternation suggests an attempt to suspend two performance codes under one performer – keeping his Kemp-like profile intact while incrementally modulating it toward the mimetic possibilities his talents began to present. In so doing, this chapter argues, Shakespeare followed Armin's lead, not vice versa, and that lead derived not from what he did in the play but from what he was doing after it. By periodically refreshing his credentials as clown, Shakespeare extended to Armin its horizon of identification and expectation, so he could reshape it himself; the contours of that secondary persona are what the dramatic type of 'the fool' traces rather than prescribes. Armin's solo practice, as we will see, ensured that an elitist company agenda could be served by fostering clowning instead of eliminating it.

This is not to suggest that Armin ever danced jigs at the Globe. From the musicality of his dramatic roles we can infer that he was hired for his singing voice, and from what we can surmise about his diminutive physique it seems equally likely he was hired because he was *not* a dancer. The Chamberlain's Men's commitment to phasing out one genre of clown postlude, however, did not necessarily relieve the demand; indeed, weaning audiences off of one appetite might well have intensified another. That intractable inertial force, the audience, brings us to the final inadequacy of any author-driven narrative of reform through warfare between playwright and player. The fundamental problem of the clown was not political merely in its aesthetics. Decorum was never the issue; the playhouse offered not just a vision of society but a real-time instance of it. What Sidney called its 'mungrelization' was for him objectionable only in virtue of the kind of comedy clowns invariably provoke, a 'laughter' of cruelty instead of a 'wonder' of ravishment. For Whetstone, the impropriety of mingling them with kings stemmed from a corruption of discourse that threatened to produce 'one order of speech for all persons.'[15] To observe degree, the drama had to exercise dominance over its own playgoers, lest that 'one order of speech' become that of the multitude. This is the chaos from which Gosson recoils in horror, where the only 'right Comedie' is 'to mark behaviour.'[16] For later critics, likewise, the core of the clown's subversion was not his self-promotion but the way it actually catapulted the audience into the main attraction – ceding them not just power over, but identity with, the theatrical event. After a tragedy, for Joseph Hall, 'mids the silent rout, / Comes leaping in some self-misformed lout, / And laughs, and grins, and frames his mimik face, / And justles straight into the princes place . . . then doth the *Theatre Eccho* all a loud' – degenerating into mass narcissism, a 'selfe-resembled show.'[17] For Dekker the trope of actualization is the same, where the inflamed crowd literally comprises 'the Sceane after the Epilogue': 'the stinkards speaking all things, yet no man understanding anything; a mutiny being amongst them, yet none in danger.'[18] In both cases the catalyst is a jig, but it was only one species of participation. By 1638, Richard Brome could declare 'the days of Tarlton and Kemp . . . purg'd': their 'barbarism,' however, consisted not so much in altering 'what the writer / with care and skill compos'd,' for the preceding scene extols the virtuosity of the actor who, 'knowing the purpose what he is to speak to,' can 'make such shifts *extempore* . . . fribble through, and move delight in others.' Rather, what Brome will not tolerate from his clown, Byplay, is just that: that 'when you are to speak to your co-actors in the scene, you hold interlocutions with the audients.'[19] Improvising for the crowd is mastery; improvising *to* them signals their priority over the script rather than the actor's, and incites them to become more enrapt in themselves than in the play. This is Hamlet's scolded 'pitiful ambition,' an ambition that debases itself. The trouble with a showstopper was that he really did 'stop' the show as a coherent transaction – erasing the barriers between performer and spectator, producer and consumer, that a legitimate professional theater and its articulation as literary artifact needed. The institutional crisis only looks to us like an internal one – for Helgerson the *platea* is still where 'authority belongs to the actor' – because the clown was a proxy for the real, ubiquitous obstacle to social improvement.[20]

The groundlings could not be cowed, moreover, by representations of discipline that had force only in the *locus*. The clown returned to shed his fictive identity, and to his fans this was the only aspect of his – of *the* – performance that mattered. From a financial standpoint, indeed, he was too valuable to jettison. If he undermined the theater's self-image by making the masses its masters, he only exposed an economic reality in which the masses, as paying customers, really *were* its masters, 'patrons' in the most basic sense. Court sponsorship would merely protect the profitability that players already enjoyed, making the satisfaction of public taste both the roadblock to preferment and at the same time its whole point. 'Dost thou not know a play cannot be without a clown?' the Cambridge *Pilgrimage to Parnassus* wryly asks, reassuring its own that 'clowns have been thrust into plays – ever since Kemp could make a scurvy face,' and that whether he 'say somewhat for thyself, or hang and be *non plus*,' the crowd would do the rest.[21] He was what people paid to see, and as John Davies tells us, what they stormed the gate to see at play's end; if his appearance could spark a riot, so could his absence.[22] More than an abstract correlative of victimization, the clown was an expression of collective will, the transformer that reversed the flow of energy back to its source; as long as theater began with an audience, he was a figure not so much resistant as irresistible.

Launching their bid for exclusivity from the inclusive Globe, competing with Kemp and Singer, the daily task thus facing the Chamberlain's Men was how to give people what they wanted while simultaneously withholding it. Necessity became a virtue. Since the clown always stood between the audience and its reform, he was the only one that could reform the audience; you train a beast by feeding it. Infinite jest had to defuse itself. If the transformer could be engineered to emit control instead of release, he might actually become a bulwark, where theater entrenched ownership over itself rather than surrendered it. Here, as at many points in early modern drama, such ownership and its discursive formations would hinge on textualizing the authority not of the playwright but the clown: he had to perform into being the idea of the dramatic author. But how do you reclaim the *platea* from the *platea*? How do you regiment the empowerment of laughter, or divert cacophony into the univocal? How do you get a clown to do it for you, to euthanize his theatrical function, to bury himself? If you took the cue of the *Parnassus* actor, you got someone who, not knowing what to say, recited 'a new love letter of mine' – someone, that is, whose improvisation generated its own text.[23] If you were the Chamberlain's Men in 1599, you hired Robert Armin – the man in the grave of Hamlet's clown, and whose job it was, even as he resurrected him, to dig it.

Armin's stage persona is graced with a foundation myth that, in certifying his comic pedigree, foreshadowed the fate of that *translatio*. In 1600, his first year as company clown, the anonymously-compiled *Tarltons Jests* gave Armin an endorsement that even Kemp never received – nor, perhaps, needed. As an apprentice to a goldsmith owed money by Tarlton's tavern-keeper, Armin was sent to collect and was repeatedly rebuffed; in retaliation, 'with chalk on a Wain-scote,' he scrawled a verse graffito ribbing the debtor's poverty. Tarlton, admiring it, added a reply: 'A wagge thou art, none can prevent thee . . . As I am, so thou'lt be the same, / My adopted sonne therefore be / To enjoy my clownes sute after me.'[24]

Armin 'so loved *Tarlton* after' that he became his protégé; 'private practice brought him to present playing, and at this houre performes the same, where, at the Globe on the Banks side men may see him.'[25] Less a jest that transmits anything funny than a genealogy of how funniness is transmitted, the anecdote exceeds the volume's preservation of Tarlton by prophesying his living incarnation, to whose enactment of 'the same,' 'at this houre,' the book must defer. But in so doing it also posits a disciplinary structure to clowning that embeds the successor in the very medium clowning is supposed to transcend. The transfer of vatic authority takes place both in writing and as a function of writing, the once and future comedians appraising each other through dueling epigrams; the intimacy of training devolves into the solitude of 'private practice.' Is this or Tarlton 'the same' that he now acts? For Armin an attenuation is already at work, wherein a textual distance intercedes between performance and its agent.

That may be because Armin's 'private practice,' in fact rather than myth, was not as a player but actually *as* a writer. Prior to surfacing in the late 1590s with Lord Chandos' Men, and even before becoming free of the goldsmiths in 1592, he had evidently made a modest literary reputation for himself. Nashe in *Strange Newes* classes him with Thomas Deloney and Philip Stubbes; Harvey lumps him among 'the common pamfletters of London.'[26] None of his early publications survives,[27] but by 1590 he was sufficiently regarded to attach a sober commendation to the even soberer *Brief Resolution of Right Religion* – hardly an arena befitting the heir of Tarlton's 'clownes sute,' and perhaps indicative of why Armin never wore it in quite the same way. 1590 was not a year for casual sallies into ecclesiastic debate, and among the tract's targets he includes the Martinists, who are a 'vitious and detestable sect.'[28] The possibility raised by such partisan affiliation, that Armin cut his polemical teeth as a satirist in the Marprelate controversy, has important implications for how the discursive attitude he brought to the theater informed not just his literary activities outside it but the parameters of his performance within it. In this seminal conjunction of print and public sphere, he would have engaged in rapid-fire skirmishes where today's attacker was tomorrow's prey, where the very power of utterance to outpace its speaker also made it vulnerable to returning carved into ridicule or perverted into character assassination. Before he was ever Armin the clown, Armin the pamphleteer would have been attuned to the anxiety of controlling the circulation and reception of a persona that instantly became public domain, and poised to appreciate the tactical value of an idiom whose every locution anticipated, contained and thereby disarmed a counterfactual response. Under such paranoid conditions, the best defense was a calculated schizophrenia. As the glossolalias of Nashe and Greene typify, maintaining the authority of 'who is speaking' came to rest in partly dissolving its integrity, in having many speaking at once, assuming and assimilating the subjectivity of imaginary opponents.[29] If an analogous mode of mimetic pre-emption, proper to print, turns out to be crucial to Armin's theatrical practice, it is because print already focalized the anxiety of performance to which it reacted. Shuttling between the self-publications of page and stage, for Armin their interpenetration became precisely the key to their respective negotiation.

We can see half of this formula unfolding in one of two pamphlets Armin published in 1600. *Foole Upon Foole* is an album of story-length jests, extracted from the 'lives, humours and behauiours' of 'six sortes of sottes,' from local idiots like Jack Miller of Wales and Blue John of Christ's Hospital, to jesters like Will Summers and Archie Andrews (see Figure 45). Modern critics, seduced by the collection's documentary flavor into the belief that Armin was founding his theatrical persona in relation to these originals, ignore F.P. Wilson's reminder that foolbooks were a fad at the turn of the century, with two others appearing the same year and five more over the next decade.[30] The pathology of Armin's imitation is sketched not in the pamphlet's text but in its paratext, where 'the fool' becomes merely the name for a deeper operation of rhetorical self-dispersal – ironically fulfilled by our misprision of it as historical self-location. That process begins in the title page motto, 'he that made it mar'd it' – a standard humility posture, to be sure, but one whose pretzel ontology is expanded in the preface Armin then addresses to the Printer and the Binder of the very book he is writing, entreating diligence in its assembly. Or, more precisely, the book itself conveys the request: 'He that made me doth persuade thee, to print pure.'[31] Before this ambiguity can clarify itself, the exhortation to 'be waking when you work' spawns a conversation with the workmen: 'You muse why I greet you thus,' Armin (or Armin's book) says, allaying their doubts that there should be profit in folly, and that their cares are worthwhile. The result is a compact, in which 'every man shall carry his own burthen,' lest the parties blame each other: 'You'll say, if my writing had been better, your printing had had more profit; I say that if your printing be perfect, my unperfect writing will the better passe: is not this good than, when one can help another?' Sealing their solidarity, however, with the pledge that 'so we two liue t'is no matter if all the world dye,' the polyphonic performance yields what Nora Johnson calls a 'Swiftian cynicism': 'Yet,' he continues, 'if…all els dye, what shall the seller doe? Nay what shall people doe, when none liues to buy his bookes?' Johnson, fixated on fool tradition as merely the content of Armin's authorship rather than its instrument of self-inscription, reads in this moment of callousness a remorse for his commercial appropriation of figures linked with a charity economy, and in the conciliatory tenor of his preface an attempt to mitigate it with 'the collaborative nature of textual transmission.' But Armin is far out ahead of the conflicted, hybrid authorial stance she assigns him, for that theft here includes appropriating the very collaboration he invokes: he acknowledges communal production not to disavow his possession but to cement it. As Johnson puts it, making 'the death of the entire reading public…a tragedy of unprofitable investment in the printing of a book' does not so much regretfully 'register the privatization of shared property' as gleefully perform it – insofar as it reinforces the conceit of the whole preface, a book that exists independent of its consumption, and that indeed precedes its own producers.[32] This entity – the text – becomes coterminous with Armin precisely to the extent that it cedes space to other agencies it can then surround and swallow. If the heterogeneous material life of his book involves sources, intermediaries, and validations that compromise its status as his property, Armin dramatizes that life as an already circumscribed process. He incorporates the book's incorporators to subsume and negate their contribution;

FOOLE
VPON FOOLE,
OR
Six sortes of Sottes.

A flat foole		A fatt foole.
A leane foole	and	A cleane foole.
A merry foole		A verry foole.

Shewing their liues, humours and behauiours, with their want of wit in their shew of wisdome. Not so strange as true

Omnia sunt sex.

Written by one, seeming to haue his mothers witte, when some say he is fild with his fathers fopperie, and hopes he liues not without companie.

Clonnico de Curtanio Snuffe.

Not amisse to be read, no matter to regard it :
Yet stands in some stead, though he that made it mar'd it.

LONDON
Printed for William Ferbrand , dwelling neere
Guild-hall gate ouer against the Maiden-head.
1600.

Figure 45 Title-page of *Foole Upon Foole, Or Six Sortes of Sottes* (1600). Reproduced by permission of the Folger Shakespeare Library

he forbears its reception – 'What ist a new booke sayes one, I sayes another' – only to foreclose it, even inducing it to 'say the Author keeps his six fooles company,' thus annexing his very subjects as self-refractions.[33] Dilating an interior world both populated by and devoid of any agency but his own, Armin is nowhere in *Foole upon Foole* because he is everywhere. His contract lets each man 'carry his own burthen' only if he can play each man; 'burthen' also meant voice.

On the page, Armin can invent the collaborators and critics he impersonates in order to insinuate proprietary control over public speech. On the stage, they were right there. 'The fool' as an authorial subterfuge took on discursive stakes where it intersected the theatrical realities of the clown: while Armin was encircling his textual identity with performance, he was simultaneously encasing that performance in textuality. The by-line of *Foole upon Foole* is the same as the other book, *Quips upon Questions*, that Armin published in 1600 – 'Clonnico de Curtanio Snuff' ('Snuff the Clown of the Curtain') (see Figure 46); he would retain the pseudonym, adapting it to 'del Mondo' (of the Globe), in every edition until 1608. For the bulk of his career in the King's Men, then, this was the unlikely figure, not 'Robert Armin,' whom he contrived as both benefactor and beneficiary of his forays into print. Why? And why make those forays? A clown's name had never helped sell a book before he was dead – especially if that book were an anthology of *actual* clowning, as *Quips* seems to be, whose pleasure was a spontaneous, participatory effusion inaccessible second-hand and thus futile to transcribe. This was less true of the jig than of the genre *Quips* depicts, the volleying of themes, where not even a rudimentary dramatic apparatus intervened between clown and audience to keep him the center of attention – which is exactly what Armin hoped thereby to install.[34] Unlike his precursors, Armin had no athleticism at his disposal, ironically reliant on his vocal gifts to individuate himself in an auditory din. Though he had the homely visage necessary to elicit laughter, it was accompanied by a dwarfishness – his characters are frequently belittled as dogs, frogs, pigs, sparrows, lice, vermin – that made his physical command of the stage, in a forum where it would be strenuously tested, a serious concern.[35] But the same liabilities that imperiled him as a player – just as he deviously invoked them as a writer – also made him an ideal candidate. If he sutured the dependencies of the author through the interchange of the clown, his precariousness onstage likewise inclined him to see the clown's position as the author's position, and to suture that real interchange into the sovereignty of the performer. This required more than disingenuously entertaining collaboration *in* print, however, but reducing collaborative entertainment *to* print. Armin had to impose a textual buffer that could absorb, and thus delimit, a live audience's constitutive role in a dialogic ritual. But the stage demanded immersion in the moment, and afforded no playbook; nor could such a playbook really be codified after the fact as a raw aggregate of past moments. It is not clear, in fact, that *Quips* aims to be either script or transcript – which is perhaps what made it both.

Unlike *Foole upon Foole*, *Quips* avoids maneuvering itself into a unitary relation with its producer, refusing to plot itself anywhere along the continuum of theatrical experience. Its subtitle calls it 'A Clownes conceite on occasion offered,' either

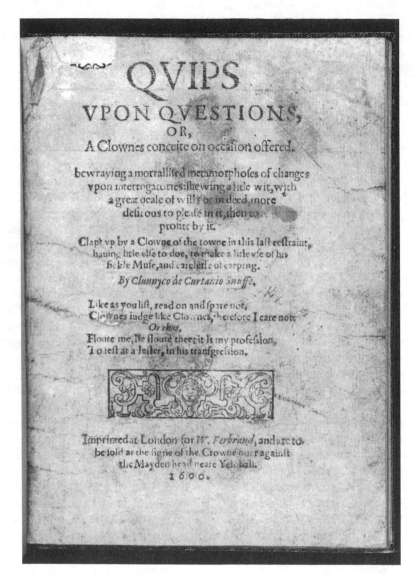

Figure 46   Title-page of Armin's *Quips Upon Questions* (1600). Reproduced by permission of the British Library

printed specially or uttered habitually; they 'bewray morallised metamorphoses of changes upon interrogatories,' a palimpsestic genesis nearly perfect in its opacity. 'Clapt up by a Clowne of the towne in this last restraint to make a little use of his fickle Muse' suggests a content both freely drafted while the Curtain lay shut in June 1600 and drawn from material already applauded while it was open. If anything, the temporality of the theatrical event *Quips* realizes is neither before nor after, but now. The title-page's twin quips mutually calibrate the affects of playhouse and bookstall: 'Like as you list, read on and spare not, Clownes judge like Clownes, therefore I care not: *Or thus*, Floute me, Ile floute thee, it is my profession, To jest at a jester, in his transgression.' Note the reversal of encroachment this simultaneity engenders: in this real-time rehearsal of his stage practice, Armin seems to recognize, the fool cannot play everyone because everyone is also playing his part; collaboration is not something he can contain but inescapably contains him. As a result – using a text to mediate his performance rather than the other way round – the tacit move of that text becomes an abdication of authority. The dissociative strategies that once totalized Armin now minimize him, leaving him abjected and exposed. Unable to put words in his interlocutors' mouths, he speaks instead to his slapstick, appealing to 'Sir Timothie Truncheon' to 'protect me from incision, or from dirrision, in which I am now to wade deeply.'[36] In this print version of stage fright, it is the bauble that must walk among the bookshops and 'bastinado them, that bobadillo like as they censure,' fending off enemies just as viscerally present as Dekker's stinkards, 'whose teeth are blacke with rancor…whose tongues are milk white with burning heate.' 'Confess[ing] mine owne weaknesse,' meanwhile, Armin absents himself from the imagined encounter: 'say I am out of towne and heare not their ribald mockes.' If the motifs of literary reception and theatrical production are fusing, his epistle to the reader further conflates impotence *over* the book with impotence *in* the book. As if going onstage, the body he prepares to exhibit is corporal: 'my blood be layd to your charge. Glut with gazing, surfet with seeing, rellish with reading…use me at your pleasure.'[37] Public scrutiny becomes unilateral violence, preposterously stifling his own voice: 'a man may liue after to requite his aduersarie,' he blusters, even though quipping supposedly offers such requital; 'a man shall not be slain hugger mugger, but shall be warned to defend,' even though quipping should be that defense. Armin thereby figures his own theater practice, like its publication, as an engulfment he perpetually flees – 'and so a thousand times making legs, I go still backward, till I am out of sight' – and from whose corresponding representation his agency will be utterly obliterated.

We should thus expect the audience to dominate *Quips upon Questions*, but it does not; at least not transparently. Having preordained a hermeneutic, Armin proceeds so thoroughly to implement it as to turn it inside out. The volume holds 45 themes, of varying verse form and ranging from one to ten stanzas in length, each headed by the originating prompt and concluded by a single couplet or quatrain. Their straightforwardness ends there. Rhymed dialogues, trialogues, decalogues, they interpolate multiple perspectives that object, correct, concur, deflect, cancel, and reverse the argument flow; yet none of these vocalic fluctuations, whether developing discrete personae across stanzas or flitting wildly within a single line, is ever prefixed or tagged. 'Who then I prethee? Faith I do not know. Harken to me, and I will tell thee what' – in a typographic environment largely free of punctuation, the effect of such crossed verbal streams (here only the first two lines of a typical response) is to foreground an overarching and familiar question: who is speaking?[38] Is Armin only the quipper, confined to refereeing with a last word? Or does he frame the debate, by posing the initial question? Are the pieces gleaned wholesale from playhouse events, as the referential particularity of themes like 'Why barks that dogge,' or an earless felon asking 'What have I lost,' seems to suggest? Conversely, does the declarative abstraction of topics like 'He builds a house,' and 'A Poet pawned' – coupled with Armin's startling admission of 'Writing these emble[m]s on an idle time, looking about, and studying for a Rime' – indicate private composition and revision?

Such categorical suppositions do not so much alleviate the unreadability of the book as illustrate it at work. Making attribution impossible makes attribution visible as a criterion of discourse, and begins to consolidate it in self-ramifying ways. The fidelity of *Quips upon Questions* to real performance cannot be recovered and so does not finally matter; what does is the expectation of similitude it courts. Armin superimposes the experience of theatrical participation and the experience of reading, and by disorienting the phenomenology of one medium is able to defamiliarize that of the other. The very proliferation of indiscriminate speech that on the playhouse floor galvanizes the audience's affect confounds it on paper: removed from the aural scene of its social production, forced to parse and individuate the baffling conglomeration of what they are told is that same speech, Armin's readers are alienated from their own expression. That dispossession, in turn, coincides with the heuristic they must adopt to decipher it: the slippery slope of ascribing to Armin the quips, then the questions, to David Wiles's insight that 'we may as easily conceive the clown's interlocutors to be the clown himself using different voices.'[39] More than just an easier approach to the text, collapsing all the personae into a chameleonic ventriloquism emanating from a single source becomes in fact the only way to make sense of the text *as* a text – which is all *Quips* is, and exactly what it thereby makes the performance it purports to convey.

We cannot know if Armin was already conducting the playhouse postlude this way, since he deliberately clouds its derivation here. But we should hardly be surprised if he were. Such a manufactured dissent would only be the theatrical mirror image of his rhetorical self-construction in print, and its authority is likewise premised, here almost literally and all the more paradoxically, on a profound resection of autonomy. Reversing the equation wherein the clown's charisma vied against the polyvocality of the crowd, Armin, rather than perform himself, constituted his singularity in performing everyone else. The smallness that made him especially a target thus became his comedic capital: he kept shrinking that target until it was impossible to hit – and at the same time, coalescing as a microcosm of the entire playhouse, became impossible to mistake. Personifying the interjections of would-be antagonists, who critique his wit and his versification, who call him a liar and a fool, he stimulated and even aggrandized the audience's febrile participation. But he also simulated and domesticated that interference, wresting it from them even as they seem to wrest the stage from him. Not only can Armin's virtual rivals say nothing he does not already want them to say, but he forces them to say it one at a time, neutralizing and disintegrating a multiplicity of voices in the very semblance of capitulating to it. Elevated to mimetically sealed spectacle, improvising *to* the crowd turned into an improvisation *of* them, and restructured its reception as a form of reading. So insulated is Armin within the crowd's own expropriated predations, indeed, that at many points he can even arrest the illusion of exchange. A catechism on 'Who is happy?' ends by valorizing the very democracy that Armin's performance has short-circuited – that 'no man shall answere one anothers part, but each man for himselfe shall: O my hart!' It is an audacious irony, like 'every man shall carry his own burthen,' that nonetheless mystifies more than it outrages. 'Why startst thou back for feare?' the quip asks what may as well be the whole playhouse, '& dost thou quake? I see thou knowst no answere what to make.'[40]

When Armin fields the question 'Wheres Tarlton?' however, he faces a moment rife with both challenge and opportunity, and his response exemplifies the overgoing *occupatio* of his technique. Armin externalizes both himself and his questioner into a dizzying repartee between 'Asse' and 'Foole.' 'One asks where Tarlton is, yet knows he's dead,' says Foole, and tells the story of a collier who, disbelieving rumors of Tarlton's death, calls for him after the play; because the clown's picture was used onstage during the show, the collier is certain he is alive and merely recused.[41] Asse, says Foole, is insisting on just such literality, doubting Foole's claim that Tarlton can survive in memory: 'What, is his name letters, and no more?' Foole chides him, 'Can letters liue, that breathe not? No no, his Fame liues, who hath laid in store his acts and deedes.' A heckler has brandished Tarlton to indict Armin: if his name is a rallying cry for confrontational immediacy, Armin retreats into a closed-circuit display of that very confrontation – 'conclude this strife,' Foole warns, 'else all that hear us...breede this mutenie, will bid us keep the collier foole for company.' Unlike the one Dekker described, this 'mutenie' *cannot* 'breede'; Armin's sterile reprise of a Tarltonian animus is yet another lifelike picture onstage, an exhumation expressly for re-burial.[42] As such, it redefines the call for presence so absence can take its place, naturalizing Armin's relation to his model. Tarlton is not an irreplaceable material body but a body of material to be replayed, not 'letters' but 'actes and deedes'. 'You say not, whers his Body,' Foole confutes, 'But, whers *Tarleton*? whers his name alone? His name is here.' 'Here' would encompass the whole theater were that theater not already encapsulated by the performer who speaks the lines; 'here' is equally the space occupied by Armin's universalized mouth. Though he genuflects that 'few clowns will have [Tarlton's] wit,' Armin actually eclipses him, not colliding with but disappearing into collective, anonymous speech in order to resurface as its sole producer and owner.

And yet 'here' is also, of course, the pages of a book, Armin's engrossment of the 'actes and deedes' of others itself channeled into – and by – 'Letters' that breathe more life than they necessarily get. *Quips* neither wishes nor requires us to know if these performances ever really took place; it is ambidextrously designed both to reinforce a *de facto* concentration of theatrical agency and to initiate one. Perhaps the efficacy of publishing it at all, indeed, lies not in monumentalizing an already achieved dramatic authority but precisely in enabling it. *Quips* can more powerfully be situated somewhere between reflecting the monological stage routine Armin enacted and actively advancing the kind he wanted. To whatever extent a past performance does not underlie this text, that is, the text creates future ones in its own image, redoubling its discursive police-work in the process of duplicating it. For if all the voices in the book – let alone in the playhouse – were not originally Armin's, the reader's benumbed accreditation ultimately makes them his. *Quips* compounds its performance by inviting its readership to silence themselves, to participate in their own banishment from participation. Its final theme, 'He begins well, but endes ill,' can retroactively repackage the entire volume as *Armin*'s 'labors': multiplicity has reverted into a lopsided dualism, in which, though 'the Author feares the Reader vowes to haue him by the ears,' the Author by now has the Reader by the throat.[43] Armin's stage practice is thus both textualizing and already textualized, aware that it is crossing theater with graphic technology. One retort is dismissed as 'scrapt out like a parchment blurre,' and later, given the nonsense theme 'Are you there with your beares?' Armin breaks his vocalic spell by revealing the device that casts it: 'One *takes my penn* and *writes* this question.'[44] Berating the playgoer's 'transgression' – it is the only theme that tries to address Amin directly – he plants his authority at the point where voice and pen become fortifying, indissoluble extensions of each other. In a wholly solipsistic moment of discipline, *Quips upon Questions* refigures the clown's stage as a literary space: when that stage is a text, to speak is no longer to constitute theater, but to violate property. Learning the boundaries of a new game, what successive audiences come to see is eventually the re-performance of a book – a book that wrote them in to write them out, a book that scripted them.

The clown had become a playwright. This proved literally true in Armin's case, for he went on to publish a play, *The History of the Two Maides of More-clacke*, in 1609 (see Figure 47). Perhaps an early showcase of his skills, it was printed for a revival in which he could not perform – nor need he have done, fittingly, because by now that performance had become accessible only through a veil of texts.[45] *More-clacke* echoes phrases strewn about the Shakespeare canon, and a whole plot is devoted to parodying *Hamlet* – a youth named 'Humil' laments his mother's adultery, not on behalf of his dead father (who turns out to be not really dead and in fact her lover), but out of naïve loyalty to his stepfather, who still wants Humil killed. Armin played Blue John, whose pranks are lifted verbatim from *Foole upon Foole*, as well as the jester Tutch, who later also dresses up as John. Every time *More-clacke* parts its dramatic illusion, it reveals not a material event but other books. They are the stars of the show, and Armin's identity – like the frontispiece, Armin-as-John – is now scripted by them as well; if his first direction is '*Enter Tutch the Clowne, writing*,' he also enters reading and being read.[46] Indeed, it is not even Armin at all, but someone else he directs to play him playing his own textual fragmentations. Exchanging only with himself, he had finally made himself exchangeable. The 'real' Armin no longer existed outside the looped regression of print and performance into which he had receded. He had become the ghost of its machine, all its voices and yet none of them, having traded the volatile here-and-now for the security – and obscurity – of being *hic et ubique*.

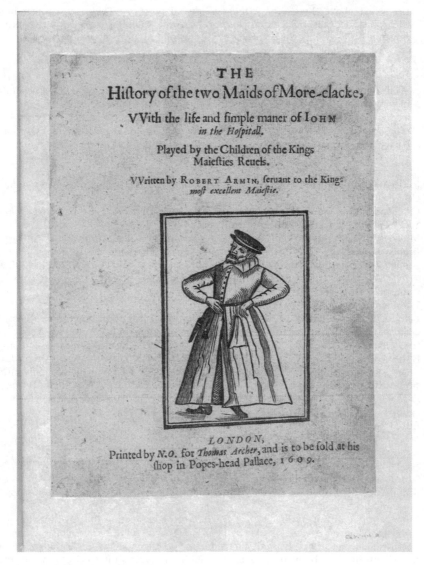

Figure 47 Robert Armin, costumed as 'Blue John' or John-of-the-Hospital, the real-life 'natural' he portrayed in *The Historie of the Two Maids of More-clacke*. Reproduced by permission of The Huntington Library, San Marino, California

Notes

1. William Shakespeare, *Hamlet*, ed. G.R. Hibbard (Oxford: Oxford University Press, 1987), 5.1.175-9.
2. Marston's parody of *Hamlet*'s spectral apostrophes is quite pronounced. The murdered Andrugio has just completed one of the rarer speeches in early modern drama – a soliloquy by a ghost – when he is answered by a voice *'from under the stage'*:

Ho, who's above there, ho? A murrain on all proverbs! They say, hunger breaks through stone walls; but I am as gaunt as lean-ribb'd famine, yet I can burst through no stone walls. O now, Sir Jeffrey, show thy valor; break prison and be hang'd.
> Nor shall the darkest nook of hell contain
> The discontented Sir Balurdo's ghost.
>
> *(He climbs out.)*

Well, I am out well; I have put off the prison to put on the rope. O poor shotten herring, what a pickle art thou in! O hunger, how thou domineer'st in my guts! O for a fat leg of ewe mutton in stew'd broth, or drunken song to feed on. I could belch rarely, for I am all wind. O cold, cold, cold, cold, cold! O poor knight, O poor Sir Jeffrey! Sing like an unicorn before thou dost dip thy horn in the water of death. O cold, O sing, O cold, O poor Sir Jeffrey, sing, sing!   (5.2.1-15)

John Marston, *Antonio's Revenge*, ed. W. Reavley Gair (Manchester: Manchester University Press, 1978).

3. C.L. Barber, *Shakespeare's Festive Comedy: A Study of Dramatic Form and its Relation to Social Custom* (Princeton: Princeton University Press, 1959).
4. Michael Bristol, *Carnival and Theater: Plebeian Culture and the Structure of Authority in Renaissance England* (New York: Methuen, 1985); Robert Weimann, *Shakespeare and the Popular Tradition in the Theater* (Baltimore: Johns Hopkins University Press, 1978), and *Actor's Voice and Author's Pen: Playing and Writing in Shakespeare's Theatre* (Cambridge: Cambridge University Press, 2000).
5. Weimann, *Popular Tradition*, 120–60; 215–36.
6. I am indebted throughout to Helgerson's exfoliation of this question, but it will become clear that it is crucially misguided: if 'the players' theater was becoming what retrospectively looks like an authors' theater' (199) this is precisely the effect of hindsight, and it is the central claim of this chapter that such a transition would have been – indeed, had to be – imperceptible to audiences, mediated by the very performance conventions supposedly resistant to it. See his *Forms of Nationhood: The Elizabethan Writing of England* (Chicago: University of Chicago Press, 1992), 195–246, from which this synopsis is abstracted.
7. Alfred Harbage, *Shakespeare and The Rival Traditions* (New York: Macmillan, 1952); Colin MacCabe, 'Abusing Self and Others: Puritan Accounts of the Shakespearian Stage,' *Critical Quarterly* 30.3 (1988), 3–17.
8. See Andrew Gurr, *The Shakespearean Playing Companies* (Oxford: Clarendon, 1996) 247, 320.
9. Gurr thoroughly backgrounds Shanke's transfer in *The Shakespeare Company, 1594–1642* (Cambridge: Cambridge University Press, 2004), 72–3. He also prints the text of the 1612 Middlesex jig ban.
10. I have omitted consideration here of David Grote's conjecture that Armin's tenure in the King's Men was preceded by Lawrence Fletcher, which I find unpersuasive. Fletcher, a Scottish clown admired by James, appears on the King's Men's inaugural charter and sharers' list in 1603; he died in 1608, at which point, according to Grote, Armin resurfaced to replace him. What limbo Armin occupied in the interim (or why they should have been mutually exclusive, given that his name also appears on the charter) Grote does not say, but on his view the bulkier Fletcher would have satisfied the traditional clown roles Kemp had vacated. This vacancy was by then four years old, however, and would have been acutely felt only if the King's Men had continued offering jigs at the Globe, which they probably did not; Grote ignores both the idiosyncratic personality that clowns projected, which would have made it difficult for Fletcher to 'do' Kemp, as well as the company's likely reasons for not *wanting* him imitated. The only new clown role, indeed, seemingly contrived for a larger actor is *Measure for Measure*'s Pompey Bum, whose sole anatomical requisite could easily enough have been supplied, as many productions have done, with gluteal padding. Fletcher does not appear, moreover, in the First Folio's actors list or in that of *The Alchemist*, and Grote's suggestion that for a

(putative) revival of *Mucedorus* in 1606 the King's Men actually renamed Mouse, its signature character, to accommodate Fletcher's size is utterly absurd. James imported Fletcher for his personal service, and that is all his nominal inclusion in the King's Men reflects. See *The Best Actors in the World: Shakespeare and His Acting Company* (Westport: Greenwood Press, 2002), 126–30.

11. Helgerson, 223; Leslie Hotson's *Shakespeare's Motley* (London: Rupert Hart-Davis, 1952), 84–128, gives the most orthodox catalog of these binaries. See also Dana Aspinall, 'Robert Armin,' in Vicki K. Janik and Emmanuel S. Nelson, eds, *Fools and Jesters in Literature, Art and History: A Bio-Bibliographical Sourcebook* (Westport: Greenwood Press, 1998), 41–9; Charles S. Felver, *Robert Armin, Shakespeare's Fool: A Biographical Essay* (Kent, OH: Kent State University Press, 1961); Olive M. Busby, *Studies in the Development of the Fool* (London: Oxford University Press, 1923); Austin K. Gray, 'Robert Armine, The Foole,' *PMLA 42* (1927), 673–85; Nevil Coghill, 'Wags, Clowns and Jesters,' in John Garrett, ed. *More Talking of Shakespeare* (London, Longmans, 1959), 1–16.

12. David Wiles, *Shakespeare's Clown: Actor and Text in the Elizabethan Playhouse* (Cambridge: Cambridge University Press, 1987), 149. Primarily devoted to Kemp, this is a groundbreaking and undervalued study, on whose perspicuity this essay continually draws. For his lucid distinction between 'clown' and 'fool' as theatrical and colloquial terms, see 61–72; for his discussion of Armin, see 136–64.

13. Felver, 47. He is unconscious of how the fool socially encodes the new subservience to the dramatist for which he advocates; he is, indeed, not even aware that he is advocating it. His analysis simply forecloses Armin's autonomy as a performer, psychologizing him as an extension of his roles.

14. In a dedication to *The Italian Taylor and his Boy* (1609), Armin calls himself 'a Begger, who hath been writ downe for an Asse in his time...notwithstanding his Constableship and Office' (A3r) – often taken to refer to the role of Dogberry. All Armin quotes reference original page signatures, reproduced in facsimile in *The Collected Works of Robert Armin*, 2 vols (New York: Johnson Reprint Corp., 1972).

15. George Whetstone, *The Right Excellent and Famous Historye of Promos and Cassandra* (1578), A2v. Reprinted in E.K. Chambers, *The Elizabethan Stage*, 4 vols (Oxford: Clarendon, 1923) iv, 201–2.

16. Stephen Gosson, *The Schoole of Abuse* (1579), C1v.

17. Joseph Hall, *Virgidemiarum* (1597), Lib.I Satire 3. One especially savors his detail of the clown's bared 'teeth in double-rotten row.'

18. Thomas Dekker, *A Strange Horse-Race* (1613), C4v. The 'torrent' of pleasure he goes on to describe, it merits noting, is merely 'about a nasty bawdy Jigge' rather than the jig itself, its reception 'more blacke...then the most horrid Sceane in the Play was.'

19. Richard Brome, *The Antipodes*, ed. Ann Haaker (Lincoln: University of Nebraska Press, 1966), 2.1.17-24 and 2.2.39-56.

20. Helgerson 224.

21. Anon., *The Pilgrimage to Parnassus* (c.1598), 662–74, in J.B. Leishman, ed. *The Three Parnassus Plays* (London: Ivor Nicholson & Watson, 1949).

22. 'For as we see at all the play house dores, / When ended is the play, the daunce, and song; / A thousand townsmen, gentlemen and whores, / Porters and serving-men together throng', Epigram 17, 'In Cosmum,' in *The Poems of Sir John Davies*, ed. Robert Krueger (Oxford: Clarendon, 1975), 136. The anonymous *Jacke Drums Entertainment* (c.1600) speaks of the 'Jigge' being 'cal'd for when the play is done' (C1v).

23. *Pilgrimage to Parnassus*, 675–92.

24. Anon., *Tarltons Jests* (c. 1600, rep. 1638), C2r.

25. Ibid.

26. Thomas Nashe, *Strange Newes* (1592) D4v; Gabriel Harvey, *Pierce's Supererogation* (1593), in Alexander Grosart, ed. *The Works of Gabriel Harvey*, 3 vols (London, 1884–85), 2.280.

27. I am discounting here the (admittedly delicious) prospect, advanced by John Feather, that Armin was the pseudonymous 'Robin Goodfellow' who composed *Tarltons Newes*

Out of Purgatorie (1590), a collection of Continental fabliaux narrated by the dead clown's ghost. One of its stories derives from Straparola's *Le Piacevoli Notti* (untranslated in England), which also yielded a source for Armin's *Italian Taylor* (1609); but this is almost 20 years later, and Feather's argument must remain speculation.

28. *A Brief Resolution of a Right Religion* (1590), A4v.

29. Rhetorical constructions of humanist authority during and after the Marprelate affair, I argue at length elsewhere, themselves borrowed from clowning and specifically from Tarlton; Armin's stage persona was merely a repatriation of theatrical material that had been processed through another medium. See Barber, 51–7, and Patrick Collinson, 'Ecclesiastical Vitriol: Religious Satire in the 1590s and the Invention of Puritanism,' in John Guy, ed. *The Reign of Elizabeth: Court and Culture in the Last Decade* (Cambridge: Cambridge University Press, 1995), 150–70; also Alexandra Halasz, *The Marketplace of Print: Pamphlets and the Public Sphere in Early Modern England* (Cambridge: Cambridge University Press, 1997), 82–113.

30. See F.P. Wilson, 'The English Jest-books of the Sixteenth and Early Seventeenth Centuries,' in F.P. Wilson, *Shakespearian and Other Studies* (Oxford: Clarendon Press, 1969), 285–324. Among the titles are *Pasquils Foolescap* (1600), *The Hospitall of Incurable Fooles* (1600), *Jack of Dover, His Quest of Inquirie . . . For the Veriest Foole in England* (1604), *The Penniles Parliament of Thread-Bare Poets* (1608), *Roome for a Messe of Knaves* (1610), and *More Fooles Yet* (1610); see H.F. Lippincott, '*King Lear* and the Fools of Robert Armin,' *Shakespeare Quarterly* 26 (1975), 243–53.

31. *Foole Upon Foole, Or Six Sortes of Sottes* (1600), A2r.

32. Nora Johnson, *The Actor as Playwright in Early Modern Drama* (Cambridge: Cambridge University Press, 2003), 39–40; but see more generally 1–53. Johnson draws much-needed attention to the relation between performance and dramatic authorship, and at many points our readings of Armin's authorial moves are remarkably parallel. Our major divergence, however, is in emphasis. As she does with Field, Munday and Heywood, Johnson analyzes Armin's work simply as 'efforts to carry over complex forms of theatrical subjectivity . . . into print', unidirectional translations that suggest 'possible versions of authorship we have failed to consider' (6). The 'authorial permeability' they thus project (12), though, is 'extraordinary' only next to a Romantic absolutism whose critical normativity Johnson vastly overstates; when we recall, more importantly, that Armin's texts exchange and interact with his performance, how they convert collectivity into singularity – how 'Armin establishes himself as an author [precisely] without using the rhetoric of textual ownership' (13) – becomes far more interesting as an active negotiation of authorship in the theater than as a passive (and apologetic) index of how theatrical authorship is always negotiated.

33. *Foole*, A2v ('To the Reader') and F4r.

34. *Tarltons Jests*, albeit at considerable remove, gives us several examples of such combative 'themes,' with which Armin's practice may be usefully contrasted; see n. 42 below. Perhaps the most paradigmatic is 'Tarltons Jest of a Gridiron.' While the Queen's Men lay in Worcester, 'it was his custom for to sing *ex tempore* of Theames given him'; one young wit, hoping to 'put him to a *non plus*,'

> gave him his invention in two lines, which was this: / *Me thinkes it is a thing unfit, / To see a Gridiron turne the Spit.* The people laughed at this . . . which angered Tarleton exceedingly, and presently with a smile looking about, when they expected wonders, he put it off thus: / *Me thinks it is a thing unfit / to see an ass have any wit.* The people hooted for joy, to see the Theame-giuer dasht, who like a dog with his taile betweene his legs, left the place. (C4r-v)

35. Within plays, Wiles notes, dramatists offset his insufficiency by buttressing him with comic trios (Feste, Toby, and Sir Andrew in *Twelfth Night*, for example, or Caliban, Stephano, and Trinculo in *The Tempest*); see 148ff. for his discussion of Armin's deformity

and its impact on his roles. What concerns me here, however, is that after the play they left him *solus*, seemingly keen to see him compensate for it himself.

36. *Quips Upon Questions* (1600), A2r.
37. Ibid., A3r.
38. Ibid. ('Who dyed first?'), E1v.
39. Wiles, 138.
40. *Quips*, C3v-C4r.
41. Ibid., D4r-E1r. This is probably an allusion to Robert Wilson's *Three Lords and Three Ladies of London* (c. 1590), which memorialized Tarlton with a similar iconic device.
42. In the theme 'Whats unfit,' indeed, the textual logic of Armin's Tarltonian agon is rendered explicit. After moving through several stanzas of variation, the theme concludes on a four-line quip that simulates and ossifies both the prompt and the response of Tarlton's signature interpersonal exchange: '*A wonder how, me thinks it is unfit / To see an Iron Gridiron turn the Spit. / No, no, mee thinks that it is more unfit / to see a blockhead ass have any wit*' (B2r). See n. 34 above.
43. Ibid., F3v-F4r.
44. Ibid., A4v, C3r-C3v (my emphasis).
45. To 'the friendly peruser' Armin writes that, perhaps because it is being 'acted by the boyes of the Reuels . . . I would haue againe inacted *John* my selfe, but *Tempora mutantur in illis*, & I cannot do as I would.' He goes on to explain that 'being requested . . . to shew him in prîuate, I have therefore printed him in publike' – a telling equation between performance and publication, as this chapter has argued, as is Armin's subsequent comparison of the text (the words, not the action) to a 'dumbe show.' *The History of the Two Maids of More-clacke, with the Life and Simple Maner of John in the Hospital* (1609), ¶2r.
46. Ibid., A2v.

Part IV
Shakespeare Reconstructed

11
Hamlet's Smile

Margreta de Grazia

It is the climactic moment. Hamlet, having at last established Claudius's guilt, happens upon him alone at prayer, unarmed and unguarded. It is the perfect opportunity to exact revenge. He draws his sword, resolving, 'Now might I do it pat, now a is a-praying. And now I'll do't' (3.3.73–4).[1] Then reconsidering, he pulls it back, 'No./Up, sword, and know thou a more horrid hent' (87–8). Hamlet anti-climactically refrains from performing the act he has until then been gearing up to perform. Without this conspicuous suspension of action, the question dominating *Hamlet* criticism would never have arisen: 'Why does Hamlet delay?' Great minds have been pondering this question for some 200 years now, from Coleridge and Schlegel around the turn of the eighteenth century to Bradley and Freud around the turn of the nineteenth, to Adorno, Levinas, and Lacan in the middle of the twentieth and Derrida and Žižek at its end. There have been times, certainly, when critics have given up on the question, dismissing it as passé, moot, uninteresting, or, worst of all, – purely academic. But it continues to resurface, so that it is hard to find a reading that does not propose or imply a solution, even among today's most theoretically sophisticated literary critics who purport to have left characterological criticism behind.[2] So now in the early years of the twenty-first century it can still hold claim to being the question of questions, the riddle or sphinx of modern times, the Mona Lisa of literature.

And yet until around 1800 the prayer scene was problematic not because of Hamlet's delay but because of the excuse he gives for his delay. He says he wants to catch Claudius in some act that has 'no relish of salvation in it': in a drunken stupor, making incestuous love, swearing while gambling.

> Then trip him, that his heels may kick at heaven
> And that his soul may be as damn'd and black
> As hell, whereto it goes. (93–5)

Hamlet's intention not only to kill a man but to damn him shocked eighteenth-century critics. To slay a body was one thing, to consign an immortal soul to eternal perdition, another. Every major commentary on *Hamlet* in the eighteenth century condemns him for this intent. In a criticism whose task it was to find

Beauties and Faults in Shakespeare, Hamlet received his fair share of criticism, for his obscene remarks to Ophelia, for example, or his insolence to Polonius. But in this instance, his conduct was more than unmannerly: it was inhuman – 'savage,' 'monstrous,' 'fiendish.' In the notes to his 1765 edition of the play, Samuel Johnson condemns the lines in the most extreme terms possible: 'This speech, in which *Hamlet*, represented as a virtuous character, is not content with taking blood for blood, but contrives damnation for the man that he would punish, *is too horrible to be read or to be uttered*' (italics added).[3]

Indeed after the Restoration, Hamlet's offending speech appears not to have been uttered on stage, at least not the last three lines voicing his execrable intent. The Players' Quarto of 1676, the basis for the acting versions performed until the very end of the nineteenth century, ticked the lines with inverted commas to indicate their omission on stage.[4] For a good 200 years after that, from Betterton in 1663 to Forbes Robertson in 1897, they were routinely omitted from production.[5] To be safe, Garrick cut the entire prayer scene from his production.[6]

Editors and commentators could not so easily eliminate the problem. Only Thomas Bowdler took the liberty of expurgating Hamlet's entire speech from his *The Family Shakspeare: In Which Nothing Is Added to the Original Text, but Those Words and Expressions Are Omitted Which Cannot with Propriety Be Read in a Family* (1807). Other editors, however, could do no more than flag and censure the lines in their notes, as did Johnson and his successors, often by quoting Johnson, their attention only highlighting what they would have expunged. Later in the century, however, critics found a defense, one which exonerated both Hamlet and Shakespeare, or at least allowed for extenuating circumstances.

The offending lines were blamed on the period in which Shakespeare wrote. From the vantage of the eighteenth century, the period before the Restoration was crude and rough in its sensibilities, lacking in the refinement and polish introduced by Augustan neo-classicism.[7] Whatever late eighteenth-century critics deemed offensive in Shakespeare – for example, his wordplay or his eroticization of male friendship – might be attributed to the vulgar taste of his times. The same relativism surfaced in defense of Hamlet's contrivance of damnation. Scholars combed through dramas of the period in order to find precedents for his repugnant resolve to exceed 'blood for blood.' Malone's edition of 1790 collects six instances in which stage avengers express similarly fiendish intentions, hoping to catch their victims in some godless or damnable state – cursing at tennis, dead drunk, consumed by lechery – before cutting them off.[8] The only trouble with these examples was that they were all published after *Hamlet*. Looking for precedents, scholars could only locate imitations.[9] Hamlet, it appeared, was not only guilty but the cause of guilt in others.

Toward the end of the eighteenth century, however, a more successful and ingenious defense is devised, not by turning back to stage conventions but by looking to the emergent study of the operations of the mind, shortly to be named *psychology*.[10] The study had been developing primarily in Scotland, following the groundbreaking lead of both Thomas Reid and David Hume, and it is two Scottish critics, one Professor of Humanity at Glasgow and the other Doctor of Divinity at

Edinburgh, who turn to this new study to champion the passage considered 'the most difficult to be defended in the whole character of HAMLET.'[11] Both William Richardson and Thomas Robertson independently light on the same 'hypothesis': what Hamlet says is not what he means; the diabolical wishes he utters 'are not his real sentiments.'[12] What Hamlet really feels as he prepares to strike Claudius is not ferocity but its precise opposite: 'the ascendant of a gentle disposition,' not a 'savage enormity' but rather a 'delicate disposition.'[13] Hamlet's words are diametrically at odds with his feelings. In short, he pretends to intend the very horror that in fact repels him.

These critics might have looked to Hamlet himself for an instance of sheep in wolf's clothing. After browbeating his mother and stabbing Polonius, he offers as apology, 'I must be cruel only to be kind' (3.4.180). The self-conferred mandate to assume the role of heaven's 'scourge' (3.4.177) would seem to require supernal harshness. As he announced before the closet scene, his 'heart' and 'soul' are to play no part in the castigations of his tongue (3.2.384–90). But, of course, as he explains, it is for the sake of his mother that he puts on such a show; his rough treatment forces her to see the begrimed condition of her soul. In the prayer scene, however, Hamlet is effectively alone. Claudius is on stage, but absorbed in prayer, he neither sees nor hears Hamlet. For whose sake, then, does Hamlet feign to be 'cruel' when he is in truth 'kind'? What is the point of being deceptive when there is no one around to deceive?

And what is deceit doing in a passage spoken as a soliloquy or aside? Convention teaches that a character speaks the truth when not overheard by other characters.[14] In solitude or isolation, there is no reason for concealment. So for whom is Hamlet's pretense in the prayer scene intended? Herein lies the novelty and marvel of the new theory. According to the two Scots critics, the pretense is for the benefit of Hamlet himself. It is to himself that he conceals his revulsion at the deed, thereby exhibiting 'a most exquisite picture of amiable self-deceit'; 'he endeavours to hide it from himself'; he 'shelters himself under the subterfuge' of a monstrous intention.[15] Lines formerly regarded as indefensible (*'too horrible to be read or to be uttered'*) are now justified as a cover-up, devised by Hamlet to convince Hamlet that he is capable of vengeance *in extremis* when in fact – that is, deep down inside – he shrinks from the prospect.

The attempt to clear Hamlet of the vile wish to damn a soul gives rise to a new form of self-reflexivity, at least in respect to dramatic character. The theory of 'self-deceit' is applied to a genre which had previously known only the deceit of others. According to Coleridge, even the greatest of critics went astray without this theory, 'Dr. Johnson did not understand the character of Hamlet, and censured accordingly.' Johnson had taken for words of 'horror-striking fiendishness' what was merely 'a pretext,' 'the excuse Hamlet made to himself.'[16] Schlegel, Coleridge's German counterpart, had resorted to the same explanation, '[Hamlet] is a hypocrite towards himself.'[17] By the time of the great variorum Shakespeare of 1821, the solution is familiar enough to require no explanation. The editor simply alludes to the psychological phenomenon that accounts for Hamlet's repellent wish: he attempts 'to hide from his own knowledge his incurable incapacity.'[18] *Hiding knowledge from oneself, deceiving oneself, making excuses to oneself, being a hypocrite to oneself*: these are all terms for a new form of self-reflexivity in the drama, imported from the emergent study of psychology. It is not that Hamlet is just saying what he does not mean. If he were (and we believed him), it would be a case of simple deceit. Rather he is saying what he does-not-know-he-does-not-mean. In the deceit of others, the speaker knows full well when his tongue and soul are discrepant, as does Hamlet when before the closet scene he announces his intent, 'My tongue and soul in this be hypocrites' (3.2.388). In deceit of the self, however, the speaker has no such knowledge. In short, in cases of self-deceit, some part of the psyche remains unknown to the psyche – a part that is inaccessible to consciousness. Toward the end of the next century, that repressed part of the psyche will be the focus of a study (and a therapy) all of its own.

That this new theory should have been embraced as a solution to a dramatic problem is indeed remarkable. For how is self-deceit to be performed on stage? To be sure, deceit is at the very heart of the theatrical enterprise, as anti-theatricalists never tired of proclaiming. *Hypocrite* derives from the Greek for actor, *hupocritēs*. A player pretends to be a character, and that character must at times, as the plot requires, pretend to be other than he is. In this play, the hypocrite *par excellence* is Claudius. He appears a jovial king when he is in reality a guilt-ridden murderer: while smiling on the outside, he gnashes his teeth within. After the Ghost's harrowing appearance and disclosure, Hamlet jots down only one bit of wisdom in his newly cleansed table book: 'One may smile, and smile, and be a villain' (1.5.108). But Claudius's hypocrisy is quite different from Hamlet's alleged self-hypocrisy. Claudius knows all too well that he is deceitful, and admits his deceit, to the audience if not to the other characters, in an aside (3.1.51–4) as well as in his private prayer. Hamlet, however, rather than hiding something from the knowledge of another or others, is imagined to be hiding it from himself: he is at once both deceiver and deceived.

On stage, an actor can stage a number of self-reflexives. He can, for example, go through the motions of talking to himself, debating with himself, even killing himself: but how can he perform the act of deceiving himself? If the character himself has no knowledge of his intent to deceive, he can not communicate it to the audience, not even in a soul-searching aside or soliloquy. How then is self-deceit to be staged? How can an audience distinguish the monstrous words a character speaks and means from the monstrous words he speaks in order to deceive himself? Imagine a placard dropping down from the rafters and reading, 'This man is self-deceived.' Imagine one character saying to another, 'Have you noticed how Hamlet has been deceiving himself of late?' (Hamlet might ask himself the same question.) A 'tragedy of thought,' as both Schlegel and Coleridge famously dubbed the play, is hard enough to enact; a number of nineteenth-century critics, including Lamb and Hazlitt, believed his ruminations rendered his part impossible to perform.[19] But how would a 'tragedy of self-deception' be staged? A post-Freudian audience, of course, would be more prepared for such a possibility, though even then, some prior account (in the program? in a review?) might be needed to explain that mechanisms of repression, resistance, or denial may be at work and accounting for otherwise inexplicable language and behavior.

The appeal to psychology to defend Hamlet's ignominious lines is the beginning of a brave new world of hermeneutic inquiry.[20] Characters move out of a world in which they possess motives of which they are aware (and can disclose or conceal, as they choose) into a world of motives of which they are not aware (and cannot choose to disclose or conceal). This is not to say – and this must be stressed – that not until 1800 is Hamlet's interiority discovered. Hamlet always possessed an area within and beyond show. What Hamlet does not possess until around 1800 is an area of consciousness which he cannot show even to himself. A new model of mind is applied to a theatrical character. It is no longer a cogitating Cartesian mind that has access to its own processes: Descartes' thoughts, as he sits alone in his study doubting the reality of the wax on his desk, are entirely accessible to Descartes. His very existence depends on their accessibility, as do his transcriptions of those thoughts, the *Meditations on First Philosophy* (1632). But by 1800, we are in a Kantian world in which relations to the self are mediated by categories of time and space, just as are relations to others and to the external world; the immediate and certain have given way to the mediated and hypothetical. There are recesses of the mind that consciousness cannot tap, even the mind of the character known for his excessive thought or 'ratiocinative meditativeness,' in Coleridge's appropriately extravagant coinage.[21] This is what Freud's disciple Ernest Jones saw as the advantage of the Oedipal theory: it alone could explain why Hamlet does not himself understand the cause of his delay.[22] Nor, according to Freud, was it understood by anyone else – not even Shakespeare – until some 300 years after the play's first production, when in 1900 Hamlet's unconscious workings were brought to light in a footnote to Freud's *Interpretation of Dreams*.[23] Once the area of the unconscious has been posited, Hamlet's expressed wish to damn Claudius loses its shock value. It is lumped in with his various other 'alleged motives' for not acting (cowardice, melancholy, suspicion of the Ghost's word), all of which, according to Jones, can be dismissed 'as being more or less successful attempts on his part to blind himself with self-deception.'[24] All these pretexts are so-many evasions or rationalizations of the deeply embedded condition which Hamlet can in no way fathom.

In attempting to redeem Hamlet's unconscionable three-line excuse, critics light upon the theory of self-deceit that in turn inaugurates a long hermeneutic tradition of that part of the mind unknown to itself. Hamlet can now be said to be the hero of the unconscious as well as of consciousness. But let us return to the other attempt to defend Hamlet's fiendish outburst: the one which dead-ended when it found no precedents in stage history, only descendants. For there certainly was a model for Hamlet's diabolism: it dated back centuries to the medieval mystery plays of the Last Judgment in which devils rushed on stage to claim reprobate souls. It is from these fiends that Hamlet learns his wicked desire, for their full-time business was the damning of souls. Their sole purpose and pleasure in life was to get back at their maker by drawing souls to eternal damnation.

In manuals on the art of dying, fiends were depicted hovering around the deathbed in hope of snatching a despairing soul. (Othello, after strangling Desdemona, imagines such fiends lying in wait for his soul.[25]) In illustrations of the Last Judgment, devils lurk at the left hand of Christ tugging the wretched souls of the damned down to searing tortures. In recent years, scores of frescoes dating from the fifteenth and early sixteenth centuries have been discovered on the chancels of English parish churches, beneath Reformation white-wash or Victorian painting. The most frequently depicted scene is the Doom or Last Judgment representing the weighing of souls, the blessed ones swooped up to heaven by angels, the damned yanked down into hell by gleefully grinning devils.[26]

As John Cox has recently established, devils from before *Mankind* to long after Marlowe, indeed all the way up to the closing of the theaters, appeared on stage, often at the final hour to seize the souls of those who had abjured God, hilariously abducting them, dragging or lugging them off stage, riding them off piggyback, or yanking them into the gaping mouth of hell.[27] The memory of those devils lingered in the trap of the stage itself, the opening to the traditional theatrical location of hell, the area beneath the scaffolding. At the Globe, this area would have been activated by the Ghost's descent and eerie intonations from that space. The Arden editor suggests that the epithets with which Hamlet addresses the Ghost – 'boy,' 'true penny' (158), 'fellow' (159) – recall the familiar manner in which the stage Vice traditionally addressed the Devil. He also notes the applicability of '*hic et ubique*' (164), 'old mole' (170), and 'worthy pioner' (171) to the ubiquitous subterranean activity of devils.[28]

The provenance of the Ghost is, of course, of some concern in *Hamlet*. This spectral 'thing' (1.1.24) appears in such 'questionable shape' (1.4.43) that Hamlet wonders if it might not have come from hell: it may be 'a goblin damned' (1.4.40), attended by 'blasts from hell' (41) and bearing 'intents wicked' (42). As he acknowledges, the fact that it bears the endearing form of his father's likeness offers no reassurance.

> The spirit that I have seen
> May be a devil, and the devil hath power
> T'assume a pleasing shape, yea, and perhaps
> Out of my weakness and my melancholy,
> As he is very potent with such spirits,
> Abuses me to damn me. (2.2.594–9)

His companions express the same concern for his soul when the Ghost beckons Hamlet alone to 'a more removed ground' (1.4.61). They struggle to hold him back, fearing the worst:

> What if it tempt you toward the flood, my lord,
> Or to the dreadful summit of the cliff
> That beetles o'er his base into the sea,
> And there assume some other horrible form
> Which might deprive your sovereignty of reason
> And draw you into madness? (69–74)

The fiend legendarily singles out those weakened by melancholy or guilt and unsettles them further with images of the abysmal void prompting 'thoughts beyond the reaches of [their] souls' (56), impelling them to despair and suicide. From the vantage of that 'dreadful summit,' 'every brain/That looks so many fathoms to the sea/And hears it roar beneath' (76–7) feels a touch of despair, the demonic sublime; and if the devil were there to 'assume some other horrible form' – some monstrous phantasma – the weak-minded would renounce all faith and topple over the edge of the precipice, into the clutches of the devil. (Edgar in *King Lear* convinces his guilt-ridden father that such a hideously fiendish figure drove him to his suicidal leap from the cliffs of Dover.[29])

But it is not only the Ghost who brings the devil to mind. 'I have been so affrighted,' admits Ophelia after Hamlet in his antic disposition has entered her closet, 'As if he had been loosed out of hell/To speak of horrors' (2.1.83–4). She gives a detailed report of his transformed appearance; as Claudius later comments, 'nor th'exterior nor the inward man/Resembles that it was' (2.2.6–7). He has lost the control of his body: his knees knock, his head shakes, indeed his whole frame heaves: 'He rais'd a sigh so piteous and profound/As it did seem to shatter all this bulk/And end his being' (2.1.83). His convulsive movements have been hard on his clothing: his braces tear apart, his cap flings off, his garters snap.

Like Ophelia, the earliest audiences of the play remembered Hamlet as one who had just been loosed out of hell. The earliest recorded references imagine him literally 'running mad.' In the early decades of its performance, Hamlet's signature action may have been not paralysing thought but frenzied motion. In two separate works, Dekker alludes to entrances by Hamlet in distracted motion, 'break[ing] loose like a Beare from the stake' and 'rush[ing] in by violence.'[30] In Chapman, Jonson, and Marston's *Eastward Ho!* a madcap character named Hamlet makes a similarly disruptive entrance: 'Enter Hamlet a footeman in haste,' reads the stage direction, and as an attendant's response indicates, his haste is quite frantic, 'Sfoote Hamlet; are you madde? whether run you now...?'[31] This must have been a favorite stage stunt, a frantic and frenzied routine not unlike that of demonic possession in which the possessed wretch ran as if chased by a devil from whom he could not possibly escape since that devil lodged within his own body.

The devilish strain of Hamlet's antic disposition has a long genealogy. Both devil and antic are versions of the grotesque, that combination of the sinister and ludicrous that violates both classical symmetry and godly perfection. The word 'anticke' according to Robert Cawdrey's 1604 *A Table Alphabeticall* denotes a disguise, particularly grotesque heads or masks.[32] Antic masks and demons heads share similar distortions and disfigurations, at once comical and terrifying. Characteristic to both is the exaggerated expanse of the mouth, tautly-stretched in one direction or another: in a smile, in a frown. The grimace is also shared by the Antic death, the *risus sardonicus* that like Yorick's skull 'mocks [its] own grinning' (5.1.185–6). And so, too, is it by the clown who enters and shows 'his teeth in double rotten row.' Richard Tarlton famously contorted what is imagined to have been a naturally ugly face when he routinely poked his head out of the tiring-house tapestry to make a 'scurvy face' at the audience.[33] According to Henry Peacham, clowns '[s]et all the multitude in such a laughter,/They could not hold for scarce an houre after.'[34] An exaggeration, one assumes, but one that suggests that this kind of mugging might have held up the show as long as the laughter continued in what is now termed an 'elastic gag.'[35] It is this practice, of course, which Hamlet targets in his interdiction against the unscripted antics of the clown, who sets the audience laughing (and even laughs himself) 'though in the meantime some necessary question of the play be then to be considered' (3.2.42–3).

Among the itinerant players in Elsinore, there is no clown, but there is a villain or vice figure. In 'The Murder of Gonzago,' he plays Lucianus. Although there are no grounds for thinking he speaks more than is set down, he certainly holds up 'some necessary question of the play.' In fact, it might be said that by delaying the pouring of the poison in the Player King's ear, he holds up *two* necessary questions: the climactic act of the play-within-the play (the one named by its title) as well as the one intended to produce the epiphanic effect of 'unkennel[ing]' Claudius's 'occulted guilt' (3.2.80–1). As Hamlet's impatient Senecan outburst indicates, Lucianus (or rather the-actor-playing-Lucianus), has been taking his time. 'Begin, murderer. Leave thy damnable faces and begin./Come. The croaking raven doth bellow for revenge' (246–7).

Lucianus is on stage (or rather the stage-within-the-stage) for ten lines waiting for Hamlet, who is scurrilously bantering with Ophelia, to shut up. For this duration, Lucianus has the stage to himself, all eyes (of the court audience) are upon him, and he takes the opportunity to indulge what Hamlet has called 'pitiful ambition' by making 'damnable faces.' He plays the scene for laughs by making diabolical faces, an instance of dilational clowning, drawing out the interim or meanwhile, the very vice Hamlet deplores in clowns.

When Hamlet is done, Lucianus stops mugging and recites his lines.

> *Thoughts black, hands apt, drugs fit, and time agreeing,*
> *Confederate season, else no creature seeing,*
> *Thou mixture rank, of midnight weeds collected,*
> *With Hecate's ban thrice blasted, thrice infected,*
> *Thy natural magic and dire property*
> *On wholesome life usurps immediately.* (249–54)

Some critics have taken these couplets to belong to the 'speech of some dozen or sixteen lines' (2.2.535) which Hamlet says he will set down and insert into the script. And indeed, there is a generic and atmospheric if not stylistic similarity to the ghoulish speech Hamlet gives right after the Mousetrap play:

> 'Tis now the very witching time of night,
> When churchyards yawn and itself breathes out
> Contagion to this world. Now could I drink hot blood. (3.3.379).

If Lucianus has 'thoughts black,' Hamlet could 'drink hot blood.' If Lucianus's infernal poison is distilled in a little flask, Hamlet's contagion would blast the whole world. If Lucianus makes damnable faces in anticipation of trickling poison into his victim's ear, might not then Hamlet also make them while contemplating the drinking of hot blood?

Hamlet is similarly inspired by the representation of another treacherous murder: 'hellish Pyrrhus' (2.2.459). After hearing the player's recitation of Priam's slaughter he tries to whip himself into a comparable state of villainy: 'Bloody, bawdy villain,/Remorseless, treacherous, lecherous, kindless villain!' (2.2.576–7). By these epithets, he presumably intends Claudius, but they occur in a monologue in which he berates himself for not being sufficiently bloodthirsty. In desire at least, he would outdo Pyrrhus's butchery. 'The hellish Pyrrhus' made 'malicious sport,/ In mincing with his sword [Hecuba's] husband's limbs' (2.2.509–10), but Hamlet would do him one better. Like his Greek counterpart, he would make mincemeat of his victim, but then, just for bad measure, he would serve it up to the vultures: 'I would ere this have fatted all the region kites/With this slave's offal' (2.2.575).

Lucianus and Priam are stand-ins for Hamlet's real rival, of course, the one he terms 'vice of kings' (3.4.98). Claudius must be all smiles in the opening court scene to make sense of Hamlet's vituperative apostrophe: 'O villain, villain, smiling damned villain!' (1.5.106) Claudius exemplifies the maxim Hamlet has jotted into his newly-wiped table book – 'one may smile, and smile, and be a villain' (108). The King's response to Hamlet's concession to remain in Denmark clearly calls for an ear-to-ear grin: 'This gentle and unforc'd accord of Hamlet/Sits smiling to my heart' (1.2.123–4). The smile is the badge of hypocrisy or dissimulation and therefore of the actor's craft: it is the simplest way of pretending to be something you are not: of 'sugar[ing] o'er/The devil himself' (3.1.48–9). The mere tightening of the facial muscles covers a multitude of sins. While registering the axiom in his table book, Hamlet might himself illustrate it by baring his teeth in sinister imitation of Claudius. Another wide smile might follow when he gives a tautological variant on the axiom. In order to deflect the watch's anxious inquiry for 'news' of the ghost, he offers only the circular, 'There's never a villain dwelling in all Denmark/But he's an arrant knave' (1.5.129–30). One may smile, and smile, and be an arrant knave.

On Shakespeare's stage, Hamlet's fiendish lines may well have been intended to give an audience what they came to a revenge play to see: how far the avenger will go. Claudius asks another avenger just this question, 'what would you undertake/To show yourself in deed your father's son?' (5.7.124–6). 'To cut his throat/I'th'church' (125), responds Laertes, indicating that he would not stop at sacrilege. 'Revenge should have no bounds' (127), commends Claudius. In fact Laertes' willingness to slay Hamlet at church, perhaps at prayer, suggests his indifference to the circumstances that stay Hamlet's hand, for surely there is some 'relish of salvation' in church attendance. Laertes's revenge, then, *does* remain within bounds, for it is limited to the here and now: *blood for blood*. Hamlet goes beyond the pale, in egregious violation of his own precept to the players to 'o'erstep not the modesty of nature' (3.2.19). As is indicated by the scandalized responses of eighteenth-century critics, always sensitive to indecorum, Hamlet *does* overstep natural modesty: by crossing the divide between the human and the monstrous, between intending to kill a man and intending to damn him, between the stage avenger and the stage devil.

As Johnson noted, Hamlet 'is not content with taking blood for blood.' He wants Claudius's soul thrown into the bargain. If the soul of Hamlet's father ('Unhousel'd, disappointed, unanel'd' [1.577]) was unready for Judgment, what revenge would there be in sending Claudius there well-prepared: 'fit and season'd' for his passage' (3.3.87), relishing of salvation? What justice in wafting a man to heaven for murder?

> A villain kills my father, and for that
> I, his sole son, do this same villain send
> To heaven. (76–8)

Yet soul for soul is not what this 'sole son' wants either. While his father was killed in the ostensibly harmless act of sleeping in the garden, his uncle must be taken in some act so vicious as to preclude salvation: 'that his heels may kick at heaven/And that his soul may be as damn'd and black/As hell, whereto it goes' (93–5). This is overkill, not retaliation, and a reminder that both *iniquity* and *inequity* have incommensurability at their semantic root.[36] It is also a reminder of the Senecan avenger's ethos that found its way into numerous Tudor and Stuart revenge plots, both narrative and dramatic: '*Scelera non ulcisceris, nisi vincis.*' In *Antonio's Revenge* Marston repeats and translates this tag from *Thyestes*: 'Crimes are not Avenged Unless they are Exceeded' (3.1.51). The state of King Hamlet's soul at death sent him to purgatory, not hell, and between the two destinations there is a world of difference.[37] Punishment in purgatory may be long and hard, but it is finite.[38] As the Ghost specifies, he has been sentenced for a definite period – 'Doom'd for a certain term' (1.5.10) – at which point 'the foul crimes done in my days of nature/Are burnt and purg'd away'(12–13). That is bad enough: 'O horrible! O horrible! Most horrible!' (80). But Hamlet wishes worse upon Claudius: the 'more horrid hent' of never-ending punishment, the eternal agony of the godforsaken pains of hell. With such fiendishness, Hamlet would outdo his rival, the smiling villain, the 'vice of kings' the 'bloody, bawdy villain' whose malice is merely of this world. With his execrable lines, Hamlet out-vilifies all the play's villains: Lucianus, Pyrrhus, Laertes, Claudius. But his triumph is greater still. For the revenge Hamlet entertains the audience by entertaining goes beyond anything available to the Senecan avenger, for while ancient villains could devise all kinds of atrocities for their victims, this particular refinement had to await Christian revelation. The damnable lines, then, show Hamlet to be the most iniquitous stage villain of them all. And to prove it, might he not in delivering them celebrate his thespian one-upmanship with a smile so wickedly – fiendishly – broad as to outsmile the smiling arch-villain?

The tradition of the stage devil may have survived the Reformation, but not the Restoration. Cut off from the histrionics of salvational drama, Hamlet's diabolical determination to damn Claudius loses its performative flair, and shocks the neo-classicized sensibilities of eighteenth-century critics. His sentiment becomes acceptable only when psychology discovers a mechanism for attributing it to the unconscious defenses of the mind. But by that point the destination of the soul is no longer a dramatic concern. The *psyche* under examination is mind, not soul. Hamlet's lines no longer attract much attention, except as one pretext among many for his problematic delay. A strong and supple hermeneutic fills the gap left by a forgotten stage convention. Thereafter it is not a stagey display of diabolical virtuosity which holds up the action of the play, but a deeply interiorized psychic complexity.

Notes

1. All quotations from *Hamlet* are taken from Harold Jenkins's Arden edition (London: Methuen, 1982), and references will henceforth appear in text.
2. For a discussion of the emergence of this question around 1800 and its duration into the present, see Margreta de Grazia, '*Hamlet* before Its Time,' *Modern Language Quarterly* 62 (2001), 355–75.
3. *The Plays of William Shakespeare* (1765), in *Shakespeare: The Critical Heritage*, ed. Brian Vickers (London: Routledge and Kegan Paul, 1979), 5:159.
4. *The Tragedy of Hamlet* (London, 1676), To the Reader.
5. As his 1859 acting edition attests, Edwin Booth reintroduced the lines, but they were subsequently eliminated. See Philip Edwards, *Hamlet, Prince of Denmark* (Cambridge: Cambridge University Press, 1985), 63–7.
6. Edwards, 64.
7. See Jack Lynch's fine account of the eighteenth-century periodizing of Shakespeare's time, in *The Age of Elizabeth in the Age of Johnson* (Cambridge: Cambridge University Press, 2003).
8. *The Plays and Poems of William Shakspeare*, 21 vols (London: F. C., J. Rivington [etc].: 1821), 7:382–3.
9. Eleanor Prosser lists 23 instances of similar fiendishness in stage avengers, but none in drama before Shakespeare, *Hamlet and Revenge* (Stanford: Stanford University Press, 1967), 261–75.
10. According to Blancard's 1693 *Physicians' Dictionary*, '*Anthropologia* or the Description of Man' is divided into two parts, '*Anatomy*, which treats of the Body, and *Psycology* [sic], which treats of the Soul,' OED, 1.a. In 1800 Coleridge prefaced his introduction of the term to literary criticism by observing that, 'We have no single term to express the Philosophy of the Human Mind.' S. T. Coleridge's *Treatise on Method*, ed. Alice D. Snyder (London: Constable, 1934), 32 n. 3; for his application of *psychology* to Hamlet's mental processes, see de Grazia, 'When did Hamlet become modern?' *Textual Practice* 17 (2003), 492–4.
11. Thomas Robertson, 'An Essay on the Character of Hamlet' (1788), in Vickers, 6:486.
12. William Richardson, *Essays on Shakespeare's Dramatic Characters* (1783), in Vickers, 6:367. Robertson notes the coincidence: 'Since writing this Essay, I have had the pleasure to find that the same idea has occurred to Mr. Professor RICHARDSON . . . .' (486 n.).
13. See Vickers, 6: 367, 368.
14. For a demystifying discussion of *soliloquy*, see Raymond Williams, 'On Dramatic Dialogue and Monologue,' *Writing in Society* (London: Verso Editions: n.d.), 31–64, and de Grazia, 'Soliloquies and Wages in the Age of Emergent Consciousness,' *Textual Practice*, 9 (Spring, 1995), 67–92.

15. See Vickers, 6: 368, 486.

16. From John Payne Collier's notes on Lecture 12 (1811–12), in *Coleridge's Criticism of Shakespeare*, ed. R. A. Foakes (Detroit: Wayne State University Press, 1989), 71.

17. A. W. Schlegel, *Course of Lectures on Dramatic Art and Literature*, trans. John Black (Philadelphia: Hogan & Thompson, 1833), 329.

18. James Boswell's endnote to *Hamlet*, in *The Plays and Poems of William Shakespeare*, (London: F. C. and J. Rivington [etc.], 1821), 7:537.

19. See Charles Lamb, *The Tragedies of Shakespeare* (1811) and William Hazlitt, *Characters of Shakespear's Plays* (1817), in *Critical Responses to 'Hamlet,' 1600–1900*, ed. David Farley-Hills, 4 vols (New York: AMS Press, 1995–), 2:102–3 and 110–11.

20. On the use of psychology to defend Hamlet from moral censure, see Brian Vickers, 'The Emergence of Character Criticism,' *Shakespeare Survey 34* (Cambridge: Cambridge University Press, 1981), 14–15.

21. See Foakes, 83.

22. See Ernest Jones, *Hamlet and Oedipus* (New York: Norton, 1976), 48–9.

23. Freud raised this footnote into the text in 1914. In *The Basic Writings of Sigmund Freud*, ed. and trans. A. A. Brill (New York: Modern Library, 1938), 309.

24. See Jones, 55.

25. 'When we shall meet at count/This look of thine will hurl my soul from heaven,/And fiends will snatch at it,' *Othello*, 5.2.280–3, *The Norton Shakespeare*, ed. Stephen Greenblatt *et al.* (New York: W. W. Norton, 1997).

26. These remarkable images can be seen in the developing catalogue of 'Medieval Wall Painting in the English Parish Church,' at <http://www.paintedchurch.org.conpage.htm>.

27. For the ubiquity of devils in the medieval mysteries and moralities as well as their surprising longevity on the London public stage up to the closing of the theaters, see John D. Cox. *The Devil and the Sacred in English Drama, 1350–1642* (Cambridge and New York: Cambridge University Press, 2000).

28. Jenkins, 458.

29. 'As I stood here below, methought his eyes/Were two full moons; he had a thousand noses,/Horns whelked and waved like the enridged sea:/It was some fiend.' See *King Lear*, 4.6. 69–72, in the Conflated Text of *The Norton Shakespeare*.

30. See Paul S. Conklin, *A History of 'Hamlet' Criticism 1601–1821* (London: Cass, 1967), 18–19.

31. *Eastward Ho!*, quoted in Farley-Hills, 1:3.

32. See Jenkins, 226, n. 1.5.180.

33. See Anon., *Pilgrimage to Parnassus* in J.B. Leishman, ed. *The Three Parnassus Plays, 1598–1601* (London: Ivor Nicholson & Watson, 1949), 223.

34. Quoted by Andrew Gurr, *The Shakespearean Stage 1574–1642* (Cambridge: Cambridge University Press,1994), 88.

35. On the 'elastic gag' and the semantics of the somatic on the Shakespearean stage, see Simon Shepherd, 'Revels Ends, and the Gentle Body Starts,' *Shakespeare Survey 55* (Cambridge: Cambridge University Press, 2002), 237–56.

36. Like Christ's mercy, Hamlet's villainy tips the scales of justice. I am indebted to John Parker for noting the uneasy kinship between *inequity* and *iniquity* in Christological thought. See 'God Among Thieves: Marx's Christological Theory of Value and the Literature of the English Reformation,' Ph.D. Dissertation, University of Pennsylvania, 1999.

37. As Stephen Greenblatt has demonstrated, the abolition of purgatory by the Thirty-Nine Articles of 1563 in no way silenced the play's multiple allusions to the place. See *Hamlet in Purgatory* (Princeton and Oxford: Princeton University Press, 2001), esp. 235–7.

38. On the identification of 'for a certain term' with the determinate duration of purgatorial pains as opposed the eternal pains of hell, see Greenblatt, 230.

12

'The technique of it is mature': Inventing the Late Plays in Print and in Performance

Gordon McMullan

I

This is a brief case history of a phenomenon – or, perhaps better, of an alleged phenomenon – that manifests itself in the way we read certain plays in the Shakespeare canon and that relates both to the way those plays first appeared in the world and to our understanding of two relationships – that of playwright and play in Jacobean England and that of theatre history and literary criticism. I use the word 'alleged' because I do not, myself, believe it exists – or at least I do not believe it exists in the form that critics have come to accept. This (alleged) phenomenon is lateness, late writing, late style – a subject that was a principal preoccupation of Edward Said before his death. Said, unlike me, did believe, and perhaps for very good and obvious personal reasons, in the idea of late writing, and in a review in *The Nation* of a recent book on late Beethoven, he approvingly cited a 1947 essay by the Austrian critic Hermann Broch which celebrates late writing as

> the reaching of a new level of expression, such as the old Titian's discovery of the all-penetrating light which dissolves the human flesh and the human soul to a higher unity; or such as the finding by Rembrandt and Goya, both at the height of their manhood, of the metaphysical surface which underlies the visible in man and thing, and which nevertheless can be painted; or such as the *Art of the Fugue* which Bach in his old age dictated without having a concrete instrument in mind, because what he had to express was either beneath or beyond the audible surface of music; or such as the last quartets of Beethoven, in which he – only then in his fifties but already near to death – found the way from earthly music to the music of the infinite.[1]

Choosing not to address the wilder romanticisms in Broch's description, Said outlines the distinctive features of Beethoven's last works which, he argues,

> form an identifiable group and show marked evidence of a considerable transformation in his actual compositional style from the romantic heroism of

his middle-period works to a difficult, highly personal and (to the listener and even his contemporaries) a somewhat unattractive, not to say repellent, idiom.[2]

Said goes on to quote Theodor Adorno's (as he puts it) 'impossibly gnomic' account of this 'unattractive idiom', noting that 'late-style Beethoven is not, as one might expect, all about reconciliation and a kind of restful summing-up of a long, productive career' and adding:

> That is what one finds, for example, in Shakespeare's late romances like *The Tempest, The Winter's Tale* and *Cymbeline*, or in Sophocles' *Oedipus at Colonus*, where, to borrow from another context, ripeness is all.[3]

There are two aspects of this account that interest me. One is the persistence it demonstrates – this account of Shakespeare's late plays by a cultural theorist of Said's stature – of an understanding of those plays that Shakespeareans tend to assume is long gone – that is, the subjectivist reading of the late plays as externalizations of the particular emotional state of the playwright at the time of writing. The other is the puzzling contradiction at the heart of lateness studies which suggests that late work is, on the one hand (as Said suggests of Shakespeare), a serene return to the early, a reconciliation of former with later forms of selfhood from the peaceful perspective of the end, and, on the other (as Said suggests of, and celebrates in, Beethoven), a complex, difficult and fragmented pre-empting of what for a later generation would manifest itself as the avant garde. It is this apparently irreconcilable contradiction that I wish to address in this essay by tracing a particular instance of Shakespearean theatre history.

II

I want to take the idea of late work as a means of focusing on the disjunction between early modern and post-romantic understandings of Shakespearean authorship and on the gulf between later critical and performance accretions of the plays we call the 'late plays' and their origins. Lateness is not an obvious subject for theatre history, but I want to suggest today that in at least one important instance the two topics are in fact closely connected. In order to do so, I need to address the two apparently very different accounts of lateness that I have outlined. I will come back in due course to the version of lateness that Said, via Adorno, associates primarily with Beethoven – the idea of late work as difficult, fragmentary, prophetic, cyclical. But first I want to explore the origins of the particular definition of Shakespearean lateness assumed by Said in his review – lateness as serene, reconciliatory, unifying – a definition perhaps best summed up in Sir Walter Raleigh's 1926 observation that

> [m]any a life has been wrecked on a tenth part of the accumulated suffering which finds a voice in the Tragedies. The Romances are our warrant that

Shakespeare regained a perfect calm of mind. If *Timon of Athens* had been his last play, who could feel any assurance that he dies at peace with the world?[4]

The attitude to lateness apparent in Raleigh – the belief that the last plays embody a profound Shakespearean serenity – was sustained across the twentieth century by critics such as Kenneth Muir and David Grene, who in the 1960s wrote books (the latter apparently unaware of the former) thematically connecting the late works of Shakespeare with those of Sophocles, Racine and Ibsen. In each case, the connections drawn suggest both that late writing is a hallmark of individual genius and that it is a phenomenon beyond time and context, manifesting itself similarly in ancient Greece, Jacobean England or nineteenth-century Norway. The first critic to delineate the particular understanding of Shakespeare's late plays that Muir and Grene celebrate and that Said echoes is usually – and accurately enough – held to be Edward Dowden, who sought to establish an overview of Shakespeare's career so as, as he put it, 'to observe, as far as is possible, in its several stages the growth of his intellect and character from youth to full maturity.'[5] He divided the life into four periods – personal phases that correspond to generic categories: comedies, histories, tragedies and romances – culminating in the phase he called 'On the Heights,' a last period in which the artist, after the crisis of 'dissonance' embodied in *King Lear* and *Timon of Athens*, emerges with a 'clear and solemn vision' to write plays in which 'there is a resolution of the dissonance, a reconciliation' expressed as a 'pathetic yet august serenity' (Dowden, 403, 406, 380). For Dowden, late-period Shakespeare 'is 'serenely victorious, infinitely charitable, wise with all the wisdom of the intellect and the heart'.[6]

But to what extent was Dowden saying something new? Edmond Malone, writing almost a century before Dowden, was the first to establish a comprehensive chronology for Shakespeare.[7] For him, though, 'late' simply meant the second half of Shakespeare's career, not a special category for the very end of the life. And we know that Malone's chronology was, in our terms, inaccurate: he was for a long time convinced that *Twelfth Night* was the last play and he dated *The Winter's Tale*, initially at least, to 1594. There is no concept of a 'late phase' in the modern sense in Malone, just a series of plays with dates assigned and a belief that the writing went on into 1614. Without a chronology, needless to say, there can be no late work: the *quality* of lateness can only be established after the *fact* of lateness has been determined. And there is in Malone an assumption at least that the more finished and perfect the play the more likely it is to be late. He dated *Twelfth Night* to 1614 partly because he saw it as an unusually 'complete' play and read this completeness as a result of the leisure afforded by 'rural retirement':

When Shakespeare quitted London and his profession, for the tranquillity of a rural retirement, it is improbable that such an excursive genius should have been immediately reconciled to a state of mental inactivity. It is more natural to conceive, that he should have occasionally bent his thoughts towards the theatre, which his muse had supported, and the interest of his associates whom he had left behind him to struggle with the capricious vicissitudes of publick taste, and whom, his last Will shews us, he had not forgotten. To the necessity, therefore, of literary amusement to every cultivated mind, or to the dictates of friendship, or to both these incentives, we are perhaps indebted for the comedy of *Twelfth Night*; which bears evident marks of having been composed at leisure, as most of the characters that it contains, are finished to a higher degree of dramatick perfection, than is discoverable in some of our author's earlier comick performances.[8]

This is an early instance of an underlying assumption – that commercial play-wrighting militates against aesthetic completeness – which sets Shakespearean late writing against the practice of the professional dramatist and thus tends to situate discussions of Shakespearean lateness apart from theatre history. It is also an instance of the implicit association of Stratford with the late plays. Treated as the objective correlative of the pastoral tendencies of those plays, Stratford allows lateness to be defined, through the last days of the National Poet, with England: it is Stratford's quintessential green Englishness, in the end, not commercial, cosmopolitan London, that embodies the final serenity of the master.

Dowden probably derived his idea not from Malone but from Henry Hallam, who in the late 1830s suggested that

> there seems to have been a period of Shakespeare's life when his heart was ill at ease, and ill content with the world or his own conscience; the memory of hours misspent, the pang of affection misplaced or unrequited, the experience of man's worser nature which intercourse with unworthy associates, by choice or circumstance, peculiarly teaches; – these, as they sank down into the depths of his great mind, seem not only to have inspired into it the conception of Lear and Timon, but that of one primary character, the censurer of mankind.[9]

From Hallam, then, Dowden drew his 'Third Period' and the implication that Shakespeare moved past this moment of darkness and doubt to a later, less oppressive phase, though Hallam didn't flesh this out. Meanwhile, Thomas Campbell in his 1838 *Dramatic Works* was the first to make a direct equation of Shakespeare and Prospero as retiring geniuses:

> Shakspeare, as if conscious that it would be his last [play], and as if inspired to typify himself, has made its hero a natural, a dignified, and benevolent magician....Here Shakspeare himself is Prospero....But the time was approaching when the potent sorcerer was to break his staff, and to bury it fathoms in the ocean.[10]

By 1840, then, the scene had already been set for Dowden's later synthesis – although all of this had in a way been pre-empted by Coleridge 20 years earlier, who in outlining a series of wildly differing chronologies for Shakespeare (largely ignoring Malone's hard-won ordering) presented the playwright's life as a five-act drama and, in his third and last chronology (from lecture notes of 1819), invoked the concept of the 'cycle of genius' in order to characterize the acts. The 'Fifth and last Aera' he defines, drawing on Schelling for his terminology, as appearing

> [w]hen the energies of intellect in the cycle of genius were, tho' in a richer and potentiated form, becoming predominant over passion and creative self-modification . . .

in other words, something similar to Dowden's period 'On the heights.' Coleridge, however, assigns to his 'fifth aera' a series of, to our eyes, inappropriate plays – *Measure for Measure, Timon, Coriolanus, Julius Caesar, Antony and Cleopatra*, and *Troilus and Cressida* – thereby largely forfeiting his place in the history of lateness. Nonetheless, it underlines the obvious point – that lateness is, at its root, a Romantic construct, a byproduct or subcategory of Genius, a concept unavailable to Shakespeare's contemporaries which begins to emerge in the years after Malone's chronology and is, somewhat belatedly, given its full shape by Dowden. Lateness, in Romantic terms, is the evidence of the genius's return, as he nears death, to the borders of the sublime last patrolled in early childhood, a return in which he can engage with, brush close to, death, the ultimate sublime, and draw on this experience to create profound images of resignation and of spiritual reconciliation. Any reading of Shakespeare that draws on this understanding of late work remains fundamentally Romantic.

III

Twentieth-century criticism split fairly consistently down the middle in regard to lateness, some, such as Muir and Grene, sustaining the Romantic conception, others, resistant to the excesses of subjectivism, turning to a range of material or institutional contexts instead, seeking the impetus for the late plays beyond the personal. Of the latter, C. J. Sisson's British Academy lecture of 1934 – in which he mocked the idea that 'dramatists write tragedies when their mood is tragic and comedies when they are feeling pleased with life' – was perhaps the most effective attack on the persistence of Dowden's assumptions.[11] But to establish a sense of the state of late-play criticism by this time, it is helpful to turn to Harley Granville Barker's somewhat fragmentary opening comments in his 1930 preface to *Cymbeline*:

> *Cymbeline* is said to have been a product, probably the first, of Shakespeare's leisured retirement to Stratford. Professor Ashley Thorndike thinks it was written in emulation of Beaumont and Fletcher's successful *Philaster*. There are signs that it was intended for the 'private' theatre of the Blackfriars. More than one editor has scented a collaborator; the late Dr. Furness, in particular, put many of the play's weaknesses to this account. . . . The Folio labels it tragedy, but it is not; it is tragi-comedy rather, or romance.[12]

Commenting on what he calls the play's 'sophisticated artlessness,' Barker adds:

> This art that displays art is a thing very likely to be to the taste of the mature and rather wearied artist. When you are exhausted with hammering great tragic themes into shape it is a relief to find a subject you can play with, and to be safely able to take more interest in the doing than the thing done. For once you can exercise your skill for its own sake. The pretty subject itself seems to invite a certain artlessness of treatment. But the product will have a sophisticated air about it. (247)

Subjectivism persists here in a hybrid form, with an echo (in the idea of Shakespeare as 'wearied') of the best-known attack on Dowden, that of Lytton Strachey (to which I will return later in this essay). At the same time, institutional contexts override the personal. On the one hand, the last plays are read, in a way familiar from Malone, as the product not of the practicalities of commercial theatre but rather of the tranquillity of a Stratford retirement; on the other, the change in style they represent in Shakespeare's output makes them the product of the King's Men's occupation of the Blackfriars, a markedly different theatre from the Globe. Equally, the plays, as the product of Shakespeare's 'leisured retirement,' stand free of the input of the world; yet they are written either 'in emulation' of other writers or in collaboration with them – the latter, according to Furness at least, introducing 'weaknesses'.

Barker's preface lists the various contradictory options considered by critics after Dowden to account for the differences between the late plays and the rest of the canon: Shakespeare's alleged departure for Stratford and the mental and spiritual elbow-room this was thought to have given him; the effect of the acquisition of the Blackfriars on the company repertory; the input of other playwrights in the form both of collaboration (writing with Wilkins or Fletcher) and of influence (Barker mentions Ashley Thorndike, whose book *The Influence of Beaumont and Fletcher on Shakspere* was so splendidly offensive to bardolaters); and the question of genre and the problematic terms 'tragicomedy' and 'romance.'[13] Of these, the explanation that most explicitly derives from theatre history is that of the influence of the newly-acquired performance space at the Blackfriars. The argument as it stood until relatively recently (first articulated by G. E. Bentley in the inaugural issue of *Shakespeare Survey*) goes as follows. Once they knew the Blackfriars was going to become available, the core members of the company gathered, Bentley surmises, for a series of 'conferences'. One of the key policy decisions they made at these conferences was 'that William Shakespeare should write henceforth with the Blackfriars in mind and not the Globe.'[14] Bentley outlines various reasons for this decision – that the new theatre was a risky proposition and they needed the playwright who knew the actors best to ensure its success, that the Globe 'could be left to take care of itself with an old repertory as the Blackfriars could not' (46), and that since Shakespeare had invested personally in the new space he would work hard to ensure that it ran smoothly.

The evidence for this argument, Bentley argues, is the late plays. As he puts it, '[n]o competent critic who has read carefully through the Shakespeare canon has failed to notice that there is something different about *Cymbeline, The Winter's Tale, The Tempest*, and *The Two Noble Kinsmen*' (47–8). This 'difference' he attributes directly to the move to the Blackfriars, an attribution which, Bentley asserts,

> accords with the known facts of theatre history, . . . with the biographical evidence of Shakespeare's long and close association with all the enterprises of the Lord Chamberlain's-King's men for twenty years [and] with his fabulously acute sense of the theatre and the problems of the actor; and it does no violence to his artistic integrity or to his poetic genius. (48–9)

This remained the received wisdom for most of the second half of the twentieth century. Over the last ten or 20 years, however, Bentley's assumptions have run into a certain amount of trouble. Andrew Gurr argues bluntly that 'too much has been made about the possible effects on Shakespeare's writing when, after a thirteen-year delay, the Blackfriars playhouse finally came into the possession of Shakespeare's company' – and it is hard to disagree, not least because there are two obvious omissions from Bentley's list of plays whose 'difference' can be attributed to the acquisition of the indoor playhouse.[15] These are, first of all, *Pericles*, which of course shares a great deal with the others and is usually these days accepted without question as a late play (even when *Henry VIII*, the lost *Cardenio* and *The Two Noble Kinsmen* continue conveniently to be forgotten) but which unfortunately and inescapably predates the company's acquisition of the Black-friars and, secondly, *Henry VIII*, which we know for certain was performed at the first Globe, not the Blackfriars, in June 1613, because it was responsible for the destruction of the building.[16]

The latter play (on which I will briefly focus) exhibits a series of features consistent with those considered characteristic of the late plays – what Irwin Smith calls 'Blackfriars Conventions' – dancing and masque-like events (Wolsey's party and Katherine's vision) and the use of a descent (for the angels in the vision), as well as the absence (notable in an apparent 'history' play) of battles, and some arguably rather claustrophobic action – all of which might reasonably be thought to point towards the Blackfriars as the expected venue, despite the evidence of at least one catastrophic performance at the Globe.[17] More to the point, the historical resonance of performance in the Blackfriars space was considerable, since the very same building had been used for the 1529 divorce hearing of Henry and Katherine of Aragon that is dramatized in 2.4, and the play makes sure nobody misses the connection: 'The most convenient place that I can think of / For such receipt of learning,' says King Henry, unnecessarily, at the end of 2.2, 'is Blackfriars' (2.2.136–7) – making it highly unlikely that the play was not written with performance there in mind (even if, in the Globe context, the reference could serve simply as promotion for the company's new space). Yet at the same time, not only are we certain, because of the fire, that the play was performed at the Globe, we can also see certain characteristics that make it seem out of place as a Blackfriars play. It features not just 'hautboys' and 'cornets,' instruments perhaps feasible for use in the low-key environment of the music room at the Blackfriars, but also trumpets, which are not thought to have been usable in such a confined space. Moreover, the Folio text's uniquely full stage directions – which do not derive (as John Jowett has persuasively argued *The Tempest*'s do) from later scribal embellishment but are drawn near-verbatim from Holinshed, a hybrid form of stage direction, in other words, at once literary and theatrical – make it clear that the play needs a considerable amount of stage-space.[18] Constructing a doubling chart for *Henry VIII* makes it clear that the play in the form it exists in the Folio could not have been performed at the Blackfriars on a stage that was, to use Gurr's figures, perhaps 20 feet by 16 compared with the Globe's 44 feet by 27: 24 people need to process onto stage at once in the divorce-trial scene, for instance. In Gurr's colourful words, '[t]he smallish Blackfriars stage, already encumbered with fifteen stool-sitting gallants wearing ostrich-plumed hats and smoking long pipes, would not have taken large crowds easily' (97). The obvious conclusions are that *Henry VIII* must have been performed at both theatres; that it was written either with both playhouses in mind or first of all for the Blackfriars but with immediate adaptation for the Globe; and that the Folio text represents the Globe version. We know that the company shifted to the five-act structure that had not been necessary for plays performed solely in an open-air theatre and that they installed a descent machine at the Globe in order to be able to replicate action possible at the Blackfriars but not previously feasible at the Globe; we also know that a clear divergence of repertory between the two theatres was still a few years off when the late plays were written. It certainly seems unlikely that the play as it exists in the First Folio and perhaps therefore as it was performed at the Globe can be identical with the play as it was performed at the Blackfriars. And since, as Tiffany Stern puts it in *Making Shakespeare*, '[w]hat works within a small artificially lit theatre can . . . be adapted to work outdoors on a large naturally lit stage [but] the reverse is not necessarily the case', it seems that the Folio text in all likelihood represents the spatially-expanded Globe version of the play.[19] For Gurr, only *The Tempest*, of the entire canon, bears unequivocal signs – in its music and its clear-cut five-act structure – of being written specifically for the company's new space. If this is the case, and if therefore the other Folio late plays are Globe versions written for both theatres, then the blanket assumption that the Blackfriars provided a radical break in staging for the King's Men's repertory and that this explains the 'difference' of the late plays is questionable.

IV

I have laboured this point for two reasons, one concerned with theatre history, the other with the construction of lateness. The alleged relationship between the late plays and the King's company's beginning work at the Blackfriars serves as a classic instance of the way in which a retrogressive quest for authenticity on debatable theatre-historical grounds can sometimes produce outcomes which, while being quite other than the expectations of those who initiated the quest (and having very little to do with 'authenticity'), are nonetheless exciting. It also provides us – by way of the Modernist repositioning of Shakespeare's late plays as vanguard theatre – with a point of access to the fundamental shift in the understanding both of those plays and of late work in general that took place in the early part of the twentieth century. For this point of access I want to turn back to Harley Granville Barker, who is, I wish to suggest, a pivotal figure in the history of Shakespearean lateness. When he came to direct one of the late plays, Barker sought to negotiate the contradictions in his account of the late plays in the *Cymbeline* preface by way of a production that was both a landmark in Shakespearean theatre history and – I want to argue – the beginning of a new phase in the history of lateness. Conflicting motivations have been attributed to Barker for his choice of *The Winter's Tale* for production at London's Savoy Theatre in 1912. One critic at the time suggested that it was because the audience did not know the play at all well or have much investment in it and that this made it more available than better-loved plays for Barker's radical purposes – 'throwing one,' as he put it, 'to the wolves'.[20] But the more constructive, more likely motivation is that Barker was deliberately choosing a play with a performance history characterized by drastic cuts and distracting sets, a play whose difficulties had been met by previous directors with the simple expedient of evasion, because this gave him the opportunity to celebrate what others had ignored or cut.

As his preface to the 'Acting Edition' of the play makes clear, his decision to choose – and to trust in – *The Winter's Tale* was premised on grounds at once biographical and theatrical: 'The technique of it,' he argues, 'is mature, that of a man who knows that he can do what he will, lets himself in for difficulties with apparent carelessness, and overcomes them at his ease.'[21] Trusting in this 'technique' – derived as it is from a particular understanding of late creativity – Barker directed the play in its entirety or near-entirety: J. L. Styan suggests that he cut only 11 lines of the Folio text, where eighteenth- and nineteenth-century directors had cut entire acts (Styan, 87). For reviewers, however, the most important of Barker's directorial decisions was not the absence of cuts but the use of a thrust stage. John Palmer, writing in the *Saturday Review*, argued that

> [t]he value of Mr Barker's revival . . . rests almost wholly upon his projection of the stage into the auditorium, for thereby hangs all that distinguishes Elizabethan plays and playing from Restoration comedy. Mr Barker's innovation . . . is not a merely topographical trick of stage management. There were precious moments in the Savoy Theatre on Saturday when it was possible to be thrillingly conscious of precisely the appeal which Burbage made as he issued from the tiring-house to the vacant platform before Elsinore.[22]

Palmer's reaction is, not surprisingly, endorsed by Styan, who sees Barker's production as the first to recreate something that might be thought of as authentically Shakespearean – that is, non-naturalistic and thus, in Styan's terms, 'theatrical':

> The cumulative effect of these elements was to return *The Winter's Tale* to its proper mode and style. The supers seemed to move like automata, lending an air of burlesque to the indictment of the trial scene. The frank asides of Leontes's first scene permitted that awkward and unnatural assertion of his jealous thoughts to work as good theatre. (89)

Styan's enthusiasm for the propriety of the Savoy production is echoed by Dennis Bartholomeusz in his performance history of *The Winter's Tale*, who treads dangerous Bradleian ground in speaking on Shakespeare's behalf:

> Had Shakespeare been present [he suggests] when Granville-Barker presented *The Winter's Tale* on the stage in England … he would not … have wanted to sue for damages, as he almost certainly would have done had he been there when Garrick staged the second half of his play only. (5)

For the critics, then, the key features of Barker's production were its truth to Shakespeare's original intentions and its bringing into mainstream London theatre the *fin de siècle* innovations of William Poel and others in reconstructing and reclaiming the thrust stage associated with the Globe.

Barker, though, as we have seen, knew his theatre history – knew about the Blackfriars – and this enabled him to re-read this late play on specifically theatrical grounds. In the preface to *Cymbeline* he writes,

> One speculates upon what might have happened had Shakespeare reached London as a young man, not when he did, but a generation later, to serve his apprenticeship at the Blackfriars instead of at the Theatre, the Rose and the Curtain. As it is he is an old hand when the change comes, and will live out the rest of his life retired, more or less, from the stage. But while he still wrote for it he would remain a most practical playwright. We might look to find in his latest plays signs that he was as sensitive as the youngest to this shift of direction. If *Cymbeline* was written for the Blackfriars it may well owe a few of its idiosyncrasies to that mere fact. (Preface to *Cymbeline*, 250)

Of *The Winter's Tale*, he argues that '[t]he signs of an association with the Blackfriars must be looked into carefully when we come to consider the play's staging,' adding – and this, I think, is significant – that this should be done 'if for no other reason than that there was a theatre far liker to our own than the open-air Globe' (Preface to *Cymbeline*, 234). Not only does this physical, commercial change provide an alternative, non-subjectivist reason to engage with and rethink a late play, then, it also situates those plays as closer in practical expectation to modern forms of theatre than any other plays in the Shakespeare canon. The turn to the early evidenced by Barker's incorporation of the thrust stage at the Savoy is in fact paradoxically a turn to the modern; the play is chosen precisely because of all Shakespeare's plays it (along with its fellow late plays) looks forward to the conditions and modes of modern theatre. And I would argue that this marks the moment at which modernism, overriding the romantic heritage, begins to appropriate the concept of lateness.

By far the best-known modernist intervention in the question of Shakespearean lateness, of course, is one I briefly mentioned earlier – that of Lytton Strachey in his essay 'Shakespeare's Final Period' (first published in 1906 though most fully circulated in his 1922 collection *Books and Characters*), in which he argues with relishable shamelessness that, as far as the late plays are concerned,

> [i]t is difficult to resist the conclusion that [Shakespeare] was getting bored.... Bored with people, bored with real life, bored with drama, bored, in fact, with everything except poetry and poetical dreams.[23]

Warming to the task of crushing Dowden, he points out the grimnesses and savageries of the late plays – 'nowhere,' he claims, 'does [Shakespeare] verge more often upon a sort of brutality of phrase, a cruel coarseness' (54) – by way of contrast with Dowden's insistence on serenity and reconciliation, and he asks of the lines 'You taught me language, and my profit on't / Is, I know how to curse': 'Is this Caliban addressing Prospero, or Job addressing God? It may be either; but it is not serene, nor benign, nor pastoral, nor "On the Heights" ' (64). Outspoken this may be, yet Strachey's intervention does not in fact mark a paradigm shift. 'Violently as Dowden and Strachey differ,' Bentley points out, 'they agree in seeking subjective interpretations' (48). 'Both portraits,' explains Samuel Schoenbaum, 'require us to assume a one-to-one correspondence between what an author writes and his mood at the time,' and he suggests mischievously that '[e]ven the boredom may be a cynic's version of serenity.'[24]

Strachey, then, despite his modernist credentials, does not take us so very far from Dowden and romanticism. For a fully-fledged modernist characterization of lateness, we need, in fact, to look beyond Shakespeare criticism to Said's landmark theorists of lateness, Adorno and Broch, for whom lateness and modernity are intimately connected. Broch, writing just after the Second World War, reads the modern period as a period of *epochal* lateness:

> Coming from myth, returning to myth: the whole, or nearly the whole, history of European literature is strung between Homer and Tolstoy. But what a strange development of the human expression, since, apparently, it returns to its mythical source. Is this not like a late homecoming? And if it be such – does it not portend the dusk before the night? Is it not the curve that drops back into childhood? (9–10)

Broch here uses the idea of late style and the return to the early that is an insistent characteristic of lateness to read modernity as a kind of late phenomenon, the ending of an epoch which is also a return to roots.

It was in the first decades of the twentieth century that art history began, belatedly, to theorize lateness, to develop the characteristics of *spätwerk* or *altersstil*, late work or old-age style, seeing it as difficult and fragmentary, as what Sam Smiles calls 'a radical reconsideration of what art can achieve that somehow points proleptically to the advances yet to be made by the artist's successors.'[25] A little later, Adorno addressed late Beethoven in ways that echo this, contrasting profoundly with the kind of lateness championed by Dowden. For Adorno, age and death drive a particular creative response in which

> there is altogether something like a tendency towards dissociation, decay, dissolution, but not in the sense of a process of composition which no longer holds things together: the dissociation and disintegration themselves become artistic means, and works which have been brought to a rounded conclusion take on through these means, despite their roundedness, something spiritually fragmentary. (189)

For Adorno, in late work,

> [t]he compulsion of identity is broken and the conventions are its fragments. The music speaks the language of the archaic, of children, of savages and of God, but not of the individual. (157)

This, then, is the genuine paradigm-shift that Strachey did not achieve. Not only is lateness no longer comforting, serene or reconciling; it is no longer an individual or a personal phenomenon at all. Moreover, in its turning back to the past it is also a prophecy of the future. For Adorno, Beethoven's late writing is not so much the last phase of the music of Beethoven as Beethoven's inhabiting the last phase of music, in (that is) its recognizable form as tonal and conventional. Beethoven is both central and incidental to this epochal change, a change which immediately falls into abeyance until the arrival of Schoenberg, Berg and Webern. It is this status of late work as a foretaste of the avant garde that offers us a way back into Shakespearean lateness as the oft-remarked *difficulty* of the late plays, glossed over by Dowden in his emphasis on serenity and reconciliation but often mentioned (not least by Strachey) in relation both to style and structure, becomes something for modernism to celebrate.

In an *Observer* interview at the time of the Savoy Theatre production, George Bernard Shaw praised Granville Barker's changes in lighting and staging for *The Winter's Tale*, and, when the interviewer pointed out that by no means all the critics had liked these changes, he exclaimed:

> Nonsense! They never noticed the change. It was so right that they took it as a matter of course. What they didn't like was Shakespeare. It will take them ten years to acquire the taste for Shakespeare's late plays, and to learn his language.... On the whole, they don't like art. They always speak of it as something new and disagreeable. To Barker it is something eternal and delightful. That is what nerves him to these astonishing adventures.[26]

This is a classic statement of the avant garde – and it is echoed in a typical and much better-known context just a year after Barker's production. At rehearsals for the riotous première of Stravinsky's *Rite of Spring*, the conductor Pierre Monteux felt (he later wrote) that 'the same instinct that had prompted me to recognize [Stravinsky's] genius made me realize that in this ballet he was far, far in advance of his time and that while the public might not accept it, musicians would delight in the new, weird though logical expression of dissonance.'[27] This engagement with vanguard art, I want to suggest, offered Barker a way to make the alleged difficulty of *The Winter's Tale* and the other late plays something to revel in, not to fret about.

The comparison is not, in fact, entirely arbitrary. Stravinsky's biographer Stephen Walsh, referring to a discussion between the composer and his collaborator Robert Craft, makes a direct contrast between *The Rite of Spring* and *The Winter's Tale*:

> in reply to Craft's question 'What did you love most in Russia?', Stravinsky recalled 'the violent Russian spring that seemed to begin in an hour and was like the whole earth cracking.' It is an image as far as possible from the Arcadian idea of spring more familiar in the art of western and southern Europe and enshrined in works as far apart as *The Winter's Tale* and *Parsifal*.[28]

Barker's production, I would argue, specifically resists Walsh's assumption (echoed by Broch and Said) that Shakespearean lateness necessarily embodies an aesthetic based in serene, negotiable pastoral. On the contrary, Barker remakes *The Winter's Tale* as at the same time a precursor and a contemporary of the *Ballets Russes* and of modernist performance in general. Costume and set design alone make the point (see illustrations Figures 48–50). Barker's production and a series of contemporary *Ballets Russes* productions share a common aesthetic in wintry Russian folk-grotesque, and it is apparent – as it was at the time, when the critic A. B. Walkley referred to the production as 'post-Impressionist Shakespeare' – that Barker's designer Albert Rothenstein – far from drawing on designs by Giulio Romano, as he claimed ('our pattern designer recommended in the play itself') – was in fact heavily influenced by Bakst and Benois and Golovine and other designers for the newly triumphant *Ballets Russes* in his costumes and sets for the Savoy (Barker, Preface to *The Winter's Tale*, x).[29] This landmark production of a Shakespearean late play, then, with its actors moving 'like automata' and its *Ballets Russes* costumes, consciously adopts a modernist aesthetic, and I would argue that this rediscovery of *The Winter's Tale* marks the appropriability of the late plays to a modernist vision in which the plays are seen as difficult, fragmented engagements with ritual and the cycle of the seasons which look forward to modern forms of art as much as they look back to primitive expression – in other words, as modernist texts. Criticism lagged, as so often, behind theatre but by the mid-century the late plays had become a focus for the kind of myth-and-ritual analyses that emerged from modernism's fascination with folk art.

In this light, Barker's observation that 'the technique of [*The Winter's Tale*] is mature, that of a man who knows that he can do what he will, lets himself in for

Figure 48　Four costume designs by Albert Rothenstein for Granville Barker's production of *The Winter's Tale* at the Savoy Theatre, 1912. Reproduced by permission of the Harvard Theatre Collection

Figure 49 Henry Ainley as Leontes, Savoy Theatre, 1912. Reproduced by permission of the Illustrated London News Picture Library

difficulties with apparent carelessness, and overcomes them at his ease' casually offers a potted history of the construction of Shakespearean lateness, beginning with subjectivism, incorporating both the 'ease' highlighted by Dowden and the 'carelessness' championed by Strachey into a narrative that, in the ostensible cause of rediscovering original theatrical experience, appropriates late – that is, post-Blackfriars – Shakespeare for modernism through its avant garde looking-forward to modern theatre, and thus marks the origins of the internally contradictory concept of late work or late style that is still current. Shakespeare's modernist sensibility, his new-found status as early modern precursor of modern theatre, is grounded in the shift to the Blackfriars, a theatre treated as if it were a modern post-proscenium space. It was an idea, moreover, that caught on. Roger Warren recalls that Peter Hall's starting-point for his 1988 cycle of late plays at the National Theatre

Figure 50   The pastoral scene (*The Winter's Tale* 4.4.), Savoy Theatre, 1912. Reproduced by permission of the Illustrated London News Picture Library

was the coincidence that the Cottesloe is roughly the same size as the Black-friars Theatre, for which many commentators believe these plays were specifi-cally designed, and which may have influenced the way they are written. He thought, therefore, that this would be an appropriate space in which to explore Shakespeare's late writing.[30]

Paradoxically, then, in Barker's hands, despite the theatrical rather than subjectivist premise of grouping the late plays as the products of the company's Blackfriars move, this shift of interest still marks a facet of lateness – that is, lateness as the precursor of the avant garde, lateness as prophecy. The 'return' to the full text and to the thrust stage thus comes about only when early contexts have in fact been forgotten, and the revitalization of the play in performance is premised on grounds that wholly reinvent the original processes of production.

V

Granville Barker's 1912 *Winter's Tale* thus inhabits a significant moment in the history of the construction both of lateness as a critical concept and of Shakespeare's late plays as a group, marking the appropriation of both the plays and the concept for modernism, renegotiating the terms of lateness in order to incorporate not only serenity and retrospection, the turn back to the early both epochally and personally, but also difficulty and prospection, the historical genius capable of looking forward to the conditions of modernity. In rediscovering *The Winter's Tale* as a contemporary of the *Ballets Russes* even as he was ostensibly returning the play to an 'original' context that probably never was, Barker drew Shakespearean lateness away from Dowden and toward Adorno, staging the modern moment at which the overarching concept of lateness both blossoms and fragments. I would argue that the basic contradictions in the idea of late work as it now stands – its alleged unifying serenity and fragmenting difficulty, its looking back which is in fact a prophecy of future forms – stem from its emergence out of and appropriation to antithetical yet consequent modes of artistic engagement, Romanticism and Modernism. It is the contradictions between these modes that inform the continuing critical and theatrical unease underlying our readings of Shakespeare's late plays and the critical failure fully to engage with them in their theatrical contexts, modern and early modern.

Notes

I am grateful to the Leverhulme Trust for providing me with a fellowship in 2002 to begin work on the idea of late writing.

1. Hermann Broch, 'The Style of the Mythical Age,' introductory essay to Rachel Bespaloff, *On The Iliad*, trans. Mary McCarthy (New York: Pantheon Books, 1947), 10–11.
2. Said, 40. Edward Said, 'Untimely Meditations,' review of Maynard Solomon, *Late Beethoven: Music, Thought, Imagination*, in *The Nation* 277 (Sept 2003), 38–42 (38).
3. For Adorno's understanding of lateness, see Theodor Adorno, *Beethoven: The Philosophy of Music*, ed. Rolf Tiedemann, trans. Edmund Jephcott (Cambridge: Polity P, 1998), 123–93.
4. Walter Raleigh, *Shakespeare*, 'English Men of Letters' series (London: Macmillan, 1926), 212. I am grateful to Kevin de Ornellas for directing me to Raleigh's comments on Shakespearean lateness.
5. Edward Dowden, *Shakspere: A Critical Study of his Mind and Art* (London: Henry S. King, 1875), v.
6. William Shakespeare, *Sonnets*, ed. Edward Dowden (London, 1881), 11.
7. On Malone's chronology and its impact, see Margreta De Grazia, *Shakespeare Verbatim: The Reproduction of Authenticity and the 1790 Apparatus* (Oxford: Clarendon P, 1991), 132–76.
8. Edmond Malone, 'An Attempt to Ascertain the Order in which the Plays Attributed to Shakspeare were Written,' in *The Plays of William Shakspeare*, ed. Samuel Johnson and George Steevens, 10 vols (London, 1778), 344.
9. Henry Hallam, *Introduction to the Literature of Europe, in the Fifteenth, Sixteenth, and Seventeenth Centuries* (London, 1837–39), 3. 85.
10. Thomas Campbell, *Dramatic Works* (London, 1838), lxiii.
11. C. J. Sisson, *The Mythical Sorrows of Shakespeare*, 'Annual Shakespeare Lecture of the British Academy' (London: Humphrey Milford, 1934).
12. Harley Granville-Barker, *Prefaces to Shakespeare, Second Series* (London: Sidgwick & Jackson, 1930), 'Cymbeline,' 234.
13. Ashley Thorndike, *The Influence of Beaumont and Fletcher on Shakspere* (Worcester, MA: Oliver B. Wood, 1901).
14. G. E. Bentley, 'Shakespeare and the Blackfriars Theatre,' *Shakespeare Survey 1* (Cambridge: Cambridge University Press, 1948), 38–50 (46).
15. Andrew Gurr, '*The Tempest*'s Tempest at Blackfriars,' *Shakespeare Survey 41* (Cambridge: Cambridge University Press, 1988), 91–102 (92).
16. On *Henry VIII* and the Globe fire, see William Shakespeare and John Fletcher, *Henry VIII (All is True)*, ed. Gordon McMullan (London: Arden Shakespeare, 2000), 57–63.

17. Irwin Smith, *Shakespeare's Blackfriars Playhouse: Its History and Design* (London: Peter Owen, 1966), 220–42.
18. John Jowett, 'New Created Creatures: Ralph Crane and the Stage Directions in *The Tempest,'* *Shakespeare Survey 36* (Cambridge: Cambridge University Press, 1983), 107–20.
19. Tiffany Stern, *Making Shakespeare: From Stage to Page* (London: Routledge, 2004), 29.
20. See J. L. Styan, *The Shakespeare Revolution: Criticism and Performance in the Twentieth Century* (Cambridge: Cambridge University Press, 1977), 85.
21. Harley Granville Barker, preface to *The Winter's Tale by William Shakespeare*, 'An Acting Edition' (London: Heinemann, 1912), iii.
22. John Palmer, review of Barker's *Winter's Tale*, *Saturday Review*, 28 September 1912; see Dennis Bartholomeusz, *'The Winter's Tale' in Performance in England and America 1611–1976* (Cambridge: Cambridge University Press, 1982), 148.
23. Lytton Strachey, 'Shakespeare's Final Period,' in *Book and Characters, French and English* (London: Chatto & Windus, 1922), 47–64 (60).
24. S[amuel] Schoenbaum, *Shakespeare's Lives*, 2nd edition (Oxford: Oxford University Press, 1993), 479.
25. Sam Smiles, 'Late Turner: Some Problems,' unpublished paper, 'Turner 2004' conference, University of Birmingham, January 2004. On the development of the idea of late style in art history, see *Art Journal* 46 (1987), a special issue devoted to 'Old-Age Style'.
26. George Bernard Shaw, review of Barker's *Winter's Tale*, *Observer*, 29 September 1912.
27. Pierre Monteux, 'Appreciation,' in Minna Lederman, ed., *Stravinsky in the Theatre* (London: Peter Owen, 1951), 129.
28. Stephen Walsh, *The Music of Stravinsky* (London: Routledge, 1988), 41. On the influence of Russian folk ritual on Stravinsky's work for the *Ballets Russes*, see also Richard Taruskin, *Stravinsky and the Russian Traditions*, 2 vols (Oxford: Oxford University Press, 1996), esp. 1: 849–966.
29. A. B. Walkley, review of Barker's *Winter's Tale*, *The Times*, 23 September 1912.
30. Roger Warren, *Staging Shakespeare's Late Plays* (Oxford: Clarendon Press, 1990), 1–2.

Index

3 5282 00618 0510